Cold War Country

Studies in United States Culture

Grace Elizabeth Hale, *editor*

Studies in United States Culture publishes provocative books that explore US culture in its many forms and spheres of influence. Bringing together big ideas, brisk prose, bold storytelling, and sophisticated analysis, books published in the series serve as an intellectual meeting ground where scholars from different disciplinary and methodological perspectives can build common lines of inquiry around matters such as race, ethnicity, gender, sexuality, power, and empire in an American context.

A complete list of books published in Studies in United States Culture is available at https://uncpress.org/series/studies-united-states-culture.

Cold War Country

How Nashville's Music Row and the
Pentagon Created the Sound of
American Patriotism

. . . .

JOSEPH M. THOMPSON

The University of North Carolina Press Chapel Hill

Library of Congress Cataloging-in-Publication Data
Names: Thompson, Joseph M., author.
Title: Cold War country : how Nashville's Music Row and the Pentagon
   created the sound of American patriotism / Joseph M. Thompson.
Other titles: Studies in United States culture.
Description: Chapel Hill : The University of North Carolina Press, 2024. |
   Series: Studies in United States culture | Includes bibliographical
   references and index.
Identifiers: LCCN 2023044338 | ISBN 9781469678351 (cloth ; alk. paper) |
   ISBN 9781469678368 (paperback ; alk. paper) | ISBN 9781469678375
   (epub)
Subjects: LCSH: Country music—History and criticism. | Country
   music—Political aspects—History—20th century. | Music trade—
   Tennessee—Nashville—History—20th century. | United States—Armed
   Forces—Recruiting, enlistment, etc.—History—20th century. | BISAC:
   HISTORY / United States / 20th Century | SOCIAL SCIENCE / Popular
   Culture
Classification: LCC ML3524 .T46 2024 | DDC 782.421642/0904—dc23/
   eng/20231004
LC record available at https://lccn.loc.gov/2023044338

Cover illustration: Cover photo of "Western Jamboree" USO show in Korea
from Staff Section Report, October 1951; A-1 Entry 252, Eighth US Army,
Special Services Section, Staff Section Reports, 1950–1958; Records of US
Army Operational, Tactical, and Support Organizations (World War II and
Thereafter), Record Group 338; National Archives at College Park, MD.

To Jennifer, Evie, Virginia, and Joseph,
for all of their love

Contents

List of Illustrations, ix

Introduction, 1

1 Big Government Country, 15
Connie B. Gay and the Roots of Country Music Militarization

2 A GI Bill for Country Music, 47
How Country Music and Military Recruitment Merged in the 1950s

3 Singing in the Ranks, 83
Memphis, Militarization, and the Country Roots of Rock and Roll

4 All-American Boy, 113
Elvis Presley and the Cold War's Musical and Military Integration

5 Best Liked World-Wide, 146
Selling the Armed Forces and the World on Country Music

6 Tell Them What We're Fighting For, 176
The CMA, Country Artists, and the Politics of the Vietnam War

7 Proud to Be an American, 219
Country Music Militarization and Patriotism after Vietnam

Conclusion, 252

Acknowledgments, 259
Notes, 263
Bibliography, 303
Index, 321

Illustrations

I.1 Roy Acuff, USO poster, 9

1.1 Connie B. Gay with FSA, 20

1.2 Grandpa Jones in Korea program, 32

1.3 "Europe Goes Hillbilly" in *Country Song Roundup*, 37

1.4 Private Cecil Gant advertisement in *Billboard*, 41

2.1 Faron Young on the cover of *Country Song Roundup*, 62

2.2 "The Army Goes Country & Western" in *Country & Western Jamboree*, 64

2.3 A screen still from *Country Style, U.S.A.*, 72

3.1 Students exercising at the Naval Air Technical Training Center, 89

4.1 Cover of Citizens' Council publication *The Southerner*, 126

4.2 Fort McClellan article from *The Southerner*, 126

4.3 Cover of Hank Locklin's *Foreign Love* album, 128

4.4 "Has Elvis Surrendered to 'Pop' Music?" article in *Country Song Roundup*, 143

4.5 Collection of images in *Country Song Roundup*, 143

5.1 CMA's "Best Liked World-Wide" logo, 150

5.2 Joe Allison, 172

6.1 Stars for Goldwater advertisement, 181

6.2 Roy Acuff performs for soldiers in Vietnam, 184

6.3 Program for a CMTS tour featuring the Wagon Wheels, 194

6.4 Soldiers tour the Country Music Hall of Fame in 1968, 196

6.5 An artillery piece with "COUNTRY MUSIC" along the barrel, 215

7.1 Crew members of the USS *Kitty Hawk* honor Lee Greenwood, 246

7.2 Lee Greenwood performs for a USO concert, 251

Introduction

· ·

"My music tastes changed on 9/11." Senator Ted Cruz (R-TX) gave that answer to a softball question floated to him by Gayle King on *CBS This Morning* in March 2015. Cruz was a contender for the Republican presidential nomination at the time, and King had asked the White House hopeful about his musical tastes near the end of the interview as a way for voters to get to know the man behind the sound bites. Quick to seize a political moment, Cruz continued, "On 9/11, I didn't like how rock music responded. And country music, collectively, the way they responded, it resonated with me, and I have to say . . . I had an emotional reaction that said, 'These are my people.'"[1]

Whether genuine or politically calculated, there was good reason for Cruz's answer. Shortly after the attacks of September 11, 2001, several country music artists went to their studios to wrestle with what it meant to live in a newly vulnerable United States. Country music has a long-standing reputation as an exceptionally patriotic genre, from the Vietnam-era backlash of Merle Haggard's "Fightin' Side of Me" to the Cold War nationalism of Lee Greenwood's "God Bless the U.S.A." Many country performers took the opportunity to record songs that voiced support for the troops during the first months of what became the multidecade War on Terror. As US servicemembers deployed to the Middle East, country radio promoted a string of these 9/11-inspired songs, and artists released a stream of patriotic tunes in the weeks before the US invasions of Afghanistan and Iraq. These included Alan Jackson's "Where Were You (When the World Stopped Turning)," Darryl Worley's "Have You Forgotten?," Aaron Tippin's "Where the Stars and Stripes and the Eagle Fly," and Toby Keith's "Courtesy of the Red, White, and Blue (The Angry American)."

In 2002, a trio of women then known as the Dixie Chicks (renamed the Chicks in 2020) released their addition to country's wartime playlist, a song called "Travelin' Soldier." It earned them a number-one hit with its lyrics about the doomed love between a teenaged waitress and a young man who dies fighting in Vietnam. The song's message was ambivalent. While one listener might hear the story of heartbreak and death as an indictment of US military policies, another could hear it as honoring the men who give their lives in sacrifice to military duty, as well as the loved ones they leave behind on the home front. Or it could be both. Either way, the Chicks enjoyed unparalleled success in the early 2000s, and "Travelin' Soldier" spoke to the mixture of pride and fear that gripped the nation.

The band's success nosedived, however, after lead singer Natalie Maines denounced President George W. Bush from a stage in London, England, on March 10, 2003, shortly before the United States invaded Iraq for the second time in little more than a decade. She told the British crowd how she felt "ashamed" of sharing her home state of Texas with the Republican president, before playing "Travelin' Soldier" to affirming cheers. When word reached the United States, many country radio disc jockeys responded with political outrage and misogynistic insults for the band's perceived unpatriotic views. Encouraged by right-wing media, stations began boycotting the Chicks' music and holding rallies to destroy their records. These protests amounted to more than bad publicity. Band members received death threats for their dissent, and with the exception of one album in 2006, the group did not release any new music until 2020.[2]

The outrage against the Chicks' alleged apostasy suggested that the group had crossed a line. The Chicks had failed an unspoken loyalty test in which country disc jockeys and fans demanded that artists offer unconditional support for the troops and the government officials who made the hard decisions to send servicemembers off to fight.

Two months after the Chicks' fallout, *Billboard* magazine asked members of the country music industry about the particular bond between the music, the fans, and the military. Dennis Hannon, senior vice president of Nashville's Curb Records, admitted that "it's a fine line that you have to walk" between showing real patriotic feeling and appearing to capitalize off the most recent war. He believed that country songwriters penned wartime songs as authentic reflections of the average American in flyover country, not as an opportunistic money grab. In Hannon's estimation, country writers knew how to speak for the "silent majority that typifies the country consumer. Country music has never been driven by the East Coast or West Coast. It's driven by middle America, the heartland. That's where the more conservative approach comes in; the more patriotic approach." The singer Daryl Worley trusted that people who "listen to country music are hard-working, working-class American people" and believed that "country listeners tend to back us guys when we put out something pro-America [or] pro-military." As for the specific role of musicians, Aaron Tippin put country artists' relationship to the military even more bluntly: "We're the cheerleaders."[3]

The responses given by these record executives and artists echoed the political and racial stories that academics and journalists often cite when writing about country music's association with the US Armed Forces. A common historical explanation posits that, in the late 1960s, as the peace movement defied the authority of the government to wage the war in Vietnam and as the Black freedom struggle notched landmark legal victories, a white "silent majority" cleaved to the ostensibly all-American virtues of white supremacist law and order, evangelical Christianity, and patriarchal social values. This constituency heard their feelings expressed in country music songs like Merle Haggard's "Okie from Muskogee" and "The Fightin' Side of Me," songs that earned him an invitation to the Nixon White House and the loyalty of fans who believed that Haggard spoke for them. The political views of these songs, along with country music's historical association with white southerners, appeared to offer cultural validation for Nixon's "Southern Strategy," which began in the late 1960s. Ever since, country music has delivered anthems that have draped the nationalistic support for war in patriotic bunting, from Greenwood's "God Bless the U.S.A." to Keith's "Courtesy of the Red, White, and Blue."[4] In this calculus, country music's support for the troops reflects some cultural predisposition that ties the genre's fans to the politics of US militarization.

But country music's relationship to the US military is more complex than artists acting as "cheerleaders," and it did not spring fully formed from the silent majority's simmering indignation. This book traces how the Pentagon and the country music industry created an economic relationship that benefited the growth of the genre's commercial power while also encouraging country listeners to enlist in and support the Cold War military. In the pages that follow, I refer to this reciprocal relationship between the Defense Department and the genre as "country music militarization."[5] This phrase emphasizes how the US military influenced the business and politics of the country music industry. I use it as shorthand to describe the personal, economic, and symbolic connections between a genre usually associated in the popular imagination with white southerners and the expansion of the Cold War defense state that delivered a financial boon to their region. Relying on music industry archives, oral histories, and military records, I show how this partnership transformed country music into the sound of white allegiance to US militarization over the late twentieth century.

Cold War Country forwards three main arguments that cover the development of the country music industry's connection to the Pentagon. First, I show how the genre's entrepreneurs latched onto the expansion of the Cold War military to help grow their businesses during the formative years of the genre's industry. Beginning in the 1950s, the Defense Department sponsored country music radio and television programs aimed at recruiting the music's predominantly white fan base. This relationship gave Music Row, the metonym for what became Nashville's neighborhood of publishing companies and recording studios, a promotional partner to sell its products and a distribution network to expand its audiences around the globe. The Armed Forces Radio and Television Service (AFRTS) networks, now known as the American Forces Network, aired thousands of hours of country music programs for military and foreign civilian listeners during the Cold War.[6] These radio and television stations provided Nashville's white artists with a government-sponsored media outlet to promote their records and expand their audiences around the globe. Additionally, the global system of installations maintained by the US Armed Forces acted as a de facto touring route for country music artists looking to increase their audience, create positive publicity, and entertain the troops. These installations also housed Army and Air Force Exchange stores, commonly referred to as the Post Exchange or PX, where record companies could sell their products to servicemembers in need of entertainment. Soldiers steadily increased the number of country music records they bought over the 1950s and 1960s. By 1968, the PXs in Europe sold more country records than any other category, giving Music Row's artists around 65 percent of the soldier market share.[7]

Second, I argue that country music militarization helped white southerners see the expansion of the military as a part of their regional culture rather than an intrusion of state power into everyday life. Because of its themes of masculine individualism and working-class pride, country music provided the populist cover for white southerners who joined the military to receive federally funded benefits like the GI Bill. When those white southerners enlisted, they began to request more country music on AFRTS stations, and some began using the armed forces as a space to explore their own talents for playing the music. Dozens of country musicians, including future stars Faron Young, Johnny Cash, Mel Tillis, and George Strait, used their time in the ranks to hone their craft. Many of these men participated in the military's Special Services, the division in charge of troop morale and entertainment, as a springboard into a civilian music career once they left the military. Artists who had served their nation in this way established personal connections between the genre and the military, making armed service seem like a natural part of the country industry and, by extension, white southern culture.

Third, I argue that the country music industry's relationship with the military turned the genre's politics toward political conservatism over the last third of the twentieth century. The expansion of the defense state had enjoyed broad support in the early years of the Cold War, when Americans of virtually all political persuasions shared a belief in a strong standing military that could fight communists. As debates over the Vietnam War fractured that consensus, an unflinching commitment to the armed forces became a central tenet of politicians who painted their opponents and anyone who dared to question military foreign policies as something less than patriotic. Politicians on the right, conservative Republicans and southern Democrats, built a movement that warned, ironically, against the increasing size of the federal government even as they supported the hawkish policies that increased the power and scope of the Defense Department. When President Ronald Reagan upped defense spending to unprecedented peacetime levels, the Republican Party conflated support for the military with support for the nation itself as way to win votes for its partisan agenda.[8]

The country industry located along Nashville's Music Row generally followed this political trajectory toward conservatism, not because of some inherent ideology within its artists and fans but because of the lucrative partnerships it had established with the Pentagon during the Cold War consensus of the 1950s. Cold War defense policies assured a demand for more soldiers. More soldiers meant steady pay, government benefits, and the creation of defense contractor jobs in the civilian sector to supply those troops. Those soldiers bought more country records and demanded that AFRTS stations play them. The Pentagon then used more country music in its recruitment and entertainment strategies. Simply put, the Cold War was good for the country music business.

Connecting Nashville's cultural economy and the political economy created by the Defense Department enhances our understanding of country music's class, gender, and racial politics. Since its emergence as a commercial style in the 1920s, country has cultivated a reputation as the music for the expressions and everyday experiences of the nation's working class, especially the white working class. Country songwriters have detailed the economic hardships, love lives, and social struggles of these people in their lyrics, cementing the music's connection between culture and class.[9] To further the genre's symbolic and social ties to rural America and the US South, country musicians have populated their songs with and dressed themselves as frontiersmen, farmers, miners, railroad engineers, and cowboys. The songs and stage personas of male artists celebrate the work of white men and the normative gender roles of manly labor.[10]

Soldiers, too, belong in country music's pantheon of white masculinity, as we can see by considering how working for the defense state impacted country music's fans, artists, and industry. Other writers have examined how the image of the soldier in television, popular songs, film, and literature influenced the "victory culture" of the postwar United States and informed the idealization of the warrior as a breadwinning hero for the nuclear family.[11] Yet these studies have largely overlooked the connections between country music and the job opportunities and political economy created by Cold War defense spending.[12] The military and its civilian defense contractors offered well-paying, stable government employment in the postwar South at a time when the region's economy lacked other comparable options. White southerners, including aspiring country stars, flocked to those government jobs. Those artists then sang songs about that government work and relied on their fellow defense workers to support their musical careers, completing a circle of art and labor shaped by the intersection of regional politics and Cold War military spending.

Cold War Country also adds new perspectives on the racial history of the genre and the popular music industry more broadly. Much of my work highlights how the white-dominated country music industry benefited from its connection with the Cold War military in ways that other genres did not. Although country has always featured racial and regional diversity, the recording industry has marketed the music as a genre almost exclusively associated with white performers and fans, often from the US South and Southwest.[13] During the late nineteenth and early twentieth centuries, record label executives and academic folklorists imposed their ideas of racial essentialism onto southern musical cultures. They segregated southern working-class music into two categories, with hillbilly, or what we now call country, classified as white music and the blues and other forms of Black music lumped under the category of race records. This musical color line did not reflect the actual repertoires played by musicians, and it did not reflect the way southerners listened to music. Instead, the record industry divided its products in a way that reproduced the white supremacist divisions of people and cultures in the Jim Crow United States.[14]

Because of country music's reputation as a genre for and by white Americans, the Defense Department's use of the music in its recruitment campaigns reveals the contradictions of the military's racial integration policies following World War II. President Harry Truman ordered the desegregation of the armed forces in 1948, and that executive order took practical effect during the Korean War. This newly integrated military emerged as one of the most diverse institutions in the nation thanks to the peacetime draft. Yet Black servicemembers continued to experience racism at the hands of white enlistees and civilians.[15] Likewise, country music recruitment campaigns could give the impression that the US Armed Forces, as an institution, favored white volunteers. I do not mean to suggest that all, or only, white southern soldiers loved country music or responded to these recruitment campaigns. But when the Pentagon used country music to convey its recruitment message, it imagined its audience for volunteer enlistees as white.

The government's investment in Nashville's white southern music industry echoed the infusion of military spending that had transformed the South's broader industrial economy. Beginning in the 1940s, the warfare state delivered an unprecedented level of economic growth to the South. White southern legislators in Congress used their positions of seniority within their respective Armed Services Committees to channel federal defense spending to the region. For the military and its contractors, the South offered cheap land, a temperate climate suitable for year-round training, and an underemployed workforce that lacked a sustained history of unionization. For the region's conservative Democratic leadership, defense spending supplied an infusion of government funds to the South, while skirting the tinge of socialism carried by New Deal programs.[16] This strategy of military Keynesianism boosted the US South's economy to unprecedented levels, as defense spending delivered both military installations and private contractors to the region. In 1951, southern states received around 8 percent of the military's prime contracts. By 1970, that amount grew to more than 25 percent.[17] Companies like Lockheed in Marietta, Georgia; Raytheon in Huntsville, Alabama; and Ingalls Shipbuilders in Pascagoula, Mississippi, remade the region's economy.[18]

The expansion of military spending in the postwar South disproportionately benefited white men and families in the region. White southern politicians had designed the distribution of veterans' benefits like the GI Bill to discriminate against Black veterans. Defense contractors in the region added to this racial inequality by operating under local control for as long as possible, meaning that their hiring and promotion remained rooted in the region's practices of Jim Crow segregation.[19] Through these discriminatory measures, defense spending helped turn portions of the Deep South into sites of white Sunbelt prosperity.[20]

Country music experienced a similar benefit from the federal government by building key components of its industry and infrastructure through Cold War defense spending. The country music business began coalescing on Nashville's Music Row at the same time that federal defense spending delivered concentrated economic growth to white communities around the South. Examining the reciprocal relationships between Music Row and the Pentagon reveals just how reliant these two institutions of US economic and cultural power were on one another.

Country music's connection to the military, however, predates the Cold War. Jimmie Rodgers, the "Father of Country Music," recorded the song "The Soldier's Sweetheart" during his first studio session in 1927.[21] Predictably, the number of war-themed songs exploded during World War II. In 1942, the yodeling hillbilly singer Elton Britt scored a hit with his song "There's a Star-Spangled Banner Waving Somewhere." With its lyrics about a disabled man who longs to give himself to military service, Britt's tune reportedly sold 4 million copies and became the first country song to earn a gold record distinction.[22] The country star Roy Acuff, a mainstay of the Nashville-based radio show the *Grand Ole Opry*, could attribute a portion of his soaring popularity during World War II to his tours for the United Service Organization (USO). According to wartime surveys in the soldier publications *Yank* magazine and *Stars and Stripes*, many men preferred Acuff to pop singers like Frank Sinatra.[23] For much of his career, Acuff even used a fiddle that members of the US Army's 348th Engineer Combat Battalion found in a "bombed-out" music store in Frankfurt, Germany, and shipped to their favorite country star as a gift.[24] While I reference these precedents, *Cold War Country* does not provide in-depth examinations of country music's spread before or during World War II. Nor does it offer anything close to a complete catalogue of every song about military service, anticommunism, or atomic warfare.[25]

I focus on the business, political, and racial histories of the Cold War era to show how the country industry and the government-funded defense state benefited from an underrecognized public-private partnership over the last half of the twentieth century. Part of the reasoning for this chronology is purely practical. It was not until the postwar era that the country music

FIGURE I.1 Roy Acuff began performing for military audiences during World War II and increased his participation in USO tours during the 1960s. Those performances included tours in the Pacific during the Vietnam War, where he appeared as an ambassador of the *Grand Ole Opry*. (Roy Acuff Scrapbook, courtesy of the Country Music Hall of Fame and Museum)

labels, publishers, and studios consolidated into a recognizable industry in Nashville, while the genre's business actors did not form their primary trade organization, the Country Music Association, until 1958.[26] Meanwhile, what President Dwight Eisenhower called the "military-industrial complex" emerged from the combination of private industry, academia, and the military buildup designed to deter nuclear war and the threat of communism in the Cold War.[27]

I also aim to bring a fresh outlook to the history of state expansion within this time frame. In relying on music industry archives to tell much of my story, I show how country music helped assuage Americans' historical suspicions of centralized authority. This is not to argue that conspiring powers within the Defense Department consciously plotted to convince country music's listeners to support a peacetime military of unprecedented size and scope. My hope is to highlight how this happened regardless of intent. As the military grew, its use of country music legitimized that expansion to the genre's fans. This blending of public and private sectors filtered state growth through the down-home sounds of country music.[28] It dressed Leviathan in a cowboy hat and surplus fatigues.

I begin by exploring the roots of that business relationship through Connie B. Gay, a New Deal agricultural adviser who discovered the entrepreneurial potentials of country radio in the postwar period. During the 1950s, Gay planted a flag for country music in Washington, DC, by purchasing radio and television stations and managing country musicians. He also established a partnership with the Pentagon to promote his radio stations and the artists he managed to US servicemembers around the globe. By the end of the decade, Gay had pioneered the use of country music in military recruitment radio shows, amassed a multimillion-dollar fortune based in the ownership of radio and television stations, and served as the founding president of the Country Music Association.

Gay's work laid a foundation for the military's country music recruitment campaigns in the 1950s that featured stars like Faron Young. An eventual Country Music Hall of Fame member, Young received an early career boost when the US Army drafted him and made him a voice of recruitment. The Pentagon embraced a wide range of country music recruitment programs following Young's tenure and relied on the folksy charm of other talented country stars to encourage enlistment. When the military began using those musicians to recruit white men into the service, it gave a familiar, down-home face and sound to the US Cold War military, one of the largest bureaucratic institutions in the world.

Some of those young men who joined the military in search of a better life, or who were snagged by the draft, also used their time in the service to woodshed their musical skills and broaden their artistic pursuits. One group of musically inclined white southern veterans coalesced in Memphis in the early 1950s to create a new style of country music called "rockabilly." Almost all of the songwriters, producers, and musicians who shook up Nashville with their cutting-edge sound gained their professional start in music by playing with fellow servicemembers through the US Army and Air Force Special Services Division or in more informal settings around the barracks. Their experiences support my argument that country music made its way into the ranks by two directions: from the top-down collaborations between the Defense Department and Music Row and from the servicemembers "on the ground" who did not check their talents or fandom at the installation gate.[29] Service in the racially integrated Cold War military also opened their ears to new sounds and artistic influences. Those influences came together to help make rockabilly and eventually the style of rock and roll popularized by Elvis Presley.

Presley's trajectory differed from that of his rockabilly peers in that he did not serve in the military until after he was famous, but his musical and military careers profoundly impacted the racial politics of the country industry and the South as a whole in the 1950s. I argue that racial integration on southern military installations and rockabilly's Black influence within country music represented internal threats to the white South's racial hierarchy. For southern white supremacists, military and musical integration represented a two-pronged attack on Jim Crow launched by a communist conspiracy to subvert US power by eroding the armed forces and the dominance of white culture. Elvis Presley began his career as a symbol of that threat to the white social hierarchies and the racial order of the country music industry. By the time Presley had completed his military service from 1958 to 1960, he had become a matinee star and pop-music idol stripped of his threatening image. In this sense, military service did for Presley what it promised to do for thousands of other working-class white men across the South and the country music industry itself. It opened a route to middle-class decency for someone who had grown up at the edge of respectable white southern society.

Like Presley, the country music industry learned how to increase its profits through an association with the Pentagon. Throughout the 1960s, the Country Music Association (CMA) used the Defense Department to cultivate a global network for the promotion and sale of country music. The CMA adopted "Best Liked World-Wide" as an early slogan for its marketing of country music. Although the genre had not earned that title, the CMA used the AFRTS to push country music to military and civilian audiences around the world and make its slogan into a reality. The PXs provided the necessary infrastructure for the US music business to export musical products around the world and built a global community of listeners for American music, particularly country music. The CMA reaped the benefits of country music's spread through the Cold War military, which provided a government-subsidized outlet for building wealth within a white-dominated industry.

Class, race, and recruitment dramatically shaped the politics of country music during the Vietnam War. Although I analyze reactionary anthems like Merle Haggard's "Okie from Muskogee," I contextualize them within the diversity of political opinions about the war expressed in country songs, including voices of dissent. But country artists' songs of subtle protest could not break the ties between Music Row and the Pentagon's recruitment and entertainment machines. The country music industry and the Pentagon continued their cozy relationship by sending artists on tours of military installations in Europe and Asia to help grow the genre's profits. This lucrative business relationship meant that Music Row could not afford to break with the Pentagon as support for the war became a rallying cry for conservatism in the Nixon era.

I close by showing how country music helped blur the distinctions between patriotism, nationalism, and militarization following the shift to an all-volunteer force (AVF). When Richard Nixon ended the draft in 1973, he mandated a radical restructuring of military policy that altered the demographics of the US Armed Forces. The conversion to the AVF led to an increase in minorities and women in the service, in part because the military offered a modicum of social welfare at a time that politicians cut those benefits in the civilian sector.[30] Changes to personnel policy coincided with changes to foreign policy, and the United States entered a period of warmer relations with the Soviet Union and other Cold War foes.[31] For a brief window in the late 1970s, it appeared that country music militarization had started to wane, as the armed forces no longer needed the genre to recruit enlistees in the way it had in previous decades.

The defense spending spree initiated under Ronald Reagan renewed the connection between Music Row and the Pentagon, and country music militarization took on a new guise in the Reagan-Bush era. Following the conversion to the AVF, the PXs no longer functioned as a cornerstone of country record sales. Neither did the AFRTS play as much country as it once had. Instead of country performers selling their music to soldiers, they doubled down on selling themselves as patriotic artists to civilian audiences by associating themselves with the military. No artist capitalized on patriotic pride like Lee Greenwood. After the release of his song "God Bless the U.S.A." in 1984, Greenwood became the darling performer for Reagan and other small-government conservatives while they expanded the size of the federal government through unprecedented levels of peacetime defense spending. By the time of the Soviet Union's collapse and the start of George H. W. Bush's Persian Gulf War, Greenwood proved just how profitable patriotism could be for individual artists willing to cash in on the fifty-year history of country music militarization.

My concentration on country music is not meant to obscure the way other media and other musical genres intersected with the US government's Cold War missions. The Defense Department kept close watch over images of the armed forces in film and television, developing a media relations office early in the Cold War to police the portrayal of American fighting men in Hollywood and aid in recruitment campaigns.[32] The Pentagon also used pop, rock, and soul music to achieve its recruiting goals, while the State Department used pop and jazz to portray the United States as a nation of racial inclusiveness in the face of communist propaganda that pointed to the hypocrisy of Jim Crow rule in a democratic nation.[33] Throughout the book, I offer comparative analysis of the way Black pop, jazz, R&B, and blues artists served and wrote music about their time in the armed forces.[34]

The book focuses on country music so intensely because no other genre's industry courted the financial aid of the Pentagon and used the military to build its business the way that Music Row did. And although the armed forces used other styles of music in their recruitment campaigns, no other genre's industry was primed to deliver what the military needed like country music. Throughout the Cold War, Nashville's music industry still functioned as a small-town operation with an insular community of producers, artists, and business actors. Music Row's genre-affiliated, vertically integrated industry model made it well-suited to deliver what the military needed. The Defense Department created an even cozier connection to Nashville after the birth of the CMA, which retained tight control over the image and politics of the music while keeping it in line with the military's Cold War mission. As a result, no genre bears the mark of the Cold War's militarization and normative patriotism into the present day like country music.

By bringing together musical and military histories, *Cold War Country* also reveals how culture can racialize and polarize the supposedly race-neutral, nonpartisan institutions of the US government. Although the US Armed Forces has pushed for progressive racial policies and claims no partisan affiliation, the Defense Department's close connection to Music Row branded armed service with the white sounds and symbols of country music. This book helps us understand how the Pentagon's well-funded bureaucracy not only provides for the common defense but also reflects and shapes US culture.

From a vantage point in the early twenty-first century, country music holds what seems like a naturally occurring affinity with hawkish patriotism. We expect country musicians to back the troops or, as Aaron Tippin suggested, be the "cheerleaders" of the US military. My book offers a deeper explanation. It shows that white southern men supported the military as a key to class mobility in the postwar era. Country music made the military seem like a part of white southern culture, something familiar, something that sounded like home. If country music is the sound of US patriotism, it is because Music Row spent decades cultivating a business alliance with the Pentagon.

1 Big Government Country

Connie B. Gay and the Roots of Country Music Militarization

· ·

Connie B. Gay used country music to build a media empire in the 1950s. His ascent began with a job as a radio announcer in 1946 on station WARL in Arlington, Virginia, and a hunch that listeners in the Washington, DC, suburbs might tune in for what the music business then called "hillbilly" music. He ended the 1950s as the founding president of the Country Music Association, the owner of dozens of radio stations, the producer of television shows on national networks, and a multimillionaire. Performers like Jimmy Dean, George Hamilton IV, Patsy Cline, Roy Clark, Johnny Cash, Andy Griffith, the Stoneman Family, and Grandpa Jones all received early career boosts from Gay's web of media and concert promotions based in the capital metropolitan area. Even *Grand Ole Opry* stars like Eddy Arnold and Minnie Pearl traveled to Washington, DC, to appear on Gay's radio and television programs *Radio Ranch*, *Gay Time*, and *Town and Country Time*. Others, including Elvis Presley, toured through Washington to play his "Hillbilly Cruise" aboard a yacht that sailed more than 2,000 concertgoers up and down the Potomac River.[1]

Gay's biography reads like a testament to entrepreneurial drive. In 1971, the *Washington Post* featured a front-page profile on Gay, then fifty-six years old. The headline told how "he rose from hardscrabble farm to king of the hill," and the writer described him as "country music's media magician." An accompanying photograph showed Gay, along with his second wife, an ex-model who was twenty years his junior, and their two small children. They posed on a verdant lawn in front of the family's four-columned Colonial Revival home in the affluent Washington, DC, suburb of MacLean, Virginia. When Gay was pressed about how much wealth he had accrued through this magic, he coyly told the paper, "Just say it's millions. . . . Enough to make sure it won't run out as long as I live."[2]

Country music carried Gay a long way from his humble origins. Born on a dirt farm in North Carolina in 1914, Gay struggled out of poverty to earn a college degree, worked as a New Deal agricultural adviser during the Great

Depression and World War II, and learned the radio business just in time to take advantage of the United States' postwar appetite for pop culture entertainment. He transformed country music's artists, producers, and record labels into an industry over the course of his career, having organized the Country Music Dis Jockey Association in 1953, cofounded the Country Music Association in 1958, and helped establish the Country Music Foundation in 1964. He even provided the first $10,000 donation to build the Country Music Hall of Fame.[3] Although he never made Nashville his full-time residence, Gay earned a reputation as a founding father of the industry that gave the Tennessee capital its nickname, Music City, USA.[4]

The characterization of Gay as an independent and visionary entrepreneur offers a compelling story, but he owed much of his success to his close ties with the US Department of Defense. Their relationship built gradually. Beginning in the late 1940s, Gay cultivated a country music audience made up of servicemembers, Pentagon employees, and other government workers by producing live concerts and radio programs in the Washington, DC, metropolitan area. Gay, like thousands of other natives of the rural South, as well as other regions, had moved to the capital during World War II for wartime government employment. The location of the Pentagon in Arlington, Virginia, meant that this influx of military personnel and defense contractors remained in and around the capital after the war. Gay recognized the potential to market country music in Arlington, sold the genre to this influx of government workers, and discovered some of the biggest stars of the twentieth century when they were still working for the Cold War defense state.

Gay formalized his connection between his country music businesses and the US military in 1951 when he booked Grandpa Jones and His Grandchildren on a tour of bases in Japan and the front lines of the Korean War. This tour generated a publicity boon for Gay's radio station back home in Arlington, as listeners tuned in to hear his reports from the battlefront and country music's role in the fight against communism. Gay parlayed this success into a position as an entertainment adviser for the Department of Defense, a role that he used to book country artists in the US military's global network of Cold War installations. As the Pentagon established the indefinite presence of US soldiers in Europe, Asia, and the Caribbean, Gay made sure that those troops, essentially a captive audience of young men, heard the latest stars of country music live and in person during the 1950s.

Country music was not the only form of entertainment to intersect with the United States' early Cold War mission. Pop stars, comedians, and movie stars toured bases throughout the world in the 1950s and visited the troops stationed in Korea, while the Armed Forces Radio Service (AFRS) played pop and swing jazz music more than any other genres during the decade.[5] African American R&B and blues musicians wrote about military service and the racial inequality still present in the ranks despite President Truman's Executive Order 9981 issued in 1948, which had mandated the eventual integration of the US Armed Forces.[6] But where white country artists used the Pentagon to build their stardom, Black artists confronted the predatory business practices of the recording industry. Only the white entrepreneurs of the music industry could use the military to promote its artists and records. The realization of that commercial success for country music began with Connie B. Gay.

US soldiers had demonstrated their fandom for country music going back to World War II. The AFRS had attempted to address the soldiers' desire for the genre during the 1940s with the country music show *Melody Roundup*. In the early 1950s, the network produced original country content with the programs *Redd Harper's Hollywood Roundup* and *Carolina Cotton Calls*. Additionally, the stars of radio station WSM's *Grand Ole Opry* began touring US military installations in Europe, and the AFRS aired the show for soldiers beginning in the 1940s. However, whereas those efforts represented marginal attempts to meet the soldiers' demand for country music, Gay made it a driving tenet of his business model.

The connection Gay established between country music and the Cold War military not only strengthened the genre's popularity but also helped change the music in significant ways. His concerts and radio programs in the Washington, DC, area elevated country music's class status. He booked performances in Constitution Hall and staged shows on a chartered yacht, all in an effort to sell the genre as the sound of a rising postwar middle class. Gay's use of military bases as country music concert venues also helped popularize the genre among US troops and disseminated the sound of country music to international audiences. And the connections Gay established between country music and the military paved the way for the Pentagon to use the genre as a recruitment tool. He took a genre predominantly associated with white, southern, working-class artists and fans and helped position it as a central part of the military's culture. This new relationship offered a powerful lesson at the birth of the Cold War. If you wanted to make money in the booming postwar economy, hitching yourself to the US military was a good bet.

From Lizard Lick to the Pentagon

Connie B. Gay followed an unpredictable path to becoming one of the most powerful businessmen in country music. By his own admission, Gay lacked musical talent. "I can't pick a note and can't sing a song to save my life," he conceded. "Never have been able to." Gay compensated for his lack of talent with a shrewd understanding of the music business, a willingness to capitalize on government assistance, and an understanding of country music's mass appeal.[7]

Born on August 22, 1914, in Lizard Lick, North Carolina, Gay came of age in a family of ten children and endured the typical hardships of rural southern poverty, including intense labor, little health care, and hunger. His family farmed and, for a short time, owned a general store. But prosperity eluded them. His native area of North Carolina experienced such impoverishment during the 1920s and 1930s, he recalled, that "you'd have to sit on a sack of fertilizer to raise an umbrella."[8]

Like thousands of other young men of his generation, Gay wanted out of the drudgery of manual labor. "We lived from hell to breakfast in those days, and there was always that damn mule waiting for me back home and 16 hours a day in the tobacco fields," he told a reporter in 1968, and he knew he was "tired of following a mule."[9] He was a poor white child in the US South during the first decades of the twentieth century, so his opportunities remained limited by a lack of local government investment in education; but he found a track to advancement by following an agricultural curriculum through high school and into college. He later recognized this opportunity as a benefit of the Smith-Hughes Farm Vocational Education Act of 1917.[10] This legislation had developed educational programs for rural schools in order to help students who planned to pursue a career in agriculture.[11]

At North Carolina State College, Gay paid his tuition by working at a dairy barn and busing tables. He also earned extra money by serving as a driver, booker, and announcer on radio station WPTF in Raleigh. WPTF broadcast to the rural communities throughout the North Carolina Piedmont, and that reach gave Gay his first exposure to the power of mass communication. He graduated with a degree in agricultural education and got a job with the US Department of Agriculture's Soil Erosion Service (later the Soil Conservation Service). This government work provided a source of job security and $150 per month in the middle of the Great Depression. Gay also worked as an adviser to a Civilian Conservation Corps camp in

Yanceyville, North Carolina, giving him another way to remain connected to the rural people in his native state.[12]

Although the Depression devastated southern farming, banking, and industry, it ushered in a boom time for radio. With little money and unemployment on the rise, radio offered a relatively cheap distraction for weary minds. Gay left his government post for a brief time in the 1930s to pursue a radio career and returned to WPTF as the station's farm program director. With early-morning and noontime slots, Gay hosted a commentary show on the issues facing the farmers of North Carolina's Piedmont region.[13] The station aired hillbilly music acts in between the farm programming. The Monroe Brothers, the Delmore Brothers, the Swingbillies, and the Tobacco Tags filled WPTF's airwaves in the mid-1930s, delivering the newest sounds in white string-band music and the close vocal harmonies that would help define postwar bluegrass and country duet singing.[14] These performances kept listeners tuned in to the Raleigh station, while Gay kept them informed of the latest agricultural news. It also made Gay aware of the powerful combination of radio technology, hillbilly music, and the distribution of news to suit the interests of working-class southerners.

Gay's entrepreneurial drive kept him chasing different job opportunities during the Depression, but none proved as reliable as the US government. He left the radio job in Raleigh for a brief time to try his hand as a traveling salesman. But with little luck on the streets of the southern towns still reeling from the economic downturns of the era, Gay headed for the dependable payroll offered by governmental agencies founded during the New Deal. In 1941, he returned to the Department of Agriculture as a county supervisor for the Farm Security Administration (FSA). Gay held a deep admiration for President Franklin Roosevelt and the humanitarian aspects of the New Deal. He described the FSA's mission this way: "the finest concept of humanity of its time, and for all times, in my book, because we were out there to help those who had no way of helping themselves." Gay took pride in his role "helping tenants, sharecroppers, the black, [and] the poor" and valued the Roosevelt administration's willingness to use governmental power to do so. With his sharp mind and dogged ambition, he ascended through the ranks at the FSA, quickly becoming a regional supervisor in North Carolina.[15] Rather than drive around the state promoting New Deal programs like the Farm Tenancy Act, Gay began broadcasting to farmers from radio stations in Charlotte to spread what he called "the virtues of the New Deal." "I found out by the use of the radio I could reach 1,000 people

FIGURE 1.1 Connie B. Gay (*right*) talks with a farmer, ca. 1940. Gay worked for the Farm Security Administration in his home state of North Carolina during the Great Depression before becoming a country music impresario after World War II. (Marion Post Wolcott, FSA-OWI Collection, Library of Congress)

in a day or 10,000 people in a day with a New Deal farm philosophy that it would take me a year or two to reach with my old Chevrolet."[16]

Beyond reaching tens of thousands of listeners, Gay also knew how to create radio content that would resonate with his southern audiences. One of his FSA radio spots, titled "Just Call Me Lu!," tells the story of a North Carolina widow named Lucinda, whose "man had died back in Hoover days," "had four young'uns to feed," and suffered from "confounded kidney trouble." Suspicious of government interference in her fledging tobacco farm tenancy, Lu finally acquiesced to the advice of the local vocational agriculture and home economics teachers regarding the FSA's rehabilitation program. The FSA equipped Lu with a new lease, a budget, farming advice, cooperation with local doctors for her family's medical needs, and a pressure cooker, along with instructions in canning her crops. Not only did Lu prosper with this new arrangement, but listeners learned that she had a son stationed in the Pacific and explained that it "must have been the canned goods and fresh vegetables and milk and medical care and all that. But he passed the Army's examination in nothing flat."[17] Consisting of equal parts Erskine Caldwell, hillbilly schtick, and New Deal propaganda, Gay's radio play delivered an allegorical southern character on the road from apprehension to full-throated endorsement of government action. In return for the government's assistance, Lu promised her son to the defense of the nation-state.

After the war, Gay combined his understanding of the white southern radio market, his agricultural expertise, and his experience with hillbilly music into a new entrepreneurial career in the private sector. In the mid-1940s, he began delivering agricultural news on the *Farm and Home Hour*, which broadcast over the Blue Network. "We went on the air at noon every day," he remembered. The network paired Gay's agricultural news reports with musical accompaniment but never gave much thought to genre. Gay did. "I noticed . . . that if we played music on the *Farm and Home Hour*, if the orchestra played anything with a rural flavor, we'd get mail. And I mean tons of mail. But if they just stuck to the old regular *Farm and Home Hour* type of music, you know, nothing happened. So it had given me an idea."[18] It was one of the most profitable ideas he would ever have.

Gay used what he learned to start the first hillbilly radio program in the Washington, DC, area. When station WARL in Arlington, Virginia, came up for sale in late 1946, some of Gay's business associates bought it. Gay offered to serve as the announcer, working strictly on commission of advertising sales, if the owners would let him play what he wanted. The owners agreed, and the station went on the air November 6, 1946, with Gay playing hillbilly music. He recalled the immediate positive response. "The phone started ringing. People said 'Lord, have mercy. Why hasn't somebody done this before?'"[19]

· · · · · ·

No one had done it before because the music business had just begun to realize the full commercial potential of hillbilly music in the late 1940s. Gay had stumbled on the right combination of medium, demographics, and genre at the right moment. He also recognized the role of the federal government in creating a market for the music. Arlington's WARL emerged as the home for hillbilly music in northern Virginia, Washington, DC, and Maryland, where thousands of rural people had migrated during the war for defense-related jobs. Nothing symbolized the complete transformation of northern Virginia's landscape and political economy like the location of the Pentagon building in Arlington, constructed between 1941 and 1943.

With fifty acres of parking lots, thirty miles of feeder roads, a dedicated bus station, and its own zip code, the Pentagon functioned as the "nerve center" of US military strength. New apartment cities, a $15 million shopping center, and a population boom of 50 percent in Arlington County between 1940 and 1943 transformed the once small town into a sprawling metropolis. The new Arlington represented a new South, even as Robert E. Lee's mansion, which gave the town its name, looked down from its hilltop on the Potomac River.[20]

As military personnel and civilian defense industry employees mixed along the freshly paved suburban streets, they tuned in daily to hear the latest records, as well as the live music on Gay's programs, which he named *Radio Ranch* and *Town and Country Time*.[21] In the late 1940s and early 1950s, before Nashville had established its hold on the commercial aspects of hillbilly music, hundreds of live-performance radio shows, recording studios, fan magazines, and honky-tonks distributed country music throughout the nation. Audiences could tune in to shows like WLW's *Midwestern Hayride* in Cincinnati, the *Village Barn* on NBC from New York City, Chicago's WLS *National Barndance*, or, beginning in 1951, *Town Hall Party* on Los Angeles's WXLA.[22] None was bigger than WSM's *Grand Ole Opry*, a fan favorite that broadcast from the Ryman Auditorium in Nashville, Tennessee; the station's powerful transmitter meant that it reached more of the rural South than other shows.[23]

Because of the *Opry*'s reach, Nashville claimed its title as the capital of hillbilly music, but the industry had not yet centralized there. The genre's press consisted of a few magazines like *Country Song Roundup* and *Hoedown: The Magazine of Hillbilly and Western Stars*, published in Derby, Connecticut, and Cincinnati, Ohio, respectively. In the pages of these publications, readers would learn of the hillbilly happenings in California, the Midwest, New England, and even Canada. Gay worked to make Washington, DC, the center of the hillbilly music world. When he discovered the overwhelmingly enthusiastic reception for the genre on WARL, he looked for ways to capitalize on the music's mass appeal. Gay's successes multiplied as he learned how to raise the stature of the genre from something associated with the rural, white ignorance of a character like Lu to something more befitting the rural, white transplants who had moved to the city during the war boom.

On October 31, 1947, almost one year after first taking the air on WARL, Gay scored a cultural coup for the genre and profits for himself when he booked a hillbilly show at Constitution Hall in Washington, DC. As a public trust managed by the Daughters of the American Revolution (DAR), Constitution Hall represented the staid confines of what passed as high culture in the US at midcentury. The DAR usually hosted classical and opera performances, genres that functioned as proper soundtracks for the organization's claims to atavistic Americanism. However, Gay partnered with Nashville's *Grand Ole Opry* to hire the biggest names in the business to headline the show, including Minnie Pearl, Eddy Arnold and His Tennessee Plowboys, and the Willis Brothers. He also showcased his developing stable of local talent with Pops Stoneman and the Stoneman Family. Presenting country music in this hallowed hall bordered on sacrilegious. But regardless of this uneven matching of genre and venue, no one could deny the event's popularity. Gay and company sold out two shows that night and raked in $22,000, a record for Constitution Hall at that point.[24] The previous record belonged to the Polish classical pianist Ignacy Jan Paderewski, who earned a mere $12,000.[25]

Gay turned that one night's success into a standing engagement at Constitution Hall, initially set for fifty-two Saturday nights beginning on April 17, 1948. Meanwhile, the negotiation of cultural power between the insurgent hillbilly genre and the pearl-clutching DAR played out in the press. Fred Hand, the manager of the venue, told the *Baltimore Sun* that "there is some sort of revolution going on," in reference to the debut of the hillbilly acts at the revered concert venue.[26] This revolution meant enormous profits, as both the DAR and Gay stood to benefit financially from the booking. The DAR, for its trouble, intended to make between $30,000 and $40,000 in rental fees for Gay's use of the space from 8:00 to 11:00 P.M. every Saturday night for the next year, while Gay hoped to replicate his initial success. Gay broadcast the show, which he called *Gay Time*, on WWDC-FM. According to the *Washington Daily News*, Gay wanted to make the program more popular than the *Grand Ole Opry*, basing his ambition on the fact that Constitution Hall's "seats will be softer" than the Ryman Auditorium's and his estimate that American consumers would purchase 35 million radio sets by 1950.[27] And the DAR need not have worried too much about the reputation of its venue. The *Evening Star* relayed that Gay "refers to his productions as concerts of folk music, rather than hillbilly programs."[28] By describing the music he promoted as folk, Gay skirted the more pejorative designation for the genre and, by extension, its fans.

Despite the class prejudices harbored by the DAR, the conservative women's group could rest easy knowing that Gay only booked white artists for the show. At the time, the DAR insisted that Constitution Hall remain a space for white artists to perform. The group's Jim Crow standards had caused serious public relations problems only a few years before Gay brought his hillbillies to town. In 1939, the women enforced their segregationist policy against Marian Anderson by refusing to allow the renowned Black opera singer to perform because of her race.[29] The *Daily News* announced, "In keeping with DAR policy, Mr. Gay will not be allowed to use Negro singers, altho [sic] spirituals will be an important part of his program."[30] *Gay Time* might bring the city's suspicious recent transplants, but Gay's show benefited from the record industry's marketing of hillbilly music as the genre of white artists and fans, a necessary stipulation to enter the refined space of Constitution Hall.

An all-white cast and audience not only conformed to the DAR and the city's Jim Crow laws, but it also inadvertently enabled Gay to take the show to the new medium of television. *Gay Time* made its television debut in August 1948, after sixteen weeks of sellout Saturday-night shows at Constitution Hall. The *Washington Post*'s Sonia Stein reported that the capital city hoped to emerge as "a big TV center" and noted that media outlets had discussed "televising tourist meccas around town" like monuments and museums. With a good-humored sense of irony and a bit of surprise, Stein asked, "What is now being fed to the NBC network for the folks in Boston, New York and other points along the coaxial cable from this cosmopolitan community, this reservoir of culture[?] Hillbilly music!"[31]

In a span of four months, Gay had extended his show's reach from local radio to national television on NBC's early forays into the new medium and earned a reputation as one of the leading men in the business. Gay, along with his cast and crew, made only $750 per broadcast from NBC.[32] But, combined with his collection of the ticket sales at Constitution Hall and the sponsorships from his WARL radio shows airing three times a day, Gay emerged as a commercial force in the national hillbilly scene. The *Washington Post* noted that, despite the cornpone humor associated with *Gay Time* and hillbilly music in general, "nobody kids the 'Gay Time' show. . . . Possibly that's because one million dollars a year makes even chin whiskers and nasal twangs seem like very serious matters."[33]

Gay flooded the Washington airwaves with country music thanks to his ever-growing roster of performers, which continued to mix local talent with artists from other hillbilly shows like the *Grand Ole Opry*. One of Gay's most consequential collaborations was with Louis Marshall "Grandpa" Jones at a pivotal moment in both of their careers. Jones had joined the US Army in 1944 and served for two years in a Combat Military Police battalion in

Germany. While overseas, he found success on the AFRS playing on a live radio program with four other soldiers, calling themselves the Munich Mountaineers.[34]

Jones and his band played for five months on the radio and received an overwhelmingly positive response from Americans and Germans alike. Jones remembered that the Munich Mountaineers "started getting stacks of fan mail from lonely GIs who hadn't been able to hear any real country music since they got overseas; most of the military music was brass bands, and the touring show troupes consisted of pop singers like Al Jolson." Their success on the radio turned into demand for live performances, and the Munich Mountaineers appeared at the Red Cross Hall and at beer gardens around their namesake city.[35] The fan magazine *National Hillbilly News* reported in its May–June 1950 issue that Jones "still receives mail from ex-GI's who remember his broadcasts 'over there.'"[36] He had experienced modest success before the war, serving as a regular performer on an Akron, Ohio, radio station's "Friday Night Special." However, his time on the AFRS prepared him for even more postwar success as a recording artist and as a performer on the *Grand Ole Opry* beginning in 1946.[37] Jones spent the next few years recording several successful sides for King Records and then landed a residency on Richmond, Virginia's *Old Dominion Barn Dance* radio show in 1949.[38] Gay had welcomed the rising hillbilly talent on his show for occasional appearances throughout the late 1940s, but he planned a new kind of gig for Jones in 1951.

When the United States joined the fight against North Korea and China, Gay saw an opportunity to expand his brand and endear himself to the soldiers stationed in the Pacific. Using his personal connections to officers in the Pentagon, he booked Jones for a three-week tour of Japan and the front lines of the Korean War. In turn, Gay furthered Grandpa Jones's career, boosted WARL's reputation, and cultivated an audience for hillbilly music among the nation's soldiers. This tour helped establish a pipeline for country artists to tour military installations around the globe and laid the groundwork for an increased demand for hillbilly music in the ranks. During World War II, the music industry and the military had noticed servicemembers' desire for country music and its popularity on the AFRS. Many fighting men entered the military as fans of the music, while others discovered it when serving in the ranks. With Jones at his side, Gay tapped into a market that had emerged organically during the 1940s and began to use the military's fan base to build his media empire.

Locating the GI Hillbilly Market

The War Department created the AFRS in May 1942 as a part of the mission to improve troop morale. The network established its headquarters in Los Angeles, where it took advantage of the city's concentration of talent and recording facilities. The AFRS recorded original content in their studios and produced its own line of 78 rpm records called "transcriptions" that contained rebroadcasts of civilian network programming and collections of music pulled from civilian releases. It then shipped these discs to GI stations throughout the world for broadcasting. Wartime programs included officially produced shows like *Command Performance, Hymns from Home, G.I. Journal,* and *Sports Round-Up.*[39] Each week from 1943 to 1945, AFRS studios created 126 programs, totaling 21,000 transcriptions, which the War Department shipped overseas to the 306 stations in 47 different countries.[40] This programming included the show *Melody Roundup,* a quarter hour of popular hillbilly artists that aired four to five times per week from 1942 to 1949, in order to slake the demand for what was then a niche market genre.[41]

The AFRS's music and news provided state-sanctioned entertainment and current events to the troops at home and abroad. This network also cultivated markets for American music and radio programming that led to what *Billboard* magazine described in 1944 as "Global Americanization." The reporter Lou Frankel made an analogy between this sonic Americanization process and the colonial expeditions of past empires, describing how "in the lush and lusty days of the past, it was trade and desire for virgin territories that made for empire, that carried the flag, any flag, across continents and around the world." "Today, as everyone knows," Frankel's history lesson continued, "the same chore of flag carrying is being, and has been done, by radio."[42] As the US Armed Forces spread across the globe to fight fascism, their radio network colonized the ears of the foreign listening publics. The AFRS spread the sound of US democracy, all wrapped in the tantalizing sounds of popular music.

Frankel noted the potential in using servicemembers as test markets and compared the programming available on AFRS with the content of stateside commercial networks. He also commented on a creeping preference for hillbilly music in the listening tastes of the soldiers. Pop music dominated the percentages played on both civilian and military networks, with the AFRS using pop for 44 percent of its original programming and the domestic networks using it for 35 percent of daily material. Hillbilly represented the next most popular form of music on AFRS, registering 11 percent of original programming. The domestic commercial networks' hillbilly programming accounted for only 6 percent, while light concert music provided almost 16 percent of airtime. According to Frankel, this spike in hillbilly programming represented an answer to the troops' requests for the musical style and the genre's absence from the civilian network programs issued for them. In his opinion, this design for radio offered a lesson for stateside networks. Frankel suggested that "there should be a thought or two here for the network and local station program managers, for if the men overseas want more hillbilly music maybe the networks at home should give their audiences more cowpoke music."[43]

The military demand for hillbilly music continued after the war as well. The AFRS responded to requests for the genre with a prerecorded hillbilly radio show hosted by Redd Harper, a singer and star of cowboy films. Harper recorded his show, called *Hollywood Roundup*, in Los Angeles. The AFRS then shipped transcriptions of the program to its stations for the network's disc jockeys. William T. Allen, the editor and publisher of the fan magazine *Jamboree*, highlighted Harper's efforts to bring "folk music" to the military through the AFRS. Allen, writing as a veteran of World War II, praised Harper's efforts and remembered "how hungry" servicemembers were "for Folk Music Entertainment news while overseas": "the fellows on my ship used to sit around the mess hall 'Battling-the-breeze' about the Folk Music Entertainment World" only a few years prior. "Yep," Allen concluded, "you're doing something really worthwhile, Redd."[44]

Redd Harper's show offered listeners a mixture of western-themed music, cowpoke humor, and Christianity. Each episode of his *Hollywood Roundup* began with an introduction song played by Harper's backing musicians, the Saddle Kings, who sang their promise to "roundup some songs for you / Maybe a laugh or two." The Saddle Kings played the accompanying music on accordion, fiddle, steel guitar, bass, and acoustic rhythm guitar, while Harper cut in with the welcoming message: "A Hollywood howdy to you neighbors. This is your old corral pal Redd Harper bringing you a full half hour of cowboy and country music the way you like to hear it, featuring those sweet-singing cowpokes the Saddle Kings." In a typical episode, Harper dedicated his first song to an individual serviceman. "Right now," Harper told the AFRS audiences, "I want to fill a special request from Jim White and all of his buddies up there in the navy hospital in San Francisco, with Tim Spencer's famous song 'Room Full of Roses.'" Other songs included "San Antonio Rose," "In My Little Red Book," "Hawaiian War Chant," "Yellow Rose of Texas," and "Your Green Eyes."[45]

The episode closed with Harper sending out a gospel song to two British soldiers who were fans of the show: "We have a typical cowboy gospel number for you folks today, and we'd like to dedicate it to British Corporal Tommy Lee over in Korea and also to John Perry down there in New South Wales. It's the ever-popular cowboy hymn and prayer 'Lie Low Little Doggies, Lie Low.'" The song included a recitation in which a cowboy thanks God for being his "boss" and ponders the theodicy of why God allowed a coyote to kill a prized calf. Harper ended the show by encouraging his listeners to "go to any church you please, but please, go to church."[46] Harper went on to record a string of Christian country songs directed at children in the 1950s. "I'm a Christian Cowboy," for example, reminded boys that attending Sunday school did not make one a "sissy." He also starred, along with the songwriter and AFRS artist Cindy Walker, in the 1951 film *Mr. Texas*, which Billy Graham referred to as "the first Christian Western."[47] With these religious segments, Harper helped define military service by tapping into the white gospel traditions of country music and tying those themes into the United States' Cold War antagonism with atheistic communism.

The stars of the *Grand Ole Opry* brought country music to the troops through tours of military installations during and after World War II. In 1949, the show's biggest names recorded two broadcasts of the *Opry* for the troops while on a tour of the US Air Force bases in Germany. The tobacco giant R. J. Reynolds sponsored the performance of Roy Acuff, Hank Williams, Red Foley, Minnie Pearl, the comedian Rod Brasfield, and Little Jimmy Dickens, at the Berlin Opera House. Billy Robinson, a steel guitarist on the *Opry* staff, traveled with the stars as part of the backing band. Years later, he remembered, "The most beautiful part about the whole thing was the way that the air force, the soldiers, the enlisted men and people just took us right into—it was unbelievable, the response we got from those people." R. J. Reynolds's *Prince Albert Show* portion of the *Opry* aired every Saturday night over the AFRS, so the men were already familiar with, if not fans of, the music. Robinson believed that the *Opry*'s visit represented something deeper than entertainment. "It was home. Here the show that they'd been listening to every Saturday night, all of a sudden was right in front of them, and, boy, you couldn't believe the response. I mean they wouldn't stop applauding."[48] The *Opry* gave servicemembers a sense of belonging in a genre-specific community that could feel more like a family than a marketing demographic. For Americans stationed abroad, listening to country music on the AFRS and reading about it in the genre's fan magazines offered a way to participate in both real and imagined communities that tied them to home.[49]

The *Opry*'s stars continued making appearances at installations in the early 1950s, connecting with their military fans and making converts. Minnie Pearl, Rod Brasfield, and Red Foley returned to Germany in 1950, with Pearl providing her cornpone commentary on the trip for *Country Song Roundup* as a "Furrin' Coorespndent."[50] Roy Acuff and Hank Williams also played air force bases in Alaska and Germany. *National Hillbilly News* noted how "Opry entertainers all are anxious to make the Air Force troops, but the number going has to be 'rationed,' so as not to take too many of them away from millions of listeners back home at one time."[51] Country musicians also released songs in the early 1950s that indulged the anti-communist fervor of the time. Hank Williams, as his alter ego Luke the Drifter, recorded "No, No, Joe," which repudiated Joseph Stalin's potential for aggression. Several other country artists issued songs about the Korean War that both critiqued the hardships of armed service and championed the United States' willingness to fight communists.[52] Whether during war or peace, country music stars traveled away from their regular gigs to tour the bases of the Cold War military and recorded songs that endeared themselves and the genre to the troops.

• • • • • •

Connie Gay wanted to reach those same military audiences and saw the US involvement in the Korean War as an opportunity to build his brand. On March 4, 1951, Gay, Grandpa Jones and His Grandchildren, which consisted of Jones's wife, Ramona, and fellow *Old Dominion Barn Dance* star Mary Klick, began their trek to the war-torn Korean peninsula. The journey started when the US Army flew the four-person group from Washington, DC, to Japan for a two-day tour.[53] On March 10, the army fitted the group with GI uniforms and delivered them to the AFRS station Radio Tokyo for an on-air performance. Grandpa Jones and His Grandchildren then began an intense schedule of personal appearances over the next thirty-six hours, playing hospital auditoriums and giving bedside performances for soldiers convalescing at the Tokyo Army Hospital and the 361st Station Hospital.[54] They then joined a Special Services country band known as Western Jamboree to play a free show for all Allied personnel at the Far East Armed Forces' theater in Tokyo on March 12. The soldier newspaper *Stars and Stripes* promised that the concert would offer "the greatest aggregation of western talent ever seen in Japan" and alerted readers that the AFRS would record and rebroadcast the show.[55]

The transcription aired on the AFRS program *Jamboree* hosted by Rusty Knight, who introduced Gay as "the maker of hillbilly and western stars." Taking advantage of the massive reach of AFRS, Gay wasted no time in plugging radio stations back home before introducing Grandpa Jones. "We're a powerful long way from station WRVA in Richmond and station WARL in Arlington but powerful glad to be here," Gay began. "Let's get things started by bringing out the 'old coon hunter,' a man featured on the *Old Dominion Barn Dance* at present, no, featured at present out of Tokyo, then back at the *Old Dominion Barn Dance*. You used to hear him on the *Grand Ole Opry*. He's the 'old coon hunter'—Grandpa Jones!"[56]

Only thirty-seven years old at the time, Jones performed his geriatric character, complete with banjo, a false bushy gray moustache, and wire-rimmed glasses, for the live audience and the mix of servicemembers and civilians listening over AFRS across the Far East Network. The crowd cheered as Jones stepped to the microphone to say, "Thank you, I'm awful proud to be here, too, just like Connie. We hope we can do a little good over here." He then launched into his mixture of comedy and his latest releases on King Records. Jones jokingly introduced the first song title as "Son, Get Up and Light the Lamp, I Think I Done Knocked One of Your Ma's Eyes Out," before correcting himself and playing his hit "Mountain Dew," a tribute to the glories of moonshine liquor.[57] The remainder of the show featured more of Jones's humor and duets with Mary Klick, along with the gospel number "I'll Fly Away."[58] Grandpa Jones probably felt at home singing to the soldiers. Performing for so many servicemembers could yield big results, and Jones and Gay looked to make the most of their volunteer trip to Korea.

On March 15, 1951, Grandpa Jones and His Grandchildren, along with Connie Gay, flew from Japan to Taegu, South Korea. There, they joined the men of the Eighth US Army, Korea (EUSAK), with whom they would spend the next two weeks. They played their first show to 400 patients at a field hospital only an hour and half after landing and followed that performance with another that night at the EUSAK theater.[59] Official reports relayed that "many stood outside the doors of the theater just to hear the music."[60] Gay wasted no time in his role as concert promoter and radio personality in finding ways to connect the men in the field with the radio listeners back home. Thanks to a telephone connection to WARL, Gay brought the war to his Washington, DC–area listeners on his second day in the country. "Hello, friends. How are you? I'm speaking to you from somewhere in Korea, where I'm with the Eighth United States Army," he related back to the States. "With me, of course, are Grandpa Jones and the Grandchildren and a whole lot of your GIs. . . . Out a few feet from where I stand are hundreds of fighting men, waiting for our show to start, and incidentally, they've been going wild over it." Gay wanted listeners, particularly the parents of the soldiers, to know that these men appeared in good health and spirits—and that they loved hillbilly music. The US Army simply had an errand to complete, and then they would return home in one piece. "They've got a job to do over here, and they're doing it well," he assured eager audiences back home. "That job, of course, is killing communists."[61]

Despite Gay's assurances, Americans worried about the soldiers in their families. Army officials tried to assuage these worries by sending letters and pictures to parents during basic training. Appreciative parents wrote back to the army to let them know how much they cared for their sons. After receiving one such update, the grateful mother of Private William H. Wirth wrote to an army official, "Like any mother feels, I do have a wonderful Son, he has always been good. . . . He has never been away from home, which makes me very lonesome for him, as he is the only child I have."[62] Gay did his part to connect parents and soldiers, as well. "I run into a lot of wonderful fellas from WARL land," he told his radio listeners and proceeded to interview six soldiers from northern Virginia and Maryland stationed in Korea. Speaking with Private Eddie L. Bowman from Baltimore, Gay asked if the soldier wanted to deliver a message for the folks at home. "Tell my mother that I'm all right," Private Bowman replied. Gay and the soldiers also took the opportunity to express their distaste for the Korean Peninsula. When Gay asked Sergeant Charles P. Franks, a tank commander from Alexandria, Virginia, what he thought of the place, Franks answered, "Well, I think it stinks. . . . Korea is the latrine of the world." Incidentally, the sergeant mentioned that his twenty-year-old sister worked at the Pentagon, and Gay got in a plug, telling him to write the folks back home and tell them that WARL had visited.[63]

The tour continued until the end of March, totaling thirty-four performances in fourteen days in venues ranging from combat-division encampments and field hospitals to corps headquarters and airfields. Before Gay and Grandpa Jones and His Grandchildren departed the peninsula, the hillbilly troupe had performed for more than 38,000 soldiers.[64] Their impact was even bigger when considering the intercontinental reach of the AFRS, where soldiers and civilians could hear transcriptions of their show. Meanwhile, Gay's broadcasts of the tour updates over the WARL airwaves relayed to the folks back in the Washington, DC, area that he and Grandpa Jones had experienced the war firsthand.

FIGURE 1.2 The cover of a tour program for Grandpa Jones and His Grandchildren. In 1951, Connie B. Gay booked Jones and his band for a run of shows for the US Armed Forces stationed in the Pacific, including the front lines of the Korean War. (Connie B. Gay Collection, courtesy of the Country Music Hall of Fame and Museum)

Before returning to the United States at the end of March, Gay sent one last message back to Arlington that conveyed the ill feelings he harbored toward Korea and its people. Sounding like a battle-scarred vet after his two weeks entertaining the EUSAK, Gay told WARL listeners, "I have just returned from the front lines of Korea. I can assure you that I never want to go there again. Of all the God-forsaken places on Earth, Korea is it. It's dirty, filthy. . . . It's the only country on Earth where I could not find someone to say anything nice about it." But he delivered a positive assessment of the battle operations, believing that "our boys are doing a magnificent job in Korea. They're killing more Chinese than Carter's has little liver pills," a reference to the patent medicine popular with rural customers since the nineteenth century.[65] That folksy reference signaled Gay's insider status to the other white, rural-to-urban transplants listening to his station, letting them know that one of their own had checked in on the servicemembers in their families.

Gay and the music he booked had succeeded in its mission of delivering country music to the soldiers, and it paved the way for even more. "Our hillbilly entertainment has been like a gift from heaven to the GIs," he told his home station, and he vowed, "When I get back home, I'm gonna go hogwild to get more of the stars to come over here for a visit, . . . Red Foley, Hank Snow, Eddy Arnold, and so forth. By golly, they deserve the best."[66] Hank Snow and Ernest Tubb, both of whom were stars on the *Grand Ole Opry*, did tour the Pacific in 1953, playing for more than 75,000 soldiers in Japan and Korea.[67] An official report of the tour by the Eighth US Army Special Services remarked that the "response to this type of music is overwhelming."[68]

With this first Korean tour, Gay had linked hillbilly music to patriotic service for his Washington, DC, listening public and for the men and women serving in the Far East. A favorable article in the *Washington Post* described Gay as "probably the only entertainer who prides himself on how small some of his audiences are. . . . The audiences of two and three to which the four-man Gay troupe played with pleasure were crouching in foxholes and behind Sherman tanks on the front lines of Korea." The *Post* reporter made it clear that, while Gay had spent $3,000 to take Jones and his band to Korea, the positive publicity had made the trip worth it. "The army was so pleased with the results that it has now hired two small troupes of hillbilly talent to play to the boys," including a return by Mary Klick.[69]

Other artists from other genres had toured Korea, but none had exposed themselves to the dangerous conditions experienced by soldiers in the same way as Jones's group. Pop singers and comedians like Al Jolson, Bob Hope, and Jack Benny gave camp shows for the men and women stationed in the Pacific. These entertainers could require large entourages and piano accompaniment and did not travel to the foxholes as the less famous Grandpa Jones and His Grandchildren did. Grandpa Jones and Connie Gay succeeded and made hillbilly fans out of soldiers because the sheer portability of the genre's instrumentation—a banjo, guitar, fiddle, and voice—meant that these artists could travel light and extend their tour far into the Korean zone of conflict.[70] Jones and his band had performed on the back of army "lowboy" trucks, which usually carried heavy artillery. A report from the Far East Command's Public Information Office described how these makeshift stages used "nothing but Korea's drab hills pitted with foxholes and gun emplacements as a backdrop." Colonel Dennis Moore, regimental commander of the Fifteenth Infantry, US Army Third Infantry Division, awarded Jones and His Grandchildren the division's "Can Do" award, a distinction usually bestowed on individual units.[71]

When the US Army recognized that sacrifice, a government institution recognized hillbilly music as a respectable form of labor and entertainment. The army valued the genre's contribution to the war effort. Major General Edward F. Witsell, the adjutant general of the Department of the Army, wrote to Gay, letting him know that he had received numerous reports of the tremendous reception Grandpa Jones and His Grandchildren had received in Japan and Korea. "It is a proud record," he told Gay and heaped praise on his willingness to perform "within 200 yards of the front lines." Likewise, Witsell expressed his admiration for Gay's and Jones's ability to entertain the diverse ranks of United Nations forces, who hailed from England, Australia, Greece, France, and the United States. "May I, therefore, officially and personally express the appreciation of the Department of the Army to you, and to Mr. Louis Jones, Mrs. Ramona Jones and Miss Mary Klick for your rare contribution to the welfare and morale of our Armed Forces."[72] Connie B. Gay and Grandpa Jones and His Grandchildren volunteered their time and risked their safety to entertain the troops. They earned the soldiers' respect and fandom in the process.

Race, Region, and Military Music

The popularity of country music with US servicemembers created more reasons for the AFRS to play the genre on its airwaves and more chances for the music's artists to tour the military's global network of installations. This reciprocal relationship inherently benefited the genre's white musicians and promoters who operated within a deeply segregated industry that marketed country as the music of the white working class.[73] When the military catered to the tastes of its country music fans, the government gave an implicit financial endorsement of that musical segregation.

At the same time, country music tours and AFRS programs also encouraged servicemembers' demand for the genre. Elton Britt, following the success of Jones's tour, visited the troops in Korea in late 1951. The fan magazine *Country Song Roundup* praised Britt for his willingness to make the trip, during which he appeared in formal venues and "hundreds of makeshift open-air platforms, in all kinds of weather and under all sorts of conditions, playing to more than 80,000 soldiers." Britt testified to the soldiers' appreciation, telling the magazine, "I never saw anything to compare to those soldiers, with their rifles on their backs, jammed all around the little stages we set up." The country singer knew from experience how an association with wartime patriotism could yield real profits. Britt's World War II–era release "There's a Star Spangled Banner Waving Somewhere" had produced one of the biggest hits of the 1940s, crossing over into the pop charts, where it secured the number-one position for months in 1942. And following Jones's trip to Korea, Britt recognized the power conveyed in a narrative about a musician who risked his own safety to entertain the troops.[74]

Even when civilian stars remained stateside, the troops in Korea could count on hearing live country music played by professional musicians from within their own ranks. Jesse McReynolds, one half of the bluegrass duo Jim and Jesse, spent much of his time in the US Army playing for GIs in a country band called the Dusty Roads Boys (or Ramblers) alongside Charlie Louvin of the Louvin Brothers.[75] The army also sent the country singer-songwriter Dick Curless to Korea in 1952, and he quickly became a fixture on the Armed Forces Korean Network. With the on-air nickname of "the Rice Paddy Ranger," Curless, a native of Maine, played country records, sang songs, and delivered words of encouragement to his fellow soldiers. A typical message from Curless reminded servicemembers that they were "working hand in hand with the Korean people for the common cause of freedom": "In boiling it all down friends, lets [sic] be good neighbors and stand together."[76] Curless's postwar promotional materials claimed that his "sojourn in Korea only added to his laurels" as an up-and-coming artist, and he recorded so many spots for the US Navy during the Vietnam War that the local recruitment office in Bangor made him an honorary recruiter in 1972.[77]

The enthusiasm for country music seemed to spread wherever soldiers went during the early years of the Cold War. In 1952, *Country Song Roundup* reported that country music had swept "the European continent like a prairie fire" and that as the "Music of America," country music "draws people like a magnetic force to their radio sets." European civilians and US servicemembers alike could tune in to the Armed Forces Network (AFN) broadcast from Frankfurt, Germany, six days a week to hear Sergeant First Class Bill Carrigan host the program *Hillbilly Gasthaus*. Carrigan, who went by the name "Uncle Willie" on the air, was from Columbia, Tennessee, "where he learned to love hillbilly and country music." He had also worked as a disc jockey in Nashville and became "personally acquainted with many of the stars of the Ryman Auditorium's Grand Ole Opry." Besides spinning records on the AFN, Carrigan hosted soldier bands, including one called The Country Boys and another called Seven Texans and a Yank. *Country Song Roundup* printed a photograph of The Country Boys, who posed in uniform with their instruments in front of a Confederate battle flag.[78]

AFRS stations also aired the program *Carolina Cotton Calls*, starring the hillbilly chanteuse Carolina Cotton, a native Arkansan known for her near-white, blond hair and dazzling yodeling abilities.[79] Born Helen Hagstrom, Cotton had honed her talents in California's western swing bands, singing with Spade Cooley and Bob Wills in the West Coast honky-tonk circuit, along with USO tours during World War II. Throughout the Korean War, Cotton recorded radio transcriptions of her show for the AFRS, which highlighted her fellow western swing collaborators.[80] She toured Korea in January 1953, visiting hospitals, making promotional recordings for the AFRS, and playing fourteen performances for nearly 14,000 soldiers in five days.[81] Her hair color and conventional good looks had earned Cotton the nickname "The Yodeling Blonde Bombshell." This combination of physical appearance and musical ability satisfied two soldier desires at once. By 1953, the Eighth US Army Special Services had homed in on the fact that soldiers went wild for country music, and as one report noted, the "men want leg shows above all."[82] With Carolina Cotton, they received a bit of both.

Like Redd Harper, Cotton's show followed a pattern of soldier dedications, scripted cornpone humor, western-themed music, and Christian messaging. Her backing band, the Rhythm Riders, included some of California's hottest country and western swing players, including Joe Maphis, Slim Duncan, George Bamby, Darol Rice, and Mike Barton. After a brief musical introduction on each show, Cotton would jump in with a cheerful greeting

FIGURE 1.3 Members of the US Army soldier band The Country Boys pose in front of a Confederate battle flag. Soldiers stationed in Europe formed hillbilly/country bands like these to entertain their fellow troops and found outlets for their music on military radio shows that featured the genre. These programs, like *Hillbilly Gasthaus*, hosted by Sergeant First Class Bill Carrigan, helped to grow country music's popularity with military and civilian audiences overseas. ("Europe Goes Hillbilly," *Country Song Roundup*, June 1952, author's collection)

of "Well, hi there fellas and gals. This is Carolina Cotton with fifteen minutes we've roped and tied, so you just hold that corral gate open wide while we brand a few musical mavericks for you." On one episode, the Rhythm Riders delivered a dedication of the gospel song "Steal Away," which Cotton announced was requested by Airman Second Class Albert Hollingsworth, adding, "and he said the hymn was his favorite and his family's favorite so could we beam it out to him about now?" Cotton also encouraged more requests, telling fans to write to her in care of the Armed Forces Radio Service, Hollywood, USA. She closed her appearances with the benediction, "Bye now, and may the good Lord keep his arms around you."[83]

Carolina Cotton Calls, as well as contemporaries like Redd Harper and the *Grand Ole Opry*, infused the AFRS airwaves with the sounds of white musical culture from the US South and Southwest. And while the US Armed Forces broadcast white hillbilly musicians, the military minimized the presence of African American culture on its airwaves. The AFRS had catered to Black soldiers during World War II with shows like *Jubilee*, which featured Duke Ellington, Lena Horne, and other top African American artists of the day, but had discontinued production in 1949. It reinstated *Jubilee* from 1952 to 1953, although the new episodes produced during this brief resurrection for the Korean War featured white performers like Merv Griffin and the Andrews Sisters, greatly diminishing its appeal to Black troops.[84] Ironically, the US Armed Forces had emerged as the nation's most integrated space following Truman's Executive Order 9981.[85] The military wanted Black labor and could always acquire more Black soldiers through the draft. But over the course of the 1950s, the Pentagon closed many of the outlets for African American culture in the military that had opened during World War II. The AFRS essentially replicated the color line of the civilian music industry, while the Pentagon pushed a progressive racial mandate well ahead of the nation's civilian racial policies.

The AFRS did play some Black artists. Jazz remained one of the most heavily featured genres on the network. Yet the type of jazz programmed for soldiers tended toward the revivalist sounds of Dixieland, including the shows *Kid Ory*, *Mostly Dixie*, and *Basin Street Jazz*, or the mainstream swing favored by whites on *Navy Swings*. Blues and R&B remained largely absent from the AFRS transcriptions until the network began rebroadcasting the CBS program *Camel Rock & Roll Party* in 1957, although the use of the Count Basie Orchestra as the house band made this program little more than a swing show rebranded for the times. The AFRS also featured Black choirs. The program *Fisk Jubilee* starred the choir from Nashville's Fisk University, while the program *Negro College Choir* relied on a rotating cast of singing groups from different historically Black colleges and universities.[86]

Although these shows offered exclusively Black content, they hardly represented the current trends in Black popular music. The network also did not include the blues and R&B songs that expressed dissatisfaction with military service in the early 1950s. Several songs by contemporary blues artists, like Sunnyland Slim's "Back to Korea Blues" and Lightnin' Hopkins's "Sad News from Korea," dissented from the unquestioning patriotism of the usual popular song offerings as the nation went to war.[87] Instead of showcasing the latest releases in these genres or songs that might question the personal cost of US foreign policy, the AFRS played Black music that conformed to what white network programmers imagined as suitable content for the morale and well-being of the troops.

Wartime musical experience did not necessarily translate into postwar success for African American artists the way it did for someone like Grandpa Jones. Cecil Gant, a Black pianist and singer from Columbia, Tennessee, had linked military service and the uncertainty of long-distance romance to score the biggest hit of his brief career. Billing himself as "Private Cecil Gant" and wearing his army uniform on stage, Gant seemed to embody the promise of the Double V campaign and the chance for advancement through armed service. Announced by the *Pittsburgh Courier* in 1942, the Double V campaign sought to leverage African Americans' efforts in the fight against foreign fascism to deliver civil rights advances long denied Black soldiers and civilians in the United States.[88] To emphasize this sound and service connection, Gant used the tagline the "GI Sing-Station," playing piano in a style that drew comparisons to Fats Waller and singing in a baritone that split the difference between Louis Armstrong's gravelly tones and Nat "King" Cole's husky smoothness.[89]

This combination of vocal delivery and piano performance scored Gant a hit in 1944 with the ballad "I Wonder," which proved so popular that by February 1945, Louis Armstrong, Louis Prima, Roosevelt Sykes, Warren Evans, Dan Grissom, and a copycat with the sobriquet Private Lloyd Thompson had released their own versions.[90] Private Gant sang "I Wonder" in plaintive tones, seemingly resigned to the loss of his love, and accompanied himself on the piano: "Where can you be tonight? / While the moon is shining bright / I wonder." Without being near, Gant could only speculate about his lover's whereabouts, singing, "Baby, I've been through, I've been through lovers' lane / I've been making life just the same / I've been traveling for miles around / Trying to find the one I love, come on / I wonder well, well,

well, little baby / Will you think of me every day?" Gant makes clear in the last words of the song that it is he who has traveled away from his love, with the devastating tag, "Though I may be a million miles away / I wonder."[91]

In the middle of the massive social disruption caused by World War II, Gant's sentiment undoubtedly resonated with military personnel of all races who experienced separation from their partners. The sparse production of this tune, solo vocal and piano with only the natural reverb of the room, matches the resignation in Gant's voice and lyrics. Heard as such, the titular refrain, "I Wonder," came off with a sardonic, almost sarcastic tone. Gant knew that his love was gone. He knew that, in his absence, another had taken his place—perhaps because he met his beloved the same way, taking the place of another soldier shipped overseas to win the Double V. Regardless of these circumstances, Gant betrayed an acceptance that his woman had already gone to another man. Domestic bliss, like racial equality, remained in the realm of fantasy for many soldiers who were deployed or recently returned home in the wake of a world war.

While Gant began playing in Nashville and would end his career there, "I Wonder" first hit in Los Angeles, where the army had stationed the Tennessee native. The initial response in 1944 proved so great that Johnny Otis (best known for his 1958 hit "Willie and the Hand Jive") recalled how he heard Gant's tune "on the jukeboxes all over Central Avenue" in Los Angeles. "I Wonder" generated unparalleled sales and jukebox plays while awakening the West Coast record industry to the need for labels targeting Black music and audiences. Gant did experience success in the race records market, spending twenty-eight weeks in the top ten of *Billboard*'s "Harlem" Hit Parade.[92] But Private Cecil Gant could not translate his martial image into a lasting career, and he could not embark on tours for the military crowds that had initially boosted his success.

After the war, Gant spent the late 1940s building Nashville's reputation as a force in the recording industry, playing on more than one hundred songs for Bullet Records, the first recording company headquartered in the city. Bullet recorded a mixture of country and R&B artists, and owner Jim Bulleit recalled that the country music records his label released failed to make much of a splash in the immediate postwar years. He recorded white country artists like Minnie Pearl, Pee Wee King, Sheb Wooley, and Clyde Moody, an artist in Connie Gay's stable, but never sold these records in large numbers. The label "had a good sale" if it "got between 25,000 and 50,000" on a hillbilly record, Bulleit remembered years later, and "that didn't amount

PRIVATE CECIL *(I WONDER)* GANT

THE G. I. SINGSATION

EXCLUSIVE GILT EDGE RECORDING ARTIST

NOW ON NATION-WIDE PERSONAL APPEARANCE TOUR

FOR OPEN DATES

Wire 4 STAR ARTISTS' BUREAU

500 N. WESTERN, LOS ANGELES 4, CALIF.

Phone HOLLYWOOD 5816

FIGURE 1.4 This tour announcement for Private Cecil Gant in *Billboard* shows how Gant and his record label used his time in the US Army to promote his concerts and record sales. After the war, Gant's hit songs and talent as a pianist helped build the early success of Bullet Records, the first label headquartered in Nashville. (*Billboard,* November 10, 1945)

to much." He struck gold with the R&B artists Wynonie Harris and Cecil Gant. The label could always bank on selling at least 100,000 copies of a Gant record and could more than recoup the costs because, according to Bulleit's recollection, artists like Harris and Gant only wanted payment as a one-time, flat fee rather than opting to receive royalty checks on their records. This arrangement meant that Bulleit and the label would collect money on all the records sold from these artists in perpetuity. Bulleit described how the label made a "killing" on these artists, revealing that for Cecil Gant, the label "paid $60" for each session, "and then the two sidemen $30, which was $120": "we always made money on Cecil."[93]

These predatory business practices extended to encouraging Gant's alcoholism. Ernie Newton, a white bassist, recalled how he would join his fellow session musician Owen Bradley and producer Paul Cohen in plying Gant with booze and listening to him improvise blues songs. Gant would "make them up as he went along," Newton claimed. "He'd tell Paul, he'd say,

'Pour me some more words.' Cohen would pour him some more booze in a glass, and he'd sit up there and drink it. He'd make those things up as he went along." Clearly enamored with Gant's abilities, Newton enthused, "Boy, you talk about playing the blues. Man, we played just exactly what we wanted to play, and Cecil sang and played the piano, played great."[94]

On March 28, 1948, Nashville's white newspaper the *Tennessean* featured a profile of Bullet records, noting its position as the first record company headquartered in Nashville, its role in establishing the first record-pressing plant in the South, and the importance of Private Cecil Gant to the label's success. The paper described Gant as Bullet's "most prolific recorder and top individual artist." The profile noted the popularity of his recordings "Nashville Jumps" and "Boozie Boogie" while perpetuating the common story that Gant could sit down at the piano and spontaneously compose dozens of songs. "Bulleit and Gant never discuss what tunes he is to record," the reporter claimed, "and Gant, whose formal musical education doesn't go much further than an ability to distinguish the white keys from the black, just sits down at the piano, messes around a little, and comes up with a tune." The report also described that Gant sold so well because so many of his songs conveyed a "morbid, 'Gloomy Sunday' like fascination for Negroes, who customarily buy two copies of it at a time. It seems that they play them over and over, to induce melancholy—when one is worn out they start on the second."[95] In the space of a few lines, this reporter managed to devalue Gant's talent by ascribing it to an inborn gift rather than the outcome of years of labor on the road, while essentializing his appeal to African American audiences as the result of a biological hardwiring for sad songs. The white press could demean Black talent, labor, and taste even in its attempts to praise a Black man who helped build Music City, USA.

Besides cutting bankable sides for Bullet Records, Gant contributed memorable piano work to a few of the songs by white artists recorded in Nashville's growing number of studios. He logged work as a session pianist for Red Foley, taking driving piano breaks on the songs "Hobo Boogie" and "Paging Mister Jackson."[96] But while Foley enjoyed success as a member of the *Grand Ole Opry* and toured the world through the network of military bases, Gant struggled as a Black road musician in the Jim Crow South. A life of self-abuse hastened his demise. Just as he prepared to leave Nashville for a road gig, Gant died suddenly, reportedly from a heart attack, in February 1951 at just thirty-eight years old. His family buried him in the veterans' section of Highland Park Cemetery in Cleveland, Ohio.[97]

Connie B. Gay Gets Rich

Connie Gay, meanwhile, was just getting started, and the US Armed Forces opened the doors of opportunity to more partnerships. In October 1951, only six months after his return from Korea, Gay took another group of country music performers on a twenty-one-day tour of installations in the Caribbean, playing shows in Puerto Rico, Cuba, and Trinidad and across the sea in Panama's Canal Zone. The Armed Forces Professional Entertainment Branch of the Special Services Division and the USO Camp Shows sponsored the trip. The press for the tour touted Gay's recent tour of Korea, where he and Grandpa Jones "went from Pusan to the foxholes, [and] entertained UN troops all the way."[98] Gay opted not to take Jones on this run of the island bases. Instead, he assembled a new group that included the guitarist Billie Grammer, the fiddler Chubby Wise, the square-dance caller Ralph Case, and an accordionist-comic named Jimmy Dean.[99]

Gay remembered discovering Dean in a Washington, DC, beer joint, where the performer was "doing rube comedy and playing an accordion."[100] At that time, the young Dean's stage attire included oversized torn pants, suspenders, a ragged hat turned to the side, no shoes, blacked-out teeth, and the stage name "Screwball" Dean.[101] Gay would help change all that. A native of Plainview, Texas, Dean joined the air force in 1946 and served for three years. During his service, he entertained his fellow airmen by playing guitar, piano, and accordion while stationed at Bolling Air Force Base in Washington. Encouraged by the reception he received on base, Dean formed a musical group with a few air force friends and began playing in the local bars. Gay saw artistic and commercial potential in the unpolished comedian and singer and tutored him in the entertainment business. Dean swapped his buffoonish costume for a tailored cowboy suit, and Gay booked him on a tour of military installations throughout the Caribbean in 1951 and a tour of bases in Europe in 1953. Dean soon emerged as the star of Gay's *Town and Country Time* radio show on WARL, backed by the band Gay hired for him, the Texas Wildcats.[102] When Gay decided to turn his radio program into a syndicated television show, he chose Dean as its star.[103] By 1956, the new show aired on forty television stations across the country, and its audio was transcribed for broadcast over nearly 2,000 radio stations thanks to sponsorship by the US Defense Department.[104]

In March 1957, Dean's television exposure led to a deal with CBS in which he hosted the network's national morning program, called *The Jimmy Dean Show*, which was meant to compete with NBC's *Today*.[105] Three months later,

Dean's show landed on the cover of the *New York Times Magazine*, promoting the "Festival of the Fleets" in Norfolk, Virginia. This event brought together over one hundred ships from eighteen nations. The cover photograph showed Dean and his band on the deck of the Portuguese ship *Corte Real*. Black sailors from the Dominican ship *Generalissimo* played saxophones, tubas, and congas, while Dean and the Texas Wildcats, in their cowboy attire, played acoustic guitar and fiddle, creating what must have been a pioneering sound in interracial, global musical collaboration. The *Times* reported that "some 54,000 sailors who—despite the barrier of language—mingled, had fun and became friendly through receptions, dances and festive entertainments on ship and shore."[106]

Dean spent the week telecasting from the decks of the USS *Valley Forge* and performing shows for sailors aboard individual ships.[107] By the fall of that year, Dean's television show displaced *Today* in the ratings thanks to his mixture of down-home charm, telegenic looks, a rotating cast of country musicians, a ventriloquist, and cohost Jan Crockett, Miss Florida 1951.[108] Throughout this meteoric rise, Dean, under the tutelage of Gay, used his association with the armed forces to promote and validate himself whenever possible. One headline in Boston read simply, "Service Gave Jimmy Start."[109]

This association between country music and the military brought tremendous profits for Gay and Dean. In a matter of six years, Gay had turned a rube comic into a national television star in a stunning display of class and status ascendancy, aided in no small part by the exposure afforded Dean and Gay through tours of the nation's military installations. When Dean went national with his television show, Gay sold the show's rights to CBS, while holding onto Dean's personal contract.[110] This shrewd move enriched Gay even more than his then-growing empire of radio stations. A *New York Times* profile of Gay in 1957 divulged that he owned twenty-two television shows in Washington, DC, three country music radio stations, a car dealership, and real estate. The article claimed that Gay earned "about a $1,000,000-a-year traffic in country music," making him "the largest individual promoter of country music in the nation."[111] According to an assessment of his finances by the Securities and Exchange Commission in 1960, Connie B. Gay Broadcasting Corporation and Subsidiaries was worth more than $3 million (over $30 million in 2023 dollars)—not bad for an ex–New Dealer from Lizard Lick, North Carolina.[112]

The *Times* recognized the centrality of the military to Gay's success. The reporter began the article by joking that "anyone who has ever, in the democracy of war, shared a barracks with a knot of fiddle-scraping wahoos from the swamp country will probably not be an instant admirer of Connie B. Gay." The *Times* took it as common knowledge that legions of "wahoos," meant to imply working-class white southerners, had overrun the ranks of the US military. Gay credited the Selective Service for the growth of country music. In his words, the draft "took a little country boy from Georgia and put him in Paris and it took a lad from New York and moved him down to Georgia and that was it." He then explained the genre's appeal in exemplary down-home fashion—through a food metaphor. "It's like bread," he told the *Times*. "All the lad from New York ever had was store-bought bread. He never had any home-baked hot biscuits. But some little Georgia girl takes him home to mother for hot biscuits and pretty soon he gets so he likes them."[113] Gay had learned the profitability of those "biscuits," and he never lost sight of the military's role in his success.

All of Gay's volunteer touring had started to turn a profit in October 1955, when Dean and fourteen of his *Town and Country* castmates embarked on a ten-week tour with a contract to entertain troops in the Pacific. Walter A. Bouillet, chief entertainment officer for the Far East Command, and entertainment branch officer Colonel Joseph F. Goetz negotiated the deal with Gay.[114] Bouillet, the son of a French immigrant chef, had served as an officer in the Foreign Legion during World War II and managed the hotels used for rehabilitation on the French Riviera after the cease-fire. After a short return to civilian life, he received a reactivation notice to deploy to Korea, and the army placed him in charge of Special Services for the Far East. He spent eight years in this position, booking entertainment, including Gay's tours of Japan, the Korean Peninsula, and the occupied Pacific islands.[115]

According to *Billboard*, Gay's tour represented "the first contract-paid entertainment unit purchased by the military for the Far East Command," helping to fulfill the need for soldier entertainment at a time that the USO lacked the funds to service that part of the world. The Far East Command, under Bouillet's and Goetz's directions, supplemented military entertainment in the USO's absence by using "'non-appropriated' moneys derived from the profits of post exchanges and theaters in the Pacific area to finance the military junkets."[116] This deal proved so successful for all involved that Gay and Bouillet went into business together the next year, following the latter's departure from the military.

The partnership between Gay and Bouillet also opened another door for the military to generate new country audiences and boost profits through the use of country music in its recruitment programs. The Nashville-based trade magazine *Country Music Reporter* informed readers that the men had organized a new firm "whose aim is to expand programs of country music to a world wide [sic] basis including possible tours overseas" and that the men had established an office in Arlington, Virginia. The paper stated that Bouillet had "supervised and produced a Navy Recruiting program here known as 'Country Hoedown' which starred Jimmy Dean (Mercury) and his Texas Wildcats." Bouillet also promised Chet Atkins, Jim Reeves, and Red Sovine for the show to fulfill an order of fifty-two episodes of the program.[117]

The navy's *Country Hoedown* was neither the first nor the last country music show used in a recruitment campaign. The Pentagon had discovered that the country music programming on the AFRS airwaves, as well as Gay's tours of installations around the world, provided a blueprint and an infrastructure to use country music as a way to entice recruits. What began in the 1940s as the military's gradual recognition that soldiers enjoyed country music emerged in the mid-1950s as a conscious strategy to bring even more men, presumably white country music fans, into the armed services. The creation of country music recruitment campaigns over the 1950s signaled the formalization of a relationship between the genre and the armed forces, a relationship cultivated by the Pentagon, country music promoters, artists, and fans in the ranks of the nation's military.

2 A GI Bill for Country Music
How Country Music and Military Recruitment Merged in the 1950s

. . . .

On the afternoon of Wednesday, April 16, 1958, Tennessee's Governor Frank G. Clement testified before the US Senate Subcommittee on Communications in defense of country music. Although he claimed to love the genre, Clement made his impassioned plea not as a fan but as the leader of a state that depended on the music industry as a cornerstone of its economy. "Nashville," he told the senators, "today is one of the major music capitals of the world. More records are actually cut in Nashville than anywhere else in the United States—and I suppose that would mean in the world; except New York." He estimated that the combination of record and sheet-music sales, along with the performance fees earned by Nashville's artists, brought in $50 million every year to the state. That industry faced a political and economic attack from a piece of legislation known as the Smathers Bill, an amendment to the Communications Act of 1934 that would prohibit song publishers from owning radio and television stations. In essence, the bill accused Broadcast Music, Incorporated (BMI), the performance-rights organization (PRO) most associated with collecting royalties for country music, of a conspiracy to push its products on radio and television to the exclusion and financial detriment of pop music and its primary PRO, the American Society of Composers, Authors, and Publishers (ASCAP). Clement attempted to explain the genre's popularity based on its sheer mass appeal and moral goodness, not on a plot hatched by Nashville and BMI.[1]

Faron Young, one of the biggest country artists of the day, gave the subcommittee a different reason for country music's popularity and BMI's success, an account based in the nation's Cold War global military expansion. Although Young did not make the trip to Washington, DC, he submitted his testimony in writing to the Senate. He began by acknowledging the accusations facing his genre: "People have told you that country music is heard a lot on the air these days because BMI and the broadcasters are pushing it to the public." Young then offered a material explanation for the genre's popularity that both acknowledged the labor of country entertainers and the assistance they had received from the Cold War defense state. "I don't know how far this conspiracy is supposed to go to force country music on the public," he told the politicians, "but if there is a conspiracy maybe the United States Government is a part of it, because I and a lot of other country performers have been sent by the Government to entertain thousands and thousands of troops with our kind of music."[2]

Young understood firsthand how the federal government had developed a unique relationship with country music's artists and promoters. The connection between the US military and country music that had started with Connie B. Gay, Grandpa Jones, and the *Grand Ole Opry* had become a formal strategy by 1953, when Young, recently drafted, began serving as the voice of recruitment and entertainment for the US Army's Third Infantry Division. Thanks to this arrangement, Young toured installations, appeared on television and radio programs, and sang on Nashville's *Grand Ole Opry*, where he plugged the US Army from the stage of the Ryman Auditorium to compulsory applause cued by the *Opry*'s emcees. His career soared as a result. He received billing as the "singing soldier" and enjoyed multipage profiles in country and western fan magazines. That type of press coverage complemented the Pentagon's broader recruitment strategies. During the 1950s, the army expanded its country music enlistment campaigns, including live performances, television programs, and radio shows hosted by Connie B. Gay. The navy and air force joined in with this musical strategy, too, creating radio shows that aired on both military and civilian networks. These programs branded military recruitment with Nashville's sounds of southern whiteness while pitching armed service as a step toward well-paying jobs and education for country music fans. Country music promised to benefit the armed forces by catching the ears of young white men at a time when the military could use all the help it could get with attracting volunteers.

Tracing the growth of country music recruitment demonstrates one of the ways that the US military addressed the personnel crisis it faced in the early 1950s. The Pentagon had slashed the numbers of US Army soldiers following the Allied victory from 8 million in 1945 to about half a million only a few years later. Other branches of the service experienced dramatic reductions as well. The outbreak of the Korean War had sent the Pentagon scrambling to field a force worthy of combat, as the Defense Department sobered to the reality of its military vulnerability. Conscription slowed the depletion of the ranks, but leaders preferred recruits, not draftees, to fill out its fighting force. Selective Service remained in place during the last year of World War II and the first year of peace, but veteran status, marriage, and school deferments kept many desirable men out of the ranks. President Truman even ended the draft in 1947 in hopes of boosting enlistment. However, postwar civilian job growth had improved so much that volunteering for the military simply did not appeal to young men with better prospects. With no waves of mass enlistment, Truman reinstated the draft in 1948 while the Pentagon searched for ways to entice recruits.[3]

The US Army and Air Force Recruitment Service (RS) attempted to fill this need by inserting its messages about the economic benefits of military service, like the GI Bill, within the growing number of postwar pop-culture outlets. In the late 1940s and early 1950s, clicking on the radio or the television probably meant encountering an advertisement for the military. The RS rolled out docudramas, talent contests, live concerts, and musical entertainment programs, inundating pop culture with its cattle call for enlistees. The US Army and Air Force Service Bands provided much of the music for these shows. These bands, with their traditional instrumentation of brass, woodwinds, and orchestral percussion, played patriotic and pop fare to rouse the nation's young men to the call of duty, or at least economic opportunity. Civilian guest stars appeared on these programs to lend their star power to Cold War recruitment. The pop singer Eddie Fisher even served as the voice of recruitment from 1951 to 1953, when the army took him away from his recording career. These campaigns cast a wide net for recruits with little thought to musical genre. They simply relied on what the service bands could perform and the mass appeal of pop stars like Fisher.

When Faron Young took over for Eddie Fisher in 1953, he signaled the RS's growing investment in country music as a recruitment tool and the country music industry's willingness to cooperate with the Pentagon's Cold War personnel mission. Facilitating military recruitment tracked well with the country music industry's desire to brand itself as the sound of wholesome American culture. During the 1950s, Governor Clement embarked on a multiyear campaign to sell country music as the United States' music. It helped that country music remained extremely popular within the ranks. While the nation's Cold War defense strategies scattered country music's fans and performers around the world, US servicemembers created a global community of listeners in uniform. These listeners wrote to their favorite country music magazines and radio hosts, searching for personal connections with like-minded fans and singing the praises of their favorite artists. The military helped establish that global audience for the genre, even as, and perhaps because, country music's promoters branded the music as the sound of America.

By creating recruitment campaigns with country music, a genre closely linked with white southerners, the US military made a statement about the kind of people that it wanted in uniform. The music attracted a demographic that was a prime target for military recruitment. In exchange, an association with the military provided the emergent country music industry with legitimacy, coding it as a genre appropriate for patriotic, all-American listening. For millions of US enlistees in the mid-twentieth century, particularly white men, providing labor to the Department of Defense opened up access to economic advancement through the benefits of the GI Bill, a message they heard repeated constantly through the Pentagon's recruitment campaigns. The country music industry entered into an analogous bargain with the Pentagon and received a government-sponsored way to grow its market reach, elevate its cultural status, and increase its profits. Country music militarization gave the genre's industry its own version of the GI Bill: government funding for the building of wealth in exchange for military service.

Recruiting Pop Culture

As a teenager in Shreveport, Louisiana, Faron Young held little ambition to be a country music singer and zero interest in joining the military. He came of age working on his family's dairy farm on the outskirts of town and attending Fair Park High School, where he chased girls and tried out for the football team. Young's small stature almost kept him off the team until he struck a deal with the coach. If allowed on the team, Young agreed to sing with the coach's country band during its weekly gig at the Southern Maid Donut Shop in Shreveport. Blessed with perfect pitch and a strong tenor, Young quickly earned a reputation as a powerful vocalist in the thriving Shreveport music scene. In 1948, the city's KWKH radio station had launched *The Louisiana Hayride*, a barn-dance program modeled after the *Grand Ole Opry*. The *Hayride* ensured that a steady stream of local and national country talent came through the city, and Young quickly ascended from singing at the donut shop to fronting professional country bands on the show.[4]

The musically gifted Young joined the honky-tonk singer Webb Pierce's band in 1951 as a singer and rhythm guitarist while completing his senior year of high school. Pierce, who was also a native of northern Louisiana, began his country recording career in the 1940s and enjoyed a featured spot on the *Hayride* by the time Young joined his group. Young's ambition soon outgrew his role as a sideman in Pierce's band, and he made his solo *Hayride* debut on October 13, 1951. He began cutting records for the independent record label Gotham Records a month later. Young then hit the road promoting those records with his backing band, the Southern Valley Boys, featuring the future famed Nashville session man Floyd Cramer on piano. He also made weekly appearances on the *Hayride*. In the span of a few months, Faron Young had transformed from high school student and sideman to fronting his own honky-tonk outfit and touring the beer joints of the postwar South.[5]

By January 1952, Young had signed a management deal with the country music promoter Hubert Long and a recording contract with Capitol Records. Six months later, at the age of twenty, he packed what he called his "Alabama cardboard suitcase" and achieved the biggest moment of his career up to that point by performing onstage at the Ryman Auditorium in Nashville, Tennessee, as part of the *Grand Ole Opry*. Hank Williams, Young's professional idol at the time, greeted him backstage at the Ryman and congratulated him on a job well done. Williams then promptly stole the new star's girlfriend, Billie Jean Eshleman, the same night and married her four months later.[6] A mixture of good and bad fortune would come to characterize much of Young's career, particularly in his first months of real fame.

The next bit of misfortune came when, shortly after playing his first *Opry* shows, Young received his draft notice. Devastated, Young later recalled how he "cried like a rat eating a red onion." He desperately did not want to go into the army and tried to convince a doctor that he had heart trouble. The doctor reportedly replied, "Yeah, son, I can hear it breaking." Inducted on November 16, 1952, and assigned to Fort Jackson, South Carolina, for basic training, Young quickly fell in with other musicians, spending their days entertaining fellow troops in the servicemen's club and generally shirking any kind of military responsibility. Never one for deference to authority, Young remembered laying out of duty as long as possible before "one day somebody got wise and said we got to train this boy. Give him a gun and put him in the mud."[7]

Young's time in the mud would be brief. On January 10, 1953, his song "Goin' Steady," a single he had recorded for Capitol before entering the service, broke onto the *Billboard* charts and quickly ascended to number two.[8] Unwittingly, the army had drafted a rising country star. The commanding officers at Fort Jackson soon put him to work entertaining the men instead of toting a gun. One report stated that Young's performances at Fort Jackson "resulted in a corps of admirers who tune camp radios to parade-ground volume when one of his records is played by local radio stations, and who cheerfully help Young open his 2000 fan letters each week."[9]

Recognizing Young as a potential resource for the promotion of military service, the army put him to use. In May 1953, his commanding officers sent Young to New York City to compete on the new network television program *Talent Patrol*, a contest show hosted by Steve Allen and Arlene Francis on ABC. *Talent Patrol* tried to boost army recruitment by showcasing the diverse skills of enlisted men and casting members of the nation's largest, most powerful bureaucratic institution as ordinary folks. Young and his band from Fort Jackson won the contest and embarked on an army career that combined entertaining current soldiers and recruitment campaigns to lure others into the ranks.[10] With Young and country music, the military found an artist and a genre with populist, working-class bona fides and a respect for patriotic service. Even better, Young appeared to be an amateur plucked from obscurity and thrust into economic success through his service to the state. In the early 1950s, the Pentagon could use a few thousand more men willing to give their time, labor, and talents to their nation in exchange for a career boost in the civilian sector. Music helped convince potential recruits that economic security lay just on the other side of a tour of duty.

· · · · · ·

The *Talent Patrol* show that gave Young his first television appearance represented just one of the dozens of recruitment experiments that the Defense Department planted in pop culture during the early years of the Cold War. In May 1950, the RS began a campaign of one-minute recruiting messages on 1,400 radio stations in 1,100 cities across the nation. These ads targeted high school– and college-aged young men, particularly college graduates who might qualify for the Aviation Cadet Pilot and Navigator Programs. The messages aired during sports broadcasts in hopes of hitting their target demographic. Likewise, the RS inserted ads in national and local newspapers, store window displays, direct mail, and magazines like *Popular Mechanics*, *Outdoor Life*, and *Look*.[11] The Pentagon adopted early television technology as well, filling a slot every Sunday evening on NBC with *The Armed Forces Hour*.[12] With this wide net, recruiters hoped to enlist the most qualified and willing recruits to fight in Korea and defend the nation against the ever-present threat of destruction at the hands of the Soviet Union.

Consuming entertainment in the 1950s often meant consuming some message from the US Army Recruiting Service. According to one study, the Defense Department spent approximately $2.7 million (around $27 million in 2023 dollars) of tax payers' money on its print, radio, and television recruitment efforts every year during the decade. While not an exorbitant number by defense budget standards, that expenditure bought an enormous amount of possible exposure for recruitment messaging, potentially reaching 50 million homes with radio sets and 47 million homes with televisions by 1960. Although the draft still offered the cheapest way of acquiring personnel, the short term of service meant that the peacetime military did not always receive a return on its investment in the training of conscripted servicemembers. Additionally, the quality of conscripted personnel did not always meet the same standard as volunteers who wanted to make a career in military service. In order to attract top-rated recruits with an interest in bettering themselves through armed service, the RS took to the page, the airwaves, and the cathode-ray tube.[13]

All of this advertising meant that when a young person flipped open a magazine or adjusted their radio and television dials during the 1950s, they probably saw an advertisement beckoning them to increase their career prospects by joining the military. A private advertising agency contracted by the army found that the prospect of vocational training offered the most effective message for the recruitment campaigns. In turn, the army placed ads in national magazines like *Life, Scholastic, Mechanics Illustrated, Hot Rod, Scouting,* and the *American Journal of Nursing.* It also used nearly 100,000 posters of various sizes, printed on paper and metal, and hundreds of billboards to deliver the good news that Uncle Sam could help them brighten their educational or occupational futures.[14]

The army's budget also allowed for the production of films that recruiters could send to local television stations and high schools. These films continued to place emphasis on the potential enlistees' real-world economic prospects. In 1960, the army paid Columbia Pictures $60,000 to make a color film called *The Hurrying Kind,* which pushed the importance of education when pursuing advancement in and out of the armed forces. This was just one of nine films made by the army at the turn of the decade that highlighted the service's vocational opportunities. The RS sent these directly to high schools, where, for twenty-eight minutes, teenagers might listen to and watch a recruitment pitch rather than their teachers. The production choice of keeping the films under thirty minutes also meant that recruiters could send them to local television stations for integration into their broadcast schedules.[15]

In fact, television offered a potent new medium for the soft-power propaganda made under the direction, or at least with the approval, of the Pentagon during the 1950s that boosted recruitment and popular opinion about the US military. Spy shows, military documentaries, sitcoms, and dramas with military settings proliferated on civilian networks during the decade. These shows cast the US Armed Forces and the nation itself as the authorities of upright morality and democratic freedom in the recent global struggle against fascism and the new fight against atheistic communism. NBC led the way with its series *Victory at Sea*, a twenty-six-episode documentary that aired from 1952 to 1953 and covered the Pacific Theater during World War II. *Victory at Sea* ran in 206 television markets, won both an Emmy and a Peabody, and included a soundtrack written by Richard Rodgers for the NBC Orchestra. Beyond these portrayals of US military might, television humanized and endeared the armed services to audiences with sitcom characters like Sergeant Bilko on *The Phil Silvers Show* (1955–1959) and light dramas set at service academies called *Men of Annapolis* (1957–1958) and *The West Point Story* (1956–1957), all of which aired dozens of episodes in the late 1950s.[16] These types of shows relied on Pentagon officials as advisers to maintain the accuracy of their military lingo, marching formations, and on-location scenes. This dedication to detail delivered real returns for the Defense Department's time. Enrollment rose at both service academies as a result of the television series based in Annapolis and West Point.[17]

The music provided by the US Army and US Air Force Service Bands also played an essential role in the RS's efforts to increase enlistment in the early 1950s. These brass and woodwind ensembles recorded the soundtracks for live radio and television recruitment shows like the radio programs *Air Force Hour*, which aired on Friday nights on the Mutual Broadcasting System, and *Time for Defense*, featured on ABC every Tuesday night. The RS also created transcriptions of dramatic and documentary radio programs that it distributed to thousands of stations around the nation. One such show, *Proudly We Hail*, provided stories of patriotic service and heroic bravery narrated by film and radio stars of the day and was meant to inspire young men to join and fulfill their masculine duty to their country. The musical program *Stars on Parade* presented civilian pop singers fronting one of the service bands to blend recruitment messages with what the RS determined as appealing music for potential recruits.[18] In each program, the military relied on its in-house talent to provide accompaniment for visiting stars, theme songs, and background music in its pitches to join the military. Yet these musical efforts remained constrained by the instrumentation and training of military service bands. The RS simply presented patriotic tunes and the pop music of the day adapted for brass and woodwinds with little thought to its audiences' tastes.

Recruiters also used music for shorter radio advertisements and live performances. One campaign featured the jazz stride pianist Johnny Guarnieri providing the backing music while the Satisfiers, a pop harmony quartet, chanted the slogans, "The Army has a career for you" and "The Air Force has a career for you." The Guarnieri/Satisfiers spots paired this musical jingle with what the RS called "'selling' dialogue," which told the details of how to enlist and the benefits of armed service.[19]

Service bands contributed to the effort by offering live performances for local recruiting events. The air force band stationed at Fort Mason outside San Francisco performed a series of outdoor concerts for area high school students during the final two weeks of classes in the summer of 1950. Six thousand students attended the shows thanks to the cooperation of their principals, and the RS distributed over 2,500 pieces of recruitment literature to this audience.[20] These types of shows occurred throughout the country during the early 1950s as the RS struggled to boost enlistment numbers and capture the attention of the United States' best and brightest recruits. Service bands undoubtedly provided professional and pleasing concerts and accompaniment, but their styles remained hamstrung by the traditional instrumentation of military bands. Their selections also had to conform to the armed forces' branding as an institution of patriotism and moral decency, which limited their repertoires.

In the summer of 1950, Captain Joseph Gigandet took over the radio section of the RS and began to broaden the service's musical strategies. Gigandet held experience in military radio broadcasting dating back to World War II, when he had produced a soldier radio show at Camp Tyson, Tennessee, as well as the music shows *On Target* and *Serenade in Khaki* for the AFRS. After the war, the army transferred him to West Germany, where his radio work continued as the executive director of the AFRS in Europe and the Military Amateur Radio System. Gigandet managed stations in three West German cities, including Munich-Stuttgart, site of the most powerful AFRS station in the world, with a 200,000-watt transmitter capable of pushing a signal hundreds of miles.[21] These jobs provided Gigandet with intimate knowledge of soldiers' musical tastes and their love for radio, and he applied that understanding to his role as the director of radio recruitment.

By early 1951, Gigandet attempted to update the sound of recruitment by introducing a radio series featuring the US Army Dance Band. The dance-band show aired from its home station in Fort Myer, Virginia, and received distribution on the Liberty Broadcast System every Saturday evening.[22] Next, Gigandet began producing a television program called *Front and Center* to showcase the array of service bands, including the US Army Band and the US Army Field Band, that provided soldier entertainment and the musical accompaniment of recruitment. The *Recruiting Journal* reported in the spring of 1951 that the show would also incorporate "former professional entertainers now in the Army and top names in show business will perform on the series each week," along with a soldier emcee to guide the program. ABC aired the show every Wednesday for half an hour at 8:00 P.M. Eastern Standard Time as a public service announcement.[23] With these efforts, Gigandet sought to attract attention to careers in the army for men and women while relying on the time and talents of soldier musicians to create the public sound of armed service.

Gigandet broke new ground when he launched a musical recruitment program called *At Ease with Pvt. Eddie Fisher*, starring the titular pop star who was then serving as a vocalist for the US Army Band.[24] Fisher had earned a moderate amount of success when he received his draft notice in 1951, but like Faron Young after him, the army made him a star. Born in 1928 to Russian Jewish immigrants, Fisher had grown up in poverty as one of seven children in Philadelphia. He discovered his talent for singing at a young age and won *Arthur Godfrey's Talent Scouts* while in elementary school. The crooner Eddie Cantor mentored the aspiring singer, and Fisher enjoyed a contract with Paramount Records and regular appearances on television shows like the *Milton Berle Show* when he received his draft notice. "How could they do that to me?" he wrote in his memoir years later. "I was Eddie Fisher. I had hits on the *Billboard* charts! How could they stop my career just when everything was starting to pay off?" He entered the service as Private Edwin Jack Fisher on April 11, 1951, and began basic training at Fort Hood, an installation outside Killeen, Texas, that would serve as the site of Elvis Presley's basic training seven years later.[25]

Fisher endured the rigors of basic training at Fort Hood alongside soldiers from southern states like Mississippi, Alabama, and Texas, many of whom Fisher believed had never seen a Jew or spoken to a northerner. He bonded with these southerners, but the army separated Fisher from his fellow enlisted men just before the end of basic training, transferring the singer to Special Services duty with the US Army Band at Fort Myer.[26] The transfer brought accusations that the army was coddling the star. A Senate committee began investigating the alleged preferential treatment that celebrities seemed to enjoy in the service. Fisher claimed in his defense, "I did everything in camp that every other guy in basic did. . . . I didn't ask for the job. . . . I was ordered to go by my superiors and obeyed orders like every soldier does."[27]

Fisher advanced his career because of his service in uniform, not in spite of that time in the army. As *Billboard* noted, "Eddie Fisher, who in civilian life hadn't quite reached the point where he could boast a radio show of his own, oddly enough achieved this goal of most singing actors by getting himself drafted."[28] While stationed at Fort Myer with the army band, Fisher lived in a private apartment in Washington, DC, and spent his time singing for radio and television programs, blood drives, and recruitment campaigns like *At Ease*. Within eight months of joining Special Services, Fisher appeared on over 150 television and radio programs and onstage at Carnegie Hall, the Philadelphia Music Festival to a crowd of 90,000, and at a July 4 celebration at the Washington Monument for more than 250,000. Additionally, he spent forty-six days touring Korea, playing to soldiers on the front and to large crowds around the peninsula, totaling audiences of more than 150,000 United Nations soldiers. He continued on with a tour of installations around Europe.[29] For these appearances, Fisher sang a mixture of his hits and requests from the crowd before leading the troops in community singalongs.[30] He even found time to complete his high school equivalency degree while working for the RS. "I felt like I'd become an adult," he remembered after receiving his discharge in April 1953, "and an even bigger star."[31]

The pop-culture press recognized the army's role in Fisher's success, too. In 1954, the Hollywood reporter Bob Thomas asked, "How do you figure a success like Eddie Fisher's? . . . His take may reach a million dollars this year. All this without having been in a movie! How has he done it?" Thomas credited Fisher's full voice, his relationship with Eddie Cantor, and the savvy handling by his management. Fisher credited the military, claiming, "I think my Army service helped me too. I look back on them as two of the best years of my life. I got to troupe [tour], which most young people don't have a chance to do these days. I sang before all kinds of audiences all over the world." To ward off potential accusations of coddling and emphasize the rigors of incessant performances, Fisher added, "I was a GI like the rest of them, but I was on a spot too."[32] The benefits Fisher received from his army service continued after his time in the ranks ended in 1953. The army sponsored the singer's radio show into the mid-1950s, using the affiliation with one of the nation's biggest pop singers to sell young people on a career in the armed forces.

Country's Soldier Talent

Captain Gigandet and the RS recognized the appeal of showcasing celebrity soldiers in uniform like Fisher, but they also wanted to highlight the entertainment chops of the amateur servicemembers as a means of boosting recruitment. In late 1952, the RS began planning a televised talent show for soldiers to be hosted by a civilian celebrity and produced in New York City. The *Recruiting Journal* noted that part of the plan was to show the diversity and abundance of entertaining talents among soldiers, suggesting that "the various acts for 1 week would be from one Army post, the following week from some Air Force base, until the country has witnessed on their TV screens the wide variety of talent available from the servicepeople."[33] By January 1953, the *Talent Patrol* contest show made its debut on Monday evenings on ABC. Steve Allen, the comedian and musician who had also guest hosted *Arthur Godfrey's Talent Scouts*, served as the master of ceremonies. Allen's time on Godfrey's show made an appropriate introduction to the format of *Talent Patrol*. *Arthur Godfrey's Talent Scouts* had propelled hundreds of performers out of obscurity, first as a radio show and then on television, by exposing amateur talent to a wider audience who could then vote on their favorites. The first run of *Talent Patrol* shows highlighted performers from the Fifth Army, with the winner chosen by the television audience just as it was on Godfrey's program.[34] The actress Arlene Francis joined the show as a co-host that summer, and the RS continued the broadcast into the fall of 1953.[35]

When *Talent Patrol* featured the skills of the Third Army in the spring of 1953, Faron Young made his television debut. *Billboard* reported that Young, the "Capitol country warbler," had won on the contest. The victory meant that Young would make appearances on the country recruitment shows and appear on the Prince Albert portion of the *Grand Ole Opry* on NBC to promote the army.[36] Gigandet traveled to Nashville to "study country handling" and direct Young on the recruitment appearances.[37] The country music newspaper *Pickin' and Singin' News* reported that "Young was so satisfactory on the big TV show that his Uncle Sam is transferring him from Ft. Jackson to Washington, DC." In the nation's capital, Young aided the enlistment effort by recording transcribed programs to be aired as public service announcements for radio stations around the country. "Rather than be exploited Young is getting a real break in his career even in military uniform," the *News* told readers.[38] Young had reason to rejoice. He had just embarked on an eighteen-month promotional tour for both the army and himself, performing in front of thousands of soldiers in personal appearances and over the radio, all at the expense of American taxpayers. The US Army and the country music industry recognized overlapping interests in the market of young men created by Cold War military service, and they went into business together.

Not only did Young possess the sound and the timing to win the hearts of country fans, but his apparent enthusiasm to serve his country further endeared him to the country music press. The country magazine *Hoedown* featured a picture of Young in his uniform, complete with helmet, and holding his guitar in a section called "Hogtied," in which the soldier-singer described his favorite food, color, and cowgirl singer.[39] *Pickin' and Singin' News* wrote admirably that "some with lesser courage and philosophy might have decried the interruption of a budding career by Uncle Sam's beck and call, but not Pvt. Faron Young." Instead, Young put a cheerful spin on his situation, telling the paper, "I'm lucky! It will give me a chance to meet people from all over America, and at the same time to do something worthwhile." The *News* could not have agreed more. The article concluded by saying, "that's the American spirit and the attitude of most Country Musicians."[40]

While other artists struggled for press and radio airplay, Young could not have bought the kind of exposure that the army provided. Commenting to *Country Song Roundup*, Young stated that the army tours were not "the easiest job on earth": "We were doing two and three and four shows a day and traveling a thousand miles a week in GI vehicles, but it was worth it." Young could hardly argue with the results of this kind of government-sponsored publicity. "The men in the Army had always been mighty nice to me as a civilian, but when they saw that I was just a private, too, they were even nicer. I'm just glad that I could give them a little entertainment." The *Roundup* interview included a six-page profile of the "Singin' Soldier" with over thirty pictures of Young, many of which showed him in dress uniform or fatigues, guitar in hand and in mid-song, reminding readers of the connection between the singer and themselves or their loved ones serving in the Cold War military. With a carefully crafted image of a clean-cut, country-singing soldier deployed for recruitment, readers could believe that Young "was 'just another guy' after all" and yet "a GI blessed with the kind of voice you hear once in a generation."[41]

Country music made the perfect genre for this story about the common soldier, plucked from obscurity on the basis of his natural talent, and given an opportunity for economic and social advancement through service to the nation-state. Beginning in the early twentieth century, tastemakers and the pop music industry of Tin Pan Alley did not consider country music worthy of consideration as a professional style of music. According to the standards of the pop industry, professional musicians read music, performed songs written by professional songwriters, and belonged to the American Federation of Musicians. By contrast, the pop industry assumed that country musicians did not read music, and country artists often wrote and performed their own songs instead of relying on the output of Tin Pan Alley publishers.[42] The pop industry also refused to include many hillbilly songwriters, as well as most of the Black artists who performed on "race records," in ASCAP, the pop-centric royalty-collection and licensing organization founded in 1914. ASCAP held contracts that dominated an ever-evolving music media, from sheet music, vaudeville, and nickelodeons to radio and jukeboxes. By the time radio emerged as the most popular medium in the 1920s and 1930s, ASCAP enjoyed an almost complete monopolization of music licensing and demanded exclusive contracts with radio stations to play songs from its catalogue. This meant that if listeners heard recorded music on their radio, the station was legally bound to pay for the rights to air these tunes.[43]

The music licensed by ASCAP skewed heavily toward the songs of Tin Pan Alley, leaving many race and hillbilly artists—those working in genres most associated with the South—without a mechanism to get their records played on radio. The ASCAP monopoly and its exclusionary financial practices shattered on December 31, 1940, when thousands of stations boycotted its material and formed BMI with a catalogue of previously ostracized genres and artists. This boycott temporarily removed the entire collections of songwriters like Cole Porter, Jerome Kern, and George Gershwin from the air and substituted music from Latin America, Stephen Foster songs, hillbilly music, and race records in their place.[44] Hillbilly and race music, normally considered the domain of amateurs, now flooded the airwaves and opened a way for those artists to collect mechanical royalties. Ten years later in 1950, following the enormous success of Patti Page's country-to-pop-crossover cover of Pee Wee King and Redd Stewart's "Tennessee Waltz," ASCAP accused the amateurs of country music of invading and nefariously taking over the record market.[45] ASCAP maintained those accusations until finally bringing legislation against BMI in the form of the Smathers Bill in 1958, which forced members of the country music industry, including Faron Young, to defend their style of music to US lawmakers.

Young's ascent from "amateur" musician and soldier on *Talent Patrol* to the national airwaves and the stage of the *Grand Ole Opry* tracked with what military recruitment campaigns promised to do for any soldier. Namely, it vowed to professionalize them in their given trade and place them on the track for economic success. In 1953, the army transferred Young to Fort McPherson outside Atlanta and bought his army band new instruments and tan business suits with the Third Army insignia, the letter *A* inside of a circle, sown on the pocket. The band took the name the Circle A Wranglers, creating a double entendre that stacked military nomenclature on top of what sounded like cowboy lingo for a ranch's cattle brand. Young and the Wranglers made several appearances on the *Grand Ole Opry* during their time in the service, and the singer closed by reminding listeners that he "appeared on the show through the courtesy of the Commanding General, Third Army."[46]

The Circle A Wranglers stayed busy playing for active troops and hitting the airwaves for recruitment campaigns. They toured installations throughout the South, including Fort Bragg, where they entertained thousands of troops stationed there for a large-scale atomic training program called Exercise Flash Burn in April 1954.[47] They also played for special events organized for the Third Army. In August 1954, Young and the Circle A Wranglers joined with other musicians stationed at Fort McPherson to perform at an event called "Southland Panorama" at Atlanta's Chastain Park. *Army Times* stated that the Third Army Special Services designed this event to "recall the grandeur and charm of the old South." A "Civil War atmosphere will prevail," the paper predicted of the event, which featured a narrative portion that would include "a soldier of Gen. Joseph E. Johnston's Army telling the saga of a growing Southland with all its spirit and proud heritage."[48]

Capitol Records continued to release singles throughout Young's time in the army, including "I Can't Wait (for the Sun to Go Down)" and "A Place for Girls Like You," both of which hit the *Billboard* top ten.[49] By September 1954, Young starred in *The Faron Young Show*, produced by the Third Army and broadcast throughout the formation's recruiting district.[50] These musical recruiting efforts aided the Third Army's boom in recruitment. Commanding officer Lieutenant General A. R. Bolling commended the unit's personnel procurement officers for the achievement of securing 137 percent of their recruitment quota from July 1953 to June 1954.[51]

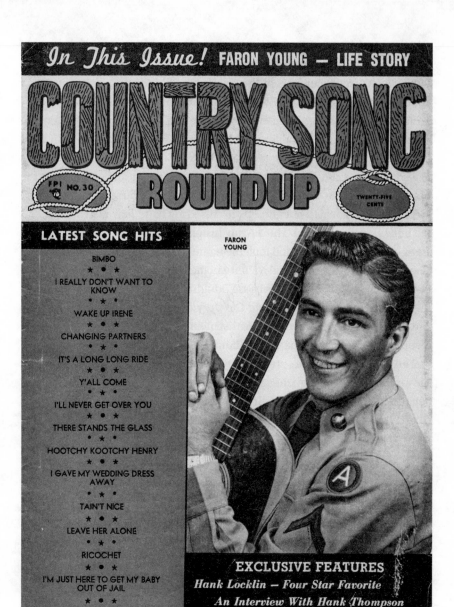

FIGURE 2.1 Pfc. Faron Young pictured in uniform on the cover of fan magazine *Country Song Roundup*. Young's performances for military entertainment and recruitment programs provided an early career boost. Here, the encircled *A* insignia on his left shoulder represents his assignment to the Third US Army stationed in Fort McPherson, Georgia. Young also called his band of soldiers the Circle A Wranglers in a nod to this assignment. (*Country Song Roundup*, July 1954, author's collection)

Young's emergence as a voice of recruitment marked the beginning of the RS's embrace of country music as a new sound for enlistment pitches. That same year, the army and the air force repackaged Connie Gay's *Town and Country Time* to produce another country music recruitment program.[52] A writer in the June 1953 edition of *Recruiting Journal,* the RS's newsletter, enthused, "In the planning state since the first of the year, now it can be told! A new program series, 'Town and Country Time' is the newest recruiting vehicle for the airwaves, and features top-notch country music." It noted that Gay, "an authority on folk music whose fans already number in the thousands in the Washington area," remained at the helm as emcee of the show, which the RS distributed to 2,200 radio stations around the country.[53] The Radio Section of the US Army Publicity Branch produced the show as fifteen-minute transcriptions of the "top stars of WSM's 'Grand Ole Opry which emanates from Nashville, Tenn.,'" playing their "folk and Western" hits with a pitch to join the service alongside the tunes. The impetus for the show emerged when the Military Personnel Procurement Department of the Adjutant General's Office discovered "through reports that the largest percentage of Army enlistees came from the Southeastern States where country music is very popular."[54]

The army recognized a regional discrepancy in the location of its enlistees. White southern men seemed to flow through a personnel pipeline into the military. Country music, the recruiters reasoned, could keep that pipeline moving. In return, the country music industry received an unprecedented boost in exposure. With the initiation of the *Town and Country Time* recruitment show, Gay received his first nationwide distribution, while the military created a new way to entice potential recruits, namely, white recruits, into the ranks. Between the successes of Faron Young, Connie B. Gay, and Jimmy Dean, the US military had emerged as the single biggest booster for country music in the world. The Pentagon essentially acted as a publicity arm for the genre, pushing country artists and their songs as the sound of armed service and, by extension, patriotic devotion to the nation.

Faron Young's career facilitated the military's embrace of this genre as a recruitment tool, and his involvement established a direct connection between army promotion and Nashville's country music industry. The fan magazine *Country & Western Jamboree* profiled this phenomenon in an article titled "The Army Goes Country and Western." "Take some good country music, mix it with a dash of sophistication," the writer enthused, "and you have a formula for a popular network radio show." Young's successes

The Army Goes Country & Western

FIGURE 2.2 Fan magazine *Country & Western Jamboree* enthused about the growing connections between the Defense Department and the country music industry in the mid-1950s. (*Country & Western Jamboree*, July 1955, author's collection)

on *Talent Patrol*, later renamed *Soldier Parade*, made the army realize that it needed more country music recruitment programming. It did not take long to correct this oversight. Besides *Town and Country Time*, the army created another new country music recruitment show called *Country Jamboree*, which aired on the Mutual Radio Network. It featured emcee Mark Hamilton and music by country stars of the day like Young. In a testament to the seduction of musical recruitment, Hamilton, a former radio announcer on Connie B. Gay's WARL in Arlington, Virginia, had joined the army himself after meeting Eddie Fisher during a radio interview. Seeing the opportunity to fuse military recruitment with country music, Hamilton based *Country Jamboree* on the format of *Town and Country Time*.[55] With a roster of country stars and the support of the US Army Recruiting Service, *Country Jamboree* joined the effort to reach out to the United States' young people with a mixture of patriotism, martial spirit, and country music.

Even Young's departure from the army earned publicity and praise. The city of Atlanta, Georgia, proclaimed Wednesday, November 17, 1954, as "Faron Young Day" in recognition of the country and western singer's recent career accomplishments. To mark the occasion, at nine that morning, Young appeared on the city's television station WSB's *Today in Georgia*, where local and national authorities met the rising country star with handshakes and words of honor. Lee Evans, president of the Board of

Alderman, presented the singer with a letter of commendation. Young then received a certificate of achievement from Lieutenant General Bolling. Glenn Wallichs, president of Capitol Records and the director of the Boy Scouts of America, participated as well, thanking Young for all he had done in the past two years.[56] Young continued to celebrate his namesake day with concerts in Atlanta that night and left the next day for Nashville, where the adorations continued. Tennessee's Governor Clement greeted Young with a scroll that heaped more praise on country and western music's favorite son of the moment.[57] Young would turn this heightened notoriety into lucrative advancements in the entertainment business, including acting roles in westerns like *Hidden Guns* and *Daniel Boone—Trailblazer.*[58] Young's music-to-military-to-film trajectory set a pattern that Elvis Presley would follow by serving in the army, gaining publicity and respect from that service, and turning that new status into a film career.

When the army chose Young, it created an alternative to the musical branding associated with Eddie Fisher's crooning and the swing music that constituted much of the early 1950s pop genre. Fisher's music harked back to the artists preferred by the urban working class of the Great Depression and World War II, artists like Duke Ellington, Benny Goodman, and Ella Fitzgerald.[59] Swing and pop coded as urban, northern, ethnic, and potentially nonwhite.[60] By contrast, country music coded as rural, southern, and white, despite the actual racial and geographic diversity of the genre's fans, artists, and influences.[61]

The use of Faron Young and country music as tools of recruitment also reflected a shift in US labor and racial politics. Deindustrialization of northern and midwestern manufacturing cities had begun as early as 1945, aided by the passage in 1946 of the Taft-Hartley Act, which gutted the strength of unions. Much like the mushrooming of the nation's military installations, industrial employers headed south to the emergent Sunbelt. By the early 1950s, white workers began their abandonment of widespread unionism as a relic of the previous decade and embraced the postwar suburban prosperity that funded white flight from what would become the cities of the Rust Belt. Places like Atlanta, Phoenix, Dallas, Houston, and the bedroom communities of Orange County, California, displaced Detroit, Pittsburgh, and Philadelphia as the nation's economic boomtowns.[62] Likewise, southern politicians ensured that military growth benefited their states, bringing more defense contractors and soldiers to the region than ever before. Country music and Faron Young created an appropriately southern soundtrack for this move.

The use of country music in recruitment campaigns signaled the genre's growing commercial power, which coincided with the centralization of the industry in Nashville. The historian Diane Pecknold has described how the consolidation of country music's studios, record labels, performers, and songwriters in Nashville made the city "the closest equivalent to Tin Pan Alley to survive the midcentury passage to fully realized mass culture." In 1953, WSM, the radio home of the *Grand Ole Opry*, helped enable this consolidation of power by gaining control of the Country Music Disc Jockey Association, an organization founded by Connie B. Gay. The station located the disc jockey's convention in Nashville and renamed it the WSM Disc Jockey Festival, essentially conflating all country music with WSM and the *Grand Ole Opry*.[63]

Country music's popularity also grew thanks to increased coverage in national trade magazines and newspapers. This boost began in 1952 when country radio gained more notice in *Billboard*'s new column "Folk Talent & Tunes." The death of Hank Williams on January 1, 1953, and the creation of the Jimmie Rodgers Memorial Festival later that year, designed as a tribute to the "father of country music," propelled the genre into national headlines just as the Nashville industry ramped up its production.[64] Williams's death created an increased demand for recordings of his songs, which enriched the publishing firm Acuff-Rose, a company owned by two of Nashville's most powerful men, Roy Acuff and Fred Rose. Fans even wanted to buy records by artists who *sounded* like Hank Williams. This phenomenon undoubtedly helped Faron Young's 1953 breakout single, "Goin' Steady," which sounded so much like a Williams composition that other performers accused Young of plagiarism.[65] Pecknold describes these leaps in notoriety for the genre as "a series of events that combined to propel the country music industry into the biggest promotional windfall it had experienced in its short history."[66]

The windfall found in the combination of professional organizations, press coverage, and celebrity death could not compare to the boost in publicity that country music earned through its association with the military. US Armed Forces recruitment had propelled Connie B. Gay and Jimmy Dean to national prominence and transformed Faron Young into a Nashville star. In return, the Pentagon enjoyed a direct line to the genre's audiences. The RS relied on country music to sell careers in military service at a time when it desperately needed recruits. It noticed a steady stream of enlistees from the South and put its resources into keeping that stream flowing. Soldiers did love country music. They hungered for it when stationed overseas and begged for news of their favorite stars, who reminded them of home. Country music not only enticed its fans into joining the military but also provided the soundtrack to their service.

· · · · · ·

The AFRS had acted as an essential tool for country music's promotion since the late 1940s, and it only increased its importance as the popularity of the genre began to grow in the early 1950s. *Country & Western Jamboree* reported on the demand for the genre among both US soldiers and foreign civilians in Germany who listened on the AFN stations in Europe. "American-style music has become as much a part of the average European's listening habits as have the familiar melodies from Stateside to the American either at home or stationed overseas," the magazine claimed in the summer of 1955. Country music proved particularly popular with civilians on the continent. As the *Jamboree* stated, "Here in Germany, a large majority of the listening audience . . . is composed of the native European 'eavesdropping' to hear what this 'American music is all about.' Needless to say, country-style music is considered a large item on the music agenda here." Both military and civilians wrote letters to the AFRS, with many letters coming from the US requesting that disc jockeys dedicate a song to an individual soldier. Three programs produced by US soldiers stationed in West Germany, *Hillbilly Gasthaus, Western Swing,* and *Stick-Buddy Jamboree,* obliged these requests and helped spread the sound of country music on the continent.[67]

These radio broadcasts, along with the Special Services concerts and country tours booked by Connie B. Gay and the *Grand Ole Opry,* kept soldiers entertained with the sounds of home and provided an outlet for the newest country music to reach audiences overseas. Groups like the Roadside Ramblers, made up of eight soldiers from the Ninth Infantry Division stationed in West Germany, performed benefit concerts for German orphanages, hospitals, curious civilian concertgoers, and soldiers at the army's service clubs. The Ramblers had risen in popularity thanks to winning a service club talent contest. They went on to win their regional talent show, which awarded them an appearance on the AFN for two half-hour programs. In explaining the Germans' interest in the music, Private First Class Harry L. Reckhart, leader of the Ramblers, suggested that "music is an international language" that transcended cultural differences. "Although most Germans don't understand the words," Reckhart contended, "the tempo and melody of American folk songs are just as novel to them as German folk songs are to us in America." Two members of the Ramblers hoped to turn their military musical experience into a civilian profession when their hitch ended, a recurring theme for the country musicians who received their start in the armed forces.[68]

While live music and radio programs kept soldiers and civilians tuned in to country sounds, the growing country music press kept soldiers stationed around the globe informed of the latest releases and news about their favorite artists. One airman, who referred to himself as Ed (Tiny) Tims, worked as a disc jockey in Laurel, Mississippi, before joining the service. The air force stationed him on Misaswa Air Base in Japan in 1955, and the *Country & Western Jamboree* kept him up-to-date on the latest country music news. He wrote to the magazine to praise its coverage. "I just read the April and May issues of your new magazine and think they are just a shade above terrific. I especially enjoyed the stories on Carl Smith and Hank Thompson." Country music helped Tims maintain his connection to his friends and his profession back home in Mississippi. His letter to the *Jamboree* included how he had heard "from back stateside that Jimmy Martin and the Osborne Brothers have made themselves quite a place in the country field with their recording of *Save It! Save It!* Certainly would like to see a write-up and pics of the boys."[69] Tims wrote back three months later to compliment the magazine's reviews of new music. "Many thanks for publishing my letter," he told the *Jamboree* editors, adding, "Your record review column sure keeps me posted on ordering my records. You sure have a magazine that's here to stay, and by far the finest in its field."[70]

Other servicemembers used the pages to make connections with other musicians and with the country music industry. Corporal Anthony Warrenfelt wrote to the magazine to request an article on Connie B. Gay and his *Radio Ranch* in Arlington, Virginia, which he claimed used to be his favorite program back home. He also wanted to know the whereabouts of Buck Ryan, a champion fiddler whom he had heard was working in Baltimore.[71] Another servicemember, US Air Force Staff Sergeant M. V. Hinorn, wrote to the *Jamboree* to ask an array of questions about breaking into the country music business. "Man, am I ever glad I subscribed to your fine magazine," Hinorn told the editors. Besides wanting to know about the careers of particular musicians, Hinorn inquired about song publishing, purchasing radio transcriptions, and contacting the executives in charge of country at Capitol, RCA Victor, Decca, and Columbia. He closed by telling the editors how their "publication is in itself the answer to a great need."[72]

The *Jamboree* did address a growing need shared by many aspiring country musicians in the military, like Hinorn. Namely, how does one become a professional musician after one's time in the service? These men had every right to think that such a move was possible. They had witnessed the success of Faron Young, who, in a matter of a few months, had risen from a virtual unknown to an undisputed celebrity. Just as other servicemembers used military service and the subsequent benefits of the GI Bill to professionalize in trades ranging from radio technicians to auto mechanics, others wanted to use their time in the ranks to professionalize their musical skill. They knew that the military could provide a springboard into the country music business. Meanwhile, the Pentagon knew that country music could help push potential volunteers into the service. In the late 1950s, the RS embraced the combined tools of radio, television, and country music to maintain the pipeline of country music listeners entering the military with dreams of economic advancement.

Country Recruitment Grows

Over the course of the 1950s, the US Army increased its recruitment campaigns to target fans of country music, still considered a niche genre at the time. Following the pattern of Faron Young's radio recruitment spots, *Town and Country Time*, and *Country Jamboree*, the US Army began producing two new radio series, one called *The George Hamilton IV Show* and another called *Country Style, U.S.A.* Hamilton's program pitched service in the National Guard and featured music by the show's namesake, who had risen to stardom under the management of Connie B. Gay. Hamilton also welcomed guests like Faron Young and Jim Reeves. This short-lived show lasted all of eight episodes and only cost the National Guard $6,800. *Country Style, U.S.A.* ran for fifty-two episodes and presented fifteen minutes of country music by top names in the genre, like Hank Snow, Eddy Arnold, and Jim Reeves, along with a message about the career opportunities available through the armed forces. The army spent almost $50,000 (nearly $500,000 in 2023 dollars) for the production of *Country Style, U.S.A.*, which entered the rotation at over 2,000 radio stations around the nation.[73]

The proliferation of country music recruitment did not mean that the Defense Department gave up on pop music. By 1960, the RS distributed eight radio shows that mixed mainstream pop music of the day with recruitment messaging. Private First Class Steve Lawrence, a pop singer and veteran of *The Steve Allen Show*, hosted fifty-two episodes of *The Steve Lawrence Show*, which cost the army $37,719 (approximately $383,000 in 2023 dollars) to produce. This fifteen-minute program featured music, interviews with teenagers, and celebrity guests. Lawrence also hosted *Army Bandstand*, another fifteen-minute show, that presented the singer backed by the US Army Band and a rotating cast of other popular orchestras to accompany the singer. The fifty-two episodes of that show ran the army $36,695. Other programs included the US Army Reserve's five-minute disc jockey show called *Whitaker's Wax*, as well as *Mostly Music*, which played concerts by vocalists backed by the US Army Band. The National Guard embedded its solicitations to join on the programs *Let's Go to Town*, *The Bob Crosby Show*, and *Andy Williams Sings*, all of which featured pop stars like the eponymous hosts, Rosemary Clooney, Connie Francis, and Bobby Darin. Lastly, a show called *Keep in Step with the Guard* highlighted music by the US Army Field Band and the US Air Force Band, drumming up enlistment and general patriotic spirit at the same time.[74]

Still, country music programming accounted for more than one-third of the US Army's televised recruitment campaigns by 1960, equaling the amount of air time given to the documentary-style recruitment shows and doubling all other types of musical recruitment on television. The National Guard contributed to that total with ten episodes of the country show *Community Jamboree*, but the bulk of the on-screen twang came from the televised version of *Country Style, U.S.A.* This version lasted for over three years and cost the army around $216,000 (over $2 million in 2023 dollars). Each fifteen-minute, live segment featured a top name in country music as a master of ceremonies, while Private First Class Charlie Applewhite, a former *Milton Berle Show* cohost, served as its first announcer.[75] Applewhite also worked as an announcer for a pop music recruitment show, giving him cross-genre experience in selling armed service as a career for the nation's young people.[76]

Although *Country Style, U.S.A.* was originally slated for just thirteen episodes beginning in 1957, the army eventually created fifty-two, a testament to the successful collaboration between Nashville's thriving music industry and the Cold War demand for young men, particularly white men, to join the ranks. The lineup included artists like Roy Acuff, Minnie Pearl, Rod Brasfield, Faron Young, Little Jimmy Dickens, and Jim Reeves.[77] The Nashville newspaper the *Tennessean* reported that the *Country Style, U.S.A.* episodes "are said to be the first of their kind featuring country musicians" and that the show would be distributed to "television stations over the nation by [the] recruiting office as a public service."[78] With this roster of country stars, the army capitalized on country music fandom. And the production of *Country Style, U.S.A.* made the connections between the military and country music even more concrete thanks to the use of Owen Bradley's studio, a US Army surplus Quonset hut that sat adjacent to his original studio on Sixteenth Avenue South in Nashville. Bradley, the legendary producer behind Patsy Cline, Willie Nelson, and Johnny Cash, also produced the army's television show.[79] With a country music recruitment show filmed in a Quonset-hut-turned-studio, the infrastructure of the warfare state literally, if inadvertently, provided the recording infrastructure on the street that would become the heart of Music Row.

Every episode of *Country Style, U.S.A.* kicked off and ended the same way, with a chorus of the western swing standard "Stay All Night (Stay a Little Longer)," which Bob Wills and Tommy Duncan had written and sent to number three on the *Billboard* country and western charts in 1946. The *Country Style, U.S.A.* house band played the Wills-Duncan tune, while square dancers clapped and danced to the music. This opening sequence played out in front of a scene of constructed rusticity. Bales of hay, piled behind the band and scattered around on the floor, added three-dimensional props to the flat, painted barn on the backdrop, where the guest emcee would stand, guitar in hand, to sing his songs. And it was always *his* songs. *Country Style, U.S.A.* cast a male performer as the emcee on every episode, while the show would cut away to a featured female performer who sang one song before the cameras returned to the male hosts.

A typical episode featured Marty Robbins as emcee. He kicked things off with two of his hit releases, "I Can't Quit" and "Singin' the Blues." He then welcomed Applewhite, who, wearing his dress uniform, alerted viewers to the "new career fields open in the United States Army." "And you know," Applewhite reminded the audience, "in the army, artillery is a career that starts with a bang!" The scene cut to footage of soldiers firing a 280-millimeter atomic cannon, and a voice-over stated how the skills gained in the army would transfer to the private sector.[80] Country musicians had wrestled with the significance of atomic warfare ever since the dropping of the bombs on Hiroshima and Nagasaki. In 1945, the hillbilly singer Fred Kirby wrote "Atomic Power," a song made famous by the Buchanan Brothers that questioned the wisdom in unleashing such a destructive force. Perhaps more famously, in 1952, the Louvin Brothers released "The Great Atomic Power," which urged listeners to "give your heart and soul to Jesus" rather than risk eternal torment following the all-but-certain nuclear annihilation that awaited humankind.[81] But in 1958 and with the airing of *Country Style, U.S.A.*, that trepidation had disappeared. In one fifteen-minute segment, the army made its intentions and cultural allegiances known. Framed between the soaring glissandos of a steel guitar and the roaring cacophony of an

FIGURE 2.3 Pfc. Charlie Applewhite, Marty Robbins, and Joyce Paul pitch the US Army as a career on an episode of *Country Style, U.S.A.* The US Army paid the country music producer Owen Bradley to use his studio for this program in the late 1950s and early 1960s. (Season 1, episode 8, Bear Family Records, DVD)

atomic missile, the army invited young men to join the peacetime ranks in a promise of economic advancement and armed adventure, all set to country music's latest hits.

Country Style, U.S.A. also made its pitch for young women to join the Women's Army Corps (WAC). In a different episode hosted by Robbins, the singer invited another of the army's announcers, Private Jody McCrae, an actor in a series of teen beach movies who had replaced Applewhite, to introduce a segment directed at women. "Tell me, you've really got something important for all these young ladies that are college graduates, is that right?" Robbins prompted McCrae. "Yeah, I really do, Marty," McCrae replied. "It's something real special." The camera then cut to a segment called "Fashion News for College Graduate" with a female voice-over, describing the latest styles in uniforms for the women's corps. "You'll look your best as an officer in the Women's Army Corps. Look at this chic taupe uniform by one of the country's foremost designers, accentuating smooth flowing

lines," a female narrator confided in a self-assured delivery. "It comple-
ments your responsible army job, for as a WAC officer, you'll start as an executive with a truly important job." With promises of traveling the globe in
your dress uniform, the army offered adventures in exotic locations to young
American women, all while maintaining their feminine image. The army
also presented the prospect of heterosexual love when the narrator reassured
viewers that "for those enchanted evenings at the officers club, you're free to
wear your own frothiest gown."[82] Plagued by rumors of lesbianism in the
ranks, WACs needed to dispel any misgivings that Americans might feel
about women in the otherwise masculine attire of an army uniform.[83]

Pop music had long functioned as a recruitment tool for the WACs, particularly since Gigandet had taken over the radio section of the RS. He had
begun reaching out to potential recruits with a show called *The WAC on
Parade*, which he produced for the radio's Mutual Broadcasting System beginning in 1951. The show featured a message from the secretary of the
army, several testimonials from active WACs, and the sounds of three official WAC musical groups called the Bar-B Sharps vocal quartette, the WAC
chorus, and the WAC Dixieland group.[84] In the summer of 1951, the RS also
produced a special episode of the radio series *Stars on Parade*, featuring
the pop star Rosemary Clooney. This show celebrated the ninth anniversary
of the WAC's founding and a recent call for 30,000 new women recruits.
Clooney joined musicians in The Army Blues, the army dance band at Fort
Myer, Virginia, to record a selection of her hits.[85] Patti Page, who had experienced an enormous career boost in the early 1950s thanks to the success
of her pop cover of the country tune "Tennessee Waltz," filled in for Eddie
Fisher on his show *At Ease* in the fall of 1952 with a special message for
potential WACs. "I've always been fascinated with these bright young
women . . . with the way they wear that pretty uniform, . . . the way they
tackle every job with real zest!" she told her listeners. Page testified, "I've
seen with my own eyes how the WACs have taken hold and learned how to
be real technicians . . . skilled in hundreds of jobs." She then made her pitch
to join, relaying that the corps could do even more for the country "if only
more of you young women would take advantage of the chance to be a
WAC. . . . There are so many benefits waiting for you, believe me!"[86]

The combination of television and country music on *Country Style,
U.S.A.* offered yet another way to reach white female fans. Service as a
WAC promised a semblance of independence for young women in the 1950s.
The RS embedded that message of personal freedom in the slogan, "Get
choice, not chance, from your Army Recruiter," a phrase coined during the

Korean War to attract career-oriented soldiers. In a 1958 episode hosted by Faron Young, the army made another pitch to young women on this promise of career choice. As Young finished a version of his 1957 tune "Vacation's Over," he thanked his quartet of backup singers, the Southlanders, as well as his band, the Country Deputies, before segueing into the recruitment spot. "We have more fun when we get to work for the army, I'll guarantee you," Young confessed, reprising his role as a recruitment leader. He then lamented, "We don't get to mention the girls enough" on *Country Style, U.S.A.* "So right now, we'd like to get Charlie Applewhite to tell you girls how you can keep up with the boys in the army by choosing a career for your future, too. Charlie?"[87]

Applewhite introduced the clip, which was accompanied again by a female voice-over. The camera pans over the Arc de Triomphe. "This is the Champs Elysees, the loveliest street in Paris," the woman's voice told the audience, "and here's the loveliest thing on the Champs Elysees, Sally Brown, American." A young brunette woman in a suit-dress holds a translation book while happily talking with a Parisian police officer, who gives her directions. The narrator then described how Sally had achieved a level of independence to which many working- and middle-class women could only aspire, describing her as a "world traveler at twenty-two and a very important person to her country." "During business hours, she's Corporal Sally Brown, Women's Army Corps," the voice-over told viewers, "an expert army photographer. Assignment: Europe." The narrator made clear that Sally earned this glamorous independence because of the opportunities provided by the army, reminding viewers that "life wasn't always this interesting, and neither was Sally." The camera cuts to Sally in civilian dress, folding clothes in a department store and explaining how, "grinding away at her routine job," Sally felt "rather routine herself."[88]

The civilian Sally Brown resented the drudgery of working in the postwar nation's service economy, where she struggled with the boredom of retail labor. The narrator told viewers that "the Women's Army Corps changed all that. Her army recruiter helped plan her career," and "she chose from twenty-six exciting courses in photography, medicine, radio, and many more." As the scene faded, Sally walked along on the arm of a male soldier, while the narrator conveyed that if "you want to be like Sally, see your army recruiter now. Learn how you too can enjoy life in the Women's Army Corps." Faron Young then delivered one more pitch before introducing Skeeter Davis, the episode's female guest star, saying, "And remember girls, now more than ever before, you get choice, not chance, in the United States Army."[89]

The country music press raved about the program. *Country & Western Jamboree* described *Country Style, U.S.A.* as "probably the 'best' Country Music television films ever made." Colonel Vernon Rice and Major Jim Hickman, two RS officers, previewed the series backstage at the *Grand Ole Opry*. Minnie Pearl served as hostess for the RS officials during their Nashville visit, and the article declared that the show "won acclaim for fine singing, good music, and strikingly simple production features coupled with excellent technical work done by Owen Bradley and his studio staff."[90] From the perspective of the country music industry, the mission behind *Country Style, U.S.A.* did not warrant a mention beyond the RS officers who screened the films. What mattered to the country industry was that *Country Style* provided Nashville's stars with an unprecedented reach into new television markets and the chance to spread the music to more consumers.

Both the AFRTS and civilian radio networks continued broadcasting country music recruitment shows during the late 1950s to address the perpetual need for volunteers. Connie B. Gay and Walter Bouillet had sold the US Navy on the program *Country Hoedown* in 1957 and used it as a tool to promote Jimmy Dean. *Country Hoedown* relied on a rotating cast of country artists as the hosts and guest stars, including Dean, Faron Young, Tex Ritter, and Ernest Tubb. Similar to *Country Style, U.S.A.*, these radio shows began with a string band performing a square-dance tune while a caller announced, "It's the *Country Hoedown*!" In a 1957 episode hosted by Faron Young, the singer greeted listeners like old acquaintances: "Well, greetings, friends and neighbors. This is the Young Sheriff Faron Young, presiding over the doings here at the Country Hoedown."[91]

Young could speak to them in this way because he was, in fact, a familiar voice to many of them, having donated his time and talent to military recruitment for nearly five years at that point. He encouraged his listeners, "Throw your cares away and join in on the fun 'cause we have plenty of music and song coming right at you." Ernest Tubb then joined Young for a bit of country humor about the hardships of growing up in rural poverty. Tubb claimed that his family was so poor that his mother used sand instead of talcum powder, while Young joked that he had twenty-eight siblings because his parents could not get along and his father wanted to "get lost in the crowd." To complete the show, Young and Tubb traded turns playing songs, Tennessee Ernie Ford gave a Bible reading, and an armed forces spokesperson encouraged listeners to continue their educations while in the service by enrolling in a telecourse. The spot ended with Young reminding listeners that the US Navy sponsored the *Country Hoedown*.[92]

All episodes of *Country Hoedown* took the basic form and content of this particular one hosted by Young, and the show followed the pattern of its contemporary country music shows like Connie B. Gay's *Town and Country Time* and Owen Bradley's *Country Style, U.S.A. Country Hoedown*'s production reinforced the usefulness of the genre as a recruitment tool and why the RS relied so heavily on country music and its stars. Both Young and Tubb sang songs in their signature styles. Tubb went first with a version of the tune "Last Blue Yodel (The Women Make a Fool Out of Me)," a song recorded by his musical idol, Jimmie Rodgers, in 1930. "I love the women," Tubb draws. "I love them all the same / But I never loved nobody well enough to change her name," followed by the song's titular refrain, "The women make a fool out of me." Young delivered the next song, his 1955 release "It's a Great Life (If You Don't Weaken)," cowritten by the wife-and-husband team Audrey and Joe Allison. With fake humility, the singer crows about not needing many worldly goods to be happy in life, just a few million dollars, dates with multiple women at once, and fancy cars to drive, before hitting the comedic refrain, "It's a great life if you don't weaken / But who wants to be strong?" The song echoed the theme of Young's first number-one hit, also written by Joe Allison, "Live Fast, Love Hard, Die Young," and helped cement his image as a raucous, hell-raisin' good ol' boy. Likewise, Tubb's rendition of the Rodgers tune boasted about a record of hard living and promiscuous sex, themes that asserted a heteronormative, albeit rebellious, version of masculinity.[93]

As Tubb's cover of a 1930 record suggested, country music had long traded in these tropes of masculine virility and hedonism but never without tempering its reported decadence with repentance and Christian devotion.[94] Young's and Tubb's performances relished in the working-class rowdiness that record producers would tone down only a few years later with the "Nashville sound," which, as the producer Billy Sherrill described, was made for "the housewife washing dishes at ten a.m. in Topeka, Kansas."[95] Yet *Country Hoedown* also made time for a Bible lesson. Tennessee Ernie Ford read a verse for these shows and offered a homily. On the Young/Tubb episode, Ford quoted from 1 Kings 3:9, stating, "Give therefore thy servant an understanding heart to judge thy people, that I may discern between good and bad." The takeaway from this passage, according to Ford, was that "while you're getting to know folks, getting to know the good and the bad in them, they're doing the same with you, yes sir. When it comes to getting along with folks, having an understanding heart is mighty important."[96] When coupled with economic advancement and military duty, the religious and gendered messages of shows like *Country Hoedown* and *Country Style, U.S.A.* sold country music as an all-American soundtrack to Cold War patriotism.

······

Frank G. Clement tirelessly promoted country music as the United States' music in the midst of these recruitment campaigns in the 1950s. Clement, a Democrat, served as Tennessee's governor from 1953 to 1959 and again from 1963 to 1967. His administrations sought to improve the state's reputation by developing industrial growth and encouraging racial moderation. He even commandeered the mic during a broadcast of the *Grand Ole Opry* in 1956 to announce the activation of National Guard troops to enforce integration in Clinton, Tennessee, when violent white supremacists terrorized the town.[97] Clement used country music to promote his state's public image by touting the genre's commercial potential. He viewed the music as a natural resource for the state, something that sprang organically from its people over generations and had modernized to meet the tastes at midcentury. Clement made a habit of appearing alongside country musicians at events, ranging from the *Opry* to the Jimmie Rodgers Memorial Festival in Meridian, Mississippi, all in an attempt to equate Nashville, and Tennessee in general, with country music and country music with the United States itself.[98]

Governor Clement took his promotional campaign to New York City in 1956, delivering the keynote address and appearing with stars of the *Grand Ole Opry* at a luncheon for the Radio and Television Executives Society held at the Hotel Roosevelt. "There are three things we folk in Tennessee take seriously," he began, "our politics, our religion, and our country music." Although he admitted to not being a historian, Clement claimed to understand the genre's roots and asserted, "Today's country music has captured and held the melodies our forefathers sang as they trudged through the tall rhododendron-covered Smokies. . . . This was the music of the pioneers. . . . It told of their sorrows and joys." Clement also acknowledged that "New York's Madison Avenue" did not always understand the music's popularity, and he tried explaining the music's attractiveness as simply as possible. "Country music is the music of the people. It's the spontaneous musical outburst of the events in their daily lives—their joys and hopes and fears," he told the crowd. He also pushed his belief in culture as a natural resource, maintaining, "Country music has always been with us. . . . It is one of the great resources of a people, of an intelligent, neighbor-loving,

God-fearing people, steeped in folk tradition and folk culture." He closed by merging personal taste, country music, and American cultural identity, claiming, "I love country music because when I hear it, I hear America singing."[99]

In 1957, the governor returned to New York City, where he addressed 350 of the city's civic and business leaders in the Rotary Club. He again recounted the genre's roots in pioneer folk culture and continued to mesh country music with Americanism in an attempt to boost the genre's image. Country music, Clement insisted, "speaks of God and faith—it sings of courage, honor, and a fundamental decency." "Thus," he continued, "I am not at all abashed or ashamed to stand before this Rotary Club of New York to some of whom even the mention of the words *Grand Ole Opry* might bring smiles of derision—and say that I like Country Music and shall help promote it." The country industry had grown steadily over the past decade. Clement cited statistics that *Opry* performers made a record high of 3,225 personal appearances in 1956 and that 25 million people had paid admission to hear these stars. On the basis of those numbers, Clement concluded that country music "is big business" and had "established itself as a permanent asset of the American way of life because it lays no claim to being anything else but the people's music."[100]

Clement rooted country music's Americanism and its commercial success in its association with the military and the *Opry* stars' willingness to perform for the troops. In the summer of 1957, the governor spoke on a telecast for *Opry* appreciation week in Nashville. He repeated his usual assessment of country as the music of pioneer stock and referred to the unprecedented commercial success it enjoyed at the time. Clement then explained its success as being because country music was "just plain good for the people of Tennessee, the nation and the world." Without mentioning Connie B. Gay, the governor recalled, "When our boys fought for us and risked their lives and shed their blood in Korea or in Germany, we found *Grand Ole Opry* stars going at no expense of the doughboy, to bring the message from home—in words and music—to the front lines where America's homes were being defended." He credited this patriotism and moral goodness with boosting country music's profile and reputation. Clement noted, "Over the past few years a revolution has taken place. . . . Those who once looked down upon what they thought was something from the hills . . . now realize that there was gold in these hills—not just of the monetary type, but of spiritual, moral, and mental values." The governor called performers like Roy Acuff, Minnie Pearl, Hank Snow, and Jim Reeves by name, complimenting them for their willingness to entertain the troops and calling them "public servants in the truest sense of the word."[101]

Clement's effusive praise for country music and its artists informed his defense of the genre during the Smathers Bill debate. In April 1958, Clement arrived in Washington, DC, to defend Nashville's industry. Country performers and music business actors joined Clement in providing testimony for the lawmakers, including the former Louisiana governor and country singer Jimmie Davis, the song publisher Wesley Rose, the producer Sam Phillips, and the artists Faron Young, Roy Acuff, Little Jimmy Dickens, Ferlin Husky, Eddy Arnold, Gene Autry, and Pee Wee King.[102] These men hoped their words would sway lawmakers to reject the Smathers Bill. Such a law threatened to hobble BMI since it was radio station owners who had founded BMI in 1940 in an attempt to circumvent ASCAP's blanket licensing fees. ASCAP brought its own defenders as well, many of whom turned the hearings into a reckoning on the state of the music industry, amateurism, and cultural taste at midcentury. Defenders of ASCAP and Tin Pan Alley, like Vance Packard, referred to country music and rock and roll as "trash," believing that these genres lowered the standards and, by extension, the collective IQ of the nation's listening public. In the opinion of pop music's defenders, the amateurs had usurped the power of the professionals, and ASCAP demanded that Congress address their grievances.[103]

Country music counted God, the Pentagon, and the free market on its side. Clement combined all three in his defense of country and BMI. Country music, he argued, "speaks of God and faith. . . . Hardly a year goes by without the American people adopting as its own a new country song with a religious significance, because in these songs they can see sincerity." He then told the senators how BMI had increased economic competition in the music market and, therefore, "immeasurably contributed to opening the door for new talent in the United States. The public has thus been given a greater choice of music than it ever had before." The government then used that new talent and newly accessible sound to promote the nation's democratic capitalist agenda around the globe. "This music," the governor continued, "and I specifically refer to country music, is being played and sung throughout the world. The State Department, the armed forces radio network, the Voice of America, and other government instrumentalities which seek to bring a message from the American people to the people of the rest of the world have relied very heavily on American country music." Country performers had traveled "hundreds of thousands of miles . . . to all parts of the world, under government sponsorship" to promote the "American way of life." Clement called these performers "ambassadors of good will," suggesting that they deserved gratitude, not scrutiny and intimidation.[104]

The artists Roy Acuff and Ferlin Huskey followed Clement's line of reasoning in their defense of country music's popularity and the rise of BMI. Acuff recounted his trips to entertain the troops during and after World War II, reminding the politicians that he had traveled to Canada, Germany, Austria, England, Japan, and Korea: "because our kind of music was the kind of thing the boys wanted to hear." For Acuff, country music's popularity in the military reflected a simple calculus of supply and demand. "The army was always very anxious to get country performers to the soldiers. We drew tremendous crowds," he relayed to the lawmakers. "We were frequently told when we played army bases that we had drawn crowds that were as large or surpassed the crowds drawn by such great comedians as Bob Hope and others."[105]

Huskey echoed that argument. He remembered how he brought his guitar along with him in 1943 when he joined the Merchant Marines. "I served on troopships and did a lot of entertaining for the servicemen. The simple songs were the kind they liked to hear because they could join in singing with me." Huskey also argued that the military gave country music unprecedented exposure, claiming, "There were lots of boys on the troopships on which I served who had never really heard country music before, and it was interesting to see how fast they acquired a taste for it. In fact, some of the most enthusiastic people were those who came from parts of the country where this kind of music was almost unknown." He pushed back against the pay-for-play narrative of BMI's success and placed the responsibility, instead, with the sociological changes of wartime. Huskey concluded with this stance by reiterating, "the thing that accounts for the national popularity of country music now is the fact that so many people had the chance to hear it during World War II who never heard it before."[106]

The *Opry* star Little Jimmy Dickens added a defense of country music's white, working-class roots in his testimony to the Senate and refuted the allegations of country music as "trash." Dickens, who hailed from a West Virginia family of coal miners and was one of eleven children, took this epithet personally. As he told the senators, when ASCAP's witnesses referred to "country and western music as trash, they are referring to the American people as trash." "My folks and their neighbors love country and western music," he testified. "They are simple, everyday, hard-working, God-fearing people, and they certainly are not trash." Dickens also emphasized his part in spreading country music via military tours. "In 1949," Dickens reminisced,

"I had the great pleasure of going to Europe with our cast of 32 country and western entertainers from our *Grand Ole Opry*. During our stay in Europe we entertained over 150,000 American servicemen and women. They loved our show. . . . We have taken our simple country and western music to the front lines of Korea to boost the morale of our fighting men." Country music lifted the spirits of US soldiers. And that, Dickens concluded, "is not my idea of trash."[107] Dickens's reiteration of the insult carried significant cultural baggage, and he showed his political savvy by situating US soldiers in this context. In defending country fans and soldiers against such insults, Dickens fought for them against the stigma of racialized poverty that would categorize them as white trash. By extension, he also insinuated that ASCAP had described US soldiers with the same term, a moral offense in the midst of the nation's Cold War mission.

No one could speak with more authority on country music, BMI, and the military than Faron Young. His testimony reminded senators, ASCAP witnesses, and the general public that country music owed as much to the Pentagon as it did to any other institution or the alleged plotting of radio station owners to line their pockets with country music royalties. "Country entertainers travel the United States, Canada, the Hawaiian Islands, Europe—in fact the world over, spreading the good faith with country music and country religious music," he testified to the senators, building on his previous statement about how the government had sent him around the world to entertain the troops. In all of that experience, Young said, "There was never any pressure put on me by radio stations or anywhere that I have worked to do BMI songs."[108] The government had given country music an economic boost. That much remained true. But what these testimonies wanted to emphasize was that country musicians and songwriters, like the soldiers they recruited and entertained, had earned those benefits fair and square.

With the promise of economic stability and personal autonomy, the US military joined with the country music industry to entice the nation's young people to join the ranks and sell them country records in the process. By 1958, when Faron Young testified for the Senate, the government's use of country music as military entertainment had helped to give the genre commercial and cultural power. If country music had grown so much that it threatened the commercial power of pop music and ASCAP, then he wanted the senators to recognize how the Department of Defense had enabled that rise. Young reflected on the army's role in his career during an interview in 1984. He told the interviewers that serving with the US Army's Special

Services Division "was a big help" to him and explained why: "because I was on 2,000 radio stations a week all over the world. Pfc. Faron Young and the Circle A Wranglers. It didn't do anything but help me." Looking back over thirty years of his time in the industry, he still thought people missed the real story of his early success, which included the 1961 number-one hit "Hello Walls," penned by a then-obscure songwriter named Willie Nelson. Young believed that people "don't realize I wasn't really that well known yet until I got in the service and went on all those radio and television things for recruiting for the service." As for those who "say 'the army really started you,'" Young continued, "well, I really can't say that it didn't."[109]

Through country musicians' relationship to the military, their music doubled as the soundtrack of both midcentury barn dances and modern military recruitment. The recruitment shows enticed listeners by promising fulfilling careers, economic independence, and world travel while promoting Nashville's white country artists to an audience of the US Cold War military. The ascendancy experienced by the country music industry, aided by its relationship to the Department of Defense, also reflected many Americans' journey into the modern middle class thanks to government programs like the GI Bill, benefits that disproportionately favored white veterans. The use of country music as a recruitment tool had targeted a demographic of young white listeners. Yet, nearly simultaneously, the Pentagon's racial integration policies had diversified the ranks. Blacks, whites, and soldiers of all races trained, ate, bunked, and fought together.

These soldiers, sailors, and airmen also played music with one another. The ironies of this institutional public image grounded in ideals of white masculinity and the increasingly diverse demographics of the troops would play out again through music that developed in conjunction and in competition with the country music industry. In the late 1950s, both country music and the military would have to reckon with the threat of a new genre called rock and roll and its country cousin, rockabilly. This new unruly genre would help country appear as the staid, mature music by comparison, making it all the more appropriate for an association with the military. Rock and roll was born, in part, as the rebellious child of country music, a child conceived, like so many baby boomers, in the downtime of military duty.

3 Singing in the Ranks

Memphis, Militarization, and the Country Roots of Rock and Roll

• •

Harold Jenkins headed for Memphis, Tennessee, as soon as he received his discharge from the army in 1956. He had heard Elvis Presley recently, and Jenkins hoped that he, too, could record for Sam Phillips's Sun Records. For the past two years, Jenkins had honed his skills as a singer, songwriter, and performer by fronting an all-soldier country band, playing for Special Services concerts and AFRTS programs. They called themselves the Fuji Mountain Boys at first, a nod to their deployment in Japan, before changing their name to The Cimarrons. According to an interview from 1959, Jenkins claimed, "I've been writing songs and singing most of my life, but things started to happen when I was in the Army in Japan."[1]

Jenkins did have some musical experience before the army drafted him. Born in the Delta town of Friars Point, Mississippi, in 1933, he learned guitar as a child and performed on the radio station KFFA out of Helena, Arkansas, before entering the service. But he gained invaluable professional experience in the army while entertaining his fellow soldiers. Jenkins learned how to hold a crowd's attention, how to collaborate with other musicians, and what instrumental lineup he liked best for his backing band. After his exit from the service, Jenkins arrived in Memphis with a handful of songs that he thought fit well with the new, happening sound of rockabilly. Phillips declined to offer Jenkins a contract, believing his sound was too derivative of Presley's, but he liked Jenkins's songs enough that Roy Orbison recorded one for Sun called "Rock House."[2]

The young songwriter rebounded quickly. Jenkins changed his name to Conway Twitty and, using personal connections made while in the army, signed a deal with manager Don Seat, who secured a recording contract for Twitty on MGM Records.[3] Twitty went to Owen Bradley's Quonset Hut in Nashville, where he cut his first hit, "It's Only Make Believe." The song shot to number one in 1958 on the *Billboard* pop chart in the United States and England, launching Twitty's career as a singer-songwriter who could straddle the genre divisions of pop, country, and R&B. When he died in 1993, he had notched more number-one country records than any other artist in his lifetime, and he received an induction into the Country Music Hall of Fame in 1999.[4]

No one could blame Twitty for heading to Memphis and Sun Studio after his stint in the military. By 1956, the city and Phillips's record label had earned a reputation for launching a new musical trend, eventually called rockabilly, that began as a style of country music played by white musicians who flaunted the influences of African American musical and visual aesthetics. Compared to Nashville's version of country music stardom, as well as the pop artists of the day, like Eddie Fisher, rockabilly performers appeared rebellious, dangerous, and wild. Elvis Presley remains the best-known performer of the genre, but the rockabilly trend included Johnny Cash, Carl Perkins, Wanda Jackson, Waylon Jennings, Charlie Rich, Jerry Lee Lewis, and Twitty. All of these artists would enjoy mainstream country success in the last half of the twentieth century. Yet, in the mid-1950s, the music industry viewed rockabilly as part of a suspicious new generation and denounced its open rebellion as a degenerate influence on the United States' youth, even as its popularity pushed both the country and pop industry to copy the new sound.[5]

Rockabilly signified and helped to create dynamic social revolutions in the South at midcentury. During the 1950s, the region continued a transformation that had begun in the 1930s, from a reliance on the mules and men of manual-labor agriculture to the economy of industry, mechanized farming, and service-sector employment. The music matched these economic and technological changes. It sounded fast, electric, modern, and young. Rockabilly also reflected and encouraged the shifting constructions of race and white supremacy at the dawn of the mass-movement phase of the civil rights movement. In contrast to the segregationists of the era, rockabilly artists, while not advocating racial equality, betrayed an open embrace of Black culture in their style, even when social conventions, sometimes coupled with their own prejudices, insisted that they maintain their distance from actual Black people.[6]

The South's economic and racial revolutions represented by rockabilly shared a common, yet underacknowledged, cause: federal defense funding. Pentagon spending priorities transformed the South in the 1950s, ushering in an economic boom time through the development of new installations and private contracts in the region that began in the 1940s and continued into the postwar period. Memphis benefited directly from the defense budget thanks to the location of the Millington Naval Air Station just north of town, as well as the contracts delivered to local factories like Precision Tools to make ammunition during the Korean War.[7] Military integration placed Black and white servicemembers in close proximity as they trained, fought, and policed the world in fulfillment of the United States' Cold War mission. Many white southerners, either drafted to serve or lured by the promise of economic advancement, found themselves sharing intimate and social spaces with Black men for the first time. For musicians in the military, that could also mean sharing a stage or a jam session with performers of a different race.

The US military's interracial, homosocial spaces and the infrastructure provided by Special Services established an incubator of creativity for the aspiring country musicians, later branded as rockabillies, who briefly pushed the sounds of Blackness to the forefront of country music. Their stories of musical experimentation, professionalization, and interracial collaboration reveal how military service influenced the sound and style of country music through the experiences of the lowliest private, rather than simply the top-down decisions of record labels or the Defense Department. Elvis Presley's guitarist Scotty Moore, as well as his Sun Records label-mates Billy Lee Riley, Johnny Cash, Sonny Burgess, and Charlie Rich; Sun producers Cowboy Jack Clement and Stan Kesler; and Jim Stewart, cofounder of Memphis's soul label Stax Records, all used their time in the military to work on their craft as country musicians. And after their time singing in the ranks, they all landed in Memphis to chase hillbilly stardom. Because of the economic relationship between the Pentagon and the country industry, the military provided these aspiring country musicians with the time and the space to develop their craft as songwriters, singers, and performers. Serving in the military also broadened their view of the world. It opened their ears to the possibilities of incorporating musical influences across the civilian color line and led to the rockabilly revolution in country music.

Memphis and the Economy of Militarization

Bernard Lansky served three and a half years in the US Army during World War II. Although he remained stateside, Lansky's time in the military took him away from his hometown of Memphis, where his father owned grocery and dry-goods stores. The army stationed Lansky at Fort Bragg, North Carolina, and Fort Knox, Kentucky, before assigning him to a troop train that shuttled other soldiers around the country. Fresh out of the army in 1946 and back home in Memphis, Lansky and his brother Guy, also a veteran, needed a way to make money. The two white men borrowed $125 from their father and opened their own store, a clothing shop at 126 Beale Street in the heart of the city's Black business district. Beale Street doubled as the Black entertainment district, where R&B and jazz musicians entertained locals and those who wandered in off the Mississippi River or from the local inland naval base. The Lansky brothers settled on a product that would appeal to thrifty shoppers on Beale. "Things were kind of breaking up, the war was over," Bernard remembered later. "We started buying fatigues and things like that." The Lanskys' original clientele "wanted this stuff because it was inexpensive, talking about a cap or something for fifty cents, a shirt, fatigue shirt or fatigue pants a dollar ninety-five cents."[8] With this business foundation built on military surplus, the Lanskys received an economic boost on their way to supplying Memphis musicians with the clothes that branded them as rock and rollers.

When the brothers ran out of leftovers from the wartime military's uniform production, they switched to what Bernard called men's "high fashion," a collection of the latest and often the most unusual trends from Dallas and other big cities. The Lanskys began stocking vibrant colors like pink and chartreuse along with the newest cuts, the pegged pants and double-cuffed shirts that gave Memphis rock and roll its material culture and aesthetic. Their merchandise contrasted with the "plain clothes" that other merchants on Beale carried. These new colors and cuts attracted a following from both sides of Memphis's segregated communities. Lansky claimed that the store drew "all the kids" from local high schools and that "the blacks and the whites used to come in and shop with us because we had fashion, we had something that nobody else had."[9] Whether they just happened upon the store or took the directive from Memphis's white R&B radio disc jockey Dewey Phillips to get down there, young Black and white men began shopping the "high fashion" sold at Lansky Brothers. The styles sold there would help define the look and attitude of the earliest rock and roll artists to emerge from Memphis.

Beginning in 1950, fifteen-year-old Elvis Presley wandered by the store whenever he could, usually on his breaks from working as an usher at the Loew's Theater in downtown Memphis. The bright colors and bold styles caught his attention, no doubt a welcome change from the ROTC uniform he wore during his sophomore and junior years at Humes High School.[10] When not in his uniform, Presley's penchant for flashy fashion made him stick out among his fellow students at his all-white high school. He also cut a conspicuous presence among the other tenants in Lauderdale Courts, the New Deal–era housing projects that he and his parents called home for a time after arriving from Tupelo, Mississippi, in 1948. For two years, the Presley family had bounced from boarding houses to rented spare bedrooms, often because of or just ahead of eviction due to his father Vernon Presley's inability to hold a job, before landing the relative luxury of all-white public housing.[11] Living in government housing and enrolling in the ROTC at Humes High, Presley joined thousands of white southerners in leaning on various arms of the state to provide economic security in the present and to help them plan for a future that might lead to a secure working-class or even a middle-class income.

The Presleys reflected the wave of rural-to-urban migrants who arrived in Memphis during the 1940s. Spread across the bluffs of the Mississippi River and creeping east into the swamps of West Tennessee, Memphis had long functioned as a hub of global capitalist exchange, beginning with the slave and cotton trades that provided the city's foundational white wealth. In the late 1940s and early 1950s, the city boomed with an infusion of private industry and people in search of a slice of postwar prosperity. Manufacturers like International Harvester and the Firestone Tire Company opened their doors in Memphis, employing the sons and a few daughters of the Mississippi River Delta and Tennessee River Valley towns that surrounded the city. International Harvester acquired a 260-acre plot in 1942, building the largest farm-equipment plant in the South, where it employed about 2,000 workers and began manufacturing combines and cotton pickers in 1947.[12] Firestone began producing tires and rubber products at its Memphis plant in 1938, quickly hitting a production of 2,500 tires every day and making gas masks and raincoats for the US Armed Forces during World War II.[13] Longing to escape or pushed out of the agricultural toil that had marked the region's free and enslaved labor for centuries, Black and white southerners descended on Memphis for those manufacturing jobs. They went to work indoors, building the machines that replaced the region's manual, tenant-farming system.[14] As these industries created a new southern economy, the city's population grew to reach 396,000, a growth of 35 percent between 1940 and 1950.[15]

The military spending that brought money and people to Memphis accounted for part of the city's quick growth. The War Department had constructed the Memphis Defense Depot in 1942 as a distribution center for wartime supplies, and a portion of the property operated as a prisoner of war camp for Nazi soldiers during World War II. With over 100 buildings, 26 miles of railroad track, 25 miles of roads, 642 acres of property, and 5 million square feet of warehouse space, the depot functioned as the largest military distribution point in the nation in the 1950s.[16] Also in 1942, the US Navy took over a World War I–era army airfield in the community of Millington, Tennessee, twenty miles north of downtown Memphis. The navy converted the field into a Naval Reserve Base and began training ground crews and pilots on the 3,500-acre property. Hundreds of aviation cadets passed through the facility between 1943 and 1945, while the ground crew training facility accommodated 10,000 students at once. In 1946, the navy transferred its headquarters of the Naval Air Technical Training Center to the Millington base and gave the installation permanent status during the Korean War, allocating $64 million for a six-year construction project on the base. The Memphis Naval Air Station became one of the largest employers in the area, with an annual payroll of $39 million by the end of the 1950s, and the largest inland naval base in the country.[17] The military brought boom times to Memphis and its surrounding communities, fundamentally altering the economy, demographics, and built environment of the mid-South's largest city.

The city's private industries also benefited from the growth of the Cold War defense state. In January 1951, the Downcraft, Incorporated, company converted its entire operation of approximately 100 workers to manufacturing sleeping bags for the soldiers deployed to the Korean War. These "Artic" bags included a new "Quick Release" zipper designed to offer a way out for the soldier without having to unzip all the way to the bottom. This contract represented just a small piece of the $3 million worth of contracts granted to the city's businesses in the first six months of the war.[18] That same month, Captain Fred G. Christianson, the public relations officer at the Memphis Depot, reported that the Pentagon had awarded nearly $1.5 million in contracts to different businesses in the city in a joint effort to refurbish pontoon bridges that the army had stored in the defense warehouse. The companies that benefited included the Hercules Construction Company, Allied Engineering, J. A. Riggs Tractor Company, and the Precision Tool Company.[19]

Precision Tool also produced ammunition for US soldiers in Korea, putting civilian Memphis residents like Elvis Presley to work in the fight against communism. Having quit his job at Loew's Theater, the sixteen-year-old Presley took a position at Precision in the summer of 1951, operating a drill press manufacturing rocket shells for $27 a week. Two of his uncles worked

FIGURE 3.1 Students at the Naval Air Technical Training Center (NATTC) take part in daily exercises in 1944. The growth of military installations and defense contractors in Memphis brought a large influx of temporary and permanent residents in the 1940s and 1950s. The NATTC on the outskirts of town helped grow the local economy and tied Memphis's musical cultures to the Cold War military. (Naval Air Technical Training Center, Millington, Tennessee, University of Memphis Digital Commons, https://digitalcommons.memphis.edu/speccoll-mss-wwtwo1/32)

there as well, and the boost in pay helped the Presley family stay afloat.[20] Presley also began to purchase small items from the Lansky brothers' store with the little bit of income he did not give to his mother and father. According to Bernard, Presley told him, "'I don't have no money, see when I get rich I'm gonna buy you out.' I said, 'Do me a favor, just buy from me, I don't want you buying me out.'"[21] With the steady pay of a government contract and the stable residence provided by government housing, Presley could afford to indulge his taste in outlandish fashion. Between drilling with the Humes High School ROTC for two years and drilling ammunition casings for the Korean War, Presley seemed ready to embrace the economic benefits of US militarization well before he embarked on a musical career. He was far from alone in this route toward rockabilly stardom.

······

Many of the artists who would define Memphis's contribution to rock and roll honed their chops in the ranks of the armed forces. Presley's future guitar player Scotty Moore joined the US Navy in 1948 and ultimately served a four-year hitch. Born to a poor farming family in the tiny West Tennessee town of Gadsden, located about eighty miles northeast of Memphis, Moore dropped out of high school and enlisted at age sixteen. Although Moore was too young to join, his father forged a false birthdate in the family Bible to trick the navy recruiter into believing that his son was seventeen, the legal age to join with a parent's permission.[22] He joined the navy with ambitions of escaping the hardscrabble life on the family farm, where hours plucking away on his guitar had provided his only means of mental escape. Introspective, shy, and prone to dreaming, Moore used the guitar as a barrier between himself and the world while growing up in Gadsden. But playing the guitar did not physically remove him from rural Tennessee, not yet. He needed the government's help for that. Moore's family also inspired him to join. Two of his three older brothers had served in the navy, and he later reflected, "I guess I kind of followed in their footsteps," when he left home for the service.[23] Having dropped out of high school, soured on farming, and longing to see the world, Moore surveyed his options and went with what he knew.

Moore's time in the navy greatly expanded the teenaged plowboy's experiences and view of the world. In July 1948, shortly after he reported for duty in San Diego, California, President Truman authorized the desegregation of the armed forces.[24] Although he had lived in relative racial isolation among his white friends and family in the segregated society of Gadsden, Tennessee, Moore now served among an integrated crew on the USS *Kent County* LST-855, a supply boat anchored at Guam and ordered to Shanghai. Moore worked the boiler room while the boat hauled food supplies up and down the Yellow River in an effort to aid the missionaries feeding Chinese citizens impacted by the war between Chiang Kai-shek's nationalists and Mao Zedong's communist rebels. He also entered into his first serious romantic relationship in China with a Russian woman who lived in Shanghai. For the child of a Depression-era farming family in West Tennessee who was barely old enough to drive a car, all of these experiences amounted to jumping, or perhaps being thrown, into the deep end of worldliness. Moore had been riding his horse named Roy to school less than a year before. Now, he ran the boilers on a ship for the US government, consorted with a foreign woman, and enjoyed the pleasures of shore leave in a Chinese city across the globe from his father's farm. He had even suffered the humbling experience of a physical altercation in which a Black sailor beat Moore while in the shower.[25] To go from barely seeing African Americans in his hometown to fighting in the nude with a Black man did more than alter Moore's perception of the racial hierarchy within the integrated military. For Moore, the whole world had changed.

The only part of Moore's life that remained constant was the time he spent alone playing the guitar. He had grown up around guitar pickers on his father's side of the family and learned to play at an early age. Yet, what started as his childhood hobby and a distraction from farm labor evolved into a life's passion and a new kind of labor while Moore served in the navy. Playing the guitar became part of his identity. "Apart from my age, I stood out from the others because I played guitar. Usually, I played below deck, but sometimes I found a private spot on the stern," he later wrote. "Music was my passion. No one had ever heard music the way I heard it. No one had ever felt it the same way I felt it. I was convinced of that."[26] In late 1949, as communists took over China and the Soviet Union successfully tested an atomic bomb, Moore worked below deck of the LST-855 on its way back to Bremerton, Washington, for decommissioning. Sailing across the Pacific, he honed a unique picking style that mixed elements from his heroes, Chet Atkins and Les Paul. It came in handy when he made port.

The decommissioning process in Bremerton took six weeks, during which time Moore formed two different country bands and met his first wife. All his woodshedding below deck began to deliver some rewards. Although the first group, the Happy Valley Boys, did not land any gigs, the second outfit snagged a weekly fifteen-minute show on the station KPRO in Bremerton. The group consisted of Moore, a guitarist/vocalist named Sparky, and a steel guitar player. "We probably didn't play very well, but we were about as good as anyone else around, so it didn't matter," Moore recalled.[27]

In the spring of 1950, Moore sailed again for the Far East, this time aboard the USS *Valley Forge*, an aircraft carrier sent to deliver planes to the US forces in the Pacific. His musical pursuits continued on his new ship. Moore fell easily into informal jam sessions with his fellow sailors. He later described, "They were just three or four guys from different parts of the country and we got [together] somehow or another, by word of mouth somebody said, 'Hey somebody in such and such division plays piano or plays guitar or something,' and, eventually everybody would get together, and whiled away the hours."[28] His navy buddy Frank Parise remembered his playing in more detail, including an interracial collaboration. Moore played guitar, Parise played harmonica, and an unidentified Black sailor sang. One such jam even resulted in an amateur recording, Moore's first. Parise remembered, "One evening we got together in the radio shack, and the three of us recorded a song. . . . I can remember Scotty played 'Double Eagle' on the guitar. He was fantastic."[29] By the time Moore received his discharge on January 4, 1952, he had spent countless hours practicing guitar and learning to collaborate with other players, and he even made a recording. He briefly returned to Gadsden but then left for the nightlife in Memphis, where he formed his most professional band yet, the honky-tonking Starlite Wranglers, with his friend Bill Black on bass.[30]

Moore was one of several aspiring artists who had served in the military and then pivoted to a career in country music. A guitar player from Pocahontas, Arkansas, named Billy Lee Riley enlisted in the US Army at the age of fifteen and served four years. Riley had worked with his family on their sharecropping farm until he turned thirteen or fourteen and learned guitar from African American players on the same plantation. The army looked like a way out of farming and the predatory structure of the sharecropping system. In his recollections, Riley placed his service in juxtaposition to his time farming. "I went into service when I was fifteen, in the army. . . . Got out just before I reached twenty. I'd served my time," he later said. "I never farmed again."[31] Not that the service fared much better than farming in his estimation. As Riley explained in one interview, "I never did like it. I went in mainly to have a place to live and something to eat!"[32]

The service professionalized Riley's nascent musical talents and gave him a platform to explore his artistic voice as a country musician. He started out with informal jams, singing Hank Williams songs. Too shy to play in front of people, Riley and his fellow soldier-musicians hid away to hone their skills. "We would go to the service club and maybe get a couple of guitars, a couple of us guys. We'd go into one of the little rooms and lock the door and play." Before he knew it, those informal picking sessions turned into his first opportunity to play in public. "We were in there one day and the service club administrator came in and heard us. . . . She talked me into being on a talent show at the service club, and I went on that show and won first place. From then on I'd had the bug."[33]

That same service club administrator urged Riley to try out for Special Services and turn his talent into a profession within the army. Riley declined to join Special Services, preferring instead to play at the local soldiers' clubs with his buddies. However, he did record himself for the first time in the army. While stationed at Fort Lawton, Washington, outside Seattle, he recorded three sides in a record booth, a coin-operated, phonebooth-sized recording studio with one microphone, choosing two Hank Williams songs and one Lefty Frizzell song among others from his repertoire of covers.[34] Riley received his discharge in 1955 and traveled across the Mississippi River from his hometown of Pocahontas to Memphis, where he joined a growing stable of white country artists creating a new sound for the genre on Sun Records. By 1957, Riley had contributed classics like "Flying Saucer Rock and Roll" and "Red Hot."[35]

Johnny Cash, a native of Dyess, Arkansas, and future Sun Records artist, remembered that he "ended up in the military the same way most other Southern country boys did, for lack of a better way out of the cotton fields."[36] After tiring of agricultural work in Arkansas, Cash migrated to Michigan, where he worked for all of three weeks in a Pontiac factory before retreating back south. He returned to Arkansas to work cleaning production tanks at a margarine plant, another job that lasted only a few weeks. Following this string of ill-suited industrial jobs, Cash recalled, "a government paycheck and a clean blue uniform looked pretty good. I enlisted for a four-year hitch." He joined the US Air Force in 1951, remembering later how he had felt "it was the thing to do. We boys wanted to serve our country."[37] Cash may have entered military service under the social pressure to protect democracy during the Cold War, but this kind of patriotic obligation offers only a partial explanation for why so many would join. He, like Moore and Riley, needed a steady check, decent working conditions, and the potential of lasting economic benefits. Cash wanted a job as a worker for the state. In the South, that often meant joining the military.

It also meant that the air force dropped Cash into its newly integrated ranks. Of course, as a white southerner, he had prior social contact with African Americans but not on the level of intimacy created by the military. Cash watched in shock as a "race riot" broke out between Black and white airmen in Bremerhaven, West Germany, not long after he arrived in the country. "I looked down, and there they were, whites and blacks, comrades in arms . . . tearing at each other with everything they had." For his own part, Cash claimed a stance of racial liberalism, recalling that he "had no problem sharing a barracks with blacks." "I couldn't imagine hating them so much," he looked back in bewilderment, "that I was willing to wage a private war on them." Cash attributed the fight to Cold War military training and close quarters. He argued that "you had a lot of men, black and white, who'd been very strongly encouraged to kill people (North Koreans, Chinese, Russians), then jam-packed together and told to behave like gentlemen. . . . They were a boiler waiting to explode."[38]

As the Cold War military demanded more personnel, the Defense Department increased the likelihood of bringing white and Black soldiers into close quarters in the newly integrated armed forces, a proposition that angered many whites, particularly in the South. Beginning in the late 1940s, Congress began batting around the proposition of Universal Military Training (UMT), an idea favored by Presidents Truman and Eisenhower. White southern politicians found themselves torn over the social, political, and moral implications of UMT. Representative James C. Davis, a Democrat from Georgia, saw UMT as a replacement for the draft and a way to reduce pressure on reservists deployed to Korea. Davis initially backed the policy but then rescinded his support. His constituents opposed this policy as a sign of creeping authoritarianism. H. C. Holland, a Methodist minister from Decatur, Georgia, wrote to Davis that UMT would represent "regimentation that is out of keeping with our free enterprise system. It would go far toward militarizing our country like Germany and Japan before World War II."[39] Others believed that compulsory military training was a tool of leftist politics. R. F. Sams of Clarkston, Georgia, considered that in approving UMT, Eisenhower was going "along with the fair-new deal ideas," which was "enuf to make any sincere American sick." He urged Davis, "do all in your power to preserve our old time American way of life & free enterprise, & keep us out of socialism."[40]

These voters need not have feared. Not only did Davis help block the UMT on the basis of these cries of government overreach, but he also objected to the 1952 bill since it mandated "that white boys and colored would live together and be trained on a non-segregated basis." In his estimation, "this is not necessary."[41] Congressional representatives like Davis and his colleague Carl Vinson had built their careers expanding the reach of the federal government in their home state via enormous installations like Fort McPherson and Fort Benning. But when the specter of universal service included the truly equal drafting of white and Black eighteen-year-old men together under the auspices of a federal mandate, white conservatives hollered "socialism." Both Truman and Eisenhower failed to rally support behind UMT, but the military still proceeded with its plans for racial integration, forcing Black and white servicemembers together for the first time in intimate spaces of peacetime and the battlefront in Korea.

The armed forces followed the order to integrate unevenly, aiming for the goal of achieving maximum efficiency, not social equality.[42] Even on the front lines of Korea, Black soldiers faced the racism of white troops who transported their domestic beliefs in white supremacy across the Pacific. Military reports of racial violence filtered back to the States, and Black veterans of the Korean War recalled serving under inept white commanding officers who received their commission on the basis of race rather than training or ability. Those race-based promotions led to the deaths and needless endangerment of Black soldiers and incidents of fragging.[43]

White southern servicemen inflamed racial division, particularly through the early-1950s trend of displaying the Confederate battle flag. On September 29, 1951, the *Pittsburgh Courier* ran with the frontpage headline, "REBEL FLAGS IN KOREA!" The article named a few of the military formations that flew the Confederate battle flag while overseas, including the First Cavalry Division, the Fifth Maryland Regiment, the "Dixie Division" of the National Guard, and the Fourth Heavy Howitzer Battalion.[44] Most of these men hailed from southern states and took the opportunity of serving in the US Armed Forces to assert their claim on a specific vision of white southern identity that praised the symbols, and by extension the cause, of the Confederacy. Presidents and the Defense Department might dictate racial integration, but white soldiers used racist actions to maintain a claim on the military as a white-dominated institution.

Black soldiers and civic leaders fought back against white southern displays of racism in the armed forces. Walter White, president of the National Association for the Advancement of Colored People, wrote a column denouncing the use of the flag anywhere but especially in the context of the military. He reported the occurrence of "certain bombastic and boastful" Texan troops who decorated their vehicles with their state flag, while "even more Southerners stuck Stars and Bars" on theirs. In a darkly comic twist, White claimed that "Korean and Chinese sharpshooters, abysmally and blissfully ignorant of the fact that the South is still fighting the Civil War of ninety years ago, assumed that the flags meant that the occupant of the decorated and beflagged car was at least a one-star general" and took aim accordingly.[45]

If a rebel flag could get you killed, country music offered another way to show one's regional pride with less overt, albeit clearly marked, racial meanings. During an interview in 1968, Johnny Cash remembered how he used country music to make a statement about white regional identity while deployed to Europe with the US Air Force, claiming, "those Yankees in my outfit bad-mouthed country and western so much I started singing it."[46] Like Scotty Moore and Billy Lee Riley, joining the military provided Cash with the space and the time to develop his craft as a musician. He bought his first guitar for twenty-nine deutsche marks while stationed in West Germany. With three other recruits, the young singer formed a group to help kill time around the barracks, and they called themselves the Landsberg Barbarians. According to a 1956 profile in *Country Song Roundup*, Cash credited the US Air Force for providing his start in music: "the best way he can explain it—Johnny Cash became a musician out of pure boredom!" The air force had stationed the singer in Germany "for three long miserable years," according to Cash, who "found that learning to play the guitar and working out a few melodies and songs seemed the only way to combat blues and boredom." The magazine also made it clear that Cash's time in the service gave him his musical education. "Having learned the basic chords from Orville Rigdon, a musician from down Nachichotes [*sic*] way," the magazine added, Cash "joined in many an impromptu session with the boys on the base and in small German honky tonks."[47] One such informal performance in Venice, Italy, reportedly drew a crowd of 300 curious spectators.[48]

The dull hours that characterized so much of military life abroad offered Cash an opportunity to develop his songwriting talents, and he penned his signature tune, "Folsom Prison Blues," sitting on his bunk in West Germany. Military life also exposed former farm boys to the latest in audio technology. Cash bought a reel-to-reel tape recorder at the PX on base and began recording the Barbarians' renditions of country songs, as well as his first original compositions. Once, a fellow soldier loaded the tape incorrectly so that it played on the wrong side. Cash liked the reversed music and used the odd sound to create the melody for one of his biggest hits, "I Walk the Line." He also worked as a radio surveillance operator. Cash even claimed to have intercepted the news of Stalin's death, making him the first American to hear of the dictator's demise.[49] When he returned to the States in 1955, Cash headed to Memphis with his newly developed talents and a handful of country songs he had written when not monitoring the Russian threat of nuclear war.

Cash's trek to Memphis followed the lead of artists like Stan Kesler, a studio musician, producer, and songwriter for Sun Studio, who received his musical start in the military. Born in 1928 on a cotton farm about seventy miles southeast of Memphis in Abbeville, Mississippi, Kesler came of age listening to blues and country. He remembered how, in North Mississippi, "you don't help but hear a lot of blues and black gospel music" but his favorite was country music. "I mean I loved the Grand Ole Opry," Kesler enthused. "I loved Bill Monroe, Eddie Arnold, all the hillbillies of the time." Raising cotton and enough corn to feed the animals left little time to learn an instrument. He found that time in the US Marine Corps. Kesler joined directly after graduating high school in 1945 and served two years. He looked back on that time with some fondness thanks to the opportunity it granted him to stoke his love of country music. "While I was in the Marine Corps that's where I really got really seriously interested in music," Kesler felt. "I loved the Hawaiian guitar. . . . I managed to buy a little lap, what we call now, a lap steel. I started playing just for my own benefit, just my own amusement there." He returned to Abbeville in 1947 to start a country band with his brother.[50] In 1950, Kesler moved to Memphis and found work as a musician at Sun Studio, playing on records with Carl Perkins, Jerry Lee Lewis, and Roy Orbison. He also penned five songs for Elvis Presley, including his country hits "I'm Left, You're Right, She's Gone" and "I Forgot to Remember to Forget," recorded in 1954 and 1955, respectively.[51]

Cash's fellow Arkansan and future Sun Records artist Sonny Burgess also landed in West Germany after the US Army drafted him in 1951. Burgess, who had already started playing music at the honky-tonks and armory dances around his hometown of Newport, furthered his skills in the army. After his basic training at Fort Chaffee, Arkansas, he quickly fell in with a group of musicians, all cooks from Texas, in the Second Armored Division stationed in Germany. The group played country and western music, with Burgess on guitar, and found success with the Special Services playing on the AFRS. Every Friday and Saturday night, the military network broadcast its version of a country music variety show called the *Yukon Grand Ole Opry* live from Frankfurt. The army selected eight bands to perform, including Burgess's group. He looked back on that time with affection, saying, "All I did was play guitar. We had a guy that sang for us. Looked like Hawkshaw Hawkins. I never will forget him. But those cooks, man, . . . I had a good time." Burgess returned to Arkansas and reformed his old band in 1954. He spent the next two years playing a repertoire that mixed the country songs of Lefty Frizzell with the blues tunes of Jimmy Reed and Big Joe Turner. By 1956, they were recording at Sun Studio, cutting songs like "We Wanna Boogie" and "Red Headed Woman" that defined the raucous, country sounds of rockabilly.[52]

Special Services and the Color of Military Entertainment

The US Army and Air Force Special Services Division created a productive space for aspiring country entertainers to hone their skills and establish their talents as musical artists, particularly through bands like the one led by Sonny Burgess. According to a report on military life prepared for President Eisenhower's Commission on Veterans' Pensions, the army began using the Special Services Division during World War II as a means of creating activities for "the off-duty use of enlisted personnel in the interests of their moral, mental, physical and social well-being." Until that time, from the Civil War to World War I, the army had allowed individual soldiers to provide their own instruments, sheet music, and entertainment. During World War I, civilian volunteer agencies like the Young Men's Christian Association, the Jewish Welfare Board, and the Knights of Columbus began staging musical performances and offering songbooks so that soldiers could sing along with what those organizations deemed to be appropriate entertainment.[53] The War Department also established a "Military Morale Section" in the spring of 1918. This represented a shift from troop morale as a concern of individual commanding officers to a centralized effort by the War Department, but the military had waited too late for the Morale Section to make meaningful changes to soldier recreation and entertainment in the First World War.[54]

These efforts to consolidate control of military morale continued during the mass mobilization for World War II and shaped the kind of entertainment that servicemembers received. Special Services oversaw both professional entertainment and soldier shows, booking USO tours and supplying amateur soldiers with sheet music, instruments, and costumes. Between 1940 and 1947, the USO staged nearly half a million shows in forty-two different counties. Total attendance for these events reached 200 million, averaging 400 attendees per show, and the expenditures for entertainer salaries, insurance, and accommodations cost over $55 million (around $772 million in 2023 dollars).[55] The centralization of soldier entertainment controlled the racial makeup of the live music heard in a military setting. More than 900 separate units of professional entertainers were sent overseas during Special Services' initial seven-year run. Although some groups were racially integrated, Special Services still maintained thirty-three "All Negro" units, and white performers dominated soldier entertainment in the 1940s. This discriminatory trend extended into the 1950s when Special Services began searching for more talent among servicemembers.[56]

During the Korean War, Special Service inaugurated a "Soldier Singing Contest," which included the categories of pop, classical, barbershop quartet, spiritual, and country and western. Winning these Special Services contests delivered real benefits in the civilian entertainment business.

The army held its first "All-Army Talent Contest" in 1954, and its finalists performed on *The Ed Sullivan Show* for an audience of 35 million viewers.[57] The next year, an estimated 45 million watched the army talent winner on *The Ed Sullivan Show*, providing even more coverage for the army's efforts at making armed service seem relatable and attractive to the general public and potential recruits. Special Services then booked the winners and finalists of the "All-Army Talent Contest" on a tour of seventy-six military installations for 100,000 troops stationed around the continental US, the Caribbean, and the Pacific. The tour, called "Rolling Along," functioned as a combination of soldier entertainment and a way to gin up civilian interest in joining the army by opening concerts to the general public.[58]

Special Services may have offered an opportunity to develop anyone's talent, but it gave a particular advantage to country musicians. Between July 1954 and June 1955, Special Services staged 38,853 concerts by soldier bands for over 7 million soldiers in total attendance. Most of these concerts presented what the army described as package shows and dance-band performances. But "hillbilly" bands accounted for 5,968 of the performances over that time period.[59] Connie B. Gay and two representatives from BMI served as the judges for the country and western portion of the All-Army Contest in 1955.[60] For a music-business actor like Gay with strong ties to the military, judging an army talent contest represented more than a patriotic donation of his time. Listening to the unsigned, amateur musicians was a scouting expedition for the next Jimmy Dean or Faron Young.

The preference given to white musicians did not go unnoticed. Special Services endured allegations of racial discrimination in the mid-1950s, including a congressional inquiry into charges that Special Services in the European Command did not hire Black entertainers.[61] In 1956, Representative Adam Clayton Powell wrote to Secretary of the Army William Brucker and claimed, "there seems to be a drift in the Army back to the days of segregation and away from the policy of integration." Powell identified five areas in which the army was accused of practicing discrimination, including the designation of "for caucasians only" on orders, unnecessary racial designations of "colored" on reports, and a low number of African American teachers at schools for army children. The other two accusations concerned soldier entertainment. Powell asserted that Blacks made up only 1 percent of the entertainers employed by Special Services and that the USO had established segregated canteens on one installation.[62] The army investigated the claims but denied any wrongdoing in hiring entertainers.[63] In 1957, Special Services added an R&B category to the All-Army contest in a nod to the diversification of soldier talents and tastes, although the bands participating in that genre may have included both Black and white performers.[64]

Despite the military's preferential treatment of country music, Special Services did expose future country and rockabilly stars to different styles of music across the color line. The piano-playing singer-songwriter Charlie Rich joined the Sun label briefly in the late 1950s after receiving his professional start with Special Services. Rich hailed from Colt, Arkansas, fifty miles west of Memphis, and like all the other early Memphis rock and rollers, he grew up chopping cotton and listening to country music. With no ambition for farming, Rich joined the US Air Force in 1952 after dropping out of the University of Arkansas. The air force stationed him at Enid Air Force Base in Oklahoma, where he played in the drum and bugle corps. He also kept busy after his official musical duties had ended by playing piano in a jazz group called the Velvetones that he formed with three other airmen who rounded out the sound on drums, clarinet, and bass.[65]

Rich's group also participated in recruitment spots. Rich remembered how the Velvetones "did some TV work, you know, representing the air force and that sort of thing, did quite a few contests and got to travel around quite a bit." He credited this experience with giving him the tools he needed to pursue music as a profession in civilian life, claiming, "During the Air Force is probably where I sang the most because we had more opportunity, I think to actually do nightclub work." Rich's experience in the air force also exposed him to the latest sounds in jazz, and he absorbed the influences of Miles Davis, Dave Brubeck, and Nat "King" Cole.[66] He channeled those eclectic influences into an R&B-infused country sound that eventually yielded enormous success in the 1960s as a Nashville recording artist. In fact, all of these white Sun Records musicians who were eventually tagged as rock and roll or rockabilly started out as aspiring country musicians, regardless of the degree to which they embraced the influence of Black music. And they all started out in the military.

The same transformative formula held true for Jim Stewart, one of the architects of the Memphis soul music industry. Another white plowboy in search of life beyond his farm in Middleton, Tennessee, Stewart graduated high school in 1948 and received his draft notice in 1951. After basic training at Fort Carson, Colorado, Stewart joined Special Services, playing fiddle in a country band that toured service clubs in the United States. He received his discharge in 1953 and was forever changed by the experience of being thrown together with other young men of different backgrounds.

Stewart expressed what the experience of military service did for him: "I think it gave us, all of us, such as myself a country boy who had never experienced anything like this before, . . . you certainly learn that you have lived in a very secluded little corner of the world, very soon."[67] Even though he stayed stateside during his tour, Stewart realized that the demographic mixing he encountered in the ranks opened the world to him. He met other young men of different races, ethnicities, and religions and found the pluralism of a foxhole democracy without ever entering a war zone.

Stewart also hinted at the demographic gamble the Pentagon had wagered in the desegregation of the military and how that policy affected his musical development. Without referring to race directly, Stewart still conveyed how diverse he found the US military. "I experienced a lot of different situations, different cultures and people from different cultures . . . from Brooklyn to Mississippi," he recalled years later. He claimed to have grown as a more accepting person from that exposure but also recognized that not everyone found that kind of mixing beneficial. In his words, contact with different types of people "broadens one's background": "It was very positive for me. It can be, on the other hand, it can be quite a shock to an individual as well and some people cannot adjust to that type of situation very easily." Stewart attributed his openness to his involvement with music. Specifically, he credited the army with giving him the willingness to listen to and appreciate musical styles beyond country. He charted this evolution in later years by saying, "I went from country to western swing, from there to rock 'n' roll and to r&b and I still love all of these. . . . I'm fortunate enough to have all this at my disposal. It's been very good for me."[68]

Inspired by the success of Sun, Stewart started his own studio and label in 1957, originally called Satellite Records. He changed the name to Stax after he went into partnership with his sister Estelle Axton, the new name taken by combining the first two letters in their last names. Stax would go on to help define southern soul music in the 1960s with artists like Carla Thomas, Booker T. and the MGs, The Mad Lads, Otis Redding, and Isaac Hayes and emerge as a beacon of interracial musical collaboration, albeit not racial equality, during the civil rights era.[69] Stewart's military experiences not only helped professionalize him as a musician but also opened him up to the possibility of working with people unlike himself. All that interracial musical collaboration still lay on the horizon in the early 1950s. For two years, Stewart fought communism as a country fiddler for the US Army, probably crossing paths with Faron Young on tour stops at installations like Fort Bragg, North Carolina.

Like Stewart, Gordon Terry, a rockabilly star and Johnny Cash collaborator from Decatur, Alabama, found his talents as a fiddler put to use in the US Army Special Services. Terry's career in country music began at age seven, when his father landed a gig on the *Grand Ole Opry* for their family band, Floyd Terry and the Young 'Uns. Seven-year-old Terry played fiddle and mandolin as a "Young 'Un," and he won the Alabama State Champion Fiddlers Contest while still a teenager. He joined Bill Monroe and the Bluegrass Boys in 1950, hitting the road with the "Father of Bluegrass Music."[70] During the early 1950s, Terry lived in Nashville, Tennessee, at Mom Upchurch's boardinghouse, a residence largely occupied by road musicians and known by the nickname "Hillbilly Heaven."[71]

During a jam session at Hillbilly Heaven, Terry struck up a friendship with a new arrival in Nashville named Faron Young. Terry received his draft notice not long after their meeting and reported for duty at Fort Jackson, South Carolina. A few months into Terry's service, Young arrived at Fort Jackson, and the two men resumed playing music together for their fellow troops. Terry then accompanied Young to Fort McPherson, where he joined the Circle A Wranglers for the duration of his military service.[72] Besides this valuable road experience, Terry also credited the army with giving him his start as a singer. In 1957, he recorded his debut single, a Boudleaux Bryant–penned tune called "Wild Honey." The song featured Terry's hiccupping rockabilly vocal and earned him television appearances on *American Bandstand* and a recurring spot on ABC's country music show *Country America*.[73] Terry spent the 1970s playing fiddle for Johnny Cash's backing band, the Tennessee Three, and Merle Haggard's band, the Strangers.[74]

Terry and Young also shared the bill with Black musicians while performing for the Third Army at Fort McPherson. Black soldiers, some of whom emerged as leaders in R&B, blues, and jazz, also found their talents used by Special Services during the 1950s. The jazz pianist Wynton Kelly served with the Third Army's Special Services from 1952 to 1954, overlapping with Young's time as the country voice of musical recruitment. Kelly had played with Dinah Washington and Dizzy Gillespie before receiving his draft notice.[75] The army sent him to Fort McClellan just outside Anniston, Alabama, before transferring him to Fort McPherson in nearby Atlanta, Georgia. He joined the Third Army traveling soldier show and recruited another draftee and future jazz luminary, Duke Pearson, to join him. Together they petitioned Lieutenant General A. R. Bolling to include more Black performers, since they represented the only two in the entire cast at the time.[76] Despite these racial disparities, Kelly led his "Wynton Kelly Trio" for the Special

Services, touring the seven states under the Third Army command for two years and even performed on the recruitment show *Talent Patrol* on March 18, 1954.[77]

Kelly's military musical career climaxed in the fall of 1954, just prior to receiving his discharge, when his trio performed for a reported crowd of 10,000 at Atlanta's Chastain Memorial Park Amphitheater. The African American newspaper the *New York Amsterdam News* described how the group played "a special 'Blues' medley during Third Army's spectacular 'Southland Panorama' musical revue which jam-packed the Atlanta Amphitheater."[78] The paper failed to mention the show's Old South theme, the fact that it praised the Confederate General Joseph Johnston, or the headlining slot given to Faron Young and the Circle A Wranglers.[79] Given that context, the details of Kelly's "blues medley" read like the Special Services' attempt to add a touch of Black authenticity to a nostalgic, antebellum-themed fantasy for an all-white audience. Following his discharge, Kelly landed gigs with Miles Davis, Cannonball Adderly, Wayne Shorter, and John Coltrane and stayed busy as an in-demand sideman for a decade after his army discharge. But that success tapered off in the late 1960s. In 1971, Kelly died after suffering an epileptic seizure, alone and broke in a hotel room.[80] For Kelly, a musical career in the armed forces offered a mixture of short-term success and struggles against the prejudices of white visions of what Black music should represent. While jazz musicians like Dizzy Gillespie and Louis Armstrong helped the US State Department fulfill its mission of promoting the United States' image as a nation of tolerance and racial inclusivity, the Black jazz musicians in the army found themselves constrained by the demands of military morale building.[81]

Other Black artists experienced a similar combination of favorable publicity but little commercial return from their time performing for military audiences. From 1954 to 1956, Clyde McPhatter sang with Special Services, appearing on more than 500 entertainment shows for the armed forces.[82] His career began with the doo-wop groups the Dominoes and the Drifters. The records he cut with those groups influenced a generation of rock and rollers, including Elvis Presley, who cited McPhatter as one of his idols.[83] McPhatter signed with Atlantic Records and cut a string of records while on furlough with the army, reflecting the fact that his career continued to grow in spite of, not because of, the military. These gospel-infused solo records bridged the gap between the doo-wop of the 1950s and the soul music of the 1960s.[84] Yet, whereas military service helped to launch artists like Faron Young, McPhatter's time in the ranks temporarily stalled the momentum of his solo career. No governors awaited him with thanks and handshakes for his service. His devotion of time and talent to Special Services did not yield glowing reviews that praised his patriotic service. The military, for musicians like McPhatter, represented an unfortunate obligation, not a marketing strategy or an incubator for artistic growth.

Similarly, the Texas blues pianist and singer Clarence "Candy" Green found work in the army but no springboard to stardom through the Special Services. Born in 1929 on Galveston Island, Green had joined the Merchant Marines at sixteen years old in 1945 and served for three years, traveling from Europe to the Pacific while always playing in clubs around Galveston and Houston whenever he returned home. He also played in bands for the Texas blues stars T-Bone Walker, Eddie "Cleanhead" Vinson, and Roy Hawkins. Green signed a record deal for himself with Don Robey's Peacock label in 1950 and cut his debut single, "Galveston Blues." But that same year, Green received his draft notice. He entered the army in January 1951 and departed for Camp Atterbury, Indiana, about forty miles south of Indianapolis. "Galveston Blues" sold well. According to the *Baltimore Afro-American*, Peacock had sold 100,000 copies by 1952. Rather than touring in support of his single, the army placed Green in Special Services, playing piano and singing in the service clubs at Camp Atterbury. He received his discharge in 1952 but could not match his pre-army success. Green moved to Mexico and then to Europe, where he spent the rest of his career playing in clubs on the continent.[85] The army could use Green's talents in the service club around base in the middle of Indiana, but modern blues and R&B did not create the kind of image that the military wanted to cultivate in the early 1950s. It was too wild, too rebellious, and too Black. For Kelly, McPhatter, and Green, the military disrupted their careers with little to no professional return for seizing their time and labor.

• • • • • •

For white, aspiring country musicians and future rockabillies, serving in the military was not a hindrance but a spark for their civilian careers. When Jim Stewart came back to Memphis in 1953, his experiences in the service made for an easy reentry into civilian life. He returned to the job at First National Bank that he had left when he entered the service and used his GI Bill to complete his college education at Memphis State College (now the University of Memphis), where he majored in business management and minored in music. He also continued making country music, playing fiddle in the house band at a nightclub called the Eagle's Nest on US Highway 78, just southwest of downtown Memphis headed toward Holly Springs, Mississippi.[86] The club sat on the second floor of a building next to Clearpool, a public swimming pool where middle-class whites from Memphis and its suburbs brought their kids for a swim while adults enjoyed a beer or a setup and listened to the band.[87]

Stewart's band entertained these audiences by emulating the style of Bob Wills, with three fiddles, drums, bass, electric guitar, pedal steel guitar, piano, and vocals.[88] A local country disc jockey named "Sleepy Eyed John" Lepley led the group, while a country-picking ex-marine who went by the name Cowboy Jack Clement served as an emcee and lead vocalist.[89] Although originally from the Whitehaven community just south of Memphis, Clement had toured the world with the Marine Corps and discovered his talent for songwriting and singing while sitting around the barracks, much like Johnny Cash. Back in Memphis, Clement, like Stewart, attended Memphis State and eventually landed a job as a session player, producer, songwriter, and engineer at Sun Studio, producing Jerry Lee Lewis's "Great Balls of Fire" and penning Cash's "Ballad of a Teenage Queen" and "Guess Things Happen That Way," both number-one hits on the *Billboard* country chart in 1958.[90] But in 1953, none of these artists had participated in or could have predicted the revolutions of popular music that lay a few months away. They played as bandmates in a western swing outfit at the Eagle's Nest while Memphis suburbanites cooled off in Clearpool or had a drink. Stewart and Clement were just two white ex-servicemen, living in a thriving industrial southern city, taking advantage of the GI Bill, and playing country music at night for other people of similar backgrounds. They cut licks and sang their tunes with skills honed in the US military, delivering western swing and honky-tonk sounds through the mingling aromas of alcohol, cigarettes, and chlorine.

In early 1954, Scotty Moore's band, the Starlite Wranglers, played to similar crowds at the Bon-Air Club, a honky-tonk on Memphis's east side. Moore had added a vocalist to the group, now calling themselves Doug Poindexter and the Starlite Wranglers. They cut a record under that name in the spring of that year, an A side called "Now She Cares No More" backed with "My Kind of Carrying On." "Now She Cares No More" featured Poindexter's twangy tenor singing over a waltz-time lament that clearly mimicked Hank Williams's "I'm So Lonesome I Could Cry," even including the lyric "I'm so lonesome / I can't wait." Moore and Bill Black combined their electric and upright bass guitars to make a clip-clop rhythm, and Millard Yow added a tremolo-soaked lap steel guitar to give it the full Hank feel. The flip side, "My Kind of Carrying On," picked up the tempo for an upbeat honky-tonker that again owed much to the style of Williams, as well as to Lefty Frizzell and Faron Young. Poindexter's tenor cuts through the production with lyrics that brag about going on "a lovin' spree."[91] *Billboard* offered an unenthusiastic review of "Now She Cares No More," reporting, "Good ditty gets an okay chanting from the nasal-voiced Poindexter." The reviewer then hinted at a rural-urban divide within country music disc jockeys and fans. "Big city country buyers might not go big for this, but it should do well in the back country."[92] Even this modestly optimistic prediction failed to materialize for Poindexter and the Wranglers. It flopped. The record sold somewhere in the neighborhood of 300 copies.[93]

The Starlite Wranglers never recorded another song, but that one record provided a connection between the ex-servicemen floating around the Memphis country music circuit and Sam Phillips's Memphis Recording Service. Originally from the northwestern Alabama town of Florence, Phillips had moved to Memphis in 1945 after a brief stint in Nashville, Tennessee. He worked in radio in all three towns and opened his recording studio in 1950, famously recording both Black and white artists who streamed into Memphis from the small towns and plantations in Arkansas, Mississippi, and Tennessee. Some of those included Harmonica Frank, Howlin' Wolf, and Jackie Brenston and His Delta Cats, who recorded the seminal "Rocket 88" with Ike Turner on piano. Phillips often leased these recordings to labels like Chess Records, which added these Memphis R&B performers to their growing roster of artists. Phillips started his own label in 1950, called Phillips Records, in partnership with the local disc jockey Dewey Phillips. After that failed, he tried again in 1952 with Sun Records and subsequently changed the name of his studio to match. The first artists recorded for Sun Records helped define blues and R&B and eventually rock and roll in the 1950s and 1960s, artists like James Cotton, Little Junior Parker, and Rufus Thomas.[94]

White country music artists barely showed up in the first offerings by Sun, but that began to shift with Doug Poindexter and the Starlite Wranglers. And that shift opened the door to recording Elvis Presley. Phillips knew Scotty Moore through the Starlite Wranglers, and he knew to pair the guitar player and his bassist, Bill Black, with Presley to round out the young singer's sound. Because of Moore's time in the navy, honing his unique sound, collaborating with different types of musicians, and living and playing with African American musicians, the guitarist did not shy away from this strange kid covering an R&B song. And because of the regional success of that first Presley single, a call went out to all those country pickers in

Memphis and the surrounding countryside who had worked their craft on the time and the dime of the US government: Come to Sun Studio. Join in creating a new sound in country music. Play and sing in a way that shows your affinity for and indebtedness to African American culture, regardless of Jim Crow.

The country music that came from Sun Studio beginning in 1954 would shine a light on the intersection of white and Black musical cultures. Sam Phillips may have taken some credit for making those records happen. But Sun Records owes as much to Uncle Sam as it did Sam Phillips for the talent that showed up at 706 Union Avenue. When the nation's Cold War military threw white country pickers into the ranks with Black soldiers, it opened their cultural and social worlds. It made them open to possibility. And it made those white country musicians into an internal threat for the country music industry.

· · · · · ·

The story of Elvis Presley's meteoric rise is a familiar one, although it warrants retelling here to show just how much he depended on Memphis's country music community created by local military veterans. It also deserves retelling to show just how much Presley both depended on and began to threaten the Nashville music establishment. On July 5, 1954, he walked into Sun Studio in an attempt to track a few songs. The aspiring singer had visited the studio before, trying his luck crooning ballads, but met with little success. Phillips declined to release any of those early sides, although Marion Keisker, Phillips's assistant, flagged Presley's demos for the potential she heard in the handsome teen performer. After struggling to come up with proper material for the first recording session with Moore and Black, Presley famously launched into an impromptu interpretation of the African American artist Arthur "Big Boy" Crudup's 1948 R&B hit "That's All Right Mama." Phillips loved it. The group followed that song by recording a fast 4/4 version of Bill Monroe's 1946 waltz "Blue Moon of Kentucky" for the B-side, and Phillips released it as a single on July 19, 1954, only two months after the Starlite Wranglers record.[95] The songs combined Presley's hiccupped vocal delivery, Black's galloping rhythm, Moore's cutting lead licks, and Phillips's slapback-delay production. With these sonic elements, these white southerners recorded two genre-blending mash-ups that did anything but flop. The local disc jockey Dewey Phillips propelled "That's All Right" to popularity on his WHBQ radio show *Red, Hot, and Blue* and reported a deluge of phone calls from listeners who inquired about the singer's race. Only when Presley confirmed that he had attended Humes High during an on-air interview with Phillips did listeners understand that the racially ambiguous voice belonged to a white man.[96]

Presley then began scaling the rungs of the local country music scene, bringing his interracial sound to the visibly all-white genre. He started as an intermission act with the Starlite Wranglers at the Bon-Air Club, but the response to the new singer proved too much. "It didn't take us but just a few weeks to realize that wasn't going to work," Scotty Moore said, because "most of the crowd [who] were coming were younger and liked that part and didn't care for the country stuff which I was playing with the whole group." He remembered the split with his old band as an amicable one. "There wasn't a falling out or anything, just everybody realized, 'Well, this is where we need to, to split off and you guys do this and we'll hang in there doing what we do.'"[97] His new trio then made a local splash opening for *Louisiana Hayride* star Slim Whitman on July 30, 1954, at the Overton Shell Amphitheater in midtown Memphis. In fact, they had named themselves Elvis Presley and the Blue Moon Boys, a nod to the popularity of their cover of a bluegrass tune, not the R&B song.[98]

Next, the group hit the Eagle's Nest, playing a few songs in between Sleepy Eyed John's band, which still featured Jim Stewart and Cowboy Jack Clement. Stewart said, "We of course noticed that there was quite a lot of enthusiasm when they came on, a little different from ours, especially from the ladies, they would just, there was this amazing reaction, we had not experienced anything like this, when he would hit the stage."[99] Clement remembered how people "would go wild, man. It was packed." Presley and the Blue Moon Boys used the economical instrumentation of acoustic guitar, electric guitar, and upright bass. By contrast, Clement described his group as being "up there with an eight-piece band and everybody's dancing and having a good time. It was a good thing but then Elvis comes on with a guitar, wasn't even amplified and a slapping bass and an electric guitar and they go nuts. Dancing every little nuance." The change in the local music scene came quickly. Clement claimed dramatically, "Elvis took Memphis by storm. It was all over the first day, man."[100]

While everyone recognized the difference between the trio's music and the country sounds of the day, Presley's race, region, and repertoire kept his music fully within the commercial structures of country music. There was nowhere else for him *to* go. Phillips booked Presley on the *Grand Ole Opry* on October 2, 1954. In three months, the group had ascended from the Bon-Air Club to the Ryman Auditorium on the local enthusiasm for one single. Presley even met Bill Monroe, who professed his appreciation of the cover and told the young singer he had recut the song to match the new interpretation. The group also played Ernest Tubb's *Midnight Jamboree* radio show after their *Opry* appearance, where Presley reportedly told Tubb that he wanted to be a country singer more than anything else.[101]

Country disc jockeys and jukeboxes gave Presley's record another boost. A week after the *Opry* appearance, his version of Monroe's tune had hit number six on *Billboard*'s "C&W Territorial Best Sellers," followed closely by "That's All Right" at number seven.[102] On October 16, 1954, Presley and the Blue Moon Boys made their debut on the *Louisiana Hayride*, a connection made through their manager, Bob Neal, a Memphis country radio disc jockey.[103] Country radio played an instrumental role in Presley's initial success. The disc jockey Tom Perryman worked for a small station in Gladewater, Texas, an oilfield town about eighty miles west of Shreveport, Louisiana, home of the *Hayride*. The show's stars often stopped in his station, KSIJ, for promotional appearances. Perryman opined, "Presley's first break on the radio came on probably country [radio] because of the 'Blue Moon of Kentucky' song and not 'That's All Right, Mama.' . . . I know that's the way I did." In late 1954, Perryman also booked the trio into East Texas honky-tonks, where Presley, Moore, and Black would play weeknights while waiting for their Saturday-night appearances on the *Hayride*.[104] These types of gigs and radio promotions established the trio as a working country band well before the mainstream pop music industry knew Presley's name. By the end of 1955, readers of *Country & Western Jamboree* had named him the genre's "Best New Male Singer" ahead of Justin Tubb, Tommy Collins, Porter Wagoner, and Bobby Lord. Faron Young, still riding his wave of postmilitary publicity, took "Best Male Singer" for the year.[105]

But while fans embraced Presley, other artists and cultural authority figures resented the change he represented for the genre. Those reactions began back at the Eagle's Nest, where Sleepy Eyed John disliked the way Presley stirred up the young folks and stole the spotlight from his band.[106] Sam Phillips had to beg Jim Denny, manager of the *Grand Ole Opry*, to let Presley perform, and Denny reportedly hated the new style the trio had brought to country music.[107] Hugh Cherry, a prominent country music disc jockey and television host in the 1950s, gave Presley no credit for musical innovation. He complained, "Elvis's contribution to American society is he gave America's youth permission to be sexual. That's all. He's a singer of minimal talent, very limited range. He never wrote a song. He didn't play two chords well."[108] Charlie Louvin, one half of the brother duo the Louvin

Brothers, toured with Presley in 1956 and lamented that "the music changed" after what was dubbed rockabilly hit the country charts. New styles cut into the bottom line for more established artists with more recognizably country sounds. Louvin observed that "people like Webb Pierce, who had had twenty-five #1s, went down the drain, and the music changed so much that it seemed like it was a terrible slump in music right then, our kind of music, right through there. So it did get lean."[109]

The country music press described Presley's impact as an injection of pop or R&B into the genre, and his repertoire backs those assertions, at least on the surface. His growing repertoire of R&B covers, including "That's All Right," "Good Rockin' Tonight," "Mystery Train," and "I Got a Woman," all recorded at Sun, certainly encouraged that interpretation. The September 1955 edition of *Country Song Roundup* featured a profile of the singer titled "Folk Music Fireball." Casting Presley as an anomaly within the genre, the author claimed that the "big (6 foot) blonde" singer's first Sun release "represented something new in records: the unusual pairing of an R&B number with a Country standard." The article also enthused about the riotous concert events that Presley caused, including an appearance for Jimmie Rodgers Day in Meridian, Mississippi. The crowd there listened to Presley's growing catalogue of country songs like "Milk Cow Blues Boogie," "You're a Heartbreaker," Stan Kesler's tune "I'm Left, You're Right, She's Gone," and the Arthur Gunter blues song "Baby, Let's Play House."[110] In December 1955, *Country & Western Jamboree* described how the country music manager and promoter Colonel Tom Parker "instituted a new policy when he presented a combination of popular and country & western music on a recent one-nighter tour." At the time, Parker managed country star Hank Snow and his son, Jimmie Rodgers Snow, and was known in the industry as having shepherded Eddy Arnold and Red Foley to superstardom. His "new policy" on this tour placed the Snows on the same bill as "pop" acts Bill Haley and Elvis Presley, even if those designations had more to do with marketing strategies rather than any clear genre demarcation.[111]

But even as Presley gradually earned a reputation as a crossover–pop star, he did so by going through Nashville. In January 1956, Presley released "Heartbreak Hotel," his first single on the major label RCA after Phillips sold his Sun contract. The song helped cement his reputation as a pop star and rock and roller with its insinuating swing, Black's descending bass line, and accents from newly added drummer D. J. Fontana's strip-tease snare. With that release, Presley secured a number-one hit on *Billboard*'s country chart, the pop chart, and a top-five hit on the R&B chart. It also earned him his first gold record. But while creating this seminal rock and roll song, Presley, in a way, recorded his most country record yet. He cut the tune at the RCA studio in Nashville, and the label's country artists and repertoire (A&R) director, Steve Sholes, produced the track. It also featured the country finger-picking wizard Chet Atkins on acoustic guitar, and session pianist Floyd Cramer, who had started a few years before as a member of Faron Young's band, gave the tune its tinkling blues runs. Additionally, "Heartbreak Hotel" presented the first hit for Tree International Publishing. Tree's president, Jack Stapp, gave credit to Presley for his firm's success. He recalled, "Elvis Presley, who had been recording, I think, country-type songs, did 'Heartbreak Hotel,' which was a Tree song, written by Mae Axton down in Jacksonville, Florida. . . . It went to the #1 position in the charts, and that's when we started making noise."[112] Tree would go on to publish songs by Roger Miller, Willie Nelson, Merle Haggard, Buck Owens, Jim Reeves, and Conway Twitty before being sold to CBS in 1989 for $40 million.[113] Presley, Axton, and "Heartbreak Hotel" provided the foundation of that Nashville institution.

Presley stayed country as he emerged as a national star on radio and television. He signed to a management contract with Colonel Tom Parker in March 1956, further embedding the "Folk Music Fireball" within the country music machine.[114] That same month, he met Connie B. Gay and made an appearance on the *Jimmy Dean Show* on Washington's WMAL television station. Gay remembered the encounter fondly: "[Presley] was just getting into the business, and he gave me, I guess, my first face-to-face confrontation with rock & roll." However, Gay did not think of him as rock and roll at the time. "I thought of him, of course, in the early days as a country singer, as did a lot of other people," he recalled. "But I recognized that here was a new state-of-the-art, so to speak, and that it probably would hang around for a few years."[115] Besides an appearance on Dean's show, Gay booked Presley on the SS *Mount Vernon*, the yacht that Gay rented for "Hillbilly Cruises" while the boat sailed up and down the Potomac.[116]

The next logical step for Presley's burgeoning country career would be a performance for the military. On April 3, 1956, Presley entertained sailors aboard the USS *Hancock*, docked in San Diego, for a special episode of the *Milton Berle Show*, followed by a two-night stand at the San Diego Arena, where the group drew over 11,000 fans each night. Scotty Moore took the time to reconnect with John Bankson, a navy buddy who was still stationed in San Diego. He brought his old friend to the shows and picked guitar with him until the early hours of the morning. Moore characterized the visit as the moment when he "closed the door" on his "Navy past": "I had to reinvent myself when I left West Tennessee to join the Navy. Once I left the Navy and moved to Memphis I had to reinvent myself once again."[117]

Presley also endured a process of reinvention in 1956, transforming from a regional star to an international success story. With that fame came the intense scrutiny of the nation's cultural authorities. In the eyes of his critics, Presley's influence over youth culture and country music made him the leader of an internal rebellion against his race. The backlash to Presley arrived just as quickly as his success. Southern politicians and religious leaders decried the racial mixing implied in the rockabilly sound and the obvious influences that Black culture had on country music's young white performers. With his hypersexual dancing, long, duck-tailed hair, eye makeup, and riot-inducing sway with female fans, Presley would help define the rebellious sound and image of rock and roll by blurring the boundaries of race.[118] Military service had given rise inadvertently to the new, Blacker sound of an ostensibly all-white genre. Ironically, Music Row would need the strength of the Cold War military to subdue the threat of racial mixing that Presley and his fellow rockabillies had brought to country music.

4 All-American Boy

Elvis Presley and the Cold War's
Musical and Military Integration

• •

In December 1957, the US Army broke its news to the nation that the draft had reached a previously unthinkable point in its Cold War mission. The army now wanted Elvis Presley as an enlisted man. Although Americans accepted the peacetime draft as part of the fight against the global threat of communism, no one could have predicted that the federal government had grown so powerful that it could conscript the nation's biggest musical star in this foreign policy strategy. For thousands of young Americans, the draft had finally overextended its reach. By early 1958, nearly a decade before the height of anti-Vietnam demonstrations, many American teens protested the drafting of Presley with an intensity found only in youth's devotion to itself. His compulsory service demonstrated both the might of the federal government to enlist whomever it chose and the willingness of the nation's young people to push back against that power. Linda Kelly, Sherry Bane, and Mickie Matson, three young women from Noxon, Montana, wrote to President Dwight D. Eisenhower with an urgent plea on the draftee's behalf. "You don't know how we feel about him," they testified to the commander in chief. "I really don't see why you have to send him in the Army at all," the three continued, "but we beg you please please don't give him a G.I. hair cut, oh please please don't! If you do we will just about die!" They signed the letter, "Elvis Presley Lovers."[1]

Shocked that the government could pluck the most popular and commercially successful artist of the 1950s for military service, these young women acted. They were not alone. Presley fans wrote letters to their government representatives, wailed, and gnashed their teeth at the thought of losing their symbol of adolescent rebellion and desire. Presley had ascended the rungs of the popular music industry by bucking conventions of genre, racial performance, and class hierarchy with his music, wanton dance moves, and disregard for white middle-class American fashion. For young women like those three "Elvis Presley Lovers," the stifling conformity of the army seemed akin to a death sentence for their rebellious idol. They took exception to what they saw as an abuse of government power when Presley finally did enter the US Army as a draftee on March 24, 1958.

What these young women and thousands of other Presley fans failed to understand was that there was, in fact, *nothing* exceptional about the star's military service. Presley's race, region, and class shaped his place within the Cold War political economy and meant that he would probably serve in the military, regardless of his success in the music business.[2] As a high school–educated white male and the son of working-class parents from the margins of southern society, Presley may have expected to serve in the armed forces at some point, whether through conscription or as an enlistee looking for the economic security granted to soldiers in the nation's standing military and sold through campaigns like *Country Style, U.S.A.*

Instead of joining voluntarily, Presley took his chances as a working artist in the country music scene. His first releases had balanced his versions of R&B and pop songs with country covers, but Presley's connection to country music extended beyond this repertoire. The country music industry had facilitated his ascent, providing his backing musicians, management, and first forays into live radio and television performances. Perhaps most importantly, the country music press considered Presley as one of its own. Thanks to his consistent hits on the country and western charts, Presley ranked as a fan favorite in the pages of *Country Song Roundup* and *Country & Western Jamboree* throughout the late 1950s. These fans understood Presley as country, even if he represented a curious new incarnation of the hillbilly sound that revealed the obvious influence of African American music and style.[3]

Presley's sexualized play with the signifiers of Black culture, however, represented a betrayal of social and political laws of the segregated South. At the same time, southern white supremacists identified another betrayal of Jim Crow norms occurring within the military through racial integration of the armed forces. In response to both of these assaults, the racist organization known as the White Citizens' Councils fought a multifront war against school desegregation, rock and roll rebellion, and the integration of the military installations that had mushroomed through the South since the 1940s. Members of one chapter of the Citizens' Council directed their fury at the military integration at Fort McClellan just outside their hometown of Anniston, Alabama. According to their worldview, the federal government had ignited an insidious social revolution by integrating the armed forces on domestic installations where men and women, both white and Black, would mix in social settings, allegedly to the strains of Black music.

These white supremacists saw the military, which had brought so much economic prosperity to the postwar South, as an internal threat to the social order of Jim Crow.

Elvis Presley represented an analogous, internal threat to the country music industry as an agent of Black-inspired culture. Scholars have rightly documented Presley's role in the appropriation of blues and R&B for white profit. There is no reason to dispute the centrality of African American musical culture and fashion in propelling him to stardom.[4] Yet this emphasis on cultural theft has elided how profoundly Presley remained embedded in the country music industry. Scholars have written Presley into this critical blind spot partly out of the need to reckon with the recording industry's white supremacy and partly out of an inability to imagine the influence of Black music within the segregated spaces of the presumably all-white genre of 1950s country. He was not only a Mailer-esque "white negro" interloper dabbling in country covers.[5] Presley's merger of the ostensibly white and Black genres represented an internal rebellion within white music by daring to flaunt his affinity for Black culture while using country music's commercial infrastructure. In Nashville during the mid-1950s, it appeared that the invaders had breached the gate. The call was coming from inside the house.

The country music industry maintained its own way of talking about race in the late 1950s that had nothing to do with African American culture or integration and everything to do with the global expansion of the US military. Beginning in 1957, country singers and songwriters initiated a hit-making trend with songs about sexual affairs between US soldiers and women of various races, nationalities, and ethnicities. Lawton Williams, an ex-military policeman turned country disc jockey and songwriter, began the craze with his tunes "Geisha Girl" and "Fraulein," recorded by Hank Locklin and Bobby Helms, respectively. Several artists, both men and women, followed suit with imitations and answer songs that charted as country hits into the early 1960s. This theme of military-transnational romance sold so well that Locklin recorded an entire album of such songs called *Foreign Love*, narrating a virtual world tour of heterosexual encounters made possible by the US military's Cold War mission to contain the spread of communism. The popularity of these songs signaled a tolerance for or even an attraction to interracial sex among country music fans, at least as it was practiced by heterosexual white soldiers who crossed any color line besides the domestic Black-white divide that Elvis dared to transgress with his music.

When Presley entered the US Army in 1958, he not only followed a familiar trajectory for white working-class men from the US South but also tracked a known pattern for male country music artists. For a country singer, armed service seemed to come with the job. And like Faron Young and others before him, Presley benefited from his time in the ranks. Presley fulfilled his masculine duty, increased demand for his music by diminishing its supply, and used his service as a springboard into middle-class respectability and a Hollywood career. Military service rid Presley of his image as a Romeo hood who dared to expose the mixed-race origins of country music.[6] Conscription into the Cold War military transformed the biggest rockabilly star. It made him even more accessible as a mass-market pop star by affirming his commitment to the white middle-class values of US nationalism and anticommunism. It cleaned him up, gave him a haircut, and wiped the mascara from his lashes. It made him wholly white. It branded him with respectability, free from suspicions of racial or sexual perversions. The army made him a man.

The Internal Threat to White Southern Manhood

By October 1956, rumors of Presley's imminent conscription filtered into the national conversation about the singer. The servicemembers' newspaper *Army Times* noted the nuisance that this hearsay had caused at installations around the country. Presley fans would write to and call these posts, insisting that they knew that the "Tennessee Troubadour" was in basic training at these locations and requesting his attention. *Billboard* ran a story about Presley's impending assignment to Fort Dix, where he would allegedly receive a shortened basic training and "extensive dental and periodontal (gum) work" before receiving his orders as part of the army's Special Services entertainment.[7] None of these details were correct, but their publication led to a bombardment of Fort Dix's mailbox and phone lines. The Fort Dix postal officer Captain Sammy Robinson stated, "I've got a whole boxful of letters for him and the telephone operators are getting lots of 'let-me-speak-to-Pvt. Presley' phone calls."[8] These rumors plagued other installations as well. An *Army Times* report stated that the officials at Fort Carson, Colorado, felt the need "to squelch the countless inquiries, principally from gasping teen-age girls, about the ducktailed hero's whereabouts."[9]

In truth, Presley avoided the service for as long as possible, as he was justifiably unwilling to give up the unprecedented success he experienced beginning in 1956. That year, Colonel Tom Parker facilitated Presley's rise from a regional to a national star signed to RCA Records with two number-one hits, "Heartbreak Hotel" and "Hound Dog." He had sold 10 million singles by the end of 1956 and costarred in his first film, *Love Me Tender*, in which he played a singing Confederate soldier, doomed in love and war.[10] None of this success could curb the steady stream of controversy that accompanied Elvis's rise to fame, particularly when it came to the pernicious influence he allegedly had on the nation's adolescents.

From ministers to politicians to concerned parents, adults in positions of authority rued the debasement of American youth caused by Presley. The Reverend W. Carter Merbreier, a Lutheran pastor from Philadelphia, Pennsylvania, claimed that American teens had turned Elvis into a subject of idolatry. Merbreier, however, placed blame with the "nervous giggling girls" and their "idiotic parents" rather than Elvis. He claimed that "even though the gesticulations of Elvis Presley are unquestionably suggestive and possibly, even immoral, the condemnation must lie with those who have by their admiration made him the golden image."[11] The Reverend Carl E. Elgena of Des Moines, Iowa, gave full culpability to Presley, alleging that the rock and roll singer was "morally insane," and believed that "the spirit of Presleyism has taken down all bars and standards": "We're living in a day of jellyfish morality."[12] American teens had embarked on a short trip toward degradation, it seemed. Presley had provided the soundtrack and pointed the way with his hips.

For proof of this social degradation, authority figures and cultural conservatives from all walks of life needed to point no further than Presley's hair. Long, unkempt, and sideburned, the singer's hair had remained a topic of fascination since his emergence from Lauderdale Courts in Memphis, Tennessee. As Presley's fame grew, so did the hysteria about his coiffure and the efforts to police those who would emulate their rock and roll idol. In late December 1956, short-haired members of the East High School football team near Knoxville, Tennessee, cut the Elvis-inspired hairdos of three students and made six other students promise to see a barber lest they receive the same tonsorial fate. The football players, all of whom wore crew cuts, claimed that the "longhairs" were "hoods" who invited bad reputations for their fellow high school boys. The crew-cut jocks held down the three offenders while another player sheared the long tops and sideburns from the boys.[13]

Young women even picked up on Presley's hair sensation. Teenagers in Arkansas started a fad bearing the alternate names "the Elvis Swirl," the "ooh, Elvis," and the "la Presley." This feminine take on the ducktail featured a short cut and sideburns. As Paulette Thomas, a thirteen-year-old from Forrest City, Arkansas, described it, "My hair dresser nearly flipped her lid when I wouldn't let her put a bobby pin in my sideburns."[14] The trend caught on outside the South as well. In Grand Rapids, Michigan, approximately 400 young women had opted for the "Presley Cut," with its bangs, sideburns, and ducktailed back.[15]

Gender subversion had played into Presley's image creation from the beginning. As early as 1954, he began wearing mascara for a heavy-lidded look. This use of makeup had helped Presley create a new form of white masculinity that flirted with feminine performance. His choice of singing "Hound Dog," a song originally recorded by the R&B artist Big Mama Thornton, meant that Presley played with the tropes of female performance, putting himself in the place of the exasperated woman who narrates the tune about a no-good man.[16] With the feminine embrace of the "Presley cut," these young women sent the gender subversion back the other way. Now, with their ducktails and sideburns, they performed Presley's feminized version of masculinity for their fellow teens. When the army sheared Presley's hair, it also ended the inspiration behind this androgynous play for young women.

Presley's hair caused such uproar and emulation partially because it accentuated the sexuality he conveyed in his personal appearances. His bangs often followed his hips, thrusting forward as he preened for the female gaze onstage. Early on, Presley took to dying his hair dark brown and then black. This color job, combined with the copious amounts of Royal Crown pomade, gave his hair a particular sheen that emulated the popular Black hairstyles of the day. As Nelson George has argued, Presley drew inspiration from the Black "process," which straightened and styled Black hair into a pompadour with the help of Royal Crown. Ironically, the process represented a Black attempt to mimic a white hairstyle. Presley brought the cycle of mimicry back full circle with his use of Royal Crown to style his wild mane into the barely tamed pompadour that became a hallmark of rockabilly style.[17] All that Presley's hair came to symbolize—the student rebellion, the racial performance, the gender bending—came under the threat of Uncle Sam's shears when his draft notice arrived in late 1956.

On January 4, 1957, Presley wore his makeup, a red jacket, a pair of black trousers, and black shoes to the Kennedy Veterans Hospital Examination Station in Memphis for his preinduction physical. The Las Vegas chorus girl Dotty Harmony accompanied the singer in a Cadillac limousine to the hospital. For her part, Harmony volunteered that she had found him to be a "fine physical specimen." Presley, too, believed he was "in good health," as far as he knew, and stated that he would serve whenever they wanted him.

Purely on presumption, the press reported how "all branches of the service are interested in nailing Presley because of his 'special service' talents as an entertainer."[18] A few days later, on January 8, 1957, the doctors had returned Presley's physical and mental test results to Captain Elwyn P. Rowan, the Army Recruiting Main Station commander. The *Memphis Press-Scimitar* teased, "GIRLS! DON'T LOOK NOW! Elvis doesn't even know it yet. But he's 1-A. '1-A' is draft board lingo. It means, 'You've had it,' 'Time to enlist,' or 'Prime draft bait'—depending how you look at it."[19] Expectant fans found relief in the report that Presley would not enter the draft for at least six months, regardless of the physician's findings.[20] Likewise, the reporters assured anxious teens that, as a condition of his assignment to the Special Services division, Presley would retain his controversial hair, foregoing the usual GI cut.[21] With Presley having an anticipated two-year hitch in the Special Services and no set date with a military barber in the near future, no one breathed easier than Presley himself, who understandably dreaded leaving the fame and life of excess he had built in the two and a half years since he stepped into Sam Phillips's studio.

But the US Army did not necessarily want the hip-swiveling symbol of adolescent rebellion and racial mixing in the ranks, whether he landed in Special Services or not. *Army Times* took Presley's mental examination as a chance to rib the draftee. A picture on its frontpage in January 1957 showed the singer with his head in hand and a frown on his face. The caption teased that Presley looked "downright houn'doggish before he's even made his first reveille," as the "noted knee-knocker thinks over a question in his pre-induction mental exam at Memphis."[22]

A spokesman for Special Services denied that the entertainment branch even wanted Presley. "Our studies indicate that his basic appeal is to young girls. Our interest in that field is somewhat limited. We have not been able to obtain affirmative evidence that he has a similar appeal to young males, particularly in the age groups we seek to reach." Regarding the image of Elvis singing about the "joys of Army life," he added, "[It] seems to us a bit grotesque. . . . That would be overdoing it, we think." The article also suggested that the army was annoyed at the stories claiming that Elvis would go into Special Services and was "particularly sore about one [reporting that] he won't have to shave off his sideburns after drafting."[23] The military wanted a certain type of performer to convey its Cold War recruitment and entertainment messages, and Presley did not fit the bill. That performer could be a white, working-class male from the South. He definitely could be a country music singer. But Presley's gender play and indebtedness to

African American culture represented two bridges too far for the army. It wanted someone who was clearly white and clearly masculine.

· · · · · ·

The South's network of White Citizens' Councils, the "respectable" face of white supremacy and segregation, emerged as the nation's most vocal opponents to the rise of Presley and the gender and racial play at the heart of his brand of rock and roll. Formed on July 11, 1954, in Indianola, Mississippi, the Citizens' Councils spread across the region, forming state and local chapters from Virginia to Texas, to apply political pressure against the Supreme Court's decision in the *Brown v. Board of Education* case, delivered on May 17, 1954. The *Brown* ruling represented the successful culmination of years of legal battles in the NAACP Legal Defense Fund's fight against the 1896 ruling of *Plessy v. Ferguson.* Both the supporters and the opponents of the *Brown* decision understood that the legal dismantling of segregation threatened to extend well beyond southern school grounds. The Citizens' Councils' campaign of "massive resistance" to the first *Brown* decision successfully stalled the desegregation of most southern schools. Then, in May 1955, the court handed down the *Brown II* decision, which only emboldened white southern segregationists, with its vague mandate of desegregating "with all deliberate speed."[24]

While the fight for integration continued in the courts, rock and roll sustained its assault on segregation in a cultural end run around the strict separation of the races. The record industry took notice of this promiscuous mixing of genres and attempted to understand what it meant for the sound and the sale of popular music. The *Billboard* reporter Bill Simon noted the predominance of R&B's influence on pop and country and western, commenting that there were "few boundary lines left in music these days, and nobody knows this better than the disk jockey, the immediate reflector as well as the frequent creator of public tastes." Most peculiarly, Simon observed that the influence of Black music had "manifested itself with the c.&w. public and those that cater to it. Southern audiences, who once craved an exclusive diet of hillbilly platters, certainly don't practice segregation in their platter preferences." Specifically, he offered "the spectacular rise of Elvis Presley" as an example for the style's ability to receive "spins on r.&b. as well as country shows, and as prominent a pop deejay as Bill Randle insists that Presley is a potentially top pop entity."[25]

The country music industry took notice as well. In October 1956, the country accordionist and songwriter Pee Wee King addressed what he saw as the negatives and positives of genre blending, in his regular column for *Country Song Roundup*. "I suppose most of you have accustomed yourselves to the fact that there is a definite change in Country-Western styled songs that are being recorded," he conferred with his readers, commenting that everyone appeared to shift to "some kind of Rock and Roll idea." He even admitted to chasing after the sound himself but justified his foray into the new style by saying that if enough artists jumped on the bandwagon, they could end the fad. King believed, "If enough of us record the Elvis Presley type of songs, we can KILL this style," the same way he thought pop singers flooded the market with covers of his song "Tennessee Waltz" and Hank Williams's "Jambalaya." On the positive side, he believed that the musical mixing present in rock and roll and other "crazes [has] wiped out the big barriers that existed between 'Pop' music, Country music and Rhythm and Blues." He also reported that jukebox and record-store owners at the recent Music Operators Convention in Chicago had discussed a future in which music would no longer be divided by genre in record stores. Instead, customers would simply "ask for the record by the name of the song and the artist you like it by."[26] This idea seemed to appeal to King on the notion that his fans would seek out *his* records and not covers of his song by someone else, like Patti Page, for instance. By extension, his fans would buy *his* covers of songs, regardless of who originated the tunes. In this new artist-based system, as opposed to a genre-based classification, fans could reward their favorite performers and not fall prey to upstart singers like Elvis Presley in meaningless fads like rock and roll.

But genres did more than divide the record store. They provided identity and reinforced racial boundaries. White supremacists recognized this. To them, a future of genre blending translated into a future of racial mixing, an unthinkable imaginary for anyone so invested in the political, social, and cultural separation of the races. The Citizens' Councils watched in disgust as Presley pushed the South's white youth into dangerous proximity with Black culture. One member claimed that his council chapter had "set up a twenty-person committee to do away with this vulgar, animalistic, n***** rock 'n' roll bop." He claimed that the committee aimed specifically at rockabilly and promised to "check with the restaurant owners and the cafes to see what Presley records is on their machines and then ask them to do away with them."[27]

Some country musicians held white supremacist attitudes toward Presley as well. Ira Louvin, Charlie's brother in the duo the Louvin Brothers, expressed a similar attitude to Presley's face. According to Charlie, one night while touring together, Presley found a piano backstage and played some gospel tunes, commenting, "You know, that's the music I really love." Ira, slightly inebriated, lashed out, "Well, you damn white n*****. Why do you play that crap on the stage if that's what you love?" Presley responded with a smile and explained that he simply gave the fans what *they* wanted, not what he always preferred.[28] For Citizens' Council members and Ira Louvin, Presley represented an internal enemy, someone who had betrayed his race and tempted the malleable minds of the South's white youth with his sexualized stage show, provocative lyrics, and open embrace of Black styles. He tempted them so easily because of his position in country music, a visibly white genre that supposedly carried the torch for all-American patriotism.

The Citizens' Council leader Asa Carter, later an infamous speechwriter for George Wallace and the novelist behind *The Rebel Outlaw Josey Wales* and *The Education of Little Tree*, emerged in the mid-1950s as one of the South's most vocal and influential critics of desegregation, popular music, and the pernicious influences of the federal government's racial policies. A native of northeast Alabama, Carter began his race-baiting career in 1953 by hosting a radio show sponsored by the white supremacist group the American States' Rights Association, on Birmingham's WILD 850 AM. Carter took to the airwaves twice a day for nearly two years, promoting racial purity and warning of the communist conspiracy behind civil rights, desegregation, and Black popular music.[29] WILD fired Carter in 1955 for his verbal attacks on the city's Jewish business community. But without skipping a beat in his pursuit of racial extremism, Carter formed the North Alabama Citizens' Council (NACC), based out of Birmingham, in October of that year, creating a working-class version of the predominantly middle-class Citizens' Council movement. He then established a chapter on his home turf of Anniston, Alabama, in February 1956, drawing members from the white steel workers, machinists, and gas-station attendants of Calhoun County. Speaking at a series of rallies before his blue-collar crowds, Carter relied on two flashpoints to raise the ever-present specter of miscegenation: Black music and Fort McClellan, the city's local military installation.[30]

Beginning in the early 1950s, Fort McClellan housed facilities for the Chemical Warfare Services and training facilities for both regular US Army and National Guard units. By 1953, the combination of Fort McClellan and the nearby Anniston Army Depot employed nearly 12,000 people, with a payroll of $20 million.[31] Located only six miles north of Anniston, Fort McClellan had also served as a massive training site for white and Black soldiers during two world wars and even hosted experiments in interracial housing for officers as early as 1942.[32] The presence of African American men in uniform threatened the racial status quo of nearby Anniston in the postwar period. Carter organized his followers in early 1956, mobilizing Citizens' Council members in Calhoun County by playing to the local racial fears, as well as the gender and class insecurities, of working whites. The alleged weakening of the "Anglo-Saxon" race through "mongrelization" at the hands of the federal government served as the overriding theme of Carter's hate-mongering tactics. As evidence of the government's insidious role in the weakening of the white race, the NACC's newsletter, the *Southerner*, detailed the role that Fort McClellan and Black music played in the demise of white power.

The February edition of the *Southerner* delivered on Carter's assessment of Fort McClellan's influence, reporting on the alleged interracial mixing between African American men and white women at the installation within the context of Black music and dancing. The article begins by positioning the federal government as an enemy of white southern mores. Referencing Truman's 1948 executive order, Carter complained that "not by choice of the people, but through dictatorial executive order, the government quite some time ago, integrated our armed forces, and consequently, the military bases." Carter, who functioned as editor of the *Southerner*, the NACC executive secretary, and the article's most likely author, indicted President Eisenhower's civil rights adviser, Max Rabb, a Jewish attorney, as "the mouthpiece of the mongrelizers to the President's ear" and the culprit for starting Fort McClellan down the road to racial amalgamation. The article claims that the government's plan for integration "was not subtle, but it was quiet," bemoaning the encampment of African American male soldiers with white soldiers just outside Anniston.[33]

By the time members of NACC and the readers of its publications had awakened to the local ramifications of the Pentagon's racial policies, the South's white political representatives had grown comfortable with receiving federal investment in the form of defense spending. These politicians had directed millions of federal defense dollars into their region in the form of military base expansion during and after World War II. When the Pentagon ordered the desegregation of the military, the federal government turned these dozens of military installations into isolated experiments in integration well ahead of any legal orders to desegregate the South's civilian population.[34]

Only 15,000 of the army's approximately 200,000 Black soldiers remained in segregated units by 1953, and the majority of those represented service units stationed in Europe.[35] The Pentagon initiated a sociological study of armed forces integration during the early 1950s under the code name Project Clear. In 1954, the reporter Lee Nichols published the study's findings as an exposé called *Breakthrough on the Color Front*. Nichols believed that the military could state with some justification that "the program, to mix white and colored servicemen and women, is nearing completion and is being described as a complete success."[36]

The South's economic reliance on defense spending meant that servicemembers and their families who were stationed in the region would need to comply with the Pentagon's racial mandate, even though federal policy clashed with local Jim Crow laws and customs. Children on posts in Germany and Japan had always attended integrated schools, while the schools on southern installations in the United States began desegregation in 1953. On January 12, 1954, Secretary of Defense Charles E. Wilson issued a memo announcing that "no new school shall be opened for operation on a segregated basis, and schools presently so conducted shall cease operating on a segregated basis, as soon as practicable, and under no circumstances later than September 1, 1955."[37] From Texas to Alabama to Maryland, schools operating on federal land and with federal funding integrated with little incident, although 28,000 federal dependents attended civilian, segregated public schools across the South.[38]

The army's integration policy also applied to the WAC, which had relocated its training headquarters from Fort Lee, Virginia, to Fort McClellan in 1954. The WAC's arrival in Alabama included the new construction of a $7 million barracks and training facility at the fort. The local paper the *Anniston Star* provided photographic coverage of the dedication ceremonies of the construction and featured staged vignettes of white women drilling, relaxing in their rooms, singing around a piano, and attending etiquette class. These images helped combat rumors that the WAC attracted women with loose morals and promiscuous sexual habits. The juxtaposition of these pictures, smiling white women marching in uniformed formation one moment and sewing in their rooms the next, created an image of white, chaste femininity in service to the state that offered an appealing image for residents of the nearby city.[39] However, not long after the WAC's relocation to Alabama, it received allegations of racial discrimination. Representative Charles C. Diggs Jr. of Michigan wrote a letter to Secretary of the Army Robert T. Stevens charging that Special Services on the post refused to admit "Negro Wac personnel and visiting civilians from nearby communities . . . to dance at regular Wednesday night 'white enlisted dances.'" Diggs alleged that civilian hostesses of Special Services ordered Black women soldiers off the floor and instructed them to return on Thursday nights for a separate dance.[40]

The realities of racism endured by Black women at Fort McClellan did nothing to dampen the paranoia of the local Citizens' Council. For the NACC, the housing of Black men and white women together under the auspices of the federal government created an intolerable situation. Where Diggs echoed charges of discrimination, the NACC saw only the potential for interracial sex, particularly related to social functions at the post. Its white supremacist vision of the world created an inverse, alternative reality from the one experienced by Black women at Fort McClellan. Black women were not victims in this racist worldview. Black men were predators. With sneering insinuation, an article about Fort McClellan's dances in the NACC newsletter described, "As the evening wears on, one can hear the music rising in tempo, the beat growing into a jungle throb, the courtesies growing more lax, until the woman is accorded no visible respect."[41] The NACC sowed the seeds of white racial violence by depicting Fort McClellan as a den of lascivious racial mixing, where white women were the innocent game hunted by Black men. For twenty-five cents per copy, white Annistonians could consume the NACC's mythmaking, reading about the collusion between the federal government and the communists, the imminent miscegenation at Fort McClellan, and the central role of Black music at every turn.

Not everyone took the NACC's bait. On March 29, 1956, the Anniston reporter Cody Hall, nephew of the Pulitzer Prize–winning, anti-Klan journalist Grover Hall, noticed Council leader Asa Carter's antipathy toward African American music and set out to survey the average Annistonian's opinion on the subject. According to Hall, Carter claimed that the Anniston Citizens' Council was then asking the city's "drug stores and restaurants . . . to remove 'rock and roll' records" from their jukeboxes. Kenneth Adams, the NACC member who would firebomb the Freedom Riders' bus outside Anniston in 1961, led the initiative and described the "animalistic" beat and "Negro origin" of the music as detrimental to the community. Anniston's jukebox owners refused to comply, and Hall quoted several high school and college-aged residents who found the council's proposal to be idiotic.[42]

On April 10, 1956, three members of Carter's NACC, including Adams, found another musical target for their pent-up racial and class resentments, when they attacked and attempted to kidnap Nat "King" Cole during a concert at Birmingham's Municipal Auditorium, sixty miles southwest of

FIGURES 4.1 & 4.2 The cover and an article from the North Alabama Citizens' Council publication the *Southerner*. The cover highlights the battle exploits of Nathan Bedford Forrest, the infamous slave trader and Confederate cavalryman. The inside article claims to show the scenes of integrated dancing at the US Army installation Fort McClellan. The North Alabama Citizens' Council claimed that military integration represented a communist-backed plot to usher in the integration of social and sexual relationships in the United States. ("Fort McClellan," *The Southerner: News of the Citizens' Council*, February 1956, 3, Alabama Room Archives, Anniston-Calhoun County Public Library, Anniston, Alabama)

Anniston. The kidnapping attempt failed, but the attack pushed the politically reticent singer to support openly the NAACP's efforts to end Jim Crow segregation.[43] Yet, despite the NACC's actual and threatened violence, certain musicians and soldiers could cross the sexual color line with impunity. And the songs they wrote and sang about these sexual exploits garnered hit records, not terroristic intimidations.

Interracial Country and Foreign Love

In 1957, a country music singer named Hank Locklin released his first crossover hit with "Geisha Girl," which reached number sixty-six on the pop charts and stayed on the country charts for thirty-nine weeks, peaking at number four.[44] The song's narrator invites the audience to empathize with his situation. He has fallen in love with a Japanese woman and does not know how to help himself. He asks listeners if they have ever been in a teahouse and "heard a love song that you didn't understand" or been lovestruck by "a pretty geisha girl dressed in Oriental style."[45] By the end of the chorus, the narrator has bid farewell to the United States and returned to Japan. He asks listeners, "Tell the folks back home I'm happy, with someone that's true, I know / I love a pretty geisha girl where the ocean breezes blow."[46]

The success of "Geisha Girl" spurred its writer, a former military policeman and disc jockey named Lawton Williams, to pen more songs detailing the joys and heartbreaks of transnational sexual affairs. He wrote "Fraulein" and placed it with singer Bobby Helms. The narrator, presumably a soldier, has left his German lover behind to return to the States, where he reminisces about his abandoned romance. While nothing about the song conjures a direct association with the military, the instrumentation provides subtle clues that connect "Fraulein" with service in the armed forces. In the background of the mix, the piano player repeats a triplet beat in the upper register, providing a near-hidden reminder of a martial drum corps. "Fraulein" reached number one on the *Billboard* country charts and crossed over to the pop charts, too, where it peaked at number thirty-six in 1957. Helms would only match this enormous success with his seasonal hit "Jingle Bell Rock" later that year.[47]

Locklin's and Helms's releases initiated a gold rush of intercontinental and often interracial love songs that reinforced the ties between country music and the Cold War military. Locklin entered the studio with Chet Atkins in December 1957 and recorded an album called *Foreign Love* that

FIGURE 4.3 The cover of Hank Locklin's *Foreign Love* from 1958. This album cast the white heterosexual US soldier as a kind of sexual tourist, collecting conquests with women of different races and ethnicities from around the world. (LP 1673, RCA Victor 1958, 33 1/3 rpm; author's collection)

included his own version of "Fraulein." Lawton Williams penned the title track, as well as the tune "Blue Grass Skirt" about a man whose "hula girl" is stolen by a "rock and roller" four years before Elvis Presley's *Blue Hawaii*. All twelve songs, including four written by Williams, addressed love affairs between a man and exoticized women of various nationalities, ethnicities, and races. These included a rewrite of the Spanish-American War / minstrel-show artifact "Filipino Baby" by the Tin Pan Alley pioneer Charles K. Harris, Cindy Walker's French/Japanese love song "Anna Marie," and Helen Stone's "Mexicali Rose" from 1923. With these tunes, Locklin took listeners on a historical world tour of US imperialism and current Cold War containment.[48]

Locklin's success inspired an outbreak of trend followers and answer songs written from a range of perspectives. Skeeter Davis delivered "Lost to a Geisha Girl" in late 1957.[49] Kitty Wells followed a similar pattern that same year, mimicking the melody and instrumentation of "Fraulein" for her tune "(I'll Always Be Your) Fraulein," about a German woman who still holds a place in her heart for her American lover.[50] Jimmie Skinner recorded a refusal to this trend of foreign love with his tune "I Found My Girl in the USA." After dismissing the exotic charms of geishas, Skinner delivers his romantic version of American exceptionalism with the line, "I was lonesome too while over there, but I waited for that day / And found my girl here in the good ol' USA."[51] The brother-and-sister duo The McCoys made their contribution with another Lawton Williams tune, "Daddy's Geisha Girl," sung from the point of view of two siblings left behind in the United States with their mother while their father travels back to his Japanese lover.[52] And in 1959, Jan Howard and Wynn Stewart teamed up to duet on "Yankee Go Home," a song that Howard's songwriting husband, Harlan, used to turn a slogan of anti-American graffiti into a refrain of hillbilly heartbreak.[53] Harlan Howard could pull inspiration from his own experience as a soldier, having learned how to play guitar and write songs while training as a US Army paratrooper stationed at Fort Benning, Georgia.[54] Locklin tried to cash in on the trend once more in 1959 with his release "Foreign Car," a comedic song set to the melody of "Geisha Girl" about trying to make love in a compact import with bucket seats.[55]

Country music fans continued buying military-themed love songs into the 1960s. In 1961, Kitty Wells scored her second and final solo number-one hit with the song "Heartbreak, USA." This tune addressed the entire "Foreign Love" trend in the form of an answer song, Wells's calling card since her first number one, "It Wasn't God Who Made Honky Tonk Angels." A chorus of background singers announce the singer's location before Wells begins a mournful tribute to her absent love, describing the depths of her loneliness and singing, "Till the trade winds bring him home to stay, I'll live in heartbreak USA." The solitude that Wells expresses in this song, another one written by Harlan Howard, implies that she will remain chaste and devoted to her lover regardless of his dalliances. She reminds her man not to let foreign women, including geisha girls, seduce him while traveling the world, although the resignation in her voice suggests the futility of her pleas.

These songs represented more than campy Cold War novelty hits. Thousands of US servicemen married Japanese women and brought their partners stateside in the late 1940s and early 1950s. The development of these marriages began with nisei Japanese American soldiers marrying Asian women while stationed in the Pacific. Thanks to activism by the Japanese American Citizen League, Congress passed a series of Soldier Brides Acts in 1945, 1947, and 1950, which permitted the women to immigrate to the United States.[56] White and Black soldiers also took advantage of these new policies. The US consulate counted over 8,000 marriages between Japanese women and US soldiers from 1945 to 1952. Seventy-three percent of those marriages occurred between white men and Japanese women.[57] In 1951, the American Red Cross established a Brides' School in Japan and at Fort Bliss outside El Paso, Texas, to minimize any impending social conflicts and to maximize assimilation.[58] *Jet* magazine even ran an article in 1953 in which Black veterans testified to the superiority of their Japanese wives as compared to Black American women.[59] By 1957, when Hank Locklin released "Geisha Girl," the Red Cross claimed to have helped 30,000 Japanese brides adapt to US culture.[60] But not all women involved with US soldiers became a bride or made their way across the Pacific. Japanese women gave birth to thousands of mixed-race children out of wedlock, and thousands more chose abortion rather than face the stigma of single motherhood.[61]

These foreign love songs not only reflected the racial and gender politics of Cold War militarization. They represented the way musicians profited from a deep tradition of interracial love songs written in the context of US empire building. Songwriters had made a tradition of chronicling love affairs with women of different races as whites made their way across the continent. Nineteenth-century ballads like "Shenandoah," "Fallen Leaf," and "Princess Pocahontas" told of white men loving "Indian maidens," while colonizers drove Indigenous peoples from their lands in the interest of Manifest Destiny.[62] The theme of white men loving Native American women reemerged in modern country music with Bob Wills's "Cherokee Maiden," Hank Thompson's "Squaws along the Yukon," George Jones's "Eskimo Pie," and Tim McGraw's "Indian Outlaw."[63] Interracial romance also offered a central theme in songs about cowboys and US law enforcement on the Mexican-US borderlands. From the cowboy ballads collected by Frank Dobie and John Lomax to Marty Robbins's "El Paso" franchise and Benny Martin's 1959 release "Border Baby," country music possessed a longstanding enchantment with singing about the charms and dangers of love with dark-haired, dark-skinned women.[64]

That same enchantment fueled the lyrics of popular songs when the US military looked to conquer land and people beyond the continental borders.

At the turn of the century, when the United States fought against Spain and flexed its military muscle on the international stage, soldiers could hear their sexual conquests with exoticized women retold in songs like "Filipino Baby," "The Queen of the Philippine Islands," and "On to Cuba, or The Cuban Girl's Song to Her Lover."[65] As these song titles suggest, US expansion could mean love, or at least sex, as part of the spoils of war. Beyond Locklin's "Geisha Girl," Cold War–era country music picked up the fascination with Asian women and churned out interracial love songs from the 1950s through the 1980s, like Dick Curless's "China Nights," Marty Robbins's "I-Eish-Tay, Mah-Su," Buck Owens's "Made in Japan," and John Anderson's "Tokyo, Oklahoma."[66] Even the country-pop heart-throb Ricky Nelson sang about the joys of crossing the color line in his song "Travelin' Man," a number-one hit in 1961 that listed a panoply of women, including a "señorita," a "sweet little Eskimo," a "China doll," and a "Polynesian baby."[67]

Artists purposefully excluded African and African American women in the country music catalogue of interracial sex, which is not to suggest that those relationships did not exist. Merle Haggard's "Irma Jackson" and Billy Joe Shaver's "Black Rose," both recorded in the late 1960s, speak of Black-white attractions, presumably set in the United States. But these songs told tales of forbidden love, shame, and fleeting, illicit pleasure in Jim Crow America—one a story of an unrequited childhood crush, the other charac-terized as a bad habit in need of divine intervention, respectively. As Shaver sings, "Lord put a handle on a simple-headed man and help me leave that black rose alone."[68] Marty Robbins recorded two songs that suggest that the female love interest is Black, both of them Caribbean themed, "Kingston Girl" and "Bahama Mama." However, Robbins sang these from the point of view of island men in an updated minstrel voice, probably in an attempt to cash in on the 1950s calypso boom.[69]

These examples remain exceptional. As a rule, country music has cre-ated an audible tradition of celebrating the crossing of any color lines other than the domestic Black/white divide in order to reinforce the racial and gender power bestowed on white men who labor in the service of empire. These songs not only reify the country performer's and listener's whiteness but also reflect the implicit anti-Blackness at the heart of the country music industry and the popular music business more broadly. The artists who par-ticipated in the "foreign love" trend, as well as the imperialist realities they represented, could pass outside the scrutiny and violence of the nation's worst white supremacists, like Asa Carter and the Citizens' Council, because their specific models of interracial sex conformed to the gendered power of white settler colonialism practiced since the founding of the nation.

The country music industry even accepted rockabillies if they could rein in their wildness and conform to the normative aesthetics of whiteness. US Air Force veteran Johnny Cash had dabbled in rockabilly but still maintained enough of a tie to the sonic and visual politics of country music to fit the military's vision of appropriate recruitment music, unlike his friend Elvis Presley. In 1957, Cash appeared on an episode of *Country Style, U.S.A.* with Charlie Applewhite to sell military enlistment to the nation's young men. Cash performed three songs, "There You Go," "Give My Love to Rose," and "Home of the Blues." He also introduced the singer Carolee Cooper, daughter of the bluegrass duo Stoney and Wilma Lee Cooper, who sang one song and joined Cash and Applewhite for the closing theme song of "Stay All Night (Stay a Little Longer)."[70] Cash still recorded for Sun Records at the time. "There You Go" had risen to number one on *Billboard*'s country and western chart the year before, his second number one in a row after "I Walk the Line," the melody for which he had picked out while still stationed in West Germany.[71]

Cash had drawn inspiration from Presley after seeing him perform at the Eagle's Nest and landed a demo session at Sun Studio in September 1954. His music fell roughly into the rockabilly mode, with songs like "Hey, Porter!" and "Get Rhythm," and he toured with Presley in the mid-1950s. Yet, whereas Presley indulged in overt displays of hip-shaking sexuality, Cash remained more staid in his presentation of the songs, abetted by the insistent *boom-chicka* train beat of Marshall Grant's bass and the calculated, durable melodic lines of Luther Perkins's tremolo-laden electric guitar. And while Presley chose to cover recent R&B hits when dabbling in Black music, Cash leaned into the folk genre, kicking off his 1957 debut album with "Rock Island Line," the work song collected by John Lomax from Kelly Pace in an Arkansas prison farm and covered by Huddie "Lead Belly" Ledbetter in 1937.[72] Cash continued this connection to folk music throughout his career, collaborating comfortably with artists like the Carter Family and Bob Dylan. But, perhaps most importantly, whereas Presley embodied the sexuality of Black singers in tunes like "That's All Right" and "Hound Dog," Cash adopted a version of Black music mediated by white folklore collectors who were fascinated with the culture of southern prisons.

With "Hey, Porter!," the A-side to his 1955 debut single, Cash offered a window into the racial politics of country music and why he would serve as an appropriate voice of military recruitment. "Hey, Porter!" gives one side of a conversation from Cash's narrator to a railroad porter on a southbound train. "Hey, porter / Hey, porter," the traveler nags, before explaining his excitement about heading home. He then suggests that the porter should have the engineer blow the train whistle to express that excitement, explaining, "I smell frost on cotton leaves / And I feel that southern breeze."[73] The porter in this song would have undoubtedly been an African American man and a member of A. Philip Randolph's Brotherhood of Sleeping Car Porters, working a rail line traveling through the Deep South.[74] Cash's narrator asks this Black worker a series of questions laced with images of cotton fields, the Mason-Dixon line, and southbound trains plucked from minstrel songs like "Are You from Dixie?"[75]

In the mid-1950s, listeners would have recognized that "porter" signified a Black man. What they would have missed in the song was that Cash wrote it about taking a train home to Arkansas after receiving his discharge from the US Air Force.[76] With that in mind, a new scene emerges from this song. It is 1955. Two uniformed men encounter each other on a train heading to the Arkansas Delta. One wears air force blue and enjoys the respect afforded a member of the nation's military currently keeping communism at bay around the globe. The other wears the dark blue of the most powerful African American labor union and civil rights organization in the twentieth century. Yet one is clearly in the service of the other. The porter suffers the persistent requests of a serviceman who apparently loves the southern landscape where they are headed together, a landscape that may very well conjure images of violence and prejudice for the Black man, who could have taken his job to escape that "southern breeze." This is a song about power, perspective, and privilege embedded in a rockabilly motif that passed as rebellious country music in the mid-1950s.

Cash combined race, military service, and region in a neat package for his musical debut. That music fit the needs of the Cold War recruitment machine, a reminder that the army continued to brand itself with the ostensibly pure white sounds of country music even as its ranks became increasingly diverse. Both Presley and Cash may have emerged from the same city and the same label at roughly the same time. But Presley's adoption of Black sexual expression in his songs meant that he embodied the threat of racial mixing in a way that Cash never did. In Cash's world of porters and cotton leaves, everyone occupied the appropriate spaces according to their race. This racial distancing meant that Cash's music remained an acceptable medium to convey the military's recruitment message.

On *Country Style, U.S.A.*, Applewhite introduced the usual pitch to join the US Army after Cash's second song, "Give My Love to Rose." The camera cuts to a cartoon of a white boy who looks like a cross between Dennis the Menace and Elroy Jetson. The boy grows into a uniformed soldier as men's voices chant in a cadence-style chorus, "Hey there chum, don't feel glum / You can be the man you want to become / Just Go, Go Army and Grow / Go, Go Army and Grow." A narrator's voice jumps in to tell viewers that they can "grow through job training": "In today's modern army, you'll get tough technical training, training that will make you a skilled expert in your field." Likewise, recruits will "grow through travel": "You'll see more of the world in the army. You'll have a chance for Europe, the Caribbean, or the Far East." A young man could also "grow through advancement": "Every step up the ladder means new confidence. Learn to lead. Learn to succeed." The narrator ends the pitch with a combination of two recruitment slogans rolled together: "You too can go army and grow. Get choice, not chance, from your local army recruiter." The last credit that audiences heard would have reminded them that "*Country Style, U.S.A.* was produced by the Recruiting Publicity Center for the United States Army Recruiting Service at the Bradley Studios in Nashville, Tennessee."[77] The army willingly integrated the newest country sounds from Memphis, but only from the artists who suited the sonic and racial politics of the military and Music Row. Other artists, like Elvis Presley, still had to prove their legitimacy to the nation's Cold War armed forces.

Making Private Presley

In early 1958, Presley could not keep the military at bay any longer. He received a six-week deferment in January to complete filming on his fourth film, *King Creole*. Colonel Parker and Hal Wallis, the film's producer, successfully petitioned the army, claiming that pulling out of a motion picture would cause financial hardship for Presley and Paramount Pictures.[78] Memphis's Draft Board No. 86 had suffered enough from the ordeal of inducting the world's biggest musical star. Milton Bowers Sr., the board's chairman, complained to the local press that he was "fed up to the teeth" with letters and calls from Presley fans who complained about the draft and detractors who complained about the deferment. Bowers told how one "crackpot" had called him at home at his bedtime and complained that they "didn't put Beethoven in the Army": "Not considering the fact that Beethoven was not an American and has been dead for some time, I suppose he felt we were discriminating against rock and roll music."[79] Fans may have felt that the army unduly targeted their rock and roll star and cried about discrimination as a result. Country fans, however, understood this move. Some may have even expected it. Serving in the military came with the territory of white working-class life. The only anomaly was that Presley went in after he had achieved success and not as a precondition to learning his craft. Readers of *Country Song Roundup* even voted Presley as "Country Music's King" at the end of 1958. Army service would do little to dampen their fervor for what the magazine called the "Folk Music Fireball."[80]

On March 24, 1958, Presley reported for his induction at the Shelby County Draft Board. He took an oath of loyalty to the US government, received the serial number US53310761, and endured another physical examination at the Kennedy Veterans' Hospital. This inspection included stripping down to his underwear alongside twenty other draftees and volunteers, including two African American men. Outside, Presley's family, friends, and fans from all over the country congregated in the rain to wish him well.[81] His mother sobbed, comforted by his then-girlfriend Anita Wood, an aspiring actor from Jackson, Tennessee. Colonel Parker, never missing an opportunity to push his product, passed out *King Creole* balloons to promote the film that Presley recently wrapped.[82] The local and national press swarmed the occasion, simultaneously fascinated with Presley's induction and his fans' reactions. The singer summed up his thoughts in an offhanded comment picked up by the press. "If you think I'm nervous," he told the onlookers, "it's really because I am."[83] At twenty-three years old with fourteen gold records and four film credits, Presley had every right to feel nervous. His whole world seemed to vanish before his eyes. And, in a way, it did. The Presley who embodied conspicuous sexuality, the possibility of racial mixing, and a rebellion within the ranks of country music was vanishing. A transformation had begun. He boarded a bus bound for Fort Chaffee, Arkansas, and did not sing a note in public for more than two years.

With this initial induction process under way, Presley began a metamorphosis from the symbol of country music mutiny into a compliant subject of state power. An image from a *Life* magazine pictorial spread showed Private Presley in his underwear, weighing in, and having his height measured. A doctor stands to his left and holds the ruler positioned directly in front of Presley so that it divides his face in perfect symmetry. Behind him and to his right, one of the African American draftees waits for his turn on the scale.[84] These pictures conveyed clear messages about the rock and roller. First, the government had quelled Presley's revolution. He could not shake his hips or drop to his knees on this new stage of notoriety. The army had tamed the body of rebellion, measuring, weighing, and cataloging his once-dangerous corporeality for processing by the Defense Department. Second, Presley would interact with actual African Americans on Uncle Sam's terms for the next two years, not simply borrowing their cultural expressions to induce young women's screaming fits of ecstasy.

Nothing demonstrated this exertion of state power over Presley like the long-feared GI haircut at Fort Chaffee. On March 25, the new private sat for his shearing by the civilian barber James B. Peterson. The long sideburns fell first, followed by the long top that had glistened and swayed to the beat of Presley's music and inspired so much adolescent lust. The army had advanced the young millionaire $7 out of his monthly $78 check to pay for the haircut. Photographers and journalists surrounded Presley in the barber chair, catching his every move and utterance. As Peterson clipped the hair down to the regulation one-inch length, Presley picked up a tuft in his hand and blew. "Hair today and gone tomorrow," he joked. Nervous and probably bothered with the close media scrutiny, Presley forgot to pay and then forgot to wait for the change from paying for his trim. Peterson had to call him back, causing an embarrassing hiccup in his transformation into a soldier. Outside, Colonel Parker handed out cards bearing Presley's official statement, which read, "Heaven knows I want to thank you very much. I hope I can live up to what people expect of me."[85]

Both pop and country artists penned songs to cash in on Presley's entrance into the armed forces. The Threeteens, an all-girl trio out of Phoenix, Arizona, released the ballad "Dear 53310761" on Rev Records in May 1958 in tribute to Presley via his army serial number. The girls sing, "Dear 53310761 . . . In the barracks when the lights are low / Please remember how I miss you so." On the bridge, they address Presley by name: "Elvis dear, I'll be true. . . . I don't want an imitation / All I want is you," while the rock and roll guitarist Duane Eddy interjects a riff that sounds like "Taps" in between each line.[86] Radio stations latched onto this release for its promotional value. A disc jockey in Fort Worth, Texas, promised $100 to anyone who could bring in a dollar bill bearing the serial number. Trinity Music, the song's publishing firm, printed 50,000 replicas of Presley's army dog tags as promotional giveaways.[87] Vern Steirman, a jockey on KJOE in Shreveport, Louisiana, dropped fifty of the tags from a single engine plane over the city to promote the record.[88] And in Boston, a disc jockey offered to give away six advance copies of the replica dog tags to boys who showed up to the station with guitars and girls who showed up in bathing suits.[89]

Country singers penned songs that poked fun at Presley's tour of duty, as if they could finally express their true feelings once he was out of earshot. Bobby Bare scored his first hit in February 1959 with the Presley-inspired song "All American Boy," released on Fraternity Records. The label issued the single under the artist name of Bill Parsons, although Bare actually sang the first-person talking-blues tune in an imitation of Presley's vocal style. The song details the rise of a nameless rock and roller from Memphis who makes it big thanks to his guitar and "a man with a big cigar," only to find himself drafted into the military. The last verse ends the singer's career thanks to the call of duty from Uncle Sam himself, who says, "I'm-a gonna cut your hair / Take this rifle, kid / Gimme that guitar." Parsons sang the B-side, a forgettable tune called "Rubber Dolly."[90] Bare had recorded "All American Boy" while Parsons served in the army. Then, in a carousel of conscription, the army drafted Bare before Fraternity released the hit, meaning that as the tune ascended the charts, Parsons went on tour singing the song. Or, in the case of his appearance on *American Bandstand*, he lip-synced to Bare's voice. The tune peaked at number two on the *Billboard* "Hot 100" in February 1959, reached the top twenty on the R&B chart, sold over one million copies, and involved Fraternity Records in the payola scandal of the late 1950s.[91] Grandpa Jones released a banjo-heavy version on Decca in 1959 backed with "Pickin' Time," a song written by Johnny Cash.[92] The military offered a gift that just kept on giving for the country music industry in the 1950s.

Presley, the actual "All American Boy," led a fairly quiet existence as a soldier in the US Army Second Armored Division. After three days at Fort Chaffee, Presley entered basic training at Fort Hood, Texas, where WAC Lieutenant Colonel Marjorie Shulten ended the media bonanza, telling reporters, "there will be no more interviews or picture taking during his training."[93] The Texas sun even returned his hair to its natural color. According to one report, "Fort Hood officials said Elvis' hair is almost blond now, blaming this on the bleaching it has taken from the sun."[94] He returned to Memphis twice during his training in Texas, once on leave in June 1958 and again in August of that year when his mother died.[95] On September 22, he shipped out for West Germany, where he maintained a low profile. Presley distinguished himself in Germany mainly by the number of women he bedded in the private residence he maintained in the resort town of Bad Nauheim, a few miles from his post in Friedberg. He also met the adopted daughter of a US Air Force captain, fourteen-year-old Priscilla Beaulieu, whom he would bring to live with him in Memphis in 1963 and marry in 1967.[96]

By the time Presley received his discharge from the US Army in 1960, he had advanced to the rank of sergeant, matured into his role as the music industry's most famous soldier, and achieved a previously inconceivable level of respectability. He did so by serving quietly and removing himself from the music scene. Not that his music disappeared. Colonel Parker wisely socked away twenty-four songs for RCA before his cash cow entered the military and then released them slowly over the following two years.[97] But hearing Presley remained a different experience from seeing him. His corporeal presence disappeared—no hair swaying, no hip swinging, no riot-inducing sexual teases. Instead, fans had to remember the old Presley or imagine him in his uniform, a wholly different experience from the outlandish Lansky Brothers attire he had sported on his rise to fame.

· · · · · ·

The country music industry never abandoned Presley during his time in the ranks, and he did not forget his roots even as he transitioned from music to movie star after the army. In the spring of 1958, when the singer entered the service, RCA Nashville's Steve Sholes drew a line through the recent history of country music, connecting the dots between the demographic mixing that occurred in World War II to the rise of Elvis. "Country-Western music gained more popularity with the advent of World War II," he wrote, "when boys from all parts of the country were thrown together and their various tastes integrated." He rightly recalled how this taste mixing created opportunity for the country music industry to grow in popularity among the soldiers, believing it "a fact that during these years Country music had a heyday overseas, and many 'converts' were made." To him, rock and roll, or whatever label the buyers preferred, simply represented the next stage in the evolution of country. He justified Presley's presence in the country music industry one last time as the singer slipped into uniform, arguing that as rock and roll grew in mainstream popularity, "the time was ripe for the great phenomenon that was to effect the final firm merger of Country music to Pop—Elvis Presley. . . . The resulting combination was coined as 'Rock-A-Billy,' which dominates the music world today."[98] Presley belonged to Nashville as much as anywhere else, including in the ranks of the US Army.

In November 1959, just four months before Presley's discharge, *Country Song Roundup* claimed the singer's country bona fides again in an article called "Elvis Presley: A Teenage Tradition." Perhaps reminding readers with short attention spans of Presley's accomplishments, the article's author recounted how the singer had hit the music industry "with the impact of an

Atom Bomb," releasing "sixteen one million record sellers—which ranks right up there with the likes of Hank Williams, Frank Sinatra and Bing Crosby." And country listeners could rightly claim him. *Country Song Roundup* told its readers, "We Country music fans can be justifiably proud of E.P. 'cause he is one of us. He's a plain ole Country boy and he'll always be." Nothing proved how relatable he was like his military service. "Our boy 'Friday' will be comin' home soon—home from serving his country in Uncle Sam's Army way across the sea in Germany." The magazine encouraged readers to show how much Presley meant to them by going out and buying his next release.[99] The magazine's readers voted Presley fourth in their 1959 poll for "Country Music's King," less than one thousand votes behind the top three, Johnny Cash, Jim Reeves, and Johnny Horton.[100]

Country and rockabilly artists sprung to the occasion again with songs about Presley's return, trying to rekindle the success of "All American Boy." Bobby Bare returned home from his stint in the service to record "I'm Hanging Up My Rifle," released on Fraternity Records like his previous hit. Using the same melody and talking-blues structure, Bare's second attempt at chronicling Presley's military career in song fell flat.[101] This formula did not bring much success for Billy Adams and the Rock-a-teens either. The group recorded a takeoff of Bare's tune called "The Return of the All American Boy" for the independent label Nau-Voo Records. Adams did his best imitation of Bare imitating Presley, singing, "Listen here, cats, and I'll tell you a story / About the return of the all American boy. / It wasn't so bad after all, you see / 'Cause he's still rockin' in Germany."[102] Lightning would not strike twice.

On March 3, 1960, Presley landed at Fort Dix, New Jersey, for a two-hour press conference. Major Mark Bottorf spoke on behalf of the Defense Department and stated that the singer had "behaved himself in a manner so as to cast great credit on the Army." Colonel Parker made an appearance to claim that Sergeant Presley had earned a gross income of $1.6 million in 1959, all while living in virtual seclusion on duty for the US government.[103] Nancy Sinatra greeted the returning rocker with a box of shirts, a symbol of Presley's passage from juvenile delinquent and "Folk Music Fireball" into the mainstream of American pop.[104] Her father helped this metamorphosis in May 1960 by appearing with Presley in the rocker's comeback television special on *The Frank Sinatra Show*. John P. Shanley, a writer for the *New York Times*, barely contained his contempt for the display, calling Presley's release from the armed forces "one of the most irritating events since the invention of itching powder." "Although Elvis became a sergeant in the

Army, as a singer he has never left the awkward squad," Shanley sneered. "There was nothing morally reprehensible about his performance" on Sinatra's show, he assured his *Times* readers; "it was merely awful."[105] Country had finally come to town, albeit to mixed reviews.

While military service transformed Presley's image, it also changed how his pre-army fans related to him. *Bye Bye Birdie*, a fictionalized version of the events around Presley's military induction, explained just how dramatically his time in the service changed his public image. A stage version of *Bye Bye Birdie* opened to positive reviews in April 1960, and it became a film in 1963. Originally titled *Let's Go Steady*, the playwright Michael Stewart wrote the script about a fictional music star named Conrad Birdie, a take-off on the army veteran and rockabilly star Conway Twitty. Despite the name, Birdie's career most closely resembled Presley's, with rabid throngs of teenaged female fans, a scheming manager, and a ducktail hairdo. The army drafts Birdie. His manager responds with a plot to boost the sales of Birdie's song "One Last Kiss" by choosing one teenaged girl for Birdie to kiss on national television before he enters the service. *Billboard* included a review that called the stage version of *Bye Bye Birdie* "a sparkling show" culled "from rather scant material." The reviewer raved about the cast, which included Dick Van Dyke as Birdie's manager and Paul Lynde, who played the father of the teenaged girl selected to kiss Birdie.[106] Van Dyke and Lynde held onto their roles for the 1963 film version, which used Ann-Margaret, Presley's sometimes off-screen romantic interest, in the lead of Kim MacAfee, the winning teenager.[107]

The film opens with an iconic scene of Ann-Margaret singing the song "Bye Bye Birdie" as she dances against a solid blue background, a song that offers a way to map the evolution of female rock and roll fandom onto its production values. She sings in a pouty, childish voice during the opening sequence, beginning with the lines, "Bye Bye Birdie / I'm gonna miss you so. / Bye Bye Birdie / Why'd you have to go?" Her voice, high and plaintive, mimics the outsized despair expressed by so many female fans when Presley entered the military five years before the film's release. The engineers recorded the vocal track dry, exaggerating the thin, reedy quality of Ann-Margaret's whining delivery. The pianist plays the song's upbeat sixteenth notes in the middle register, adding to the song's innocence, as if the girl is singing in the family living room or in her childhood bedroom. "Bye Bye Birdie," she sings, "Guess I'll always care," and she gives a quick turn from the camera. So ends the first version of the song and the beginning of the end of her innocence.[108]

Ann-Margaret reprises the song at the film's end. A tonal shift has occurred that marks the emotional transformation her character has undergone during the film. The lyrics and the production of the music signal what
the listener realizes is a physical and emotional maturation. The vocal returns with reverb, adding body and depth to the song. The piano returns
but in the lower register. And she shifts her delivery. The teenaged girl is
gone. A woman takes her place. Her voice returns full and knowing, aged
by the lesson of fawning over a pop music idol only for the government to
rip him away and the record industry to use fans' emotional investment in
him to sell their latest song. The full-bodied, reverb-heavy production of
her voice signifies the maturation of her emotional and physical self. Her
character is resolved now to lose Birdie, a change heard in lines like, "The
army's got you now / I'll try, Birdie / To forget somehow," which she sings
with facetiousness. Ann-Margaret makes it clear that her adolescent lust is
gone, and her interest lies somewhere else now: "No more sighing / Each
time you move those lips / No more dying / when you twitch those hips. . . .
Bye Bye Birdie / Ta-ta ol' sweetie pie. . . . Time to say good-bye."[109]

Birdie/Presley could go to the army or not. Ann-Margaret and all the
young women for whom she sang were on flights of their own. When she
began the song and the film, Ann-Margaret's character idolized Conrad
Birdie, as so many white middle-class girls did with Presley. She would do
anything to meet him and felt outraged that the government would draft
the music star of her fantasies, again, just like the young women who wrote
President Eisenhower about the army's drafting of Presley. But two years
in the life of a teenager might as well be a geological epoch. When Presley
left for the army, many of those young women outgrew their infatuation
with the singer or moved on to one of the pop idols who emerged in Presley's absence. Many simply aged out of the screaming teenaged masses. The
movie made it clear just how that change had happened. The combined
power of the music industry and the government had conspired to close a
chapter of Presley's career.

By the time *Bye Bye Birdie* hit theaters, Presley had undergone his own
cinematic image transformation, documented by the 1960 film *GI Blues*, a
fictionalized version of his time stationed in West Germany. Presley stars
as Tulsa MacLean, a tank soldier with the Second Armored Division guard-
ing the Cold War's European front. Presley spends the entirety of the film
flirting with frauleins, conducting training drills, giving hell to his over-
bearing sergeant, and playing music in a combo with his fellow soldiers.
The real Presley never played live music in public while overseas, but the

opening scene offers a view into the real economic decisions that would have made military service an attractive option had the music industry not made him a millionaire. In this scene, Presley and his costar load large-caliber shells into a tank, shells that Presley could have made at Precision Tools had the movie been set during the Korean War. The older soldier complains to MacLean, Presley's character, about the long hours and hard manual labor of soldiering. He even threatens to abandon his post. MacLean shuts him up by ribbing back. "Ah, quit squawking. We've got a steady job, haven't we? Room and board, lots of fresh air, good hours, what else you want?"[110] Presley's character is only half joking here. As his name and accent suggest, MacLean is a soldier from the South, specifically Texas, doing his duty and happily collecting a government paycheck. What else could a young, white, working-class southern man want?

When MacLean does complain, he does so in a good-natured way, conveying the message that serving one's country is more of an inconvenience than a hardship. MacLean lists these benign grievances against military life in the title track, performed at the end of the film when he and his bandmates finally convince a local beer-hall owner to let them play. The Americans take over the stage from a local group featuring Scotty Moore, in lederhosen, who stays onstage to accompany the soldier-musicians. "GI Blues" sticks to an AAB twelve-bar-blues song structure, through which MacLean lodges his gripes against the army. He starts with the natural surroundings, describing his room, which overlooks "the beautiful Rhine," though he would prefer "a muddy old crick in Texas any old time." He then moves on to complain about German food and longs for a "slice of Texas cow," as well as bemoaning how the frauleins supposedly lead them on. The musical arrangement and its production contribute to the military feel of the song. Snare-drum rolls kick things off and remain high in the mix throughout the tune, making the musical accompaniment more like a marching cadence than a blues-based pop song. The chorus emphasizes this militaristic arrangement with the lines, "I got those hup, 2, 3, 4 occupation GI blues. . . . And if I don't go stateside soon, I'm gonna blow my fuse."[111] MacLean expresses his grief about military life, although it is not about the politics of Cold War anticommunism or US militarization. His complaint is about his job. He embeds his grievances in a double entendre on the word "occupation," signifying both the global spread of US soldiers on permanent military installations and the daily grind of working for the Defense Department.

Through the character of Tulsa MacLean, Presley reintroduced himself to the world as a respectable citizen with a clean-cut coiffure and GI khakis.

HAS ELVIS SURRENDERED TO "POP" MUSIC?

Just ask, "Who is the greatest name in the music business today," and whether you are talking to a teen-ager in Philadelphia, a Japanese house-wife, or a German frauelein, the answer will immediately be "Elvis Presley," accompanied more than not by squeals of delight. And yet, ironically, this wonderful kid who began as a Country and Western singer, and who then drifted into rock 'n' roll, has apparently abandoned both his Country heritage and Country music, not to mention the rock 'n' roll he gambled millions with, to popular music, and even operatic songs. Has Elvis forgotten his loyal Country fans who gave him his start, put him on top, and kept him there?

Elvis' roots in Country music are deep indeed. Born in Tupelo, Mississippi, in 1935, of poor and simple farm people, he was never-the-less brought up with love and kindness, and taught right from wrong by his father at an early age. Often as a boy of eleven, he and his mother would sing hymns and Folk songs down in the cellar during storms. Elvis' love for Country music was a part of his heritage, and is as much a part of him that to forget it would be to forget his life.

There are reasons, however, why it appears that the boy who has become the gold mine of the music industry has forsaken the Country-style songs which are a basic part of him and his music. When Elvis plunked down four dollars at Sun Records in 1953 and put a slow ballad on wax, Sam Phillips,

owner of Sun and a genius at discovering new talent, recognized something different in this boy's style.

Only eight weeks after his first record was released, Elvis guested on the nation's top C&W Show, "Grand Ole Opry," in Nashville, and appeared on "Louisiana Hayride," in Shreveport, where he was immediately booked as a regular. He then toured Arkansas, Louisiana and Texas. Wherever he went, he was a sensation. It seemed that the kids adopted him as their hero, and the number of Presley fans zoomed. Then, in November of 1956, RCA Victor bought Elvis' contract for $35,000.00, and brought him to New York. The rest is history.

It was Country music, however, that gave the "King" his start. He learned his style, his feeling for music, in fact his whole musical background from the Country song heritage in which he was brought up. By singing popular songs, Elvis is merely showing his versatility. Critics of this great talent have often accused him of being able to sing only rock 'n' roll and C&W songs. By offering popular arrangements he proves his ability to handle any type of song. Yet, his loyal Country fans, whom he regards as his best and most loyal fans, will never be abandoned by Elvis. It is when he is singing an old-fashioned Country tune, the kind he loved as well as a boy in Tupelo, that he is happiest — and his fans are too. And Elvis will return to his first love soon. He must — it's part of his life.

Juliet Prowse, Elvis and the director of "G.I. Blues," huddle on location

Have no fear gals — Elvis will always remain true to all of his fans

Has Presley Deserted His Western Fans For The "City Music" Lovers....?

Lucky, lucky girl — imagine being "bussed" by the great one

The Presley star will continue to glow just as long as the guys and gals dig the very best in note sounds

COMMUNITY FAIR

FIGURES 4.4 & 4.5 An article and collection of images from the fan magazine *Country Song Roundup* questioned Elvis Presley's country authenticity after his stint in the US Army. To Presley's base of country fans, it appeared that their "hillbilly cat" had ventured too far into the pop side of the music industry. The singer's role in *GI Blues* seemed to confirm those suspicions, after which Presley presented a more sanitized version of his public persona and began his ascent toward matinee and pop star status. (*Country Song Roundup*, July 1961, courtesy of the Country Music Hall of Fame and Museum)

On the surface, this patriotic Presley bore little resemblance to the hyper-sexual star of his pre-army days. The sideburns vanished. He danced in *GI Blues*, but gone were the riot-inducing hip thrusts. And the demands of the soundtrack subdued the music to a caricature of the rocking country music that Presley had used to achieve pre-army fame. No longer "morally insane," Presley appeared to have shed his reputation as a social degenerate and reemerged as a worker in the defense of US capitalist democracy against the encroachment of Soviet communism. At least superficially, Presley appeared to have conducted one of the most striking transformations in the history of US popular music—from delinquency to duty, from punk to patriot.

Nothing signaled this transformation like the official endorsement of the government. As the opening credits rolled, audiences learned that Paramount Pictures filmed *GI Blues* "with the full cooperation of the US Army and the Department of Defense."[112] It took Presley's serving his country in isolation from the music industry, but he finally won the approval of the US military. *GI Blues* not only benefited Presley's image but also gave the US Army a powerful recruitment tool, two years after denying Presley a place in the Special Services. The following year, AFRTS even began incorporating rock and roll into its playlists for the first time.[113]

With Presley's star turn in *GI Blues*, he announced to the world that he had changed. His country fans even sensed an evolution that threatened to usher him away to the lofty heights of pop stardom. But here was the ruse. Presley never needed to change because military service was nothing out of the ordinary for someone like him. Having participated in ROTC training at Humes High School and manufactured ammunition at Precision Tool for the Korean War, he might have ended up in the military before his draft notice had his music career not taken off the way it did. Working for the federal government as a soldier offered an auspicious alternative to the manual labor to which he was probably destined for the rest of his life as a white, working-class Memphian with a high school education. Serving in the military could open collaborative opportunities and valuable woodshedding time for aspiring musicians, as his Sun Records labelmates knew. The only extraordinary thing about Presley's military career was its timing. Outside of his fame and in the eyes of the government, Presley was just another working-class draftee converted into serial number 53310761, a pretty catchy set of digits for the Threeteens.

Presley returned to Nashville for his first recording session after the army in March 1960. Back in the RCA studios, he cut "Stuck on You" and "Fame and Fortune," a single that reached number one on the *Billboard*'s Hot 100, number six on the R&B chart, and number twenty-seven on the country chart.[114] He may have sold millions of records, traveled the globe, served his country in uniform, and returned to international fanfare, but Presley knew where his musical home was. He came home to Nashville. Yet his time in the ranks improved his image to such a degree that Hollywood beckoned. No longer a threat to the racial or class hierarchies of white middle-class audiences, parents felt comfortable with post-army Presley. The newly respectable Presley spent the bulk of the 1960s as a film star, making mostly forgettable, highly formulaic, highly profitable musicals. He left Nashville and his country audiences behind in the process. After "Stuck on You," Presley would score only one other country hit, the ubiquitous "Are You Lonesome Tonight?," before his 1968 comeback.[115]

The Nashville music industry, thanks to an assist from its allies in the Defense Department, weathered Presley's threat to upset the sounds of southern whiteness that predominated in country music. In fact, Presley's tenure as a soldier reinforced the marketability and the bankability of the alliance between country music and the US military. The country industry embarked on a mission at the dawn of the 1960s to make its genre a truly global phenomenon. For nearly a decade, country artists had helped sell people on the idea of military service. It was time to use the full potential of the Cold War military to sell people on country music.

5   Best Liked World-Wide

Selling the Armed Forces and the World on Country Music

In the early 1960s, Tom Daniels held a job that allowed him to serve his country and the country music industry simultaneously. As a sergeant in the US Army, Daniels hosted two country music shows for members of the US Armed Forces, their dependents, and the millions of civilian "shadow" listeners across Europe who tuned in to the Allied Forces Network (AFN), the continent's branch of the AFRTS. His first show each day, *Hillbilly Reveille*, began with Daniels's eager announcement, "It's six-o-five, and your 'Hillbilly Reveille' is coming to you alive," before treating audiences to the latest in country and western sounds. If listeners missed that show, they could catch the next one later that day. *Stickbuddy Jamboree*, Daniels's afternoon slot, began at 3:05 every afternoon. According to the *Billboard* reporter Omer Anderson, the afternoon show attracted "the biggest listening audience of any European program—in any language—on the air at that time." Daniels already knew about the affinity that the military had for country music before he landed his AFN gig in Europe. He had served stateside as emcee for the radio version of the army recruitment program *Country Style, U.S.A.* and a similar show sponsored by the US Air Force called *Country Music Time.*[1] Now, instead of recruiting country listeners to the military, he recruited military listeners to the fold of country fans.

Although Daniels received his paycheck from the US government, his labor primarily benefited members of a newly formed organization headquartered in Nashville called the Country Music Association (CMA). Formed in 1958, the CMA acted as a "Chamber of Commerce" for country music, promoting the genre's economic growth while improving its image as a respectable style of music.[2] When the CMA formed, the country music industry had reached a point of crisis. Rock and roll had stolen many of its young fans. And though Elvis Presley's roots lay in country, his connection to the genre proved too ambiguous—and his crossover pop success too meteoric—for Nashville to claim him as its own without reservation. Record sales had waned, too, as had the amount of country music on the radio. Even when the country industry experienced success and threatened pop music's profits, critics had labeled the genre as "trash" and endangered its business model by proposing the Smathers Bill. The CMA promised to reverse those fortunes, snap the industry into shape, and deliver real economic gains for those who remained in the country corner.

One of the key players in this new organization was its founding president, Connie B. Gay. Having built his multimillion-dollar media empire with country music and burnished the genre's image in Washington, DC, Gay began to do the same for the genre as a whole. Gay's vision for the CMA included growing country music's share of radio airplay, developing more personal-appearance opportunities for the genre's artists, and increasing the number of country records purchased by fans around the globe.

The industry's ever-growing relationship with the Defense Department played a key role in making those dreams of global popularity into a reality. Sometimes that help came through the presence of country fans working at radio stations on military installations scattered around the world. Thanks to disc jockeys on Europe's AFN and the Far East Network in the Pacific, Gay and the CMA leaders could rely on their allies in the military, many of whom joined the CMA, to cater to fans in faraway places and cultivate new audiences for country music in international markets. That grassroots connection continued to grow through fandom within the military. In response to soldier demand, CMA-affiliated artists like Roy Acuff and Hank Snow committed their time and labor to the USO, touring military installations in Europe and Asia in the early 1960s.

But the growth of this connection also came from the top—through direct orders by the Defense Department. The AFRTS convinced Joe Allison, another founding member of the CMA and one of country music's most successful disc jockeys, to host a radio show for the military, called *Country Corner*, that aired from 1963 to 1970, twice a day in some markets. The US Army and Air Force Recruitment Service also continued using the genre in its efforts to encourage volunteer enlistment. Those efforts only intensified during the early 1960s, when the threat of nuclear war and communist encroachment put the Kennedy and Johnson administrations, the Pentagon, and civilian citizens on edge. Not only did the United States need men enlisting to defend capitalist democracy, but the Pentagon wanted country music to inspire citizens to take up arms and defend a specific version of US heritage that the music helped to define.

In the process, the Defense Department transformed from a pipeline for country music's promotion efforts to a vested partner. The more soldiers heard country music on the AFRTS and through live performances, the more they wanted to purchase the music by their favorite artists. This persistent country music programming delivered a significant boost in record sales for Nashville, a primary concern for the CMA, thanks to the army's network of post exchange stores (PX). In 1960, PX officials in Europe noted that country music outsold all other genres that year.[3] By the end of the decade, country would make up at least 65 percent of all records purchased at PXs on the continent.[4] And, in true soldierly fashion, the military helped defend country music by policing the public image of the genre. The Pentagon banned all denigrating descriptions of the genre as "hick" music in armed forces print or audio media in 1965.[5] Speaking ill of country music through a military channel risked running afoul of Defense Department policy, giving Nashville's musical products the official protection of the US government.

This reciprocal relationship between the Defense Department and Music Row revealed two truths about the country music business at the dawn of the 1960s. First, the industry's participation in military recruitment campaigns and the CMA's desire to grow an international audience had connected the genre with the broader Cold War aims of the US government. As the nation most identified with the ideology of capitalist democracy, the US used both soft-power propaganda and military might to stave off the spread of communism. Country music's midcentury militarization meant that the genre sat at the intersection of that need for cultural influence and military labor power.

Second, the overwhelming whiteness of the country music industry signaled that the military's musical recruitment programs would maintain the racial status quo at a time of increased civil rights activism in and out of the ranks. Music Row was only a quick, segregated bus ride away from the lunch counters where Black activists forced Nashville's businesses to end Jim Crow laws in 1960. Two years later, President Kennedy launched the Committee on Equal Opportunity in the Armed Forces to address the continual existence of racial discrimination in the military. Yet, in Nashville and in the nation's military-industrial complex, country music dominated the soundscape, helping the CMA build wealth and influence with the help of the Cold War defense state.

Selling the CMA

When the WSM Disc Jockey Convention met in November 1958, Jack Stapp, the president of Tree Publishing, announced the formation of a new organization called the Country Music Association. Hounded by bad press over the Smathers Bill hearings, the continuing popularity of rock and roll, and a nagging public image as music for "hillbillies," Nashville's music business launched a new strategy to shore up the financial future of country music. Stapp's address to the disc jockeys and other businesspeople gathered in Nashville represented nothing less than a call to arms in defense of the genre. He told the audience gathered in Music City, "Country music has helped to house you and your family, it has medicated your children," and, perhaps most importantly, the music was "helping you to utilize your American heritage to progress and gather for yourself not only the necessities of life, but some of its luxuries."[6] In essence, Stapp wanted the businesspeople gathered in Nashville that weekend to help him help themselves by growing country music's popularity. This new organization promised to give them the direction and vision to make that happen.

The creation of the CMA grew out of frustration with the Country Music Disc Jockey Association (CMDJA), a group founded in 1953 by the businessmen Ken Nelson, Connie B. Gay, and others with the mission of formally organizing the country music industry for the first time. As such, the CMDJA sought to institute professional standards for the genre's DJs and create a reputation for members as objective mediators of good taste in the music. The CMDJA even promoted itself as "the Voice of America's Music" in a bid to claim genre-specific authenticity while also suggesting that country music represented a distinctly American sound with nationwide appeal.[7] Despite the group's intentions, it did little to advance the actual commercial prospects of the genre. Gay commented that members of the CMDJA would gather annually "to do a little drinking and a little tomcatting around Nashville and telling lies to each other and so forth, arguing about whether such and such a record was really hillbilly or . . . whether or not a thing called a 45-rpm would ever work or a 33 1/3-rpm would ever work."[8] The CMDJA did not have a cohesive plan to advance the financial interests of the country industry.

In contrast, the CMA came into being with an ambitious commercial strategy that envisioned country music's worldwide popularity, if not global dominance, and enlisted members from every corner of the business. An eighteen-person board of directors would steer the executive decisions of

FIGURE 5.1
The CMA logo featuring the "Best Liked World-Wide" slogan as it appeared on issues of its monthly publication *Close-Up* from its beginning in 1959 through the mid-1970s. (Courtesy of the Country Music Hall of Fame and Museum)

the organization. These members represented different sectors of the industry, including publishers, artists, managers, disc jockeys, radio stations, record labels, trade publications, and songwriters.[9] According to its charter, this board dedicated the CMA to the "fostering, publicizing, and promoting of country music, by bringing the commercial possibilities of country music to the attention of advertisers, advertising agencies, station managers, and radio and TV networks."[10]

Those grand designs even made their way into the organization's logo, a musical note stylized to look like a globe and draped in a banner with its slogan, "Best Liked World-Wide." The CMA's newsletter, *Close-Up*, featured this design at the top of its monthly issues, which began publication in 1959. Although the logo reflected little more than a dream in the beginning, the CMA began coalescing different parts of the country music business to turn that statement of faith into real economic benefits for the fledging industry. The logo also reflected the country music industry's cultural politics. The industry's business leaders had latched onto and facilitated the broader militarization of US life following World War II. Now, the CMA aligned itself fully with the growth of the Cold War military occupation. Country music went where the armed forces went. The Pentagon's mission was country music's mission. For the CMA, becoming "World-Wide" went hand-in-hand with country music militarization.[11]

Connie B. Gay served as the CMA's founding president, and few other people possessed more potential to usher in the commercial boom that the organization hoped to find. He had positioned himself as one of the most important players in the country music business by amassing a personal fortune. As CMA president, he threw his efforts into improving the prospects of the country music industry as a whole. Looking back on the beginning of the organization, Gay gave credit to the early years of the CMA for growing the country music industry beyond its commercial plateau. In an interview conducted sixteen years after the organization's start, Gay cautioned, "And let's not forget that had it not been for CMA and those early people who started the CMA, country music would still be way, way, way down the hill, as far as I'm concerned." He also marveled at how the "CMA became a fantastically operative organization fairly fast" in the first few years under his leadership.[12] The group started with thirty-seven lifetime members and 160 annual members, but its rolls grew to include fifty lifetime members and 600 annual members by the end of 1961.[13]

The quickness of that success belied the financial struggles the CMA faced at its beginning. The organization depended on what essentially amounted to charity for its income. That altruism flowed from fundraising concerts, membership dues, and donations. A series of benefit shows in early 1959 gave the group an initial fund of around $15,000, but this money did not last long. When members gathered for the first annual CMA banquet at the end of that year, the group's treasurer told them plainly, "Money is what we need and what we have very little of." Three months later, in February 1960, the CMA had less than $800 in the bank.[14] Gay remembered, "In the early days we had no money, we had no members, we had nothing but just about a dozen of us who had a dream and had an idea." Still, the CMA just "took off," in his estimation, because "it was standing at the right place at the right time."[15]

The organization's fortunes did turn around quickly, but Gay's memory of dreams, ideas, and serendipity does little to explain the association's success. From its beginning, the CMA knew that the key to growing country music's commercial power rested in getting more music to more audiences. And, if Music Row wanted more people listening to country music, then it needed more of its artists on the radio. More artists on the air would lead to more record sales. It was, and still is, a simple formula. But pushing more country music onto radio proved harder than ever in the 1950s.

The country music industry suffered from a severe lack of its product on air, particularly in the wake of the rock and roll boom. The genre had achieved a high point in 1953, when 65 percent of domestic civilian stations played at least one country music show. This market share declined steadily

over the remainder of the decade. By 1961, the amount of AM stations playing at least one country show dropped to 36 percent.[16] Connie Gay never
lagged in his ambition to elevate the status and commercial power of the
genre. He continued to play an important part in keeping country music on
the air with the stations he owned and programmed. Besides maintaining
his *Town and Country Jamboree* and Jimmy Dean shows in the late 1950s,
he also bought station WGAY in Silver Spring, Maryland (a station whose
call letters predated his involvement), and made it the first all-country station on the FM band.[17]

Not everyone could simply purchase and convert a radio station to country. For most other promoters, one of the most effective ways of pushing
the music was placing it in advertisements. These country-themed ads could
air on any station, regardless of how many country programs it played. At
the 1958 WSM Disc Jockey Festival, the same event where Jack Stapp announced the creation of the CMA, industry leaders told record spinners and
radio station owners about the power of matching country music with the
right promotional sponsors. Two thousand attendees gathered at the War
Memorial Auditorium in Nashville for two days of workshops. The first day's
meeting featured RCA's Jack Burgess, Ray Morris of Pet Milk, and Connie B.
Gay. Morris spoke about the successful use of country music as a promotional tool for Pet Milk on 200 radio stations around the nation. He believed
that country music generated more revenue per dollar spent than any
other type of music. Gay delivered an address titled "The Growth of
Country Music and Its Place in Your Future," which predicted an upcoming
boom for the genre and received an ovation for his bullish outlook.[18] This
vision of country music's expansion included the continual growth in
overseas markets. Correspondents for the National Broadcast Corporation
from London, Berlin, and Tokyo told the disc jockeys about the popularity
of the genre in their respective cities. People in those locales loved country
music and saw it as an extension of the United States' post–World War II
military mission. To that end, the Berlin correspondent received an especially warm reception when he told the audience, "What the Russians fear
most is your country music."[19]

The next insight into country music's market potential tied into this same
understanding of the genre's relationship to Cold War militarization. Colonel
Vernon W. Rice, one of the men who had studied the *Opry* on a visit in 1957
and then launched *Country Style, U.S.A.*, gave a speech called "Your Full-
est Public Service Advantage thru Country Music." He praised the unique
qualities of country music and the music's ability to support successful re-

cruitment campaigns.[20] As the director of recruiting publicity for the US Army and Air Force, Rice was then working closely with country music labels, studios, artists, and station owners. His speech to the workshop that day reflected his use of public service announcements for the dual purpose of promoting the military and country music. He understood the genre's potential and urged others to use the music's appeal to push their particular message through public service announcements, as the Department of Defense had done. But whereas Rice's interest remained focused on gaining new soldiers through country-themed enticement, the country music industry understood those new recruits as something else: potential record buyers.

Selling Military Records

The US Armed Forces began selling records to servicemembers in 1947. That year, *Billboard* feverishly reported that the military's PXs had opened a "new retail record market, with potential sales volume of 1,000,000 disks a month and up." These outlets accounted for more than 800 domestic and foreign retail sites, including the army and air force PXs, as well as with the navy, coast guard, marine, and Veterans' Administration stores. The development of the record sections started in the foreign exchanges, where PX officers had experimented by buying several thousand records from Polish and Italian manufacturers. The PXs sold out of these foreign-made offerings quickly. In response, the exchanges decided to institute permanent record sections and to purchase from US distributors.[21]

Billboard's report could barely contain its excitement at the sales potential for the military market. The trade magazine expected record-store owners to complain about the government entering the retail record business since the armed forces could sell music without sales tax, possibly undercutting civilian retailers. However, since the military stores did not specialize in record sales and could only carry a limited amount, the magazine believed that the PX would stock and sell "just enough to get the soldier or sailor interested in disks and act as a stimulant for the dealers."[22]

The addition of phonograph records to the PX inventory promised the music industry a much-needed boost after the fifteen-year slump of the Great Depression and World War II. Consumer demand for records had plummeted during the 1930s. Likewise, a shellac shortage caused by wartime rationing had limited the available number of records for purchase in the first half of the 1940s. The desire and fandom for music never abated, and radio exploded in popularity thanks to a lull in consumer purchasing power and governmental policies. But, with the economy's reconversion to civilian products, the music industry set its sights on regaining lost ground in the retail record market.[23] According to *Billboard*, the record industry hoped that a military tour of duty might prime the pump for the soldier-consumer's demand for popular music records and eventually deliver a bonanza for the recording industry.

The PX provided government assistance to the music business by creating an outlet to reach US soldiers, sailors, and airmen who often had no other method of buying US goods. The government, as well as private retailers, had long understood that soldiers were also consumers. The War Department established the PX system in 1895 to provide a government-regulated retail outlet for soldiers. These stores replaced the civilian dealers, known as "sutlers," who had trailed US armies since the Revolution and who often took economic advantage of soldiers' lack of access to other shopping options. The PX offered something different. The War Department mandated that each installation in each branch of service have a PX, a place for soldiers and sailors to buy products beyond the basic necessities of nutrition and hygiene. The availability of comfort items like magazines and nonperishable food injected a boost to morale by enlivening the drudgery and boredom of military life.[24]

PXs expanded their list of items during World War I and then began stocking products that appealed to servicemembers and their families. By the late 1940s and the US military's extended peacetime occupation of nations in Europe and Asia, the PXs more closely resembled the domestic consumer economy's modern-day retail experience. During the Korean War, the Defense Department even initiated Operation REINDEER, which opened stores in the conflict zones so that active combat soldiers could purchase Christmas gifts. Fifteen years later in Vietnam, these frontline stores offered soldiers in the thick of battle everything from chewing gum and cigarettes to portable radios and "girlie" magazines.[25]

The number and variety of records at the PX grew steadily with the rest of its inventory over the 1950s, and the music industry took notice. *Billboard*'s Ren Grevatt reported in February 1957 that the army and air force PXs located in thirty nations around the world sold about $6 million worth of records each year. Long-playing albums (LPs) accounted for 70 percent of these sales overall and 80 percent of sales on bases located in Japan. The popularity of this format bucked the civilian buying patterns of the mid-1950s, which began trending toward the 45 rpm singles that had hit the market in 1949. Grevatt explained the disproportionate popularity of the LP with soldiers due to the format's portability. Soldiers had to maintain their readiness to move from post to post with a minimal amount of personal gear. "The buyer is aware that someday he'll have to move all his possessions back home," Grevatt told the music industry's readers. The average soldier preferred LPs because "he can get more playing time per space occupied with LPs." Grevatt also reiterated the music industry's excitement at the volume of records purchased by the United States' Cold War occupiers.[26]

The industry was as interested in the genre of the records that soldiers bought as it was in the volume of sales. Grevatt notified readers that 50 percent of soldiers' LP purchases went to pop records, 30 percent to classical, and 20 percent to jazz.[27] The age of LP buyers helped explain this ratio. PX shopping attracted older, career soldiers with dependents who bought more of these genres than anything else. *Army Times* also helped cultivate a military market for these styles, particularly jazz and pop. Beginning in the early 1950s, the paper featured a column written by Ted Sharpe called "Music on Record," which directed soldiers to the latest releases by mainstream jazz performers like Stan Getz, Oscar Peterson, and Rosemary Clooney. With Sharpe's guidance, soldiers stationed anywhere in the world could then purchase the most current recommended records at the PX and feel relatively up-to-date with the newest sounds of the domestic music scene.[28] The music industry knew and understood these types of consumers. LP buyers represented the striving postwar middle class whose consumer habits mapped onto the purchase patterns of their civilian counterparts who paid more money for long-playing records to spin on their new hi-fi component stereos.[29]

But if PX album sales mirrored what the industry understood as middle-class, adult civilian preferences, the military's singles sales also reflected civilians' love of genres like country and R&B that depended on sustained radio play to gain crossover momentum. Grevatt wrote that no genre dominated these 45 rpm sales, "owing to the fact that the same crossover of pop, rhythm and blues, and country material in effect here also exists across the water." He attributed this to "the influence of the Armed Forces Radio Service, which receives and programs at all its overseas outlets the same records that are being played on Stateside radio stations."[30]

Grevatt made a simple point for those in the music industry who were willing to listen. Soldiers bought the singles they heard on the air. If artists and labels wanted to appeal to the deployed servicemembers, they would need to get more radio airtime. Grevatt stated how "new records are received at even the most remote bases within two weeks of their release here." In particular, they bought rhythm and blues artists like Bill Doggett and Fats Domino, who had experienced some crossover pop success, along with the crooners Perry Como and Frank Sinatra. Grevatt stated that even Elvis Presley, "whom some believe has a stronger following among female teen-agers, is one of the top sellers among the military buyers."[31] AFRTS may not have officially programmed rock and roll until 1961, but it regularly spun crossover hits, making the PX another lucrative market for the niche artists with enough appeal to hit the pop charts. The 1957 report delivered an important message for the country music industry. More products on the AFRTS would equal more record sales at the PX.

This revelation marked the beginning of a change in the relationship between the government and the country music industry. No longer would Nashville rely on occasional tours, word-of-mouth promotion, and amateur performances to grow the genre's popularity. It also need not rely on proximity to country fans in the ranks in order to convert skeptics into believers. It would need to promote the recorded sounds produced in Nashville to soldiers and sailors through the armed forces radio to encourage the purchase of country records. This market analysis corresponded with the military's use of country music as a recruitment tool and reflected the strategy to push the genre's product to the armed forces. The army had announced the launch of *Country Style, U.S.A.* on television in June 1957, only a few months before the PX report.[32] If country music could turn fans into soldiers, then surely the military could help turn soldiers into country music record buyers. Music Row only needed a way to get more of its records on the air, even if no one was sure exactly how many country records servicemembers would buy.

In late 1958, on the heels of the CMA's formation, *Billboard* published the latest PX record sales numbers and called the Cold War military "the most music-conscious, music-loving, music-appreciating fighting force in the history of armies." John J. Ryan, a writer for *Army Times,* had used his connections to the Department of Defense to study the PX's sales potential and linked that sales point to the music industry. By his account, PXs had emerged as "the largest single customer for the music record industry." Soldiers and their dependents represented 6 million PX customers, who spent an estimated $8 for every soldier in the service. The armed forces bought 20 million records from the PX and spent another $7.5 million on record players each year. Like Grevatt's report, Ryan found that soldiers preferred the "unbreakable LP" over singles at a ratio of three to one. He also repeated the genre preferences among soldiers, who continued to favor pop over their second-favorite category, classical.[33]

Ryan could make these claims because he had spent ten years working for the Army Exchange Service before transitioning into a career in writing and publishing.[34] In 1957, he left the army and completed an intensive study of the PX market, describing the potential for retail sales and the centrality of the PX to morale. He published his findings as a book called *Selling the Armed Forces Consumer Market: The Military Market Handbook*. He also contributed a condensed version to *Army Times* that explained the "enigmatic nature" of the PX, which "operates stores in the most inaccessible spots, yet it must operate as efficiently as any civilian merchandising chain."[35] This paradoxical existence was what made the PX so ripe for robust record sales. The stores had to stock the items that soldiers desired, no matter their location or profit margin. And, as it turned out, one thing soldiers wanted was country music records.

The sale of 45 rpm singles hinted at the growing popularity of country music among servicemembers when they could actually access those records. Unfortunately for those fans stationed overseas, PX purchasing agents did not yet prioritize the genre. As *Billboard* reported, "only the top pop singles make it" to the international posts due to the practicality of trying to fulfill the taste preferences. Niche genres took a backseat. However, the genre of singles sold at stateside PXs matched the civilian buying patterns. Pop still dominated these 45 rpm sales, but Ryan revealed that soldiers showed "perhaps a shade of preference for country and western in certain areas."[36] He suggested selling to soldiers through mail-order record clubs, thereby bypassing the PX in order to satisfy the military's demand for specific artists and genres.

These statistics gave Ryan the confidence to predict that the military record market would grow by 7 percent in the following year. Conveniently, he thought that record sellers should market these record clubs through servicemembers' newspapers, believing that "the greatest sales promotion lies in reaching all Armed Forces personnel, both domestic and overseas, thru the world-wide editions of the Army Times, Air Force Times, Navy Times and the American Weekend."[37] Self-interest aside, Ryan was right. More and more US soldiers bought and listened to records as a way to break the boredom and monotony of peacetime service. The PX continued to provide soldiers and their dependents with easy access to the latest pop releases and a growing number of records in specialized genres like country.

If country music's record labels and artists wanted to tap the full potential of the PX market and move soldiers' interest in the genre past "a slight shade of preference," then it would need to place even more of its products on the radio.

······

Gay and the CMA worked to maintain the business connections between Nashville and the Pentagon at the same time that writers were reporting these record-purchasing patterns. In April 1960, *Close-Up* announced that Chief Warrant Officer Charles S. Brown had arrived in Nashville from his post in New York City to record "more than 30 quarter-hour shows, featuring C&W artists." The newsletter referred to Brown as one of the "brains" of the military who "realize the value of Country Music in their promotions for recruiting men."[38] Gay had known about and facilitated the military's use of country music recruitment for his personal gain since 1953. Now, as president of the CMA, he welcomed the continuation of these kinds of campaigns to boost the overall profile of the genre.

The CMA recognized the AFRTS as a partner in growing country music's popularity and seized on the military's potential to make "Best Liked World-Wide" an actuality rather than an aspiration. In July 1960, an English country music enthusiast named George Haxell wrote to *Close-Up* to tell the CMA about a magazine he had started in 1954 called *Country-Western Express* for fans in the United Kingdom. There, a small but devoted number of record collectors were obsessed with Jimmie Rodgers, the Carter Family, and other foundational artists from the first generation of hillbilly recording artists. He claimed, "The British Broadcasting Company turned a 'deaf ear' to our pleas for a country music show on disc." Still, interest in contemporary country music grew in the United Kingdom, which helped to expand the distribution of *Country-Western Express*. Haxell credited that growth primarily "to the excellent record programs aired by the American Forces Network in Germany." The US government supplemented the country music content that the British government denied these fans. Haxell could report to *Close-Up* that "Country Music records are being issued in ever-increasing quantities per month. Nearly every music magazine or daily newspaper with a music column carries some indication of the steady progress being made by Country & Western Music."[39]

The CMA celebrated news of other international country music scenes, always linking the music's proliferation to the AFRTS. An editor of the Dutch publication *Hillbilly Hayride* named B. William Schipper wrote to *Close-Up* in 1960, asking, "Are you aware of the fact that Country Music has become an international movement?" He then went on to list the major accomplishments that he and other Dutch promoters had achieved since 1956. Those achievements included issuing more country record releases, putting more country shows on the radio, generating public interest, and getting country songs in the Dutch pop charts. Schipper had written to the CMA with a request for more records and publicity material from the United States.[40] In 1961, a Swiss country music promoter named Charles Steiner founded a country music chart that would register the hottest tunes on the continent. According to *Close-Up*, he compiled his rankings "by checking tunes most requested on the American Forces Network and by checking sales reports."[41] With these kinds of details, the CMA essentially issued instructions to country artists and businesspeople: place your music on the AFRTS, and expand your market reach to encompass the globe. This type of market expansion could move the organization *that* much closer to achieving its vision of worldwide popularity.

Military broadcasters remained an active partner in the CMA's mission at the dawn of the 1960s, and country music remained part of the military's Cold War soft-power campaign. In November 1961, *Close-Up* ran four related articles on one page under the headline "Country Music Reflects Pulse of Unrest in Germany." One of the pieces detailed the weaponization of country music against the communists in East Berlin. Apparently, locals in West Berlin "fired a fusillade of Country Music across the dividing line in Berlin via the airways," which enraged the "Reds."[42] Another article described how a seventeen-year-old from West Berlin named Benno Haupl had written to *Close-Up* to declare himself a "pistol packin' son-of-a-gun and blue folksong fan #1." He hoped to join the CMA on the condition that "the Russians do not come here." To prove his loyalty, Haupl published a fan magazine and served as president of the Stickbuddy Jamboree Club of West Berlin, a reference to Sergeant Tom Daniels's show on the AFN.[43]

The same issue of *Close-Up* described the steady stream of Nashville talent making its way across the waters to US servicemembers. The Jim Denny Artist Bureau sent the *Opry* stars George Morgan and George Jones, himself a Marine Corps veteran, to Asia for weeks, with stops in Japan, Okinawa, and South Korea, and sent the Carter Family, Kitty Wells, and the bluegrasser Jimmy Martin to Europe. The piece also recognized the enduring popularity of Hank Snow and Roy Acuff among the troops. With the pipeline of musicians flowing from Nashville to international installations, the writer surmised that "the trend seems to bear out the CMA slogan to the hilt—'Country Music, Best Liked World Wide.'"[44]

These kinds of reports during the fall of 1961 cued the programmers at the AFN into the growing interest in the estimated 30 million foreign civilian listeners who tuned in daily to hear US country music. Based in West Germany, the network promised to increase the amount of what *Close-Up* called "this All-American commodity" and noted that "AFN people say C&W requests outnumber all other requests by far."[45] In response to that demand, the AFN increased the quantity of country music on air by 35 percent. *Billboard* reported that this expansion would include a "daily hour-long network program of c.&w. and in addition will schedule special Saturday programs on c.&w. themes."[46] Tom Daniels's *Stickbuddy Jamboree* and *Hillbilly Reveille* remained fan favorites on the continent, as well as the transcription broadcasts of the *Grand Ole Opry*.[47] Over in the Pacific, the CMA member US Air Force Staff Sergeant "Ol' Buddy" Al Lynch began hosting a country music show on KSBK, the "only English-language commercial station in Okinawa," in 1962.[48] Lynch also successfully petitioned the PXs in Okinawa to carry more country music records, endearing him to the CMA and earning a mention in the *Close-Up*'s international news.[49] These market reports and testimonies from country music enthusiasts in foreign lands pointed toward a correlation between record sales and spins on the AFRTS networks, signaling to the CMA that nurturing the military connection overseas was worth the effort.

The CMA had reason to believe that cultivating the military connection could boost the bottom line for Music Row and grow the popularity of the genre overseas. Near the end of 1961, *Billboard* reported that country music sales in the European PXs had jumped from 65 to 75 percent during the Christmas shopping season. One GI described the appeal of country music in relation to US foreign policy and homesickness. He owned hundreds of country records and claimed that soldiers stationed abroad "are all a little keyed up": "We don't know what's ahead. We're all thinking of home more than ever before, and country music is the music of home for all of us." The desire for country music also translated into successful ticket sales for artists. Country performers from the United States drew sellout crowds on their tours of the European bases. The tour manager for Hank Snow relayed, "Americans overseas are starved for country and western music. The boys played to packed houses at every stop, and the foot-stomping and cheering applause was tremendous. Never saw anything like it." That enthusiasm for the music increased sales so much that the PXs could not keep up with the demand due to the limited number of records sent by domestic record companies. One PX buyer said, "Some American producers seem to regard c.&w. with lofty disdain, as something too vulgar to soil their hands with. From our point of view, this is a tragic mistake."[50]

The "lofty disdain" identified by this Exchange officer was real. For many critics and PX purchasing agents, country music muddled the distinction between hominess and hokum. It marked the taste of the unwashed and unread. In 1961, *Stars and Stripes* stirred the debate over musical taste and the question of country music's cultural value when it printed the UPI entertainment writer Vernon Scott's review of the television program *Five Star Jubilee*. His article, derisively titled "Twang, Twang, Twang," opened with the salvo, "the big question about country music is which country should take the blame for it." The *Five Star Jubilee* television variety show offered a half hour of country music performances. The singer Carl Smith hosted the show, and the episode under Scott's review featured song performances by Jimmy Wakely, Rex Allen, Tex Ritter, Roy Acuff, and a country comedian named Bun Wilson, whom Scott described as "a rustic Mort Sahl." Smith received the brunt of Scott's condescension. "You've got to see this guy to believe him," the Hollywood reporter wrote. "He strolled before the camera with a big ol' grin, a Herbert Hoover collar, shiny-buttoned vest, and a voice that would fetch the cops in any city with a population greater than 500." Scott went on to deride every moment of the performances, describing the songs as sentimental schlock and Acuff's voice as "only slightly less pleasant, say, than running your fingers down a blackboard." Even his closing line delivered the barb, "on the bright side, there were the refreshing commercials dealing with farm machinery."[51]

Letters in defense of country music and critical of Scott poured into the *Stars and Stripes*. Technical Sergeant Paul J. Graupp expressed that he found the article "distasteful and insulting." Graupp spoke for himself, as well as many of his fellow airmen, who felt that the article was "in poor taste and written by a man who seems to be as distant from the entertainment world as the article was from reality." He went on to take a shot at *Stars and Stripes* and suggested that its dearth of country music coverage, combined with the Scott article, reflected an innate bias against the genre at the editorial level. Graupp believed that a "retraction would be in order" if the *Stars and Stripes* were "an ordinary newspaper." However, the deep bias that he saw in print meant that the "viewpoint one gets from reading the various columns is that only the white collar, blue nose and socially listed parties have any business reading the newspaper." To make matters worse, the paper printed weekly columns reviewing jazz records and pop records, while country rarely received a mention outside of coverage for the occasional tour from one of the genre's stars.[52]

Despite critics' low opinion of country music, the desire for the genre's records continued to grow so fast that PX purchasers could not keep pace with the demand. West German record companies supplemented the PX shortage of country platters with their own pressings of albums, and both German and American musicians increased their performances of country music to meet the demands for the genre. Gus Backus, an airman in the US Air Force, stayed in West Germany after his discharge and began recording German-language country hits like "Da sprach der alte Hauptling (So Said the Old Indian Chief)," which was used as a campaign song for Chancellor Konrad Adenauer. Backus had started his military-musical career by joining the interracial doo-wop group The Del-Vikings, all of whose members were in the air force and formed the group while stationed in Pittsburgh, Pennsylvania. However, Backus converted to country music after his deployment to West Germany.[53] Another ex-GI, named Bill Ramsey, rode country music popularity to fame in West Germany, recording the tunes "Old Johnny War ein Wunderkind" and "Hilly Billy Banjo Joe." West German performers joined the trend, too. Jupp Schmitz and His Backyard Musicians performed for German audiences, and the singer Caterina Valente sold hundreds of thousands of her country sides like "Der Sheriff von Arkansas" to local and American disc buyers.[54] The military had turned country music into a viable, respectable genre on the continent, so much so that politicians and pop stars embraced the American sounds of the white South.

Gay's desire to plant more country music in the recruitment campaigns, the proliferation of country on the AFRTS, and the continued increase in PX sales for the genre seemed to signal that the Nashville-Pentagon connection was paying off for the CMA. But these plans also set the CMA inadvertently at odds with the civil rights activism growing locally in Nashville and the national movement that began to sway leaders in Washington, DC. Despite the industry's efforts to reach more listeners, the genre remained the domain of white artists and fans. There might not have been a "whites only" policy stopping African Americans from entering the studios and publishing firms on Music Row, but then there was no need for anything so obvious. When recruiters partnered with a white-dominated music industry headquartered in the South, they branded the military with the racial assumptions that went along with that music. A country music military remained a white military, and that fact exposed a demographic problem occurring within the Cold War armed services. A predominantly white military did not reflect the racial makeup of the nation. The lack of Black servicemembers, in conjunction with the ongoing complaints of discrimination from the relatively few who did join, revealed the problem of using country music to entice new recruits. A genre as self-consciously white as country music mostly drew white listeners. To think otherwise would have ignored the cultivation of its specific listening public over the previous twenty-five years.

Military Music and Civil Rights

A few blocks away from where the Recruiting Service used the all-white spaces of Music Row, African American activists developed the strategy of nonviolent resistance to insist on their social equality in Nashville. In February 1960, James Lawson, an African American seminary student attending Vanderbilt University, began training local college students in the methods of peaceful protest. Lawson was an anticolonial activist and had studied the methods of nonviolent civil disobedience taught by Mahatma Gandhi. After arriving in Nashville for his graduate training, he began meeting with students like Diane Nash from Fisk University and John Lewis from the American Baptist Theological Seminary who were interested in applying those methods to integrate the city's businesses. Through their organizing efforts and sit-in demonstrations at the Kress lunch-counter chain, these activists pressured Mayor Ben West to end Jim Crow segregation or risk bringing shame on a city that many leaders still considered the "Athens of the South," in a nod to the city's reputation as a beacon of enlightenment in a benighted region.[55]

Not long after these grassroots activists forced Nashville's white city officials to end segregation, the federal government looked to the military as a barometer of racial progress and found it lacking. More than a decade had passed since President Truman issued his executive order desegregating the military, a move that had helped ignite Strom Thurmond's Dixiecrat revolt during the 1948 election.[56] The Korean War had forced the military to accept the realities of what it meant for Black and white soldiers to train, live, and fight next to each other and, in the process, unmasked the deep-seated racism within the armed forces.[57] President Kennedy had campaigned in 1960 on soft promises to move the cause of civil rights forward but had frustrated activists and aides with inaction after he took office. To make matters more complex, the Democratic Party still counted southern segregationists like Thurmond as members, and Kennedy walked the political tightrope of addressing racial inequality while not alienating conservative legislators in his own party.[58]

Despite this political hazard, Kennedy's secretary of defense, Robert McNamara, established the President's Committee on Equal Opportunity in the Armed Forces in June 1962 as a "fact-finding team" charged with investigating the racial discrimination that was faced by African American servicemembers and that threatened the efficiency and morale of the troops.[59] The committee, led by Gerhard Gesell, investigated low enlistment rates among African Americans, charges of racial violence between servicemembers, and instances of discrimination experienced by Black servicemembers in the civilian communities surrounding their installations. Gesell was a Yale-trained attorney who had worked for the Securities and Exchange Commission in the early 1940s and as Democratic counsel during the Pearl Harbor hearings. As a federal judge in the 1970s and 1980s, he ruled on such high-profile cases as Watergate, the Pentagon Papers, and Oliver North's conviction in the Iran-Contra Affair. But during the early 1960s, Gesell's name became synonymous with the interracial committee's investigation into the military's racial discrimination. The committee members, all of whom were civilians, spent the next year visiting bases on occasion and compiling research from statistical surveys generated by the federal Civil Rights Commission. They could not make policy, but they could make recommendations based on their data.[60]

The Gesell Committee delivered its initial report to the White House in June 1963 and revealed a disturbing pattern in the demographics of the armed forces. The long-standing policy of integration and the career opportunities made available through military service suggested that the armed forces should have attracted a large number of African Americans for voluntary enlistment. The committee's report told a different story. African Americans made up 11 percent of the overall civilian population but only 8 percent of servicemembers.[61] The committee's work also exposed the educational and class disparities embedded within these racial divisions. Few African Americans had achieved a commissioned officer rank. Only one branch, the US Air Force, could count a Black general. The US Army held the highest percentage of Black commissioned officers, with African Americans making up a little over 5 percent of captains. African Americans accounted for less than 1 percent of any officer classification in the Marine Corps.[62]

While the Gesell Committee researched and reported on the low enlistment rates of African Americans, Music Row strengthened its ties to the recruitment efforts and created more programming aimed at attracting white men. The Recruiting Services officer Charles Brown retired from the armed forces in 1961, moved to Nashville, joined the CMA, and opened an office as a booker for concerts, radio, and television.[63] In 1962, with his new job as a civilian country music promoter, Brown booked a radio series for the US Marines called *Leatherneck Jamboree*. The CMA's *Close-Up* reported on these sessions, announcing that "Uncle Sam enlisted C&W recently for the purpose of pointing the long arm to say Uncle Sam needs *you*." The newsletter also gave CMA members instructions on how to obtain copies of the show for their stations by writing to their local recruiters or to the US Marine Corps in Washington, DC. The show featured some of the biggest names in the business, including Faron Young, Patsy Cline, Flatt and Scruggs and the Foggy Mountain Boys, the Everly Brothers, June Carter, Wilma Lee and Stoney Cooper, Benny Martin, Hawkshaw Hawkins, and Cowboy Copas.[64] And, in a continuation of the *Country Style, U.S.A.* sessions, Brown used Owen Bradley's studio to record the show.[65] This kind of reciprocity boosted the profiles of the participating artists and delivered government funds to pay for the studio time, co-opting the country music industry to aid the Pentagon's mission of filling the Cold War ranks.

Although the Gesell Committee failed to mention the country music campaigns as a contributing factor, the committee did blame the absence of Black representation in the military's recruitment material for the low numbers. "Negroes rarely appear in recruiting literature," it told President Kennedy, "and then almost never on the cover together with other personnel or in the more appealing action shots."[66] The committee also noted that the Recruiting Service should make "affirmative steps . . . to ensure that no recruiting personnel, consciously or unconsciously, channel Negroes to particular career fields, disregarding their aptitudes."[67]

The Gesell Committee found that no branch of the armed forces had developed a strategy of recruitment that would appeal to the specific interests and tastes of African Americans. In its estimation, the military needed to craft a public image that showed Black servicemembers contributing to the service in meaningful ways. It expressed special concern over the low numbers of Black officers and recommended that the armed forces target Black colleges, use literature that would be "appealing to Negroes," and "make wider use of Negro officers in recruiting assignments."[68] Different service branches responded to this urging by soliciting information and flattering publicity on the duties of Black officers. The navy, for instance, issued a memo instructing recruiters to "direct publicity materials towards the local ethnic community showing photographs of naval personnel which are interacial [sic] in composition, particularly when the photographs are to be released in home town newspapers."[69] The Gesell Committee's suggestions reflected a progressive understanding of the need for the military to undergo a makeover, one that created the public perception of the US Armed Forces as a racially diverse and inclusive institution.

The report moved beyond recruiting to take aim at on-base discrimination and segregation in the civilian communities that surrounded military installations. To address on-base racial conflict, the committee initially recommended creating a system through which soldiers could report instances of discrimination efficiently. The committee also believed that the services should monitor recreational activities, personal relationships, public transportation, and military police actions for signs of racism.[70] These changes to racial policies on domestic installations proved to be relatively simple to implement since, on paper, the military should have practiced full integration for over a decade at that point. The Gesell Committee noted that local commanders reacted promptly to racial discrimination once the committee brought these practices to their attention. That meant that the military corrected lingering cases of segregation in housing or in service clubs on installations. In fact, the committee praised the armed services' ability to institute these changes so quickly and efficiently, writing, "The base commander not only enjoys an independence which permits him to do so; he can also point to the successful program of equality of treatment and opportunity which exists on his base and to the economic dependence of the community upon the base."[71]

To ensure that all local commanders supported the integration of troops on and off base, the Gesell Committee's report prescribed the creation of a policy that would prohibit the removal of Black servicemembers from public-facing assignments in musical units and sports teams. The committee complimented commanders who "refused to permit [musical] groups from a base to participate outside the base in events where elimination or segregation of Negro personnel would be required because of civilian attitudes." However, the committee also noted that the removal of Black musicians, indeed, had occurred on occasion to satisfy white civilians, a fact that the report called "an indefensible form of discrimination within the Services."[72] Not only did Gesell and his fellow committee members recognize that some commanders had bent to the will of local segregationists, but those commanders recognized how race and music intersected in the minds of southern racists. It was one thing to have Black soldiers stationed at southern installations. It was wholly another to have them represent the United States' military as musicians, potentially sullying the sounds of service with their allegedly degrading influence and tarnishing the reputation of the nation's fighting force.

The Gesell Committee also used the power of the federal government to enforce integration at the USO clubs where servicemembers went to dance to the sounds of jukeboxes and live bands. At the time, the USO operated 139 clubs across the nation. Although the USO had formally adopted racial integration in 1951, it had not actively enforced this policy. The organization, with the help of the Gesell Committee, identified twenty communities in Texas, Florida, Georgia, South Carolina, and Virginia where the USO maintained two separate clubs, one white and one Black.[73] By enforcing integration, the USO invited Black and white men to congregate with women of both races, raising the prospect of interracial sex in the process. Gesell believed that this "sex thing" was crucial to the project of ending segregation.[74] Without embracing integration and all its interracial implications, the armed forces risked degrading troop morale and discouraging future recruitment of African Americans.

And yet, regardless of the discrimination in the military's entertainment venues, Black soldiers still found ways to make music and pursue professional opportunities while serving their country in the early 1960s. Jimi, then known as James Marshall, Hendrix joined the US Army for a three-year hitch in May 1961, partially in an effort to avoid a conviction for car theft. Hendrix went through basic training at Fort Ord, California, received an assignment to work in a supply warehouse at Fort Campbell, Kentucky, and earned his Screaming Eagle patch as part of the 101st Airborne. His interest in the army waned after his father shipped his beloved Danelectro guitar to the post in Kentucky. Hendrix had played in a few amateur bands around his native Seattle before joining the military at eighteen years old, but his time in the army propelled him toward a real career in music. One day while practicing guitar in a service club at Fort Campbell, Hendrix met Billy Cox, a fellow soldier and bass player. The two men struck up a musical friendship and immediately formed a band that played at the segregated Black-only clubs in nearby Clarksville, Tennessee, and in Nashville, some sixty miles south of Fort Campbell. Soon, Hendrix was playing the guitar as much as possible. He shirked his army duties and came under the close scrutiny of his commanding officers who did not look fondly on the young guitarist's incessant practicing. He played constantly around the barracks and even slept with his Danelectro on his chest. For Hendrix, military service ultimately acted as an impediment to finding success in the music business. When he finagled a premature discharge from the army in May 1962, he hung around Clarksville until Cox's enlistment ended, and the two men headed for Nashville to join the vibrant R&B scene in Music City.[75]

Allen Toussaint, the producer, singer-songwriter, and pianist from New Orleans, spent two years in the US Army from 1963 to 1965. Already twenty-five years old at the time of his enlistment, Toussaint had written hit songs for singers like Jessie Hill, Ernie K-Doe, Irma Thomas, and Lee Dorsey when the draft stole him from the Crescent City. He had also released his own record of piano-centric instrumentals called *The Wild Sounds of New Orleans* under the pseudonym Tousan in 1958. But whereas Hendrix felt thwarted by his military duties, Toussaint embraced his lot and thrived in the musical community he found on Fort Hood near Killeen, Texas. The piano player joined a soldiers' chorus as its accompanist and believed that the experience gave him a lesson in the power of musical dynamics. He also formed a rhythm and blues group on base called the Stokes and wrote what he described as a "joke" song called "Whipped Cream" for it. That instrumental tune would prove to be one of Toussaint's most lucrative songwriting efforts. Herb Alpert's Tijuana Brass featured the tune as the title track and the inspiration for the cover art for the group's hit album *Whipped Cream & Other Delights* in 1965, and it gained another life when *The Dating Game* adopted Alpert's version as its theme song.[76]

Around the same time that Toussaint found a temporary outlet for his music in the military, the army's on-base race relations received some much-needed positive press. In September 1963, the husband-and-wife writing team of Ruth and Edward Brecher published an article in *Harper's*, giving their insights on the success of military integration and the conflict that these policies created with local communities in the South. The Brechers traveled over 3,200 miles through several southern states, touring installations, interviewing servicemembers, and gauging the impact that an integrated military had on a segregated region. In many instances, they found a commendable level of integration, in which they witnessed white and Black soldiers eating, playing, attending religious services, and living together. Families, too, socialized together regardless of color where servicemembers were allowed to live with their wives and children. According to the Brechers, many of the Black soldiers and the wives they interviewed told them "that nowhere else had they ever experienced such complete or such successful neighbor-to-neighbor integration" than on a US military installation. Putting it in the context of recent civil rights events like the

Birmingham Children's Crusade, the Brechers admitted, "Seeing such activities in the heart of the South, we found it hard to realize that a few miles away, Negroes were being arrested and beaten for seeking a cup of coffee at a lunch counter."[77]

Off-base living conditions remained another matter. The South's white supremacist racial order threatened the morale and safety of Black troops. As the Brechers put it, "The sorry truth is that integration stops abruptly at the gates of the military reservations," after which point, the southern laws and customs of Jim Crow still reigned. The authors collected stories of Black soldiers stationed in the South who struggled to find livable housing for their families and sufficient education opportunities for their children. These conditions left Black servicemembers demoralized and disillusioned. Even interracial fraternizing in the community could lead to civilian and military punishment. The Brechers told the story of eleven soldiers, eight white and three Black, who received a transfer order to move from Germany to rural Georgia. These men had developed tightknit friendships while overseas and continued their social life by searching for a bar to have a few beers one night. After a white establishment refused them service, they landed at a Black bar, only to have the Black bartender immediately call the police on them before they could finish one beer. The men spent a night in civilian jail and had their off-base privileges revoked for a month on a false charge of "drunkenness."[78]

The Brechers' also revealed the persistent "isolated remnants of on-base discrimination" on a handful of southern installations and the role of music in maintaining that division of the races in social situations. They discovered that, regardless of the order to desegregate the armed forces and the Gesell Committee's then-current investigation, some white commanders found understated ways to maintain racial divisions. These policy-savvy segregationists knew the law well enough not to prohibit the movement of Black soldiers or prevent their access to certain parts of the post. That kind of violation might allow Black men to file a formal complaint with documentable evidence. Instead, the Brechers described how "a commander can set up several clubs, staff one of them with a Negro manager, load its jukebox with Negro records, and hire Negro bands for gala events." According to their research, "Negro personnel get the message *quickly*."[79]

Despite the Defense Department's awareness of the need for messaging tailored to African American communities and its push for integration in social settings, the continued use of country music in its recruitment campaigns and entertainment programming undercut McNamara's inclusive

vision. It also probably bolstered the kind of "subtle" discrimination described by the Brechers. Defense leaders knew that music could mark a
military space as white or Black, depending on the genre and the race of
a performing artist. Every time the CMA encouraged the growth of country music programming and record sales in the military, it claimed the
US Armed Forces as a federal institution that carried the endorsement of
Nashville's white music industry.

Uncle Joe Joins the Army

The amount of country music on the AFRTS continued to grow in the early
1960s. The CMA found its most lasting and most lucrative connection to the
military's radio listeners in Joe Allison, a disc jockey, songwriter, and producer, who emerged as the key figure in the creation of format country radio and hosted a long-running show for the AFRTS beginning in 1963. Born
in McKinney, Texas, in 1924, Allison received his start in country music in
the late 1940s when he went on the road as an announcer for Tex Ritter.
In 1949, he landed a job on Nashville's WMAK and quickly rose to the top
of the country music disc jockey field.[80] He wrote several successful country songs, including the hillbilly rocker "Live Fast, Love Hard, Die Young,"
which turned out to be Faron Young's first hit after receiving his discharge
from the army.[81] The record peaked at number two on *Billboard*'s country
charts and remained Young's biggest hit until he reached number one in 1961
with Willie Nelson's "Hello Walls."[82]

Country Song Roundup boosted Allison's visibility in the early 1950s by
giving the DJ a regular column called "Music City, USA." The column offered evidence of Allison's early on-air personality and the way he connected
listeners to the music with his friendly, even familial style. He invited *Country Song Roundup* readers to tune in to WMAK, where he hosted "a couple
of disc jockey shows each day." He then asked them to write to him for
more information on the music that he spun. Simply address a letter to
"Uncle Joe Allison" at the WMAK studios in the Maxwell House Hotel,
Nashville, Tennessee, he told them. "Let me hear from you," Allison wrote,
"and I'll bet you half a gallon of red ants I'll cooperate with you in any way
I can."[83] His listeners were like friends and family. Just get in touch with
Uncle Joe for your country music needs.

Allison also participated in the consolidation of music industry power
in Nashville while he cultivated this down-home appeal. In the early 1950s,
Allison had moved to California after answering a call from Tennessee

Ernie Ford to join the disc jockey staff at KXLA in Pasadena.[84] The country music industry wanted to grow beyond its loyal demographic base, and the Southern California communities of second-generation Dust Bowl transplants represented a prime market for the music to thrive.[85] The children of white migrants now living in San Pedro, Bakersfield, and Orange County could tune in to hear Uncle Joe spin the latest country platters while on their on their way to work in the shipyards and aircraft factories that fueled the region's exponential postwar growth.

Allison broadened the reach of country music even further in the last half of the 1950s by leading the industry in the new field of format radio. A Nebraska radio programmer named Todd Storz had pioneered the pop-oriented Top 40 format radio in 1955. One night, Storz watched a waitress at an Omaha bar play the same song three times in a row on the jukebox after all the other customers had left, even though patrons had played the selection repeatedly throughout the evening. Inspired by the woman's desire to hear a song she liked on repeat, Storz envisioned a constricted radio playlist of thirty or forty pop songs that would ingrain the hits into listeners' minds.[86]

Country radio stations caught onto this formula slowly. Although KDAV in Lubbock, Texas, had switched to all country 1953, format programming was different than simply sticking exclusively to one sound.[87] Instead, format radio sought to catch specific market demographics by repeatedly playing selections from a tightly curated list of songs.[88] After brief stints at stations in Akron, Ohio, and Nashville, Allison returned to the West Coast in 1956.[89] He joined other veteran country DJs in converting KRKD, a radio station in downtown Los Angeles, to an all-country format. KRKD began its broadcast as Los Angeles's first full-time all-country station on October 1, 1956.[90] Over the next decade, Allison slowly helped to convert a growing number of radio stations around the nation to the format, pushing a select list of country hits to broader audiences in larger listening markets.

The emergence of country format radio gave the industry a way to push its releases in concentrated campaigns, and it soon found a way to transfer that model to armed forces radio. Allison brought country music to those military listeners from 1963 to 1970 with a show called *Country Corner*. He recorded the show in Los Angeles at the AFRTS studios, where the tapes were then transcribed onto discs for shipment around the world. Once a week, the pioneer of the country format went into the AFRTS studio with a box of records that he selected and recorded five hours of country music hits while inserting his commentary and readings from letters he received from around the world. "They made it easy for me," he remembered.

FIGURE 5.2 Joe Allison, pioneer of country format radio and host of *Country Corner* on the AFRTS. Allison claimed to reach an audience of 600 million listeners with his show. (*Music City News*, October 1970, courtesy of the Country Music Hall of Fame and Museum)

"I would go down to the Armed Forces studios one day a week. . . . My show was fifty-five minutes a day in length." He recorded every show for an entire week in one sitting. He later described, "We would do it almost in five hours. I mean, we just didn't stop."[91] These recording sessions created an efficient way to reach what the network told Allison was an international audience of 600 million listeners. The reach of the AFRTS did wonders for exposing potential new fans to the sounds of country music. Many stations played Allison's show two times a day to meet their listeners demand for the genre.

Unlike most other military country programs, *Country Corner* did not contain any recruitment efforts. Allison recalled, "There was no propaganda of any kind, not even any recruiting things or no reenlistment propaganda, no nothing. We were employed to do strict entertainment."[92] This arrangement gave Allison free range over the playlist and his on-air personality. Each episode of *Country Corner* began with "Main Street Rag" played by Chet

Atkins as the theme song before Allison broke in with his mixture of country music insider knowledge and countryfied comedy. He delighted in confiding personal details about the musicians that he played on air, letting the audience become familiar with artists vicariously through his persona as Uncle Joe.

According to Allison, more foreign civilians than GIs wrote to him requesting songs and information on their favorite country artists, and he relished reading selections from these hundreds of letters on the air. Allison mixed in his humor and industry connection in a typical episode to answer one Dutch letter writer. "Dear sir," Allison read before inserting a joke in his Texan accent: "They always call me 'dear,' and that's a funny way to spell 'sir,' 'c-u-r.' So, I have both jokes out the way, all right?" He then read the listener's sincere request: "I am a fan of the *Country Corner* music in Holland, and I would like to ask you to send me some pictures of Buck Owens, Jim Reeves, Ray Price, Norma Jean, Kitty Wells, Connie Smith, and Skeeter Davis."[93] Both military and civilian listeners could hear Allison instruct this particular fan on how to obtain the desired memorabilia, feeling connected to the country industry and the United States in general through the down-home tone of *Country Corner*.

All that country music on the AFRTS, whether it was from Uncle Joe or a military disc jockey, began to increase the number of records sold at the PXs in the mid-1960s. Having witnessed this rise in country popularity, one European Exchange Service (EES) official told *Billboard* in 1963, "Our advice to any young composer with talent, and impatient for instant success, is to write country music. The demand is insatiable right here with our own military forces." "Nashville," he said, "doesn't have any real idea of the European demand for country music. The surface has hardly been touched."[94] The EES official obviously exaggerated Nashville's lack of interest in the military and the overseas markets it created. Country music's business actors had fostered that demand for the genre among the nation's fighting men. But he did identify an important point for the commercial growth of the genre overseas. Military audiences and foreign civilians might genuinely enjoy country music. But, if Music Row wanted to grow the genre's market reach, it would need to maintain a steady inundation of the European airwaves, concert stages, and the PX record sections.

By 1965, military officials knew that country's growing popularity with the troops was making the music synonymous with the United States itself. Omer Anderson reported for *Billboard* that the US Armed Forces had begun a "campaign in Europe to present country music as 'an integral part of the American cultural heritage and of the American way of life.'" Officials announced a four-point plan to boost country music's image as a piece of the US cultural fabric. That plan included a concerted effort to stop the "disparagement of country as 'hick' or 'hillbilly' music," a plan to place more country records in the PXs, an increase in country radio shows for AFN, and a priority to book more European tours for country artists. The explicit promotion of country music addressed what Anderson called "a matter of morale." According to his report, "virtually all military personnel prefer— or at least listen regularly to—country music," and the genre had a way of "instilling loyalty and a sense of duty to country into members of the Armed Forces." The military attributed this phenomenon to the music's roots in the folk music of the United States and believed that "no music has as strong an emotional appeal to soldiers." As such, the AFRTS received orders to refrain from referring to country music with the descriptors "'hick,' 'hillbilly,' and 'music from the sticks.'" Instead, it stressed the "American folk character of the idiom." The military suggested referring to the genre as "'country,' 'western,' 'c&w,' 'American folk music,'" or, in terms that repeated the 1950s campaigns of Governor Frank Clement and the CMDJA, the "music of America."[95]

The military's description of country as the "music of America" merged national identity with a genre synonymous with the white South. In actuality, country was no more the music of an entire nation than jazz, pop, blues, or soul music were. Other institutions, like the State Department and Voice of America, relied on other genres to express different images of the nation. Jazz and pop served propaganda missions to boost the United States' image as a country of tolerance, inclusivity, and democratic, capitalist freedom.[96] Some within the country industry attempted to use their music this way, too. Alvin S. Bennett, president of Liberty Records in Los Angeles, solicited his fellow CMA members for financial contributions in support of Radio Free Europe. *Close-Up* encouraged its readers to donate to the organization's mission of "broadcasting the truth behind the iron curtain," truth that presumably included country music songs.[97]

Yet, the government not only used country music and the industry's money to boost the image of the nation in the Cold War's ideological struggle, but it also used the infrastructure created by its own military might to boost the image of country music. That governmental influence helped change perceptions about the genre from its reputation as the sound of rural white ignorance to the modern incarnation of atavistic folk purity and patriotic devotion. The Pentagon recognized that country music had become indelibly linked with military service thanks to more than a decade of recruitment campaigns, live entertainment programs, and AFRTS radio airplay. Rather than fight that association, the military wanted to brand the genre as an expression of authentic US culture, a music that echoed and shaped the experience of armed service.

The CMA must have welcomed the results of these propaganda campaigns. More country radio shows meant more military listeners. More listeners meant more loyal customers. By 1968, country records accounted for approximately 65 percent of the records sold in European PXs. Those totals equaled about $4.2 million in sales for country records alone, a total worth around $37 million in 2023 dollars. Charles Hendrickson, an EES record buyer, told *Billboard*, "Country, rhythm and blues, and pop account for 85 per cent of all our record sales. But country dominates the market. This is proved, not only by our sales, but also by letters to the Allied Forces Network." According to Hendrickson, country programs drew 1,200 letters per week from soldier and civilian listeners. That represented a "fantastic number" when compared to the volume of correspondence from fans of other genres.[98] Country offered more than musical entertainment. It offered an identity, music that made a person exceptional among the larger audience of pop listeners and particularly patriotic as a supporter of the "music of America." The CMA could not have asked for a better sales pitch.

Although it had been a long time in the making, Music Row began to reap the financial rewards of its close connections with the Defense Department in the 1960s. Over the years between World War II and this sales boom, the country music industry had persisted in enmeshing itself with the spread of the US military. Because of that persistence, the CMA had moved country music closer to being truly "Best Liked World-Wide." And yet, that success came with a political cost. The CMA had wedded itself commercially and symbolically to the military when support for the armed forces was still part of the midcentury political consensus. By the late 1960s, with the US fighting a highly unpopular war against the North Vietnamese communists, the country industry felt the social and political consequences of that marriage of sound and state.

6 Tell Them What We're Fighting For

The CMA, Country Artists, and the
Politics of the Vietnam War

. . . .

In February 1968, at the height of North Vietnam's Tet Offensive, the CMA announced the release of a compilation album called *Country Music Salutes the Armed Forces*. The organization had designed the album to sell at PXs around the world. The twenty-four-song track list spanned several decades of country music, featuring classic songs like Roy Acuff's "Wabash Cannonball" and more recent releases from Mel Tillis and Bobby Bare. Only Elton Britt's "There's a Star-Spangled Banner Waving Somewhere" carried any overtly patriotic themes. What tied these songs to the military was the CMA's desire to send, as the *Close-Up* stated, "a salute to the GI's overseas who has [sic] been one of the reasons for the spread of Country Music and for its popularity around the world." Thanks to the artists' willingness to waive the royalties from this album's sales, the CMA offered the record at "reduced prices to reward them [servicemembers] for loyalty." Still, the country industry never missed a chance to profit from the soldier's dollar. The CMA donated all profits from the sale of *Salute to the Armed Forces* to the cost of building the Country Music Hall of Fame and Museum, which had opened in 1967 on Music Row. The Pentagon payroll helped fund the construction of what *Close-Up* called "the shrine of the country field . . . dedicated to the perpetuation of the lore of country music."[1]

At the time of the record's release, more Americans than not believed that sending troops to Vietnam had been a mistake.[2] But just as the CMA counted on the troops to support country music, the Defense Department counted on Music Row to support what became an increasingly unpopular fight against Vietnamese communists. Beginning with the mass deployment of US forces in 1965, country music artists consistently toured Vietnam, and they maintained their near-constant presence at military installations in Europe, the Caribbean, and Japan. Country music militarization hit an all-time high in the late 1960s, with the Pentagon and CMA bestowing awards on each other for their entwined contributions to entertaining the troops and disseminating Music Row's latest releases.

All of those servicemembers heard their own stories of sacrifice, service, and pride echoed in the songs written by country artists during the Vietnam War. Dozens of country songwriters penned songs about the war. Meanwhile, Nashville studios continued to function as recording hubs for the Recruiting Service, producing shows like the US Air Force's *Country Music Time* that touted the economic benefits of armed service. Enticing new enlistees during the Vietnam War meant appealing to young men and women regardless of flagging public support for the military as an institution. As the death toll in Vietnam mounted, antiwar protestors gained political support, and Ho Chi Minh's forces continued to thwart a US victory, many Americans had grown disillusioned and impatient with the rationale for what looked to be an increasingly irrational war.[3]

Not so on Music Row. The CMA cast its lot with the Pentagon's commitment to war, a decision that would hold far-reaching consequences for the politics of country music. Because of the Cold War political consensus that had guided the United States' anticommunist foreign policies, the country music industry's relationship with the Pentagon had never carried an overtly partisan affiliation. In fact, there was never an inherent political meaning to the genre, and politicians of all stripes courted country music fans and used its artists in their campaigns throughout the twentieth century.[4] During the Vietnam era, country artists performed in support of the presidential campaigns of Lyndon Johnson, Barry Goldwater, George Wallace, Richard Nixon, and Edmund Muskie. Having cultivated a reputation as "America's music," country music stamped these candidates with the downhome American values that the music supposedly represented. Country music was patriotic, not partisan.

The use of country music by politicians and military leaders affiliated the ostensibly color-blind institutions of the government with the genre most associated with white racial conservatives and their militarized patriotism. That gap between the integrationist policies of the US government and the entrenched white supremacy within those same institutions could lead to frustration for the growing number of African Americans in the military and the country music industry. O. B. McClinton, a Black singer-songwriter from North Mississippi, believed that he could leverage his military experience to create a career in country music. He discovered his talent for singing and writing the genre while stationed on Okinawa with the US Air Force. Yet, although his fellow airmen encouraged his talents, McClinton experienced more frustration than success within the white-dominated spaces of the domestic country music industry, no matter how much he emphasized his military service or participated in recruitment campaigns. For McClinton, the relative racial equality created by the Defense Department's integrationist policies did not translate into racial equity in the civilian music world.[5] Country music's color-blind patriotism could not make it a welcoming genre for all races, despite the token success of the African American artist Charley Pride.

By the end of the war, the country music industry's version of patriotism pushed its politics to the right when Nixon and his "silent majority" captured support for the military as a feature of modern conservatism.[6] Country music's racial reputation as a genre created by and for white Americans further cemented this political alliance between the music and the politics of the right. Historians and music critics have often considered the patriotic themes of Vietnam-era country music as emblematic of this white conservative counterrevolution against the antiwar, civil rights, and student protests of the 1960s. Songs like Merle Haggard's "The Fightin' Side of Me" allegedly reflected a deep-seated jingoism within white southerners and perhaps most country fans around the nation. Their militarized patriotism made these voters primed for the rise of Nixonian backlash politics and the Republican "Southern Strategy."[7]

The diversity of war-themed songs and the complexities of country artists' politics during the Vietnam War tell a different story. It is true that most leaders of the CMA understood the commercial value of their connection to the military and supported the armed forces as an institution. Music Row had made its bed with the militarization of US culture long before Vietnam. But it is also true that country musicians could and did dissent, often with more nuance than the antiwar anthems from the counterculture did. Songs like Tom T. Hall's "Mama Bake a Pie (Daddy Kill a Chicken)" chronicled the personal devastation experienced by wounded veterans. Country artists' ability to cheer the military in one song and think critically about the war's personal consequences in another was one of the things that attracted members of the US Armed Forces, as well as civilians, to the genre. When country musicians sang about the war, they did so not from any one ideological or exclusive partisan stance but because the midcentury political economy tied their industry and so many of their fans to the Cold War defense state. The country industry's politics followed the voting and purchasing patterns of white listeners and the military. Over the course of the Vietnam War, the needs and tastes of those demographics combined to make country music the sound of white political conservatism.

Bipartisan Country

In 1964, two cowboys pulled the country music industry in different political directions. On the left was the sitting president Lyndon B. Johnson. The Texan had risen through the ranks of the Democratic Party during the Franklin D. Roosevelt administration and embraced the progressive vision of growing the federal government to address the inequalities of US society. With his trademark Stetson hat and his ranching bona fides, Johnson married his liberal politics with a brash, no-nonsense populism associated with his rural roots in the West. He was someone who made things happen in the halls of Congress and in the White House, despite the predominance of eastern elites in the capital.[8]

On the right was Barry Goldwater. He served as a US senator from Arizona and had consciously cultivated his public persona as Gary Cooper–meets–policy wonk who rode east to Washington, DC, to end what he believed to be the tyranny of a federal government that began under the New Deal. He had also made a name for himself through his polarizing views on civil rights and communism. He opposed the Civil Rights Act of 1964, allegedly on constitutional principles, and floated ideas like using low-yield nuclear weapons in Vietnam, dissolving the Social Security Administration, and ending public education. While Johnson famously cast Goldwater as an unhinged extremist, the Republican's hardline views endeared him to the right wing of the party, also known as "movement conservatives," who saw a slippery slope toward socialism in anything resembling Democratic liberalism. And, although Goldwater had inherited a fortune as the heir to a department store chain, he performed the part of a rugged cowboy, a performance that appealed to those same movement conservatives, as well as everyday voters with populist leanings.[9] In November 1963, he posed for the cover of *Life* magazine wearing a western-cut shirt, jeans with large belt buckle, and cowboy hat, all while nuzzling his horse, Sunny.[10] Had he not been a Republican presidential candidate, readers might have mistaken Goldwater for the lead in a prime-time Western or a country singer.

The country music industry's competing partisan loyalties divided Music Row. Connie B. Gay had remained a Democrat since his days in the Roosevelt administration and welcomed Johnson's candidacy. Gay's loyalty even earned him an invitation to dine at the White House with President John F. Kennedy when Emperor Haile Selassie visited in October 1963.[11] Rubbing elbows with the president opened new commercial opportunities for Gay. In November 1963, he took his stable of country acts, including Elton Britt, the Willis Brothers, and Mary Klick, to Amsterdam. There, they performed for eighteen days as part of the United States Food and Agriculture Exhibition that promoted US farming and the foods that it provided to European markets, in a bit of soft-power Cold War propaganda. Gay and his performers met Vice President Johnson, and the two former New Dealers used their respective talents to burnish the image of US democracy through its music and agricultural production.[12] In July 1964, a new country industry newspaper called *Music City News*, owned by Faron Young, announced that Gay would serve as one of ten businessmen sent overseas by President Johnson to assess the state of free enterprise in West Germany.[13] From Gay's perspective, the Kennedy and Johnson administrations represented allies in the White House, where the most powerful men in Western democracy understood the worth of the country music business. He saw no need to change course in 1964.

Goldwater's small-government ideologies and militant anticommunism appealed to the more conservative artists and businesspeople in Nashville. Marty Robbins, a native Arizonan and navy veteran who had performed the role of the cowboy himself on the album *Gunfighter Ballads and Trail Songs*, served as chairman of an organization called "Stars for Barry." This promotional committee included some of the top artists of the genre, like Eddy Arnold, Roy Acuff, Hank Snow, Charlie Louvin, and Tompall and the Glaser Brothers. In the fall of 1964, they played concerts for the senator and placed Goldwater ads in the October edition of *Music City News* that featured the campaign's tagline of "In our hearts, we know he's right."[14] In that same issue, the paper published a profile of Goldwater that highlighted his hobby of amateur radio broadcasting. The piece included a picture of Goldwater at the desk in his Washington apartment's library, appearing to tinker with his machines, while another picture showed him at home with his wife, children, their spouses, and grandchildren.[15] The images softened Goldwater's image, suggesting that maybe the cowboy-senator bent on dismantling the modern federal government was, in fact, just a normal guy.

No amount of media boosterism could propel Goldwater into office. However, these country artists and Nashville print outlets reflected a broader right-wing media push for Goldwater's campaign, led by publishers like Henry Regnery, the talk-radio personality Clarence Manion, and the writer William F. Buckley Jr., that sought to acclimate the mainstream to the candidate's more extreme positions.[16] The "Stars for Barry" campaign also hinted at the shifting political climate on Music Row and in the South more broadly. Before 1964, few country music insiders, with the exception of Roy Acuff, would have ventured onto the campaign trail for a Republican politi-

In our hearts,
we know he's right.
Signed: Stars for Barry, Marty Robbins Chairman.
Barry Goldwater
President

FIGURE 6.1 Several country performers gave their endorsement to the Goldwater presidential campaign in 1964. (*Music City News*, October 1964, courtesy of the Country Music Hall of Fame and Museum)

cian. Acuff had run for governor of Tennessee in 1948 as a Republican, but he was fairly unique for that party affiliation among white southerners. President Johnson's signing of the Civil Rights Act in July 1964, along with Goldwater's opposition to it, had revealed a growing fissure between white southerners and the national Democratic Party that they had supported since Reconstruction. The "Stars for Barry" campaign helped claim ground for country artists on the right and primed country fans for Music Row's embrace of the Republican Party by the end of the Vietnam War.

That partisan sea change still lay ahead for Music Row in late 1964, when President Johnson designated November as "National Country Music Month." The CMA had lobbied for this proclamation since its beginnings and had won over state governments around the nation in the early 1960s. It started with Tennessee's Governor Frank G. Clement but spread to Louisiana, Florida, Georgia, Colorado, and Oregon. In September 1964, Senator Caleb Boggs, a Republican from Delaware, had entered his recommendation for the creation of National Country Music Month in the *Congressional Record*. Boggs engaged in a bit of mythmaking that boosted country music's Cold War cachet as an exceptionally American genre tied to folk traditions while also centering Nashville as the undisputed home of its commercial power. According to Boggs, Nashville's WSM was the first station to air "this folklore in word and song that is as much a part of our heritage as apple pie—as distinctly American as baseball." He also recognized the evolution of the genre and its integration within the postwar economy, calling it "wholly a child of America, expressive of her history, hopes, dreams."[17] In the run-up to the presidential election, it appeared that Johnson understood and valued the contributions of country music to the meaning and history of American identity, or at least the meaning that the CMA had crafted and curated over the past six years.

Johnson and his fellow Democrats also took a hard line against the spread of communism, a stance that benefited Music Row's military alliance. Under the direction of Robert McNamara, Kennedy's and Johnson's secretary of defense, the Pentagon deepened its commitment to the domino theory in the early 1960s in an increasingly hot Cold War. In 1962, the United States avoided nuclear war with the Soviet Union during the Cuban Missile Crisis. By 1963, North Vietnamese communists appeared to be winning popular support in a revolution against South Vietnam, where 17,000 US military advisers assisted the capitalist-backed Diem regime. To preserve military readiness for impending war, the United States maintained installations around the world and poured money into defense-industry production of proven armaments and new defense technologies.[18] The Pentagon also upheld and tried to grow its enlistment counts in an effort to address the ever-present need for more personnel in uniform.[19]

Members of the country music industry continued their military tours, and Nashville welcomed the chance to pair its product with more recruitment efforts. Roy Acuff embarked on near-annual USO tours in the early 1960s, playing over twenty shows in Spain, Portugal, and Morocco in 1961, over thirty shows in the Mediterranean and Middle East in 1962, and over twenty shows in Japan in 1964. As a measure of his commitment to the US servicemembers, Acuff missed his induction as the first living member of the Country Hall of Fame, choosing instead to tour for the nation's military members. The US Air Force's commanders of Trabzon Air Station in Turkey presented Acuff with a cake in lieu of the Nashville ceremony.[20] Back in Nashville, the US Navy increased the production of a recruitment show called *Your Navy Country Music Show*, recorded at the city's Naval Recruitment Station. The program began in the late 1950s, releasing twenty shows a month in which sailors embedded recruitment pitches in fifteen-minute blocks of current country hits. By March 1964, the recruiters had upped their production to sixty-two shows a week that went out to at least 100 radio stations in the Nashville area.[21]

While Acuff entertained the servicemembers deployed in peacetime occupation and the armed forces enticed country listeners to join their ranks, President Johnson and the Pentagon committed the nation to war, helping the South Vietnamese stave off a communist takeover by North Vietnam. The Gulf of Tonkin Resolution, approved in August 1964, gave Johnson the congressional authorization to "prevent further aggression" against US forces in Southeast Asia. In the spring of 1965, the president escalated the US involvement by increasing ground troop levels to 125,000. That summer, General William Westmoreland ordered the first offensive ground operation against the North Vietnamese Army and the Viet Cong in South Vietnam. Using what he called "expressive terms" for infantry action, Westmoreland ordered US troops to "search and destroy" communist forces and their abettors, unleashing tens of thousands of American fighting men on North Vietnamese soldiers, South Vietnamese combatants, and civilians on both sides of the conflict. The United States would not withdraw from the fight until almost ten years later, incurring nearly 60,000 US casualties.[22]

War-Torn Country

Roy Acuff joined the US Armed Forces on two different fronts in the fight against communism in 1965. In June, Acuff and a scaled-down cast of the *Opry* played a series of shows in the Dominican Republic, where President Johnson had ordered US Marines to prevent a communist takeover of the Caribbean island. Acuff told *United States Forces News*, a servicemembers' publication, that he would play his scheduled USO dates for the troops despite the heavy fighting on the island, explaining, "We don't like to change our schedule." The paper praised Acuff's willingness to deliver a taste of "down home USA" for the men stationed there, as well as his inclusion of a female singer, the "curvaceous Joyce Moore whose looks aren't exactly the kind most country boys meet on the south 40." With an innuendo as subtle as mortar fire, the writer gushed that Moore's "voice matches her appearance giving a double barreled package of 'showmanship.'"[23] Acuff's music remained basically unchanged since he rose to fame in the 1930s, eschewing the incorporation of background singers and string sections that many artists in Nashville had embraced by the early 1960s. He still sang songs about trains, family, and Christian faith in his trademark nasal tenor, with the relatively rustic backing of a scraping fiddle and plaintive sliding notes

FIGURE 6.2 Roy Acuff and His Smoky Mountain Boys perform for soldiers in Vietnam. (Roy Acuff Scrapbook, courtesy of the Country Music Hall of Fame and Museum)

on the dobro played by Bashful Brother Oswald, who always wore overalls and an old slouch hat onstage. The old-time wholesomeness of Acuff's music combined with the sex appeal of a young woman performer reminded the marines in Santo Domingo of what they were fighting to protect back home.

Acuff and his band spent Christmas 1965 in Vietnam, entertaining the troops on another USO tour and generating press about the commitment to US servicemembers from one of country music's most enduring performers. Soft-pedaling his patriotism before he left, Acuff told the *Nashville Banner*, "It's the least we can do for the boys fighting over there."[24] In fact, the trip included stops in Korea, Japan, and the Philippines and was his fifteenth military tour since 1949. The Pacific edition of *Stars and Stripes* praised Acuff for that level of dedication, noting that he had spent 167 days on tour for the troops in the past six years, with one tour lasting seventy-six days and another lasting forty-nine. "No other entertainer has compiled such a record," the soldiers' paper told readers, with a possible swipe at Bob Hope, "although some have received more public acclaim for lesser efforts."[25]

Acuff also took the time to assess the political significance of the war in Vietnam and his own partisan loyalties. "I'm out of politics for good now. But I'm still interested in 'em and in what's going on," he told *Stars and Stripes*. "That's why I wanted to make this trip. I figured it would give me a chance to gain some knowledge and at the same time we could bring the boys some downhome music."[26] What he saw must have pleased him. Acuff's politics followed the anticommunist mission of the US Armed Forces in Vietnam. He muted whatever criticisms he harbored for President Johnson under his commitment to entertaining US soldiers in times of war.

Other country music artists and entrepreneurs followed Acuff's example and rolled into action in 1965. That year, a talent agency called Hometowners, USA, Inc., created a kind of roaming house band, also named the Hometowners, to play in service clubs across Europe. The group began as the idea of five ex-servicemen who had played together in their off-duty time while stationed overseas. The Hometowners, who dressed in red, white, and blue stage outfits, returned to West Germany, where they played country music for US troops and served as the backup band for touring country music singers. The Defense Department maintained hundreds of clubs that served as the venues for the group. With so much demand for country musicians overseas, these veteran-musicians could probably work more abroad than they could back in their actual hometowns.[27]

While the Hometowners used the military to sustain their employment as working musicians, other country artists used their military experience to inform their civilian careers as songwriters. Few country songwriters could relate to the experience of military service like Tom T. Hall. Born in 1936 at Olive Hill, Kentucky, Hall left school at the age of fifteen to earn money for his family after his father suffered a debilitating gunshot wound during a hunting accident. Hall worked in factories and cut grass at a graveyard, among other short-term jobs, before seeing the military as a way out of low-waged employment. "I joined . . . with the intent of finishing high school in the army," he recalled. "I got my diploma there from that, and . . . for a short while attended Roanoke College in Roanoke, Virginia, studying to be a writer, of all things, a novelist."[28]

Hall never published a novel, but he did discover his skill as a songwriter while stationed in Germany in 1957, a skill that led to enormous success in the 1960s. As he remembered, "I was in Europe in the army, and I was singing, entertaining some of the GIs over there in some of the clubs, and we had a band. . . . So I started writing some songs to entertain the GIs. That's the first time that I realized that I had a talent for writing, because they just smashed for the GIs." The songs he wrote reflected his experiences and those of other servicemembers stationed in the network of Cold War military installations around Germany, with titles like "3,000 Gallons of Beer," "Short-Timer's Blues," "36 Months of Loneliness" (named for the standard length for a tour of duty), and "Gasthaus Rock," a reference to the German name for a nightclub. Hall said, "I was singing there and entertaining the GIs to such an extent, I thought, 'Well, when I get back to the States, maybe I can write songs and entertain people back there.'"[29]

After Hall returned from the army and after his short stint as an aspiring novelist, he began working as a disc jockey for country radio stations and continued writing songs. In 1963, the Nashville recording star Jimmy C. Newman recorded one of Hall's compositions, called "DJ for a Day," written from the perspective of a heartbroken man who wants to take over a radio station and play music for the woman who has left him. Newman's success with the song led to a recording contract for the writer. The following year, Hall released his first single, "I Washed My Face in the Morning Dew." Over the next five years, Hall achieved an astonishing level of success. He penned hit tunes like "Harper Valley PTA," which Jeannie C. Riley took to number one on the pop and country charts in 1968, making her the first woman to do so. He also wrote most of the songs on the Flatt and Scruggs album *The Story of Bonnie and Clyde* and at least seven other top-five hits for himself and other artists by 1969. Between 1967 and 1985, he wrote thirty-three top-twenty country songs, in an unparalleled hit-making career.[30] Hall's time in the army and his interest in writing about the job of armed service provided the basis of that success.

As quickly as the Pentagon increased US ground troops in Vietnam, Hall responded with a war-themed song. On August 25, 1965, the country singer Johnny Wright released Hall's "Hello Vietnam." In a solemn voice, Wright sings from the first-person perspective of a soldier on the eve of deployment. It begins with the refrain, "Kiss me good-bye and write me while I'm gone / Good-bye my sweetheart, hello Vietnam." The verses explain why the soldier must leave, how the war should inspire collective sacrifice, and how military service fits into US foreign policy. "America has heard the bugle call," Wright sings, while a guitar filtered through a heavy tremolo effect mimics a military bugle. "And you know it involves us one and all." He then reiterates the domino theory that communism must be stopped, "or freedom will start slipping through our hands." "Hello Vietnam" debuted at number one on the *Billboard* country charts, holding that position for three weeks and staying on the charts for over five months.[31] With this combination of patriotic gusto and tearful farewell, Hall's song captured the mixture of duty and trepidation that shaped soldiers' emotions on the verge of deployment to yet another war in Asia.

The song touched US servicemembers so deeply that fifty sailors assigned to an aircraft carrier off the coast of Vietnam contacted Johnny Wright to thank him for his record. They had heard the song played over the speakers on their ship and told Wright, "You've pretty well captured the spirit of how we, who are so actively involved over here, actually feel about the war itself and being away from our wives, girl friends and families." The letter also revealed the political message that the men took from Wright's delivery of Hall's lyrics. "We feel that your song says something very meaningful to the people who are causing such trouble in our colleges and cities. We hope that they'll pay close attention to the words and will think twice before condemning our position against the Communists over here."[32] The peace movement had gained momentum by late 1965, with young people like the Students for a Democratic Society leading the denunciation of what many saw as a pointless war against Vietnamese self-determination.[33] The sailors heard Hall's song as a commonsense rebuttal to those demonstrations.

"Hello Vietnam" slipped down the charts in the winter of 1965, only to be replaced by another Vietnam-themed Hall composition, Dave Dudley's release "What We're Fighting For." Dudley's song reached number four by January 1966 and spent four months on the *Billboard* country charts. Hall wrote this hit in the form of a letter from a soldier who asks his mother to tell the antiwar protestors, "There's not a soldier in this foreign land who likes this war" before pleading, "Oh mama, tell them what we're fighting for." The song casts the peace movement as a misunderstanding between soldiers willing to fight and die for democratic freedom and the people who simply must have forgotten about the way foreign adversaries can threaten the US homeland. "Tell them that we're fighting for the old red, white, and blue," the soldier instructs his mother, and he asks, "Did they forget Pearl Harbor and Korea, too?"[34]

The success of this song encouraged Dudley to build an entire album that reflected wartime patriotism, titled *There's a Star-Spangled Banner Waving Somewhere*. Every song catered to the soldier experience, including the title track, which was a reworking of Elton Britt's World War II–era hit. The album also featured three Tom T. Hall songs ("What We're Fighting For," "Hello Vietnam," and "Then I'll Come Home Again"), four songs from Hank Locklin's *Foreign Love* album ("Geisha Girl," "Lili Marlene," "Fraulein," and

"Filipino Baby"), and "Viet Nam Blues" by Kris Kristofferson, a then-unknown army veteran and aspiring songwriter.[35] "Viet Nam Blues" took the talking-blues style popularized by leftist artists like Woody Guthrie, Pete Seeger, and Bob Dylan and turned it into a critique of antiwar protestors as naïve, privileged children. Kristofferson, himself a child of privilege, had earned a degree from Pomona College and studied at Oxford as a Rhodes Scholar of English literature. He also joined the US Army, flew helicopters, earned distinction as a Ranger, and was the son of a major general in the US Air Force. He would develop a reputation as a sought-after songwriter whose poetic tendencies made him a hit-making outlaw and friends with Nashville elite like Johnny Cash and Roger Miller. But in 1965, Kristofferson leaned into country music militarization and the backlash against wartime dissent.[36]

An initial reaction to Tom T. Hall's Vietnam-themed hits might categorize them as jingoistic, prowar, anticommunist anthems or simply as kitschy Cold War propaganda. Subsequent pop-culture uses of "Hello Vietnam" have certainly supported that interpretation. The opening of Stanley Kubrick's *Full Metal Jacket* shows Marine Corps barbers shaving the heads of the film's stars in preparation for basic training on Parris Island, South Carolina, while Hall's song plays over the scene. In Kubrick's hands, "Hello Vietnam" provided an ironic, corny soundtrack to the mass conformity of military service.[37] Mercury Records undoubtedly believed that it had a statement of patriotic support with Dudley's "What We're Fighting For." The label shipped 3,000 copies of the single to Vietnam as Christmas presents for soldiers in December 1965.[38]

But there is more than flag waving at work within these songs. In each of these early tunes, Hall gives the power of first-person narration to his characters. He allows them to tell their own stories, at once fictional and yet immediately believable. One leaves his lover. The other writes to his mother. Both express fear about their future and the acts of violence their government has undertaken. Hall entrusts his listeners with the sensitivity to hear the depth of emotion in his characters. No one is happy about the war. The soldiers are merely doing a job that they were ordered to do, and Hall was merely doing his job by reflecting those soldier experiences, giving voice to the nation's servicemembers and their families. Doing his job well in this way meant that Hall could sell more records.

Hall acknowledged the marketability of these themes in times of war. In a 1969 interview, he stated, "You know, during war the country always comes to country music. . . . Country people become more country. Therefore, you sell more country records. . . . That's primarily because all the country boys fight all the wars, incidentally. The rest of them go off to college, and through politics and things, they don't get drafted. . . . So country boys fight the wars."[39] Hall was right in his demographic analysis, particularly if by "country," he meant the working class and southerners. The enlisted troops during Vietnam were approximately 25 percent poor, 55 percent working class, and only 20 percent middle class. Likewise, 30 percent of US soldiers during the war hailed from the states of the former Confederacy plus Kentucky, even though the region made up only 22 percent of the nation's population. Southern soldiers also made up 27 percent of all US deaths in Vietnam.[40]

Like Hall, Nashville's country music industry recognized the escalation of the Vietnam War as a chance to reach fans serving in the military. The idea to ship 30,000 copies of Dudley's "What We're Fighting For" had come from Dixie Deen, a *Music City News* staff reporter from England who was also a talented songwriter and future wife to Tom T. Hall. Having grown up overseas, Deen understood how the US military furthered country music fandom. She recommended sending the record, with copies of *Music City News*, to the troops in Vietnam. Her editor contacted a man named Buz Cahn, who was an active member of the Air National Guard and was a former writer for *Music City News*, to arrange the delivery. Cahn then oversaw the inclusion of the paper/record bundle onto the Guard's shipment of holiday gifts, called "Operation Christmas Star," to soldiers in the Far East. Never missing a chance for self-promotion, *Music City News* created a photo opportunity of Dave Dudley, Dixie Deen, and Mother Maybelle Carter, who had an answer song called "I've Told Them What We're Fighting For," assembling the care packages next to a Christmas tree in the paper's Nashville office.[41]

The efforts to promote Dudley's record and the *Music City News* coincided with similar campaigns from the Defense Department and the *Grand Ole Opry* to push country music to the troops. In late 1965, the US Armed Forces had announced its intention to increase the amount of country music on the AFN in Europe and ban the disparagement of the genre as "hillbilly" or "hick" music.[42] On January 14, 1966, the *Opry* filmed a special episode of the show as an inaugural program on a new AFRTS station that broadcast from Saigon. WSM, Nashville radio station and home to the *Opry*, recruited the help of emcee Roy Acuff, as well as performances by Dottie West, Connie Smith, the Willis Brothers, Charlie Louvin, the Carter Family, and several more.[43]

Near the end of 1966, Bill Williams, the promotion manager for WSM, embarked on a two-week-long airlift mission to deliver free country music records to soldiers stationed in Vietnam.[44] Williams had spent his life working in radio and had taken over the head public relations position at WSM in 1964. He had also served on US Navy submarines during World War II and earned a Silver Star for his valor.[45] With his trip to Vietnam, Williams joined together his personal experience of bravery in the line of fire, his understanding of the sacrifices that accompany military service, and his duty to country music. "Vietnam is, of course, one of the loneliest spots in the world. It's lonely in the jungle, in the elephant grass, or in the swampy Mekong Delta," he wrote in *Country Song Roundup* on his return. "Alleviating some of this loneliness was part of my intended purpose."[46]

Williams and WSM eased that loneliness by soliciting record donations for soldiers from Decca, RCA Victor, Capital, Columbia, Hickory, Starday, and Monument record companies. The Tennessee National Guard then loaded the albums on a C-97 and sent them to Saigon. Williams flew separately but rejoined the record shipment in country. The Joint United States Public Affairs Office arranged a tour for Williams to interview the troops about country music and hand out the free records. In words that Connie B. Gay could appreciate, Williams told of traveling where "there were bombs going off too close for comfort, a teargassing, and a shooting incident." He persevered to deliver country music to the soldiers, who deserved it. And just as Gay had played soldiers' messages during the Korea War, Williams "brought back dozens of tape recordings of the troops to play for their families back home." "It helped create a link," Williams told readers of *Country Song Roundup.*[47]

While Williams and WSM cemented the personal connections between country radio and the music's military fans, the CMA honored the longstanding ties between the country industry and the military brass. When the CMA's board of directors met in San Diego during the summer of 1967 to plan the organization's annual televised award show, they decided to recognize the Defense Department for the way "various military services have promoted country music in various forms, including USO tours, Armed Forces Networks, and display of country product in the P.X.'s around the world" over the past twenty-five years.[48] To accept the award, the CMA invited US Air Force Colonel Robert Eby, commander of the AFRTS, a man who understood the country music–military relationship in simple terms of supply and demand. He told *Close-Up* before the award ceremony, "What the troops want, they get, to the best of our ability."[49] According to the military's official line, mediated through the CMA, US servicemembers wanted country music at least as much as, if not more than, they wanted the cutting-edge sounds of the pop mainstream or the growing counterculture.

And, even if they did not want country music, the Music Row–military partnership would have made the music nearly inescapable.

The testimonies provided by *Close-Up* and the CMA's interest in promoting its products could make it seem as if the military only cared about country music or that only Music Row held these warm connections with the US military. In reality, servicemembers enjoyed a wide range of entertainment options that represented the far-reaching influence of the Defense Department within the US culture industries. The USO and private promoters facilitated a steady stream of entertainers on tours of Vietnam, ranging from Hollywood stars to musical acts to professional sports teams. During the first few years of the war, US troops could look forward to "handshake tours" from the likes of John Wayne, Jayne Mansfield, Robert Mitchum, the Los Angeles Lakers, Henry Fonda, James Garner, Joey Bishop, and Bob Denver, among others. The troops could also count on annual Christmas shows by Bob Hope thanks to the pull of the USO.[50] These tours gave servicemembers a chance to meet the stars, however briefly, and continued the tradition of sending celebrities to visit the US fighting forces as a means of boosting morale and lending star power to US armament. With the help of the USO, it appeared that mainstream US showbusiness, from the Duke to Gilligan, was on the side of the US soldier.

The armed forces' courtship of mainstream pop culture extended to its selection of musical acts, and GIs flooded the concert events by the thousands to catch the sights and sounds of American performers. The USO certainly booked country artists within their stable of stars, but the full scope of musical offerings bridged a wide range of tastes. Entertainment Branch records from 1966 to 1969 indicate that the Black gospel singer Clara Ward made twenty-two tour stops, performing for more than 15,000 concertgoers. The pop star and actress Connie Francis played twenty-two shows in Vietnam as well and netted nearly 60,000 attendees. The Cascades, who received their start in the US Navy and were known for their 1963 hit "Rhythm of the Rain," played nineteen shows for around 25,000 servicemembers in 1968. No one topped the sultry-voiced Nancy Sinatra, who was known for her high boots and higher blond hair. With just seventeen dates, she broke attendance records, with a combined audience of 103,500 servicemembers, probably reflecting the fact that her mixture of musical talent and conventional good looks made her particularly popular with the young men in country. By contrast, a twenty-two-date Hank Snow tour generated a total audience of around 13,000, while Roy Acuff's sixteen shows in 1967 attracted around 34,000.[51] Any number of contributing factors may have affected concert attendance, but it seems that most professional musicians could garner a decent crowd regardless of their genre affiliation. Servicemembers hungered for a respite from the alternating terror and boredom of wartime, and the USO made sure that a steady stream of musicians, athletes, and movie stars kept them as entertained as possible.

Although the troops appreciated these entertainers, the USO did not and, in fact, could not book the acts from the cutting edge of popular music for its tours. The newest and hippest music of the mid-1960s came from the counterculture, a Venn diagram of movements that included antiwar protestors, free-speech advocates, civil rights activists, psychedelic-drug zealots, and other critics of the US mainstream. That mainstream categorized the counterculture's music, namely, psychedelic rock, folk, and soul, as subversive, particularly when compared to elder statesmen of showbusiness like Bob Hope or Roy Acuff. The mission of the USO focused on building morale and patriotism. It could not book an act that carried any association with the culture of rebellion that prevailed in much of the latest popular music.[52]

Consider the summer of 1967, when the USO sponsored tours by those elder stars. Music fans could have purchased brand-new releases like the Beatles' *Sgt. Pepper's Lonely Hearts Club Band*, Jefferson Airplane's *Surrealistic Pillow*, Otis Redding's *Live in Europe*, or Aretha Franklin's *I Never Loved a Man the Way I Love You* and *Aretha Arrives*. It was the "Summer of Love," after all, and generational change seemed to be at hand. Events like the Human Be-In at San Francisco's Golden Gate Park, the rise of the Black Panther Party, and the mass antiwar protest during the spring had alerted Americans to young people's growing dissatisfaction with the status quo of white middle-class American values. The soul music and psychedelic rock of the era gave voice to that discontent and disillusionment.[53] The troops who fought in Vietnam skewed disproportionately young compared to the age of US fighting forces in previous wars, and many counted themselves fans of this countercultural music, regardless of what the CMA's *Close-Up* told its readers. And, while they may have liked country music, their tastes in the latest rock and roll music put the entertainment desires of servicemembers at odds with the vision and booking priorities of the USO, as well as with the country music boosterism of the CMA.

The US Army's Entertainment Branch addressed soldiers' desires for more current and even countercultural sounds by creating the Command Military Touring Show (CMTS), a program that took a bottom-up approach to entertainment by forming bands and theater acts from the GIs themselves.

The CMTS groups then toured Vietnam, performing at service clubs, hospitals, and makeshift stages wherever soldiers could spare a few minutes for some tunes. Because these entertainers came from the ranks of trained soldiers, the CMTS could send these bands into the thick of the fighting, far deeper than the army would allow civilian USO acts to travel. It also served the purpose of tapping into the existing musical talent and tastes of American youth without trying to book professional civilian groups. The CMTS included psychedelic rock bands that billed themselves under "heavy" or vaguely druggy names like Buzz, Fixed Water, Burning Spear, and the Electric Grunts. Special Services proudly advertised the "mind-bending sounds" of such groups and even co-opted illustrations from the hippie underground to promote their shows on posters and tour schedules.[54]

For all of the evidence that the CMTS fulfilled the need for countercultural sounds, it also opened a new avenue for country musicians to spread their music in Vietnam. The CMTS formed bands like Jamboree, the Wagon Wheels, the String-A-Longs, Nashville Cats, and the C. and W. Golds, pulling country pickers from the ranks and forming them into hot bands that received overwhelmingly positive receptions in the late 1960s and early 1970s.[55] The group Jamboree represented one of the first CMTS acts of any genre to hit the road in Vietnam. Its promotional materials touted its ability to "offer the best in country and western music" and boasted that this was a collection of "professional musicians who also happen to be servicemen," including a former member of Hank Snow's band. Jamboree proved to be a hit with the soldiers on their tour in the spring of 1967. The entertainment coordinator for each unit at each stop completed an evaluation form, with most requesting more groups like Jamboree and one noting that "the enthusiasm of this group is contagious—very well received."[56] The CMTS may have kept soldiers connected to the countercultural sounds of rock and soul, but it also kept them steeped in the sounds of country music. What soldiers seemed to appreciate the most was the willingness of any group, regardless of genre, to take them away from the stress of war, showing that someone cared enough to share their talents and time with the soldiers.

While the troops in Vietnam enjoyed this wide spectrum of musical genres in country, the country music industry maintained its courtship of the military brass. On the night of the CMA award show in November 1967, Tex Ritter presented Brigadier General Michael Paulick, commanding officer at Fort Campbell, Kentucky, with a bronze and walnut plaque engraved with the message, "The Country Music Association Salutes the United States Armed Forces Protecting Us around the World." General Paulick thanked

FIGURE 6.3 The program for a Special Services/CMTS tour by a group called the Wagon Wheels. Special Services formed all-soldier bands to supplement the need for military entertainment. While the CMTS fulfilled the desire for more countercultural sounds like psychedelic rock and soul, they also formed country bands that added to the proliferation of the genre among US fighting forces. (National Archives at College Park)

the CMA audience for their continued support of the war effort and the troops on the front lines. He also told them that he was forwarding the award to the Pentagon, where it would hang in the secretary of defense's offices.[57]

Ritter then presented Colonel Eby of the AFRTS with a separate award, a piece of parchment mounted on red velvet and framed in gold that read, "To the Armed Forces Radio and Television Service for Twenty-Five Years of Programming of Country Music to United States Military Personnel around the World." Eby told the crowd that his network only selected the best entertainment for the troops and that the large amount of country music on the air was no arbitrary decision. He repeated his previous rationalization for the proliferation of country music to the award banquet audience, explaining that the networks played more country because servicemembers requested it more than other genres.[58] His cause-and-effect description obscured the active cooperation between Nashville and Washington and masked country music militarization as a reflection of pure market forces.

That public-private partnership cultivated by Music Row and the Pentagon only grew in 1968, when the fighting intensified in Vietnam and public support for the war crested. In February, the CMA released its *Country Music*

Salutes the Armed Forces compilation record for sale in the PXs.[59] The Defense Department commissioned a television program for the AFRTS in late 1967 highlighting the history and growing popularity of country music. The short film featured interviews with Jo Walker, the CMA's executive director, and WSM's Bill Williams, both of whom described the significance of the Country Music Hall of Fame. *Close-Up* relayed how the AFRTS would use the film "in support of the overseas Federal Crusade for health and welfare funds" and how servicemembers "voted overwhelmingly for a country music theme for their campaign promotion."[60]

The Country Music Hall of Fame and Museum, operated and funded by the Country Music Foundation, also tried to turn the troops into country fans before they left for their overseas posts, with the help of General Paulick at Fort Campbell. The iconic building, with a design that split the difference between a barn and a church, had opened on Music Row at the corner of Sixteenth Avenue South and Demonbreun Street in 1967. During its first year in business, the Hall of Fame welcomed around 200 soldiers from Fort Campbell for a special tour every Sunday. *Music City News* reported, "Most of them will soon be sent to Viet Nam—the soldier who arranged for the boys to visit the foundation is there now." Before their trip to the Far East, these men took part in a red-carpet tour of the library and museum. Their visits also included performances and personal interactions with a rotating cast of country stars like Tex Ritter, Loretta Lynn, Skeeter Davis, Jim Ed Brown, Liz Anderson, and Jan Howard. These tours probably created a meaningful opportunity for Howard who had lost her son earlier in the war.[61] No matter these artists' feelings about the fight, they took time out of their Sundays to entertain the young soldiers, who undoubtedly felt a mix of pride and panic at the thought of leaving the comforts of the United States for the front lines of Vietnam.

· · · · · ·

Individual country singers also voiced their patriotic support for the troops with flag-waving hits. These songs spoke from, or at least for, a political position that loathed dissent from the antiwar movement. In 1966, Staff Sergeant Barry Sadler, a member of the US Special Forces and a Vietnam veteran, scored a number-two country hit with "Ballad of the Green Berets," a tribute to the army's elite soldiers.[62] That same year, a honky-tonker from North Carolina named Stonewall Jackson released "The Minute Men (Are Turning in Their Graves)." Written by Harlan Howard, this banjo-driven song includes a militaristic snare beat and cast suspicion on those who

FIGURE 6.4 Soldiers stationed at Fort Campbell, Kentucky, visit the Country Music Hall of Fame at its original location on Sixteenth Avenue South in Nashville, Tennessee. (*Music City News*, courtesy of the Country Music Hall of Fame and Museum)

"march in lines and carry signs, protesters one and all / They'd rather go to prison than to heed their country's call."[63]

Like so many other country musicians, Jackson discovered his talent for singing and songwriting in the late 1940s while serving in the military. He briefly joined the army at age sixteen by falsifying his birth certificate, but that stint lasted only a few weeks before his commanding officers found the truth about his age. He then joined the navy legally at seventeen. Although he had played guitar for a few years and written a handful of songs, Jackson said, "This is where most of my country music career started. I started writing more and I found my fellow sailors had quite an interest in my style of singing and pickin [*sic*]." The captain of his ship, the USS *Kittiwake*, was a fan of country music and even loaned Jackson the first "real good guitar" he had ever used.[64] For Jackson, a white southern veteran who had served during the Korean War, witnessing antiwar protests in the mid-1960s challenged his experience with the military as an institution of economic and professional uplift, and those protests challenged what many Americans defined as patriotism.

Jackson would soon find himself in the minority of Americans who still supported the war effort and its justifications.[65] But as popular support for the war waned and more Americans identified with the sentiments, if not the tactics, of the antiwar movement, a few country performers doubled down on the expressions of jingoistic pride. No artist captured that recalcitrant support for the US military and its role in anticommunist foreign policy like Merle Haggard. In 1969, Haggard released his single "Okie from Muskogee," which, on its face, exalted the thrills of small-town America and the virtues of living the square life, bragging how its residents "don't smoke marijuana," "still wave Old Glory down at the courthouse," and think that "white lightning's still the biggest thrill of all." The support for the military and the Vietnam War specifically comes through in the detail that the narrator and the other residents of Muskogee "don't burn our draft cards down on Main Street" because they believe in "livin' right, and bein' free."[66] Although many fans and journalists conflated Haggard's personal beliefs with those expressed in the song, the truth was more complicated. Haggard was born in California to Dust Bowl migrants from Oklahoma and therefore was something of an Okie himself. Anything but a square, Haggard spent time in San Quentin for his part in a robbery and cultivated a taste for marijuana at least by the late 1960s. He wrote "Okie from Muskogee," with help from his drummer, as a character study of a specific conservative mind-set, not an autobiographical endorsement.[67]

Haggard's poetic intention faded quickly once audiences began to respond to the song's surface-level meaning. He debuted "Okie" during a concert to US Army soldiers stationed at Fort Bragg, North Carolina. The men erupted in applause, hearing a rebuttal to the antiwar protestors in the voice of someone who supported the troops regardless of the mission or the popularity of the war. Encouraged by the reaction, Haggard quickly recorded the tune, and it shot to number one. He followed the single with a live album recorded in Muskogee, at which the state's governor presented him with the key to the city. Haggard proved to be a cagey interviewee when reporters pressed him on the intention of the song and how closely it reflected his own beliefs. Regardless of the singer's purpose in writing "Okie," people's enthusiasm for the song was undeniable on both sides of the political divide of the war. It earned Haggard an invitation to the Nixon White House, while countercultural groups like the Grateful Dead added the song to their repertoire in sincere admiration for Haggard as an artist and an ironic embrace of the opinions expressed in the song.[68]

When Haggard was pressed by his label, Capitol Records, to take advantage of the momentum created by "Okie," he dipped back into the well of jingoism. He returned in early 1970 with the single "The Fightin' Side of Me." This new song admonished the "people talkin' bad / About the way they have to live here in this country" and who were "Harpin' on the wars we fight / And gripin' 'bout the way things oughta be." The chorus challenged dissenters with an ultimatum and a threat of violence: "If you don't love it, leave it. . . . When you're runnin' down our country, hoss / You're walkin' on the fightin' side of me."[69]

Haggard's caricature of conservative attitudes toward the war inspired others. Ernest Tubb turned in "It's America (Love It or Leave It)" the same year as "Fightin' Side." Tubb's song began by naming the counterculture and implying that protestors were spoiled children who did not appreciate the privilege of a college education or their US citizenship. In his deadpan baritone, Tubb complained that he was tired "of seein' hippies runnin' wild / And burnin' down the schools and steppin' on the flag."[70] The Texas Troubadour had scored a moderate hit with another patriotic song "It's for God, and Country, and You Mom (That's Why I'm Fighting in Viet Nam)" in 1966, which reached number forty-eight on the *Billboard* chart.[71] "It's America" fell flat with audiences and failed to chart.

The most brazen attempt to cash in on war-themed country music came from a disc jockey named Terry Nelson. In 1971, he, accompanied by a band of studio musicians calling themselves C Company, cut the song "The Battle Hymn of Lt. Calley," which quickly sold over 1 million copies. Three years earlier, Lieutenant William Calley and his men in Company C of the Twentieth Infantry Regiment had slaughtered more than 500 unarmed Vietnamese civilians. The mass murder, known as the My Lai Massacre, came to the attention of the American people in 1969 and led to the indictment of twenty-six US Army soldiers, although only Lieutenant Calley drew a conviction.[72] "The Battle Hymn of Lt. Calley," set to the tune of "The Battle Hymn of the Republic," defended Calley as an innocent US soldier who had dreamed of serving his country in the military since boyhood, only to be betrayed by the country he loved for fulfilling his patriotic duty. The Nashville-based Plantation Records then timed the release of the single to coincide with Calley's court martial verdict, giving the label its biggest hit since Jeannie C. Riley's "Harper Valley PTA," written by Tom T. Hall.[73]

Terry Nelson spun records at WWWR in Russellville, Alabama, when he teamed up with the songwriters Julian Wilson and James M. Smith to cut "Lt. Calley" at nearby FAME Studios in Muscle Shoals. *Country Song Roundup* profiled Nelson for a two-page spread in November 1971 titled "Terry Nelson: The All-American Boy." The magazine described Nelson's speaking voice as "quiet, soft" and depicted his prefame life with signifiers of the rural South like driving a tractor, picking cotton, and feeding livestock, which gave him "a deep appreciation for the simple things in life, such as music." He had "blond hair and blue eyes," and his "pet peeve is people who pretend to be something they aren't."[74] If the backing band for "The Battle Hymn of Lt. Calley" took the name C Company, then Nelson and his "All-American" image represented Calley himself. Together, they exonerated the reputation of the most notorious soldier in the Vietnam War by depicting Nelson, and by extension Calley, as the authentic blond-haired, blue-eyed, unpretentious American patriot.

Country musicians could express more perspectives than simple wartime chauvinism. In 1966, Loretta Lynn released "Dear Uncle Sam," an epistolary song to the federal government that reminded the Pentagon of the human cost of war. She begins, "Dear Uncle Sam, I know you're a busy man / And tonight I write to you through tears with a trembling hand." Lynn goes on to describe how her man, a patriot, answered the call to serve, but that service had left her with nothing but loneliness and worry. "He proudly wears the colors of the old red, white, and blue," she sang, "While I wear a heartache since he left me for you." By the end of the song, the singer has received the worst possible news. "Dear Uncle Sam, I just got your telegram / And I can't believe that this is me shaking like I am / For it said, 'I'm sorry to inform you.'" Lynn ends abruptly, leaving the listener to imagine the confirmation of death.[75]

Mel Tillis, a singer-songwriter and US Air Force veteran, released the song "Stateside" in October 1967. In the mid-1950s, the air force had stationed Tillis on Okinawa, where he formed a country group called The Westerners and notched his first professional experience. "Stateside" reflected Tillis's own experience, as well as the emotions of servicemembers deployed to Asia for the latest war. With a nod to Hank Locklin, Tillis sang, "The geeshee girls don't understand the lonely life of a service man / When his heart is far away to a girl in the USA / I wanna go stateside."[76] He also wrote "Ruby, Don't Take Your Love to Town," which told of a paralyzed veteran who threatened violence on his lover when he could no longer satisfy her needs. Tillis found inspiration for the song from people he had known in his hometown, a World War II veteran and his British war bride. He altered the lyrics to fit the Vietnam era with the lines, "It wasn't me that started this whole crazy Asian war / But I was proud to go and do my patriotic chore." Waylon Jennings recorded the song in 1966, followed by Roger Miller, Johnny Darrell, and Tillis himself in 1967. However, it would not become a lasting radio hit until Kenny Rogers and the First Edition covered it in 1969.[77]

Tom T. Hall wrote the song "Mama Bake a Pie (Daddy Kill a Chicken)," which George Kent released in 1970, followed by Hall's own version in 1971. Like Hall's other military-themed tunes, the song uses the first-person voice, this time to relay the story of a wheelchair-bound Vietnam veteran arriving home from the war. Hall begins, "People staring at me as they wheel me down the ramp toward my plane / The war is over for me, I've forgotten everything except the pain." As the veteran comes into contact with more civilians who inquire about his condition, he makes listeners aware of their questions by giving his side of the conversation with lines like, "Thank you, sir, and yes sir / It was worth it for the ol' red, white, and blue." The titular chorus makes a simple request for his homecoming meal: "Mama bake a pie, Daddy kill a chicken / Your son is coming home, 11:35 Wednesday night."[78] Throughout the tune, audiences hear only the voice of the soldier and his projections about the reactions of his family and acquaintances. Listeners learn that the disabled veterans' parents do not know what to say, his drunk uncle makes an awkward suggestion about acquiring wooden legs, and his former girlfriend is uninterested in staying by his side. The young man depends on the self-medicating comfort of alcohol, which he keeps in a bottle under the blanket covering his legs.

With this familiar first-person narration, Hall used his song to cut through the political din of hawks versus doves and fights over who was or was not patriotic. He made people listen to the consequences of the war, consequences that included psychological isolation, chemical addiction, and a loss of physical intimacy. Hall understood the ambivalence and dread with which soldiers and their families faced the nation's role in Vietnam, and he put those emotions into words with which they might sing along, blending their voices with the voice of his anonymous, wheelchair-bound soldier. He gave his audience the tools and the permission to dissent from the Cold War political consensus that demanded loyalty to the Pentagon's mission of global intervention.

Race and Recruitment during Vietnam

While country music songwriters captured the array of responses to war, Nashville's artists continued touring military posts in Vietnam, Japan, and Germany. Established stars like Roy Acuff, Hank Snow, Little Jimmy Dickens, Bill Anderson, Buck Owens, Jeannie Seely, Red Sovine, and others toured Japan and Germany in the late 1960s and early 1970s, playing military installations for enthusiastic GI crowds and encountering a surprising number of foreign civilian fans who seemed to know every word.[79] Acuff, whom *Country Song Roundup* called the genre's "Bob Hope," had visited Vietnam and the Philippines on a GI hospital tour over the 1969 Christmas season. "I've met with many of the servicemen. I like to encourage them to go on," he told an interviewer. "We've got to do something."[80]

Military tours also offered an important, albeit risky, stepping-stone for performers looking for a way to connect with potential fans and gain valuable touring experience. The country singer-songwriter Dick Flood encountered the benefits and dangers of military-musical tours when he nearly lost his life in Vietnam. Flood began his career as a country musician in 1954 during his time in the US Army while stationed at Clark Air Force Base in the Philippines. He formed a group among his fellow soldiers called the Luzon Valley Boys, that played in service clubs around the islands, allowing him to develop as a singer and guitar player. After receiving his discharge, Flood notched his first showbiz break when Connie B. Gay heard him as part of a duo called the Country Lads and cast them on the *Town and Country Jamboree* and the *Jimmy Dean Show*. In the 1960s, Flood formed a backing band called the Pathfinders and began booking tours of military bases at home and abroad to launch his solo career.[81] His brush with death occurred in 1966 when Flood contracted dengue fever after landing in Vietnam. His health rallied to continue a three-month tour of installations and front lines, and the singer allegedly manned a gun at one point to defend the soldiers he entertained. His performances met with enthusiastic receptions from US troops, as well as from the South Vietnamese Black Dog Battalion, which gave Flood the honorary distinction of colonel. "It almost makes you cry," Flood wrote about the soldiers he met, in a letter back home. "They show me pictures of their wives and families and request songs they've 'just got to hear one more time.'"[82]

Despite the potential dangers of disease and combat duty, women country artists also continued touring Vietnam, helping to fulfill a long-standing military tradition of sending female entertainers to predominantly male troops. The armed forces sent these artists to meet the assumed heterosexual desire of the servicemen while controlling the kind of female entertainment that they consumed. In the process, military leaders hoped that seeing women onstage might curb men's appetite for Vietnamese prostitutes, although that proved to be nothing more than a naïve hope. Still, the men stationed in Vietnam relished the times when bombshells like the *Playboy* Playmate Jo Collins, Nancy Sinatra, or the actress Raquel Welch visited. But they also loved the attention they received from the Red Cross nurses and Donut Dollies, the nickname given to the hospitality volunteers who handed out Kool-Aid and snacks to men returning to base. These "girl next door" types reminded men of their girlfriends and wives—a familiar level of feminine charms that the soldiers missed in the unattainable stars like Welch.[83]

Pat Campbell, a young woman from Nashville, traveled all over the United States and the world singing country songs for soldiers. While on tour in Vietnam during the particularly violent Tet Offensive, Campbell reportedly participated in the fight, firing a 105-millimeter Howitzer cannon at Viet Cong forces, before entertaining a crowd of 1,000 cheering troops. After her return home, Campbell recalled that on one rainy day in the jungle, "the mortars started coming in," just as she walked out onto the stage. "I screamed and started looking for cover and the guys all laughed and applauded. They were accustomed to that kind of pressure, I suppose. . . . I sang until 'Charley' (G.I. term for the Viet Cong) started coming in."[84]

The military awarded Campbell several commendations for her service, including an artillery lanyard, a green beret from Special Forces, and a Combat Infantry Badge. Although these honors may have exaggerated Campbell's soldiering bona fides, they do suggest the true appreciation that men on the front lines felt for the women entertainers who made the trek to Vietnam. *Country Song Roundup* described Campbell as a "brown eyed 5′2″ package of TNT" who was "single, weighs 105 pounds and likes '. . . anything athletic.'"[85] With her showbiz sexiness chastened by the down-home goodness of country music, Campbell made the perfect kind of entertainer for the male servicemembers. Similar to Carolina Cotton's tours in the 1940s and 1950s, an aspiring star like Campbell gave the men a balance of both types of sexuality.

The steady presence of these white country acts could wear on servicemembers who wanted more racial and sonic variety in their live entertainment. The military was rife with racial conflict during Vietnam, and arguments over music served as a proxy and sometimes as a catalyst for violence between Black and white troops. African American soldiers often complained about the lack of soul music. One notorious service club in Cam Ranh Bay played country music almost exclusively, a decision that nearly led to a race riot on at least one occasion.[86] Special Services began to cater to requests for soul by forming all-Black CMTS bands like Jimmy and the Everyday People, a reference to the Sly and the Family Stone hit and the song's progressive racial attitudes.[87] Another CMTS group, the Soul Chordinators, toured encampments and frontline battle positions, playing the Motown hits "Cloud Nine" and "I Heard It Through the Grapevine," as well as rock songs by Jimi Hendrix, including "Hey Joe," "Fire," and "Purple Haze."[88]

Despite these advancements in the military's musical options, Black musicians often endured the same racial inequality in military settings as they had in civilian life. Even James Brown, the Godfather of Soul, found ill treatment at the hands of white soldiers while on a tour of Vietnam, Japan, and Korea. Brown had volunteered his time to go to Southeast Asia in June 1968 to entertain the troops and expected the army to accommodate his needs. After feeling slighted by the hospitality that the army provided, Brown contacted President Lyndon Johnson. "Mr. President," Brown handwrote on hotel stationery, "since we arrived in Korea I have received very bad treatment and no courtesy. . . . I am being very patriotic. Please sir can't you do something. Please let me come home feeling like a good American. I am a black man and I wish that I could be accepted as a man."[89]

Brown had not experienced problems with the shows, which he claimed drew "the biggest crowds ever over here," but he did complain that the "small ranking soldier finds it very hard to get in to see the show and we are doing two shows a day." He closed by thanking Johnson for having him for dinner at the White House and wishing the best for the president. He signed the letter, "Your fellow American, James Brown," and then added, "Am I an American?"[90] Brown had given his time, talent, and resources to the war effort and was one of the most successful Black artists of the 1960s. Yet, in the context of the military, he felt that soldiers treated him with disrespect, not fully a man or even a fellow American.

Not all Black servicemembers and musicians played soul music, and not all of them experienced the same kind of racism endured by Brown. O. B. McClinton, a Black man from Senatobia, Mississippi, found that performing country music for military audiences offered a way to gain fandom and respect while serving overseas. Born in 1940, McClinton's love of country music made him something of an outsider among his peers and family. He tuned in to WSM to hear the Grand Ole Opry, as well as the rhythm and blues played on WDIA out of Memphis, Tennessee, fifty miles to the north of his hometown.[91] In 1957, McClinton dropped out of high school, left Senatobia, and hitched a ride on a lumber truck that took him to Memphis, where he bused tables at a local Mexican restaurant and practiced singing to the customers.[92] During the early 1960s, McClinton received a General Educational Development certification and then entered Rust College in Holly Springs, Mississippi, where he earned a bachelor's degree and started writing songs. Two of his efforts landed with soul singers signed to local labels. Otis Redding recorded McClinton's "Keep Your Arms around Me," while James Carr cut "You've Got My Mind Messed Up."[93]

In 1966, with the draft looming, McClinton opted to join the air force rather than risk placement in the army or marines. He entered basic training at Lackland Air Force Base in San Antonio, Texas, where he heard the country music played on the radio and the bars around the city. When the air force stationed McClinton at Kadena Air Base on Okinawa, the boredom of life on base meant that he focused more on songwriting and kept up with the latest hits through the AFRTS. During his stay on Okinawa, McClinton penned a follow-up tune for Clarence Carter's "Slip Away," which he titled "Let Me Comfort You." Carter released McClinton's song in 1968. This success led to a five-year songwriting contract with the producer Rick Hall's FAME Publishing Company in Muscle Shoals, Alabama.[94]

The air force also presented McClinton with his first real opportunity to hone his craft as a performer, and when he did, he channeled his efforts into country music rather than the soul music he had written in civilian life. The then-recent success of Charley Pride, an army veteran and country music's lone Black superstar, inspired this move. McClinton discovered Pride's debut album in a fellow airman's record collection. "That's when I started," he told the author Rob Bowman. "When I was stationed on Okinawa, there was a lot of country and western bands over there." One night, his fellow airmen urged McClinton to take the mic and upstage the singer for a local country band. When McClinton belted out "Folsom Prison Blues," the bar erupted. "So after that I started working at a lot of clubs on Okinawa, the Army base, and down at the Marine base, and I would work at the Air Force NCO club. Then I started writing more country oriented songs while I was in the service."[95]

McClinton landed back in Memphis after his discharge from the service in 1970 and looked for a way to jump-start his performing career. Catching wind that Al Bell, vice president and co-owner of Stax Records, was working in Muscle Shoals, McClinton parlayed his connections in Alabama to make a visit. He booked himself into the Holiday Inn in a room next to Bell's and waited for him to return from a session at FAME Studios. McClinton then played Bell some demos by a "friend from the service" trying to break into country music. Bell loved what he heard and expressed interest in signing the unknown artist. When McClinton revealed that the demo artist was actually himself, Bell refused to believe until McClinton sang. Bell then offered McClinton a recording contract and a $10,000 advance.[96] With money in his pocket, record label backing, a batch of songs, and a well-honed stage persona, McClinton seemed to hold all the necessary cards for success in country music. Now Bell and the Stax staff only had to negotiate the odd calculus of marketing a Black man in country music.

An early Stax press release delighted in optimism about McClinton's future of breaking the Jim Crow barriers of country music, saying, "Country music for Blacks, like soul music for whites, had always had a 'do not sing' sign on it." The promotional material then absolved potential white audiences and radio programmers of any wrongdoing, noting that the "problem" with the sign "was no one knew who put it there or how it got there. However, since music has many times broken the code of category restrictions, it has become synonymous with freedom to many musicians."[97] Powered by this ebullience, McClinton and the Stax offices did their best to push this racial outsider into an almost exclusively white genre, releasing four albums between 1972 and 1974, *O. B. McClinton Country*, *Obie from Senatobie*, *Live at Randy's Rodeo*, and *If You Loved Her That Way*. Although his debut failed to produce a hit, he broke into country radio with a cover of Wilson Pickett's "Don't Let the Green Grass Fool You," as well as the title track from *Obie from Senatobie*.

As the name suggests, "Obie from Senatobie" offered a humorous play on Haggard's "Okie from Muskogee." It reiterated the singer's pride in his small-town roots and deep southern accent that coded not as white or Black but as a country voice, which seems always on the verge of breaking into laughter. The opening verse recounts his time joining the air force and how he announced that he hailed from Senatobia to his drill sergeant, rather than rounding up to the closest big city like Memphis as the other recruits had done. The chorus boasts, "You can just call me Obie from Senatobie / And you better believe, that's a Mississippi town / We still eat watermelon at the Tate County gin house / And we drink home brew when the sun goes down."[98]

A Black man bragging about eating watermelon, that symbol of alleged Black carnality and theft, situated at the gin house, that local institution of monocrop capitalism and predatory exchange, all set to a chugging country beat, created a potent statement of country pride, almost to the point of disbelief. It is possible that McClinton made a spoof of white conservative anger. After all, he did campaign for Edmund Muskie, a candidate for the Democratic presidential nomination, in 1972.[99] But more than likely, McClinton simply emphasized his true country roots, including his military service, despite his support for the antiwar Muskie, rather than caricaturing white conservatism. McClinton's skin made him an outsider, even as everything else about him, including his military service, signaled insider. Ultimately, his race proved too big an obstacle in his quest for commercial and critical legitimacy. McClinton spent the late 1970s and early 1980s relegated to constant touring, hocking albums on infomercials, and winning over audiences on Ralph Emery's *Nashville Now* before he passed away in 1987 from abdominal cancer.[100]

· · · · · ·

It made sense that O. B. McClinton found his calling for country music in the US Air Force when he did. That branch of the armed forces consistently partnered with Music Row during the Vietnam War, and the music permeated the recruitment and entertainment cultures of the service. The country stars LeRoy Van Dyke and Bill Anderson toured air force installations and generated such an affinity with the airmen that the branch designated both of them as "honorary recruiters" in 1968.[101] It also ramped up its production of the long-running recruitment radio program *Country Music Time*, originally hosted by Sergeant Tom Daniels of *Stickbuddy Jamboree* fame. Major Charlie Brown took the helm as producer for the show in 1969 and recorded a slate of artists including Bob Luman, Warner Mack, Connie Smith, and Charlie Walker. These recordings then went out to around 2,500 civilian radio stations throughout the nation. Major Brown also donated the *Country Music Time* records, as well as other US Air Force music program tapes, to the Country Music Hall of Fame in late 1969.[102] Two years after opening its doors to the public and in the peak of the nation's cultural and political crises, the Hall of Fame incorporated its military history into its archive.

Regardless of country artists' personal feelings about the war, dozens of performers participated in *Country Music Time* throughout the late 1960s and early 1970s. In 1967, a World War II veteran and former AFRTS disc jockey named Charlie Walker made an appearance on the show. At the time, Walker enjoyed a modest performing career and pushed his first hit from

1958, "Pick Me Up on Your Way Down," as well as his then-current releases "The Town That Never Sleeps," "Don't Squeeze My Sharmon," and "It's No Secret What God Can Do," to round out a set of sin, humor, and redemption.[103] In the middle of Walker's set, the music stopped for a message from Sergeant Tom Shaw, who made a pitch to listeners to consider the educational opportunities through the air force's "Operation Bootstrap." This program paid for two-thirds of an enlistee's college education and provided night classes on base taught by professors from nearby universities.[104] With messaging like this, the air force piggybacked onto the markets traditionally targeted by country music, while artists used the program to promote themselves.

Artists cut their segments for *Country Music Time* in Nashville recording facilities with session musicians, complete with a small audience (or at least the band) to provide clapping and generally aid in the organic feel of the show. Engineers later spliced these songs together with prerecorded interjections from the air force recruiter as seamlessly as possible. O. B. McClinton recorded six sessions for *Country Music Time* over his career and remembered his tour in the air force fondly to listeners. "I always feel at home on one of these good old air force shows, being an old ex-sergeant myself," he confided on one episode, telling the host, "That's right. I did four years, twenty-nine days, and a duffle bag drag."[105] Outtakes from the *Country Music Time* sessions reveal this production technique. On an episode with the Carter Family, the band members read from a script, engaging in a one-sided conversation with a silent recruiting officer, leaving space for his side of the dialogue to be punched into the recording at another time. To fit the military platform, the Carter Family sang the Civil War–era ballad "The Faded Coat of Blue," in which a mother mourns the death of her son, a Union soldier.[106] Other artists pulled off the staged dialogue a bit more convincingly, like Jeannie C. Riley's flirtatious exchange before her cover of "The Fightin' Side of Me," in which she purrs a come-on to the recruiting officer.[107]

Music Row did not hold a monopoly on musical recruitment during Vietnam. In the late 1960s and early 1970s, the army produced a recruitment program called *It's Music* that took pop and rock hits of the day, like "All You Need Is Love" by the Beatles or "The Crystal Ship" by the Doors, and embedded the songs within solicitations to join the ranks.[108] Produced at Fort Meade, Maryland, by the US Army Recruiting Command, *It's Music* compiled four fifteen-minute programs on one LP. A local disc jockey at a civilian station could then drop the needle on the record and take a quarter-hour break while a recruiter took over. A typical episode from 1971 started with the welcome message, "We're on with *It's Music*. This is Army Specialist Tom Bell with the hits for your army recruiter." Bell then introduced Chicago's jazz-rock hit "25 or 6 to 4." As the song ends, Bell returns to the mic, interjecting commentary like a cool FM jock: "Man, what a thick hit. From Chicago, '25 or 6 to 4.' Here's a chick I'd like to get next to for a long, long time, Linda Ronstadt."[109]

It's Music went beyond situating recruiting messages next to hip music. The show also included rewrites of current hits with lyrics that promoted armed service. When Ronstadt's song "Long, Long Time" ends, another tune begins that sounds remarkably like Neil Diamond's "Sweet Caroline." Yet, instead of Diamond's nostalgic ode to the initial spark of love, listeners heard lyrics encouraging them to join the Women's Army Corps: "When you are young and in love with life, there's a way you can do more / You can travel and make new friends in the Women's Army Corps. . . . You can walk through Central Park on a sunny autumn day / You can see the sun a-setting across the San Francisco Bay." A male voice cuts in while the co-opted melody fades, reminding listeners, "See your army recruiter today." On the same episode, a song with melody and instrumentation that sound nearly identical to the Four Tops' "Reach Out (I'll Be There)" spoke to young people who needed employment, telling them to join the army, where they could choose their professional route. The verse begins, "You say it's getting tougher day by day / To get a good job to come your way / And you're looking 'round for some solution / To help you get the job of your choosin'." But, where the Four Tops sang the catchy refrain "I'll be there, with a love that will shelter you / I'll be there, with a love that will see you through," the olive-drab imitators instructed that "Army's where, the future's up to you / Army's where, there's so much you can do." To close out the fifteen-minute service announcement, Specialist Bell selected "Uncle John's Band" by the Grateful Dead.[110]

Unlike the live sessions of *Country Music Time*, the rock and pop hit makers on *It's Music* had no direct involvement with the program. It strains the imagination to consider acts like the Beatles, the Grateful Dead, or the Doors purposefully pitching the option of armed service for the US government to their young fans. In fact, the army had to rewrite pop songs, probably without the express permission of the original authors, in order to mesh their message with anything remotely hip among the countercultural generation.

This is not to suggest that country musicians supported the military and its current war any more or less than their rock contemporaries did, but the production of the country shows constructed the sound of intimacy between the artist and the recruiter. Additionally, the artists on *Country Music Time* did not promote a singular political message. Since the artists cut their songs live, they could make choices about their contributions to the program rather than simply promoting their latest singles.

The live production arrangement for *Country Music Time* gave the musicians a chance to editorialize, however subtly, even as they participated in the recruitment of military personnel for a war that grew increasingly questionable with every day. For every "Fightin' Side of Me," there was the Carter Family's reworking of a Civil War–era ballad about the emotional devastation delivered to a family when a son dies in the line of battle and trades his faded coat of blue for a robe of white in heaven. In 1968, the honky-tonker Johnny Darrell performed a somber version of "Green, Green Grass of Home," a song he had first cut in 1965. Written by the World War II veteran Curly Putman, "Green, Green Grass of Home" told the story of a death-row inmate dreaming of reuniting with his loved ones, only to awaken in the reality of his cell just prior to his execution.[111] Heard in the context of a military enlistment advertisement in the midst of the Vietnam War, Darrell's delivery sounded less like the perspective of a condemned prisoner and more like empathy for the homesickness and threat of mortal danger faced by US soldiers in Vietnam.

Country Music Time also provided cover for artists traditionally associated with conservatism to try different approaches. Sergeant Barry Sadler, of "The Ballad of the Green Berets" fame, recorded a painfully stilted version of "Sunday Morning Coming Down," a song written by the army veteran Kris Kristofferson and made famous by the air force veteran Johnny Cash about a hangover's slide into existential despair.[112] Similarly, Stonewall Jackson performed his 1968 release "I Believe in Love." With a stark departure from his "Minute Men" hit, Jackson sang lines more closely identified with the hippie counterculture than with country music militarization. "I believe in love," Jackson sang. "I think that peace should rule the world to please the Lord above / Before we die, what shall we try? / I believe in love."[113] Country listeners and potential recruits may have bought into the politics that brought economic opportunity through the military-industrial complex. But that did not mean they experienced the pains of war with any less ambivalence or trepidation than did their countercultural counterparts who articulated more normative expressions of protests in more expected venues and with more predictable genres of dissent.

Country artists kept participating in these recruitment campaigns, in part, because US servicemembers and their families kept buying country records. After all, military personnel and their dependents bought more country records than any other genre by the end of the 1960s.[114] That did not mean that everyone in the country music industry was prowar. When President Johnson tried to push for an end to the conflict in 1968, Connie B. Gay received an invitation to fly to Vietnam and report on the peace-talk proposals.[115] And yet, with so many military listeners around the world and with so much money at stake, country artists naturally sang about the issues affecting the nation's servicemembers and their families. Sometimes that meant a rousing version of Merle Haggard's "The Fightin' Side of Me," and sometimes it meant something as sobering and implicitly antiwar as Tom T. Hall's "Mama Bake a Pie."

Music Row Breaks Right

Because there was no clear partisan through line to country music's ties with the military, politicians of all ideological stripes latched onto the genre to advance their agendas during the late 1960s and early 1970s. President Johnson had declared a national "Country Music Month." Johnson also grabbed the CMA's attention when Ray Price and the Cherokee Cowboys entertained the president and Ladybird Johnson during a visit to Governor John Connally's ranch outside of San Antonio, Texas, in the summer of 1968.[116] That September, Johnson invited Buck Owens and the Buckaroos to the White House to perform as part of his departure festivities.[117] As a Texan and a politician who understood the power of populist appeal, Johnson saw a chance to maintain, or at least to do no harm toward, his connection with country music audiences.

President Johnson even enlisted Music Row in the War on Poverty, which he had launched in 1964 as part of the domestic agenda known as the Great Society. In the spring of 1968, that war effort needed the help of country music. Johnson's vice president, Hubert Humphrey, wrote to Hubert Long, the newly inaugurated president of the CMA, soliciting the organization's involvement in Johnson's Council on Youth Opportunity. Praising country music's "enormous appeal," Humphrey believed that the genre could be a "logical means of communication, of encouragement, and of pleasure for vast numbers of American youngsters, including our disadvantaged." Long went to New York City that April for a conference with the president of the William Morris Agency to learn how country music might help turn underprivileged youth on to the benefits of the government's job-training programs, and he promised to enlist country artists for the job. The CMA had joined the effort to sell the nation on the most robust expansion of social welfare programs since the New Deal, aligning the country music industry, however briefly, with Johnson's progressive domestic policies just as he was leaving office.[118]

Conservative candidates created a more lasting home for country music. George C. Wallace, the multiterm governor of Alabama and three-time presidential candidate, used country music to bushwhack a political path for himself toward the national stage. His use of country music as a campaign tool dated back to his first unsuccessful run for the governor's mansion in 1958. During that effort, Wallace ran as a racial moderate and paid the *Opry* stars Webb Pierce and Minnie Pearl to perform at his rallies across Alabama. Pearl appeared again, this time with the singer George Morgan, during Wallace's successful run for governor in 1962, when he embraced the full-throated rhetoric of white supremacy, encouraged by his speechwriter and adviser, Asa Carter.[119] Wallace continued an association with country and gospel music throughout his first term, a tenure that marked his hostility toward the integration of the University of Alabama and the civil rights protests in Birmingham and Selma. He made the pages of the *Music City News* in 1965 when he invited a group called the McCormick Gospel Singers to his office in Montgomery, where he posed for a picture.[120] In 1966, shortly after his wife, Lurleen Wallace, won the state's governor's race, largely as a placeholder for her husband, Wallace visited the Ryman Auditorium for a performance of the *Grand Ole Opry*. Milling around backstage with the *Opry* artists and the staff of the *Music City News*, Wallace claimed to read the *News* every month "cover to cover."[121]

Wallace wedded the white supremacy of the southern Democratic Party with the backlash against busing and the antiwar movement emerging from the northern and western suburbs to siphon voters from both parties as an independent candidate during the 1968 presidential election.[122] Under the campaign slogan "Stand Up for America," the aggressive Alabamian made political theater out of his speaking events on college campuses, where he verbally tangled with young members of the antiwar left, taunting male protestors for their long hair and alleged effeminacy. He also took as a running mate the retired US Air Force general Curtis LeMay, who suggested the possibility of using nuclear arms in Vietnam.[123] Wallace's hostility found musical expression from a minor country artist named Hal Cass, "the singing bricklayer," who recorded a song called "Stand Up for America" for the Wallace campaign.[124] It also echoed the personal attitudes of some conservative musicians like Faron Young. In a profile from 1967, Young praised his time in the military for teaching him business sense, responsibility, and self-discipline. "I recommend it for everybody," he told interviewer Dixie Deen, "especially those sit-inners!"[125]

Country musicians performed the soundtrack to Wallace's confrontational campaigning. His late-1960s rallies included performances by the country artists George Morgan, Billy Grammer, Hank Thompson, and the Wilburn Brothers, supplemented by his personal campaign band, Sam Smith and the Alabamians. Additionally, Wallace's son performed with his own country group, called George Wallace Jr. and His Governor's Five—a band made up of musicians from the US Air Force.[126] When Wallace won reelection to the Alabama governor's office in 1970, he did so with the help of Roy Clark, Jeannie C. Riley, Hank Thompson, the Osborne Brothers, and Grandpa Jones.[127] By 1972, when he ran again for the White House unsuccessfully, Wallace questioned the wisdom of the foreign policy advisers who had gotten the nation involved in Southeast Asia. As he told one interviewer, "Maybe a fellow just ought to advise himself from the seat of his pants, just what his common sense tells him, instead of sitting down with someone who told us to get into this [Vietnam] war."[128] With a position that placed blame for the war on policy makers rather than individual servicemembers, Wallace's pugilistic campaigning, southern accent, and populist promises to fight the alleged overreach of the federal government and its bureaucratic experts made an easy fit with the country music industry's claim to the down-home values and old-time roots of the white South.

No one wanted to cash in on the political capital of country music like Richard M. Nixon. After winning election in 1968 as a peace-minded statesman who could roll back the alleged excesses of the Great Society, Nixon hardened into a culture warrior bent on permanently fracturing the voter base of the New Deal coalition to create a new era of Republican domination.[129] In late 1969, President Nixon articulated a political identity called the "silent majority" for the dutiful, presumably white, middle-class Americans who did not take part in protests but went to work, paid their taxes, and supported the military. At the same time, the Grand Old Party deployed the "Southern Strategy," which took a page from Wallace's playbook and began appealing to white racial animosity over busing, the student movement, and civil rights legislation. These political appeals resonated with white voters in the high-growth Sunbelt region and suburbs across the nation who had grown weary of the 1960s political and social upheavals.

By uniting these constituencies under the banner of Republican partisanship, Nixon flattened white class divisions under the weight of race-based cultural resentments. To be a Nixon voter was to identify with the struggles of the "real Americans"—understood as aggrieved white taxpayers—regardless of one's own class status or privilege.[130]

Nixon and his advisers embraced country music as a tool that could align their rock-ribbed Republicanism with the genre's populist appeal, inviting Johnny Cash, Merle Haggard, Roy Acuff, Jeannie C. Riley, and others to the White House for performances in the early 1970s.[131] The president's attempt to glom onto country music led to a few awkward encounters. For Johnny Cash's visit to the White House in April 1970, Nixon requested that he play Haggard's "Okie" and Guy Drake's right-wing novelty song "Welfare Cadillac," even though the songs did not belong to his repertoire. Cash declined the request and reportedly played his own songs, including "What Is Truth," which expressed the singer's sympathies with the peace movement.[132]

Although not an actual fan of the music, Nixon took care to meet and pose for pictures with these artists in a bid to endear himself to their fan bases and use country music to build his new Republican majority. The CMA's *Close-Up* reported that Glen Campbell performed for the president in 1971 as part of a "day-long tribute to the American farmer," in which the singer "moved easily through a selection of songs, sprinkling proceedings with talk about his own days on the farm" in Delight, Arkansas.[133] In October 1971, Nixon sent a personal note of congratulations to the breakthrough African American country artist Charley Pride for winning the CMA's award for "Entertainer of the Year."[134]

Nixon could use country artists in this way because Music Row maintained such a close connection to the military throughout the president's intensification of the Vietnam War. During his first year in office, Nixon committed to winning the conflict through military escalation rather than seeking "peace with honor," as he promised on the campaign trail. To achieve that victory, the president mandated a policy of "Vietnamization" that shifted the burden of battle onto the South Vietnamese while ordering massive bombing campaigns on North Vietnamese supply lines. As the US military dropped bombs on the citizens of Vietnam, Laos, and Cambodia, the mutual admiration between the country music industry and the Defense Department continued.[135] On October 18, 1969, executives at *Music City News* invited the AFRTS's Master Sergeant Bill Boyd, who would go on to lead the CMA rival the Academy of Country Music (ACM), to a live broadcast of the *Ernest Tubb Saturday Night Jamboree* on WSM. The paper presented the military entertainment network with a "Special Merit Award" to honor the network's "outstanding service to country music." The AFRTS had programmed country music for military listeners for two and a half decades at that point, and the *News* noted that those efforts had "materially benefitted the entire country music industry by promoting the popularity of our music."[136]

That admiration flowed in the opposite direction as well. The same month as the AFRTS commendation, a captain from the US Navy presented the CMA with an award at the organization's annual Awards Banquet for its efforts in promoting country music.[137] This relatively minor, completely ceremonial exchange of admiration marked a significant role reversal. The CMA did not thank the navy for its help. The US Navy thanked the CMA for promoting country music to its sailors.

Reports of country music fandom among US servicemembers trickled into the pages of the industry's papers and newsletters as the CMA and the Defense Department engaged in their merry-go-round of flattery. In June 1970, *Close-Up* published a picture of a US Army artillery piece somewhere in the "Far East" emblazoned with the nickname "COUNTRY MUSIC" painted on the barrel. The caption described how the cannon possessed the name "lovingly given by the gun team manning it." "Country Music," the writer concluded, "speaks loudly every time the weapon fires."[138] In the fall of 1971, Dennis E. Hensley, a US serviceman stationed in Vietnam, wrote to *Music City News* with his prediction that "country music will remain a favorite among Asians" long after the US troops withdrew. To prove his point, he noted the prevalence of country musicians in the ranks, the amount of country on AFRTS, and that the service clubs presented live country music at least 25 percent of the time with performers from Korea, Thailand, the Philippines, and Australia playing the sounds of Music City.[139]

The CMA produced quantitative evidence of the same point when it published statistics showing that country music trailed only Top 40 in popularity with enlisted servicemembers and actually exceeded pop music among those stationed in Korea. The organization credited the AFRTS's 350 radio and ninety television stations for promoting the genre. The AFRTS broadcast seven hours of country music television each week, with *Hee Haw*, the CMA Awards Banquet, and the variety shows hosted by Johnny Cash, Glen Campbell, Bill Anderson, and Billy Walker. As for the radio, AFRTS played weekly broadcasts of the *Opry*, a thirty-nine-hour audio documentary on the history of country music, and shows hosted by the singers Charlie Williams and Jimmy Wakely. The CMA report also reminded its

PROOF POSITIVE OF COUNTRY MUSIC APPEAL

FIGURE 6.5 An artillery piece emblazoned with the words "COUNTRY MUSIC" along the barrel. The CMA offered this image as "proof" of the genre's popularity with the troops. (*Close-Up*, June 1970, courtesy of the Country Music Hall of Fame and Museum)

members of the real financial stakes of the military broadcasts. The PX system consulted the AFRTS when creating its record inventory, a sales outlet that had grown to $17 million a year.[140] Stationed overseas and with a steady government paycheck in their pockets, US servicemembers remained one of the most reliable customer bases for Music Row.

While country music filled the military airwaves, the Pentagon continued to order the bombing of Vietnam and its neighbors. The American people approved of what they knew about Nixon's handling of the war, thanks to a drawdown of ground-troop levels and a drastic decrease in press coverage.[141] And, as Nixon's reelection campaign intensified in 1972, he continued using country music as a method of appealing to patriotic support. That summer, the president sent a letter to the country singer-songwriter Red Speeks, praising his song "The Red, White, and Blue," for the "spirit of patriotism which the composition reflects."[142] In August, the Republican Party hired the country artist Lynn Anderson to sing the opening rendition of the "Star-Spangled Banner" at its national convention in Miami, making her the first country star ever to receive that honor.[143] Not to miss out on the genre's popularity, the Democratic National Convention scheduled Tom T. Hall, Tammy Wynette, and George Jones for George McGovern's nomination party, also held in Miami that year.[144] Neither party's entertainment roster probably made a difference in swaying actual voters, as McGovern won Massachusetts and Washington, DC, while Nixon won the forty-nine other states.

Even after this landslide victory, Nixon cultivated an association with country music's more strident patriotic themes. For Pat Nixon's birthday party in 1973, the White House booked Merle Haggard and his band the Strangers. Haggard remembered receiving an icy reception as his road-weary band tore through their repertoire. The audience warmed only for the expected backlash hits "Okie from Muskogee" and "The Fightin' Side of Me."[145] What Nixon heard in those songs was his own desire to kick his opponents and the antiwar protestors to the curb. The president had floated the idea of sending members of the Teamsters Union to peace movement rallies to, in his words, "beat the shit out of these people."[146] But Nixon made the common error of conflating the singer and the song. The president assumed that country musicians like Haggard supported his hard-nosed politics and right-wing policies simply because of the characters portrayed in their songs and over two decades of country music militarization.

That assumption informed Nixon's decision to appear on the *Grand Ole Opry* on March 16, 1974, during the opening celebration of the brand-new Grand Ole Opry House on the outskirts of Nashville, Tennessee. The *Opry* had moved from the Ryman Auditorium in downtown Nashville into a state-of-the-art facility in the suburbs, complete with ample parking and a country music theme park called Opryland. Dogged by Watergate and the ambivalent end to the Vietnam War, Nixon could have used a night of performatively lighthearted fun. He sought refuge with those Americans he considered his base, the "law and order" voters who made up the silent majority. He expected that the *Opry*'s fans, whether in attendance or listening over WSM's radio broadcast, remained *his* fans, part of the 24 percent of Americans who still approved of the president at his lowest point or the 29 percent who still considered Vietnam worth fighting as late as 1973.[147] Roy Acuff introduced him, telling the crowd that Nixon remained "one of our finest Presidents." "You are a great man," the singer reminded the embattled commander in chief. Speaking on behalf of Music Row, Acuff added, "We love you."[148]

More than seeking positive press coverage among friendly faces, the president diluted the negativity around his administration with the populist and patriotic sounds of country music.[149] Nixon began his appearance at the *Opry* by praising the genre as something exceptionally American. "First, country music is American. It started here, it is ours. It isn't something that we learned from some other nation," he told the faithful. "It isn't something that we inherited." He then recounted how country stars like Roy Acuff and Merle Haggard had played at his White House. Acuff had performed alongside Bob Hope for a reception of US prisoners of war recently freed from a North Vietnamese prison following the Paris Peace Talks, which ended the United States' combat role in Vietnam. Nixon claimed that when he asked the freed prisoners of war why they enjoyed country music so much, they replied, "You have got to understand, we understood it." The president then clarified the soldiers' response in terms of country music's, and specifically Acuff's, old-timey authenticity, explaining, "They knew it. In other words, it went back a few years, but they understood it, and it touched them and touched them deeply after that long time away from America."[150]

Nixon attempted to flatter the *Opry* crowd with his professed affinity for country music. Besides noting the genre's alleged ancestral Americanism, the president claimed that country music "talks about family, it talks about religion, the faith in God that is so important to our country and particularly to our family life. And as we all know," with a reference to the genre's ties to the military, "country music radiates a love of this Nation, patriotism." He asserted that country music's abiding patriotism reflected the strong "character" of its fans and artists. Americans needed that kind of character, according to the president, who was only five months away from resigning in disgrace, in order to ensure world peace for generations to come. As he told the Nashville crowd, "It is going to depend on our character, our belief in ourselves, our love of our country, our willingness to not only wear the flag but to stand up for the flag. And country music does that." The audience then sang the western swing standard "Stay All Night (Stay a Little Longer)" for the president—the same song that had been the theme to *Country Style, U.S.A.* To end his time onstage, Nixon sat down at the piano and led the crowd in a sing-along of "God Bless America."[151]

Nixon's speech and his very presence at the *Opry* melded country music patriotism, conservative political values, and military service. He wanted a public relations boost from his base. What the president and his strategists failed to realize was that country music's allegiance to the US military had less to do with partisan politics and more to do with the economics of the music business. The country music industry, not all of its individual artists and fans, had aligned itself with the armed forces. As the Cold War consensus crumbled over the Vietnam War, the country music business still benefited from its participation in recruitment programs and its sales to servicemembers. But a business relationship with the Pentagon did not mean that country artists blindly backed the president's politics.

Tom T. Hall refused to surrender country music as the soundtrack for the so-called silent majority. In a 1973 interview with *Rolling Stone*, Hall told the rock magazine, "I always believed that a writer ought to say for people what they can't say for themselves. And I think there's a lot of those people at peace marches and military bases." He then added, "I don't think George Wallace speaks for the silent majority. Lawrence Welk does."[152] With that statement, Hall dispelled the assumption that white southerners, blue-collar workers, and country music fans were solely responsible for the rise of Nixonian politics. It was also those middle-class white ethnics, those polka fans who tuned in to Welk's show for something less rustic than the *Opry*. He fired a shot in a culture war to defend servicemembers like himself who had joined the armed forces in search of a better future or simply because the draft had forced them into duty. Hall knew and had participated in the alignment of the country music industry and the military. The US Armed Forces had branded itself with the country sounds of white identity while offering its audiences an economic leg up. In return, country music received a tax-free venue to push its product and the endorsement of the federal government as an appropriate genre for patriotic consumption. But Hall also knew that country music fans did not harbor some inherent, white working-class disposition for military service or political conservatism. Artists and fans felt tied to the military because of a long history of alignment between the country music business and the political economy of the military-industrial complex. The music simply told their stories.

7 Proud to Be an American

Country Music Militarization and Patriotism after Vietnam

. . . .

On April 13, 1983, CBS viewers watched as Kenny Rogers stepped from the shadows of an impressive concert hall and walked across its mezzanine toward the camera. With a three-piece tuxedo and hair coiffed to salt-and-pepper perfection, Rogers's sophisticated appearance matched the large, dramatically lit stage of the venue and indicated that the hundreds of empty seats surrounding him would soon belong to similarly attired concertgoers. "This great auditorium is Constitution Hall in the nation's capital," he told the television audience. A prerecorded flutist played "Shenandoah" in the background, recalling the heritage of American folksongs and that tune's themes of westward expansion. Next, Rogers explained to viewers that the Daughters of the American Revolution had created the hall as a memorial to the Constitution, using a bodily metaphor to describe "that immortal document" as "the sinew, bone, and muscle of the United States of America." With a slight wince, he steeled himself against the patriotic emotion rising from within, claiming to feel "overwhelmed with the cultural history these walls embrace."[1]

Rogers then drew his audience's attention to why he, of all people, was there and what Constitution Hall had to do with his home genre of country music. His explanation may have surprised viewers, most of whom were probably not versed in country music's historical connection to the nation's capital. Reflecting on that cultural history, Rogers said that he could hear "the country sounds of Grandpa Jones, the Stoneman Family, Jimmy Dean, and Roy Clark and so many more," echoing through the revered venue. He continued to enlighten the uninitiated by explaining that "it was here in Constitution Hall on an evening in 1948 that a gentleman named Connie B. Gay produced the first country music network television program, introducing country music to a whole new audience. In 1958, that same Connie B. Gay became the founding president of the Country Music Association."[2]

With that brief history lesson, Rogers welcomed viewers to the CMA's twenty-fifth-anniversary television special and to the fulfillment of Gay's vision for country music. Over the next hour of network television, viewers saw the genre's past and present mingle. Roy Acuff delivered a tribute to Jimmie Rodgers. Contemporary artists sang several medleys of hits that spanned generations. Special duets joined older artists with new hit makers, like the pairing of Carl Perkins and Mickey Gilley. It ended with a full-cast sing-along of "America the Beautiful" led by Ray Charles.[3] Country music belonged in that hallowed hall because it reflected a history allegedly shared by all US citizens. If you took Kenny Rogers at his word, country music embodied a tradition nearly as meaningful as the Constitution itself.

The country music industry had earned a reputation as being a patriotic genre over the years, making the booking of Constitution Hall seem natural rather than the near scandal that it was in 1948. Part of that successful branding effort had come through the genre's reputation as an intrinsic part of US military culture due to the efforts of Connie B. Gay and the CMA. Yet the CMA did not rely on the armed forces on the night of the celebration. Instead, the country music industry pivoted to its claims on American identity in terms of the music's professed ties to small-town life, quaint traditions, and family values. This messaging fit well with the rhetoric favored by President Ronald Reagan, who attended the television taping and called Constitution Hall "an appropriate place to make music history with such a profoundly American tradition."[4]

Viewers might have expected to see the armed forces honored at this patriotic celebration, but country music militarization had changed since the Vietnam War. At one time, Music Row could count on the military for its record sales and talent promotion. But the country industry had to reconfigure its ties to the military due to the changing demographics of who served in the ranks and the evolution of US foreign policy. In 1973, President Nixon ended the draft and instituted an all-volunteer force (AVF). The shift to the AVF brought more minorities and more women into the armed forces, particularly in the US Army. African Americans—not the traditional target audience for country music—more than doubled their numbers over the 1970s to make up one-third of the army by 1980.[5] The nation had also entered a period of détente with the Soviet Union, leading to friendlier relations within the once-heated Cold War rivalry.[6] The Pentagon still used country music in its recruitment and entertainment efforts, but the State Department also began to see more value in the genre, sending Roy Clark and others on goodwill tours of the Soviet Union.

Country music militarization also evolved as the Pentagon revised its policies on how servicemembers consumed music at the PX and through the AFRTS. The PX system consolidated its record and tape division in the 1970s, combining most of its shipping and receiving into one massive distribution hub in suburban Atlanta. This new system promised to deliver more of the latest records to the PXs faster by tying its inventory to the *Billboard* charts. Around the same time, the AFRTS began using more syndication and automation in its programming, reducing the personnel needed to play music and cutting down on the locally produced shows that had boosted country music's global popularity. By the 1980s, the AFRTS still played country music, but nearly all of it came from tightly curated prerecorded playlists created from the *Billboard* charts rather than from the personal choices of military disc jockeys. Because the PX and the AFRTS so closely reflected what was popular with civilian audiences, the military no longer functioned as an incubator to nurture new country talent the way it once had with live, in-studio performances from soldier musicians.

Nor did Music Row need the military financially as it had in the 1960s. The industry had enjoyed record-setting prosperity beginning in the late 1970s due to the growth of country format radio and a national fascination with the culture of the Sunbelt South.[7] Country artists also pursued and won pop crossover success thanks to stars like Dolly Parton and Kenny Rogers. Buoyed by those radio spins, as well as the successive trends of outlaw country and the *Urban Cowboy* soundtrack, country music records grossed over half a billion dollars in 1980, its highest sales ever at that point.[8] Military sales remained a component of that growth, but the tastes of US servicemembers had shifted. The army introduced soul music recruitment programs in the 1970s, and the PXs sold more soul records than any other genre by 1985.[9]

Yet country music militarization evolved rather than disappeared. Following the shift to the AVF, the country industry began using the armed forces less as a way to sell soldiers on country music and more to sell civilians on the idea of country music as the most patriotic genre. The Cold War politics of Ronald Reagan further blurred the line between patriotism and support for the military in the 1980s. Country performers, most famously Lee Greenwood and his song "God Bless the U.S.A.," set up shop on that line and helped turn country music into the sound of US patriotism in the late days of the Cold War. During the Persian Gulf War, Greenwood's wartime opportunism exposed the transactional truth of country music's militarization. Country artists proclaiming that they were "proud to be an American" had always been good for Music Row's bottom line.

A New Kind of Country

In April 1975, television news cameras relayed an unfamiliar military story to American viewers. It was a story of retreat and defeat. As the Vietnamese communists pressured the South Vietnamese capital city of Saigon, US Marines assisted in loading helicopters with thousands of evacuees from the rooftop of the US embassy and onto the USS *Hancock*, the same ship that Elvis Presley had performed on for *The Milton Berle Show* in 1956. After nearly a decade-long ground offensive and an even longer intelligence campaign on behalf of South Vietnamese leaders with ties to Western democracies, the US Armed Forces abandoned the mission of securing an independent, capitalist South Vietnam. A domino had fallen. Communism had won. Nearly 60,000 American men gave their life in the effort. American pride, at least the kind bound up with midcentury militarization, took a beating.[10]

The US music industry marked that retreat as only it could—by lamenting the loss of revenue. Only seventeen days after the last helicopter had departed the embassy rooftop, *Billboard* reported that "the takeover by the communists in Vietnam was the final closing of a mart that had meant countless thousands of dollars in record sales for US labels." The North Vietnamese forces had even gone so far as to raid the US embassy in search of "records and other choice goods as the Americans pulled out."[11] In truth, the end of the US military market in Vietnam resulted from a slow withering rather than a sudden collapse. The AFRTS had closed its last station in Vietnam in April 1973 following the Paris peace talks early that year. As *Billboard* reminded its readers, the AFRTS had operated at least eight stations during the height of the US invasion, employed 170 servicemembers, and reached approximately 95 percent of the half a million troops stationed in country. The exposure provided by that airplay had "contributed to enormous sales" for domestic labels. By the mid-1970s, the Army–Air Force Exchange Services sold $50 million worth of records and the newly popular medium of tapes per year, with $30 million coming from the overseas PXs.[12]

Although the shooting war in Vietnam had ended for the United States in 1973, Music Row and the Defense Department continued their mutual admiration and mutual recruiting efforts into peacetime. At the CMA's board meeting in October 1974, Rear Admiral Robert Brock McClinton, deputy commander of navy recruiting, presented an award to the CMA that read, "With genuine appreciation for your superb support of Navy Recruiting. This support will significantly assist in attaining a quality All-Volunteer

Navy." The CMA then awarded Admiral McClinton with a membership in the organization.[13] In 1975, John Abernathy, sergeant first class, received a mention in *Close-Up* for his work as the host of a show called *Notes from Nashville* on the AFN during his deployment to West Germany. Having returned stateside, Abernathy went to work as the country music director for station WOCR in Olivet, Michigan, and served as an army recruiter. He bridged his two professions by setting up autograph sessions with country artists to entice new recruits to the AVF, booking events with Charlie Louvin, Ernest Tubb, and Dave Dudley.[14]

Recruitment had taken on a new urgency after Nixon ended the draft in 1973 and converted the military to the AVF. Young men no longer felt the pressure to volunteer for service as a means of preempting conscription and getting "choice, not chance," as the old army advertisements had promised. Instead, enlistees joined the AVF, theoretically, because they chose the military as a line of government work by their own free will. Nixon's decision to adopt this new personnel strategy revealed the influence of neoclassical economists like Milton Friedman. According to Friedman, the economy and, by extension, US society worked best when the government did not impose regulations or restrictions on how people made or spent their money. Friedman and his fellow travelers helped build the New Right's belief that the private sector, not the government, could best address society's shortcomings. They advocated policy changes like closing public schools, ceasing social welfare programs, and rolling back the New Deal regulatory state that had brought Americans a sense of security against economic and environmental hardships. These economists took aim at the draft as an example of government overreach that they compared to involuntary servitude or even slavery.[15]

Back in 1966, Friedman had assembled a meeting of like-minded economists at the University of Chicago, his home institution and a bastion of free-market thought, to discuss what the military might look like after the end of the draft. They concluded that the army should use cash inducements to attract enlistees. Rather than conscripting young men into the ranks, these economists believed that the Pentagon should have to compete with other employers just like any other business. In their thinking, even military service in exchange for in-kind benefits like the GI Bill or access to the PX perverted the self-regulating efficiency of the free market by constraining servicemembers to the choices offered by the government. That kind of government-mandated limitation smacked of socialism to these economists. With cash in hand, servicemembers could spend their money as they wished, free from the restraints of government management. The Pentagon never adopted this vision of cash-induced service, but the free-market theorists pushed Nixon into what became a radical personnel policy change that altered the political economy of military service in the late twentieth century.[16]

Filling the ranks of the AVF required enticing as many potential recruits as possible, regardless of race, and at least two branches of the armed forces began recruitment campaigns that targeted African American radio listeners. In the early 1970s, the US Air Force launched its show *Soul in Motion*, hosted by the Los Angeles–based Black disc jockey Roland Bynum. With his soft delivery, Bynum introduced album tracks from the likes of Bill Withers, Cymande, the Spinners, and the O'Jays while injecting the air force's encouragement to join. Bynum's recruitment scripts focused on promoting the employment advantages of the air force, including pitches that targeted college-aged women. "Hey, young women," Bynum addressed listeners in one episode, "you can get executive responsibility as an officer in the United States Air Force. Yes, the United States Air Force offers the young woman college graduate the opportunity to apply the knowledge she's learned in school." Instead of battling the dismal job market of the mid-1970s, women could find guaranteed employment in the force and the promise of government-regulated gender equality, where there was "no long training period and women work right along with the men."[17]

The army followed suit in the mid-1970s with *Soul Line*. The Black radio personality Vy Higginsen hosted this program, delivering sixty-second announcements about recent and historical achievements in Black entertainment and urging young listeners to pay for college by joining the ROTC—all over the top of a funky instrumental track. The Army ROTC then compiled these tracks onto an LP with twelve tracks on each side for distribution to radio stations. On a record produced for January 1976, Higginsen spotlighted news items about Stevie Wonder, Hank Aaron, and the Pointer Sisters, among others.[18] Though neither *Soul Line* nor *Soul in Motion* lasted for long, they did reflect the Defense Department's recognition that the new AVF would require a different marketing strategy than the old conscription system to maintain enlistment quotas.

While the Defense Department finally embraced musical recruitment campaigns that specifically targeted African Americans, Nashville began broadening its connections to the US government beyond the military. By the fall of 1974, Music Row cultivated a new partnership to grow the genre's international influence and spread the good news of life under a capitalist democracy. On September 12, President Gerald Ford's State Department, the state of Tennessee, and Opryland, USA sent a troupe of country music performers for a string of performance dates in the Soviet Union under the title "Country Music USA." The longtime star Tennessee Ernie Ford co-headlined the tour with an up-and-coming singer named Sandi Burnette. Their entourage included nearly two dozen dancers and musicians picked from the new Opryland, USA theme park, which featured daily concerts and dance performances alongside the roller coasters and cotton candy. The purpose of this revue, according to *Close-Up*, was to show Soviet audiences "the evolution of Country Music from its European origins to its present development." The Russians received them warmly by all reports, packing performance halls and snapping their fingers to Ford's classic "Sixteen Tons."[19] Written by the Kentucky-native Merle Travis, "Sixteen Tons" expressed the hardships of mining coal, and the communists understood the lines "Saint Peter, don't you call me 'cause I can't go / I owe my soul to the company store" as a critique of capitalist exploitation.[20]

"Country Music USA" seemed to offer proof that the easing of Cold War tensions under détente could generate real exchange while creating positive publicity for the United States as a nation that supported all cultural and racial backgrounds.[21] In this sense, the tour resembled the State Department's jazz tours in the 1950s. On those excursions, interracial jazz bands fronted by African American musicians cast the United States as a beacon of racial democracy and equal opportunity.[22] Country music could not have worked in the same way before the 1970s because of the deep-seated segregation within its industry. The mid-1960s legal wins of the civil rights movement provided cover for the nation in general, and Music Row could promote racial liberalism with some sincerity after Charley Pride's breakthrough. However, coverage of the tour revealed how awkwardly the industry's press still talked about race. To prove the music's diverse appeal, the touring cast included an African American dancer named Gary Chapman. The fan magazine *Country Music* published a profile of the tour and described that, while country music on the radio might have made a few Russian converts to the Nashville sound, "it was those final song-and-dance routines, with black Gary Chapman bouncing around the stage like a red-blooded Tennessee Cossack, that brought the various Soviet Houses down."[23] If country music was to represent the United States' music to the Soviets, then it needed to represent the nation's racial diversity, however superficially, and forestall communist criticisms of US inequality.

The Soviet tour and the country industry's affiliation with the Republican Party endeared these country musicians to the Ford administration. When the Opryland crew returned stateside in October, they gave an encore performance at the White House for the president and first lady's twenty-sixth wedding anniversary.[24] It also helped that the industry had a man on the inside. Connie B. Gay wrote a letter to the CMA during the first months of Ford's presidency announcing that Ron Nessen, the new president's press secretary, received his start in media hosting shows under the on-air name "Old Hickory" on Gay's WARL in Arlington during the mid-1950s.[25] Gay had retired from the music business by that point, but he could not turn down a chance to connect country music with the highest seats of power or to remind the CMA of his part in making country music a national phenomenon.

Opryland's cultural Cold War efforts continued into the next year. On January 8, 1975, NBC aired a film, sponsored by American Express, made from footage of the "Country Music USA" performances in Leningrad and Moscow. According to a report in *Close-Up*, a Soviet official told Tennessee Ernie Ford that the tour accomplished more than five diplomatic summits since it improved the Soviets' understanding of American people and their culture.[26] Reflecting on the tour's warm reception, one cast member believed that it had little to do with the music and more to do with the way the Americans acted onstage. "You see the people were kind of wild," he told *Country Music*, drawing a distinction between his peers and the allegedly repressed Soviets. He described how the cast members "like to have fun and party": "So when they got on stage, they'd just be natural. . . . And I was wondering if this—well, *freedom*—emanated out into the audiences. Maybe *that's* what made the tour such a success."[27]

On May 10, Voice of America (VOA), the soft-power radio network created to cultivate goodwill for the United States around the world, launched a new country music show. This program took the name *Country Music, USA* and broadcast on Saturday nights for half an hour to listeners in Asia, Europe, the Pacific, and the Middle East. VOA also invited country artists to stop by the network's studios in Washington, DC, to record guest spots.[28] Whether playing at the White House, touring the world for the State Department, or sending out songs over VOA, the country music industry found ways to use the government to stay attached to the nation's political power and burnish its patriotic qualifications, even if that meant finding civilian outlets for its work.

Automating the Army and Making Country Cool

As the VOA pushed country music to civilian listeners around the world, the Defense Department consolidated its record sales and changed how members of the new AVF purchased music. In April 1974, the PX system opened a 160,000-square-foot "buying center" warehouse at Fort Gillem in Forest Park, Georgia, a suburb just south of Atlanta. This new office consolidated inventory and functioned as the purchasing headquarters for all music stock in the Southeast exchange and capital exchange regions. These two sales areas included sixteen states (Alabama, Mississippi, Georgia, Florida, North and South Carolina, Virginia, Delaware, New Jersey, Pennsylvania, Massachusetts, Connecticut, New York, New Hampshire, Vermont, and Maine) and Washington, DC. The streamlining of record distribution worked so well that soon Fort Gillem began servicing most of the PXs around the world.[29]

The Fort Gillem facility opened with the purpose of turning US servicemembers who shopped at those stores into better music consumers by putting the newest records in their hands faster than ever. In the mid-1970s, the Army–Air Force Exchange operated 618 PX locations worldwide that sold $2.5 billion worth of merchandise a year (about $14.6 billion in 2023 dollars), including stereos, records, and tapes. Those sales figures made the tax-free government outlet a dreaded competitor for smaller stores near military installations and the third-largest US-based retailer behind Sears and J. C. Penney.[30] To service those stores, the Fort Gillem facility maintained a limited inventory of around 1,000 titles of records and tapes. Servicemembers paid around $5 for an LP that cost a civilian nearly $8, but although soldiers could count on the tax-free discount, they often complained that the PXs did not receive the latest records until well after the civilian stores did. The heads of the Fort Gillem warehouse implemented shipping changes to increase the speed of new inventory's arrival, using army and civilian trucks and planes to transport music from suburban Atlanta to New York and on to Europe. Soon, the army had the shipping time on this route down to four days, meaning soldiers in Europe could purchase the latest records from the United States in under a week of their domestic release dates. PX leaders predicted that their streamlining of the music sales would deliver a 20 percent growth in retail volume, from $39 million in 1976 to $47 million in 1977.[31] The relatively small inventory supplied from Fort Gillem ensured that the biggest hit records remained top priority for in-store stock, while soldiers with niche requests would have to place individual orders with the warehouse.

At the same time that the Defense Department changed how servicemembers bought music, it was also changing which songs made it onto military radio. The AFRTS received orders from the Defense Department in 1974 that it would begin broadcasting with cassette tape, on the promise that the format would save money for the armed forces. The Pentagon had long wanted to reduce the operating costs of the AFRTS. Beginning in 1964, the Defense Department started monitoring the service's networks by requiring annual budget reports and mandating a staff reduction. The budget reports provided a small measure of oversight, but the Defense Department never fully trusted the information that the stations provided and suspected this morale-boosting arm of the military of being a necessary, but unnecessarily costly, expense. In 1969, Nixon's Defense Secretary Melvin Laird ordered a study to determine the feasibility and potential savings of removing a large percentage of AFRTS broadcasting staff and shifting to automation, a move that would require the adoption of automated tape machines rather than the old system of live disc jockeys and transcription discs. The report found that the military would recoup the cost of this conversion to new equipment within the first year if it also reassigned servicemembers to other departments. The Defense Department deferred on this change, and the networks operated as usual into the early 1970s.[32]

Secretary Laird reassessed the AFRTS again in 1973 and again planned to save money by reducing the networks' personnel and reassigning them to positions with combat capabilities. Laird formed a working group and ordered it to conduct a new study to determine how many positions the department could cut and how much money it would save. The working group sent out questionnaires to AFRTS stations, soliciting information about their employee numbers, payroll, and programming. When the stations either ignored the questionnaires or returned them with glaring inaccuracies, Laird's group made site visits to AFRTS outlets in Europe, Asia, and Alaska and found them all lacking in areas of labor-power efficiency and cost effectiveness. In the report that the working group released in 1974, it suggested cutting 570 AFRTS staff in the course of three years, for a potential savings of $4.5 million.[33]

To eliminate staff, the Defense Department would need to adopt more syndicated programming, end most local radio production, and implement more automated broadcasting. In 1974, the AFRTS maintained 1,143 stations (929 radio and 214 television) and employed 2,657 people, 2,155 of whom were servicemembers and 502 of whom were US and foreign civilians. A majority of the networks produced their own material to add a "local flavor" rather than exclusively using what the AFRTS headquarters provided for them from the studios in Los Angeles or Washington, DC. Not only did this local programming not meet the AFRTS's professional standards, but it added to the budget of the operations, a needless expense in the opinion of the working group. The group's recommended solutions emphasized centralizing control over the AFRTS under direct oversight from the Defense Department and adopting new technologies that would reduce the number of employees. If the Defense Department eliminated these local production operations and mandated the use of more syndicated programs, the AFRTS could cut 255 of its staff, 188 of them military members, for an estimated savings of $2.8 million.[34]

In a way, the AFRTS had helped pioneer syndicated broadcasting through the use of transcription discs. Since its beginnings in World War II, the AFRTS depended on these prerecorded shows to fill the airtime and boost soldier morale. It had opened the door for influential country music programming like the *Grand Ole Opry* and *Country Corner*. But servicemembers had come to identify with military disc jockeys as part of their daily routines. Military radio hosts had also used their shows as a space for live performances by their fellow servicemembers. Those hosts, while perhaps not cost-effective, had given the AFRTS its personality. It was also one of the reasons for country music's proliferation over the airwaves thanks to men like Sergeant Tom Daniels and his *Stickbuddy Jamboree* going back to the 1960s.

In an attempt to save money and satisfy soldiers' desires for radio personalities, the AFRTS began to produce more of its own country music shows in the style of Joe Allison's *Country Corner*. Jerry Naylor, an army veteran and front man of the post–Buddy Holly version of the Crickets, hosted one called *Hit Country*, a three-hour syndicated show that he recorded in Los Angeles and Nashville. The first hour featured an extended interview with one artist, followed by an hour of current *Billboard* country hits and a final hour of several country stars performing together. When not recording these episodes, Naylor toured military bases in Europe to promote the show and his own music career.[35] The AFRTS also produced *Gene Price's Country World*, hosted by the eponymous Price, a country songwriter and Merle Haggard's bassist from the late 1960s through the early 1970s. *Country World* ran well into the 1980s, providing country fans in the service with another audible connection to someone on the "inside" of the genre's business.[36]

As the Pentagon mandated more syndicated programming as a cost-saving measure, the AFRTS grew more reliant on civilian shows that played the top songs from the *Billboard* charts, all of which brought an unprecedented consistency between military and civilian radio. Beginning in the 1970s, the military catered to the youngest servicemembers, whom they imagined as rock and soul fans, with syndicated shows like *Wolfman Jack* and the *King Biscuit Flower Hour*.[37] AFRTS also partnered with Watermark Productions, a syndication company, to deliver its latest programs to military listeners. According to AFRTS publicity, the company worked from a Xeroxed rough draft of *Billboard* each week and used that information to record Casey Kasem's *American Top 40* three days before the magazine hit newsstands to ensure that soldiers received the show. Watermark also recorded the *American Country Countdown*, which aired on both AFRTS and civilian networks.[38] The show was created by Kasem as a genre-specific alternative to the *American Top 40*, and an aspiring country artist named Don Bowman hosted it from 1973 to 1978, at which point the popular Los Angeles–based disc jockey Bob Kingsley took over the duties. If anyone from the country industry thought that these shows might distance average fans from their local radio station, Kingsley put those fears to rest. "It really knocks me out when a station tells me they get calls or mail for me," he told *Billboard*. "It means that I'm achieving the goal I set for myself when I entered the studio, and that is to sound warm and friendly with a real local feel."[39]

By 1977, the Defense Department began embracing the recommendations from Secretary Laird's working group. The AFRTS planned to replace records, live shows, and many local disc jockeys with syndicated programs that stations broadcast via the new tape decks and automated playlists that could run up to twelve hours without interruption. The stations received their new equipment early the next year, with instructions to cease all transcription disc broadcasts by March 1, 1978. The adoption of this new medium meant that stations had to install and learn to operate automated machinery. It also meant that syndicated shows like *American Top 40* and *American Country Countdown* would arrive on tape for easy continuous play from one program to the next. Aside from convenience, the new technology promised to deliver an improved listening experience for servicemembers. A memo outlining the procedures of adopting the tape system and heralding its benefits claimed that "such problems as record segue, record skip, record lock out, and . . . surface noise [are] a thing of the past." The only extraneous noise on a tape, the memo promised, "will be that noise on the medium used to record the program. You will not hear any noise from this system itself."[40]

The Pentagon hoped to appease servicemembers' entertainment and musical morale needs with syndicated shows and automation, promising a better broadcast experience to help justify the cuts to the AFRTS labor force. Although local military disc jockeys could still host their own shows, they did so with less frequency and needed approval from the Defense Department chief of information's office before launching any new programs.[41] Listeners might miss out on the "flavor" of a local disc jockey because of this policy change, but the Pentagon could save money with the transition to tape machines and the elimination of these on-air personalities. Whether the music came from a local, live disc jockey or a syndicated host probably did not matter to the businesspeople on Music Row. Their interest remained in getting their product in front of the eyes and into the ears of as many people as possible.

To that end, the syndicated shows, with their curated playlists that cleaved closely to the *Billboard* charts, benefited the industry's top labels and publishers even more than the local military disc jockeys, who could play whatever they wanted. This new consolidated model for the AFRTS also awarded hit-making artists with a larger share of the listeners. Rather than the military breaking new artists as it had in the days of Faron Young, it began functioning as a worldwide echo of country format radio. If artists wanted to crack the military market, they needed a hit big enough to make it onto one of the syndicated radio shows that predominated the AFRTS airwaves.

· · · · · ·

While these syndicated shows delivered the latest country hits to servicemembers around the globe, the country music industry experienced an unprecedented boom in radio growth. The market share for country radio rose by 52 percent between 1972 and 1977, and country stations won more listeners in major cities like San Francisco, Chicago, Los Angeles, Miami, and New York. Meanwhile, the sheer number of country format stations jumped from 1,400 in 1979 to 2,300 in 1983.[42] More radio plays translated into more record sales, particularly for artists whose styles gave them crossover appeal to rock and pop listeners. Willie Nelson, Waylon Jennings, Jessi Colter, and Tompall Glaser contributed to the lightly conceptual compilation album *Wanted! The Outlaws*, which caught the attention of many rock listeners. Released in 1976, the collaborative album rode a wave of popular fascination with these artists, who seemed to revel in bucking the traditional image of country artists as clean-cut, implicitly conservative Americans.[43]

With Willie and Waylon at the helm, country music did not sound like the music of "squares" from Muskogee. Nor was it the domain of the performers cashing in on faux patriotism whom the director Robert Altman skewered in his 1975 film *Nashville*. Suddenly, country was cool. Nelson, Jennings, and their collaborators dressed in faded jeans and leather vests and grew their hair in the style of the counterculture, while their songs celebrated making love, life on the road, and raising hell. That combination turned out to be a hit. Record buyers propelled *Wanted!* into becoming the first certified platinum country record, earning a number-one slot in the *Billboard* country charts and number ten on the pop charts.[44] It was the kind of record that US servicemembers probably heard more than their share of, with hits like "Good Hearted Woman," on the AFRTS syndicated programs.

Beyond the success of *Wanted!*, country music infiltrated the United States' popular music industry with crossover artists, variety shows, and movies in the 1970s. Kenny Rogers, John Denver, Dolly Parton, and Olivia Newton-John all recorded country-pop crossover hits, winning awards from the CMA in the process.[45] Barbara Mandrell, a multi-instrumentalist prodigy, came of age touring military bases in the United States and in Asia as a member of her parents' group, the Mandrell Family Band. In 1967, she married Ken Dudney, the band's drummer, who left music to serve as a US Navy pilot. Mandrell signed a deal with Columbia Records and released her first song to make the charts in 1969, a cover of Otis Redding's "I've Been Loving You Too Long (to Stop Now)." By the late 1970s, Mandrell had released a string of number ones, including crossover hits like her version of the soul singer Luther Ingram's "(If Loving You Is Wrong) I Don't Want to Be Right." In 1979, Mandrell won the CMA's Female Vocalist of the Year. The next year, she won the CMA's Entertainer of the Year, and in 1981, she won both. Those accolades had landed Mandrell a television deal with NBC, where she starred with Louise and Irlene Mandrell on the variety show *Barbara Mandrell and the Mandrell Sisters* from 1980 to 1982.[46]

Whether it was Willie Nelson, Dolly Parton, or the Mandrells, country music's crossover appeal helped the genre creep into pop culture's mainstream during the 1970s as part of a larger fascination with the US South. Sometimes referred to as the "reddening" or southernization of America, the national love affair with southern culture, particularly the version of white southern culture represented in country music, deepened as the nation moved from the social and political turmoil of the 1960s into the economic decline of the 1970s. Repulsed by Watergate, plagued by deindustrialization, and chastened in their consumerism by inflation and an energy crisis, Americans from around the nation turned to the once-benighted South for inspiration as it emerged as part of the Sunbelt's new suburbs and office parks that stretched from Northern Virginia to Southern California.[47]

The political-geographical phenomenon of the Sunbelt owed much of its prosperity to the politicians who directed Cold War spending in the form of defense contractors and military installations to the region. In defense-industry strongholds like Marietta, Georgia; Huntsville, Alabama; and Houston, Texas, the Sunbelt grew fat on the federal dollar and helped a narrative of redemption for the region long known for its racism and resistance to change.[48] Along with country music, other signifiers of southern and southwestern culture grew in popularity. Cowboy boots and hats, western cut jeans, and pearl-snap button shirts became fashion statements in a trend known as "redneck chic" that hit its peak with the release of the film *Urban Cowboy* and its soundtrack in 1980.[49]

This enchantment with the South also influenced the political trajectory of the late 1970s. Voters elected Georgia Democrat Jimmy Carter for president in 1976. Carter, a farmer, veteran, and graduate of the US Naval Academy, staged events with the Allman Brothers Band and Willie Nelson to sell his candidacy to the counterculture, country fans, and the people who straddled both camps.[50] The CMA jumped on the Carter bandwagon, too, recognizing a son of the South as an ally in its quest to curry political favor for the country industry. During Gerald Ford's brief tenure as president, he had maintained the obligatory connections to country music established by Richard Nixon, continuing to recognize a national Country Music Month and sending the *Hee Haw* star Roy Clark on an eighteen-day tour of the Soviet Union in early 1976.[51] Ford even sent a letter of congratulations to the CMA on the organization's seventeenth anniversary in 1975, hailing how "country music is the sound of farms, ranches and homes across rural America": "I welcome this opportunity to commend those who have helped to make it popular around the world."[52]

Jimmy Carter portrayed a different kind of connection to the music. He did not just speak of country music's ties to rural white America. Carter consciously embodied it through his salt-of-the-earth, Southern Baptist farmer credentials. With this native Georgian in the White House, Music Row could feel as if it had one of its own in the seat of power, putting aside partisanship in favor of peanuts. In April 1978, the CMA Board of Directors held its second quarterly meeting in Washington, DC, where the president and First Lady Rosalynn Carter honored the CMA with a dinner and a concert at the White House. President Carter introduced the musical performers for the night, Tom T. Hall, Loretta Lynn, and Conway Twitty, backed by a band of Nashville musicians. The country-rocker Charlie Daniels led an informal jam session in the East Room after the scheduled concert and dinner. President Carter delighted in hosting the country music luminaries, remarking, "It's good to see something from the South so popular. As a matter of fact, some people have called my campaign a crossover hit."[53]

The country industry embraced Carter's administration even as he curbed defense spending and focused on human rights as the driving force of his Cold War foreign policy. Since the Truman administration, presidents had subscribed to the idea that the United States could not cede any ground to communists, particularly its main rival, the Soviet Union. This domino theory had given purpose to the militarized peace of the mid-twentieth century, as well as the wars in Korea and Vietnam. Carter began to deviate from that strategy in his inaugural address, in which he expressed his intention for the United States to center "human rights" as its central tenet of foreign policy rather than anticommunism.[54] He made that commitment even more explicit in a commencement address at the University of Notre Dame in 1977. Carter articulated his "quiet confidence" in US democracy and its military, so much so that the nation could reduce its nuclear strength. Instead of leading with military might, the new president outlined his belief that the United States should help create a "new world that calls for a new foreign policy—a policy based on constant decency in its values and on optimism in our historical vision." He went on to name human rights, support for democratic allies, slowing the arms race with the Soviet Union, peace in the Middle East, and ending nuclear weapons proliferation worldwide as the nation's five foreign policy priorities.[55] Conservative pundits and politicians pounced on the president's agenda as weak and potentially harmful to the well-being of US allies. Ronald Reagan, by then a former actor, a former California governor, and a Republican presidential hopeful, blasted Carter's language as a cheap public relations stunt.[56]

Despite the president's new focus on peace and human rights, country artists and bookers had grown accustomed to using the armed forces as a promotional partner and still turned to the AFRTS as a powerful outlet. In May 1977, the talent manager Jim Halsey booked Roy Clark, Don Williams,

Hank Thompson, and Freddy Fender in Carnegie Hall for a show called "Country in New York." Halsey broadcast the sold-out show to what *Close-Up* called "one of the largest radio networks ever assembled in the United States, a total of sixty stations." On top of that domestic radio reach, Halsey cut a deal with AFRTS and VOA to carry the show to twenty-seven nations, including the Soviet Union.[57] Halsey continued his relationship with the AFRTS when he secured distribution for his annual Tulsa International Country Music Festival, located in Tulsa, Oklahoma, for broadcast over AFRTS and VOA in 1977 and 1978.[58] He also synced the AFRTS to the live performances at the 1979 Montreux International Jazz Festival, where he booked Roy Clark, Barbara Mandrell, the Oak Ridge Boys, and B. B. King.[59] In September 1977, the US Army produced a film promoting Opryland, USA as a place to spend one's off-duty time, and the US Army Board of Chaplains distributed the film to bases all over the globe.[60] The AFRTS also aired the 1977 CMA Awards show with a telecast that reached nineteen countries and fifty-three US Navy ships.[61] Between these broadcasts and the armed forces' syndicated shows playing the latest country hits, Music Row could rest assured that the AVF still received its share of country music.

The CMA continued its steady courtship of political power when it presented President Carter with its "First Special Award" on May 15, 1979. Willie Nelson, Charley Pride, and members of the CMA board, including Executive Director Jo Walker, met with the president in the Oval Office. Posing for pictures for the occasion, Nelson handed the president an engraved Steuben glass bowl. Pride held a framed certificate that read, "The Country Music Association is honored that the most respectful and powerful voice in the world—that of the President of the United States—should consistently speak out on behalf of Country Music." The text commended how Carter had "always given support and encouragement to this inherently American art form" and, quoting the president's words from a Country Music Month proclamation, praised him for acknowledging the music as "part of the soul and conscience of our democracy."[62]

Carter's approach to foreign policy also filtered down to the CMA's shifting attitude toward communism. In November 1979, Chinese ambassador Chai Zemin arrived in Nashville for a visit as the guest of the CMA. Executives from BMI treated Chai to a dinner and a special performance by Barbara Mandrell. Chai also dined at the governor's mansion and received private tours of the Country Music Hall of Fame, the CBS recording studios, and Andrew Jackson's Hermitage. The ambassador's musical exposure continued on Saturday night with a visit to the *Grand Ole Opry*, where

Roy Acuff introduced him to the *Opry*'s audiences. Before leaving the next day, the ambassador visited the home of Tom T. and Dixie Hall. There, Tom T. and his band performed a country version of China's de facto national song, "The East Is Red." Chai then heard from Jim and Jesse, Jimmy C. Newman, and Johnny Cash. Cash gave his guitar to the ambassador as a souvenir. Chai absorbed more class solidarity than capitalist flag-waving in the music that day, remarking, "Country music is not only famous here, but internationally as well. It reflects the lives of American people and is also the music of the working class of the world."[63]

By the end of the 1970s, country music could receive praise from the president of the United States as the "soul" of US democracy and from a communist ambassador as the sound of the international working class. The historian Bill C. Malone told *US News and World Report* in 1982 that the genre was "trying to be all things to all people. . . . Some of it appeals to the kinds of people who used to listen to Dean Martin and Perry Como, some of it attracts blue-collar working people, and some of it—'progressive' country and bluegrass—is big on college campuses."[64] The CMA's brilliance and business savviness lay in its ability to tout both sides of country music's political history while embracing the sonic diversity that fell under the umbrella of "country." The organization could play up its patriotic themes as an exceptionally American music, gaining proximity to the White House in the process. But it could also welcome a representative of the most populous communist nation in the world and allow him to cast the genre as a music with humble, proletariat roots. Country music's politics seemed to match the politics of the listener, at least those who viewed the genre in a favorable light. No perspective was wrong so long as it served the greater mission of boosting country music's reputation around the world.

The amorphousness of country music's meanings in the late 1970s resembled the slipperiness of Carter's politics. The president straddled ideological fences, leaning into the moral contradictions that came with being the leader of a geopolitical superpower and small-town southern farmer. He could rub elbows with other heads of state and also lean into his rural Georgia roots to burnish his populist reputation when needed—not to mention the good-old-boy clout he received by association with his brother Billy, a beer-drinking archetypal redneck. His desire to be all things to all people may have undercut his credibility by the time he ran for reelection in 1980, but for a moment, Carter embodied the Sunbelt ethos in his potential to shake the South's dark past and lead the nation forward toward a sunnier future. Then, Carter's political potential turned into a tragedy worthy of a country song. A national gas shortage, stubborn stagflation, a series of public relations disasters, and the Iranian hostage crisis all combined to doom the southern Democrat's presidency, and no amount of positive press from the country music industry would help.[65]

Reagan Country

In 1980, American voters cast their ballots for a California cowboy over the Deep South farmer. Ronald Reagan rode into office on the promise of removing government from people's lives and letting the market ease the nation's economic and social ills. He famously declared in his 1981 inaugural address that "government is not the solution to our problem, government is the problem."[66] Betraying his background as an actor and antileftist spokesman for big businesses like General Electric, Reagan repackaged Barry Goldwater's right-wing cowboy performance with a Hollywood sheen and telegenic star power. And, despite his experience as the president of the Screen Actors Guild, Reagan repudiated the pro-labor spirit of the New Deal for the pro-capital beliefs of free-market economists like Milton Friedman. Those beliefs guided major political and policy decisions early in his first term, like when he notoriously ended the PATCO strike by firing hundreds of air traffic controllers and cut funds for welfare benefits and public education.[67]

The president's policies attracted business conservatives and allies from within the country music industry to serve in his administration. In 1981, Reagan tapped Dan McKinnon, a country radio station owner, veteran US Navy pilot, and former president of the CMA, to serve as chairman of the Civil Aeronautics Board (CAB). The Franklin Roosevelt administration had established the CAB in 1935 to regulate commercial air service by limiting the number of airlines and monitoring ticket sales. In 1978, Jimmy Carter signed into law the Airline Deregulation Act, a bill designed to end the CAB and open the commercial airline industry to more free-market competition. Reagan chose McKinnon to oversee the dismantling of that agency, which he finished dissolving in 1985.[68] Mike Curb, a musician and owner of the country label Curb Records, had worked for Reagan's unsuccessful presidential run in 1976. He won the California lieutenant governor's office in 1978 as a Republican and served as acting governor while Jerry Brown ran for the Democratic presidential nomination in 1980. Curb also served Reagan directly as the finance chair of the Republican National Committee in 1984, helping to bring in $100 million for the incumbent's landslide win over Walter Mondale.[69]

Besides this growing political access, the country industry also celebrated the juggernaut of the genre's popularity in the early years of the Reagan era. In 1980, the National Association of Recording Manufacturers (NARM) reported that record and tape sales for country music had grown over 20 percent from the previous year to earn $526 million, its highest ever profit. Although country music amounted to 14 percent of the total sales, the genre came in second only to the rock/pop category, which claimed 51 percent. The CMA took this news as a bellwether of prosperity. Jo Walker-Meador, the CMA executive director, stated that the NARM news gave "irrefutable proof" of what the CMA had been "saying all along—country music is fast becoming one of the most dominant music forms of the decade" and was a "vital part of American culture."[70] An exponential increase in radio stations playing country music had helped to push country to music consumers. The CMA reported that nearly 45 percent of radio stations in the United States and Canada played country music as some portion of their daily programming. That meant almost 3,500 stations in North America played some country, and a little over 2,000 had converted to a full-time country format.[71]

While the amount of country music on civilian radio skyrocketed, its air-time on the AFRTS plateaued. According to typical program schedules from the mid-1980s, the AFRTS sent its radio stations as few as three country music shows. Servicemembers would have heard an hour of *Gene Price's Country World* five times a week, an hour of *Live from Gilley's* once a week, and two hours of *American Country Countdown* once a week. Out of those, the AFRTS studios produced only *Gene Price's Country World.*[72] Armed Forces Television helped spread country music by airing episodes of *Hee Haw*, *The Tommy Hunter Show*, and *Pop Goes Country*, all of which originated with civilian networks.[73] Just a few years after adopting syndicated civilian shows, the AFRTS had whittled its country offerings down to a handful of programs playing songs that soldiers could have just as easily heard on civilian stations.

The PXs continued a booming business for records and cassettes in the 1980s, but changes to their policies implemented in the 1970s and the dwindling amount of country music on the AFRTS ultimately hurt country music record sales among military purchasers. With 620 stores in 1980, the head of the Exchange Service predicted that the government retailer would earn $62 million in gross sales that year, up from $56 million in 1979. Sixty percent of that inventory passed through the Fort Gillem warehouses on its way overseas, and the biggest international sellers of that year included

Michael Jackson's *Off the Wall,* Pink Floyd's *The Wall,* and the country music soundtrack to the film *Urban Cowboy.* The head of the PX distribution revised the hit-record list every two weeks and updated the rest of the selections every month to keep inventory fresh and military consumers on top of the latest releases.[74]

In 1981, the PX revised this policy again to cater to servicemembers' demands with even more speed. Starting that year, any album that reached the top ten of *Billboard*'s pop, soul, or country charts automatically shipped to the overseas stores and received special placement in a display made for each top-ten list. The PXs sold what the Fort Gillem officials and the *Billboard* charts decided, and that was all.[75] "It's not the record business," a former Fort Gillem purchasing agent told *Billboard.* "It's just moving tonnage in and out."[76] To make matters worse for country music, the PX had instituted a rule in the early 1970s stating that PXs could only sell records pressed in the United States, ending a lucrative market for foreign subsidiary labels that issued country records overseas.[77] This reconfiguration meant that the PX would have carried the top ten country albums of the moment but lacked the wide-ranging offerings that a hard-core fan of the genre would have wanted. With less country on the AFRTS and a narrower selection of country records on the PX shelves, it looked as though the once-strong connection between Music Row and the armed forces had weakened.

The problem was not with servicemembers failing to buy music but the kind of music servicemembers bought. PX record sales soared in the mid-1980s, and the stores broadened the kinds of music they offered to suit the growing diversity of the AVF. With regard to genre, the Black gospel label Savoy Records reported an uptick in PX sales, accounting for a little more than 1 percent of the records sold by 1983.[78] The military stores also began purchasing Spanish-language records from RCA's Latin division in 1984, while the exchange system's music sales as a whole grew by 8 percent to reach nearly $72 million.[79] And then, in 1985, soul music—a catchall term for African American secular music—eclipsed pop and country to become the top-selling genre in the military exchange stores with 34 percent of the sales. Pop finished a close second with 33 percent. Country finished third with just 9 percent of the profits despite what *Billboard* described as the genre's "historic identification as a cultural mainstay of American soldiers."[80]

The writer offered no explanation as to why country held such an affiliation with the military, but obviously something had changed. Country music's popularity with servicemembers had plummeted. The US Armed

Forces' role as a seedbed of country music fandom had diminished. Personnel policy told part of that story. With more minorities joining the AVF, fewer servicemembers fell into the traditional target audience for country music. The change in PX and AFRTS policies told another part. Nashville could not flood the airwaves with its product, a strategy that had primed the pump for country record purchases throughout much of the mid-twentieth century. The relationship between Music Row and the Pentagon was becoming less of a financial reality and more of a symbolic connection, something remembered rather than something actively lived.

· · · · · ·

Although these economic connections between Music Row and the Pentagon had frayed, many of the old ties to the military remained. Two of the biggest acts of the 1980s, Alabama and George Strait, received their starts with help from the armed forces, much as artists had in the 1950s and 1960s. Alabama, a quartet from the town of Fort Payne in the northeast corner of its namesake state, broke into the country charts with hits like "Tennessee River" and "Mountain Music." Mark Herndon, the group's drummer, credited their time playing bars in Myrtle Beach, South Carolina, from 1973 to 1976 and the military audiences from nearby bases with helping them hone their sound. Herndon recalled that the band "would have had to play in a different city every day in the year to have reached that many persons from so many different places."[81]

George Strait, who won numerous CMA awards and holds the record for the most *Billboard* country number ones, did not play country music until he served in the US Army from 1971 to 1975. Stationed in Hawaii and assigned to the payroll department, Strait needed a way to entertain himself. According to his recollection, he "bought an old cheap guitar . . . and some old Hank Williams songbooks" and taught himself to play. The confidence gained from those self-taught lessons encouraged Strait to join a band on his installation and find his talent as a vocalist. By his last year in the army, Strait had earned a spot in a Special Services country band, an experience that was new to him but a well-worn trail for so many star-bound country artists. He returned home to Texas after his discharge, used his GI Bill benefits to enroll in college at Southwest Texas State University (now Texas State University) in San Marcos, and began fronting the Ace in the Hole Band at a local bar called Cheatham Street Warehouse. His career soared from there. As Strait later recalled, he had wanted to be a country artist for a long time: "but it wasn't until I ended up in Hawaii that I really got serious about it."[82]

The army gave him that opportunity and indirectly supported his civilian music career by funding his college education.

The country industry also continued to use the armed forces to promote its artists through live performances. Jerry Reed (a US Army veteran and former AFRTS disc jockey), Freddy Fender, Freddy Hart, and Margo Smith toured military installations for the USO in the early 1980s, and country music artists accounted for around 20 percent of the organization's concert tours during the decade.[83] Hank Williams Jr., Alabama, Waylon Jennings, and several other country performers filmed a concert special in 1984 for the cable channel Showtime aboard the USS *Constellation*. In 1964, this aircraft carrier had assisted the USS *Maddox* in the operations against the North Vietnamese that led to the Gulf of Tonkin Resolution. Twenty years later, the *Constellation* was docked in San Diego and in the service of country music. For nearly four hours, 5,000 crew members and 5,000 civilians watched consecutive performances alternating between two stages with a forty-foot tall cutout of a bald eagle and two F-14s between them. One of the concert producers gave his reasoning for why they chose the ship, explaining that he envisioned something different from the *Urban Cowboy* image and "wanted to get away from typical country music productions."[84] In truth, the cable special fell neatly into a long history of such events reaching all the way back to Jimmy Dean. Given the tenor of Reagan's "Morning in America" reelection campaign and nationalist excitement around the Summer Olympics in Los Angeles that year, country musicians recognized a moment of hyperpatriotism and seized on its symbolism.

Few performers merged patriotism, country music militarization, and self-promotion like Lee Greenwood, a lounge singer turned country crooner. Greenwood had landed on the country scene in 1981 with the release of his first single, "It Turns Me Inside Out." This song's lyrics told a tale of heartbreak and regret over a failed love affair that fit easily within the country music tradition, while its soft bed of strings, gently plucked acoustic guitars, and Greenwood's raspy tenor sounded more in line with adult contemporary. That combination propelled the song to number seventeen on the *Billboard* country chart and announced the arrival of another artist ready to bring contemporary pop sensibilities to Music Row. Over the next two years, Greenwood released ten consecutive singles that reached the top ten on the country charts, with two number ones. His chart success, as well as his reputation for high-energy concerts, earned Greenwood the award for Male Vocalist of the Year from the CMA in 1983 and the same award from both the CMA and ACM in 1984.[85]

Greenwood took a meandering journey to country music stardom. Born in Los Angeles in 1942, he was only one year old when his parents divorced. Rather than raise Lee as a single parent, his mother sent him to live with her parents on a farm near Sacramento, where, in his recollection, "I was either doing farm work or trying to work at the things I knew would be my life."[86] Those alternatives to farming included music. His father, Eugene, played saxophone while serving in the US Navy during World War II, and his mother, Bliss, played the piano. Greenwood followed in their footsteps, taking up both of those instruments as a child and showing prodigious talent for each of them. For young Lee, music seemed like a tool to get off the farm and out of Sacramento. Before he was old enough to drive, Greenwood landed paying gigs as a saxophonist with a local country and gospel singer named Chester Smith and with Del Reeves's band for a brief run in the late 1950s.[87] Next, he cofounded a dance band called the Apollos and, after graduating high school, began to book tours, including several USO concerts at installations from California to Alaska. Besides gaining road experience, he also met his first wife at a USO show at McClellan Air Force Base outside Sacramento. The couple married in Reno and had a son in 1961—all before Greenwood had turned nineteen.[88]

Greenwood spent the 1960s and 1970s making a living as a saxophonist, singer, and pianist in the casino lounges and nightclubs up and down the Las Vegas Strip. He experienced enough near misses with fame over those two decades in the music business to break a less determined performer, including a brief record deal with Paramount that went nowhere and a chance to stay on with a band that became the Rascals. By the late 1970s, he was fronting lounge acts and dealing blackjack with little to show for his music career except two failed marriages, a defunct record contract, and a repertoire of pop covers to please the gambling crowds. In no position to be choosy about his next music gig, he took a job as a band leader for a show at the Nugget casino in Sparks, Nevada. "I paid a lot of hard dues—which for anyone else might have dug them a grave," he later recalled. "Me, I just kept working at it til I got out."[89]

Greenwood's career turnaround and his journey to Nashville began when Larry McFaden, bassist for Mel Tillis's band, the Statesiders, saw Greenwood perform at the Nugget. Immediately impressed with Greenwood's vocal talent and multi-instrumental capabilities, McFaden convinced the struggling singer to head to Nashville, signing him to a publishing agreement and getting him a record deal with MCA. The label released his first album, containing the hit "It Turns Me Inside Out," in 1982. That same year, Greenwood turned forty years old. Typical press coverage of Greenwood's early Nashville career always noted his workaholic schedule. Jim Halsey signed Greenwood to his talent agency and began booking the rising star on a nonstop schedule of concert dates from arenas to state fairs. He also made appearances on *The Merv Griffith Show, Solid Gold, The Tonight Show, Hee Haw,* and *Good Morning America* while notching endorsement deals with Coors and McDonald's. Given that his success had arrived in middle age, Greenwood worked hard to keep a tight grip on the fickle fame of the music business.[90]

Then, on September 1, 1983, news broke that made Greenwood think that everything he had worked for might vanish. The Soviet Union had downed a Korean Air Lines flight carrying nearly 300 passengers, sixty-three of whom were Americans. War felt imminent, and Greenwood channeled his unease into a song. "It was the strike against innocent citizens that actually made me put pen to paper," he recalled in his autobiography. Within a few days, he had written "God Bless the U.S.A."[91] The song praises the nation's freedoms, conflates allegiance to the United States with allegiance to a Judeo-Christian God, and sanctifies military sacrifice. In its memorable chorus, Greenwood sings that he is "proud to be an American," is certain of his freedom, and promises that he "won't forget the men who died" to ensure his rights. The motivation to express his national pride came in a torrent of inspiration. As Greenwood later recalled, "The song just about wrote itself. It was as if, within my mind, a strong personal statement had been formulated. It's quite possible that my subconscious had been working on it for a long time." He cited his experiences as a Boy Scout in planting his first earnest feelings of patriotism, as well as the stories he heard as a child about World War II.[92] In May 1984, MCA released Greenwood's next album, *You've Got a Good Love Comin',* which included "God Bless the U.S.A." as its first single. The song peaked at number seven on the *Billboard* country chart and crossed over to reach number twelve on the adult contemporary list.[93] By the end of the year, Greenwood, in partnership with his manager and producer, had built a three-story, 14,000-square-foot modern office building with a penthouse suite for Greenwood on the top floor among the retrofitted bungalows along Music Row.[94] With a combination of pop and patriotism, Sin City had planted a flag in Music City.

Yet Greenwood's song was more than an outpouring of country music patriotism. It was a wartime song in search of a war. The fact that Reagan did not order a military retaliation against the Soviet Union did not stop Greenwood from finding a militarized peacetime narrative for the hit.

During the summer of 1984, viewers of the cable channels Country Music Television or its rival The Nashville Network would have seen Greenwood drive a tractor onto their television screens. The singer-songwriter bumps along over an open pasture for a few seconds before bringing the machine to a halt directly in front of the camera. Greenwood folds his hands over the steering wheel and lowers his head, pantomiming a word of prayer before looking contemplatively into the distance. Soft notes from an electric keyboard sketch a melody over a bed of synthesizer chords, and the pained expression on Greenwood's face tells viewers that he is worried. The first lyrics support that look of concern. As he drives the tractor into the distance, viewers hear Greenwood sing, "If tomorrow all the things were gone / I'd worked for all my life / And I had to start again with just my children and my wife." Some unseen threat, or at least the anxiety of an imagined peril, must be on the horizon.

In the next scene, the threat becomes real. Greenwood, now on foot, approaches a house with weathered clapboard siding where a group of white people, presumably his family, are loading the back of a pickup truck with furniture. Someone is moving away. These folks greet Greenwood with handshakes, smiles, and hugs, offering comfort from the unnamed threat in the first verse. The song lyrics shift to offer further reassurance as he enters the house. "I'd thank my lucky stars / To be living here today," the singer's voice tells listeners, as he passes by people in the house. Two of the men seen greeting Greenwood represent multiple generations of military service: the elder, probably a veteran of World War II, wears an American Legion–style cap, while the younger, probably a Vietnam veteran, wears an olive drab field jacket. And why does Greenwood feel so confident in the face of the hypothetical menace? Because "the flag still stands for freedom / And they can't take that away."

The family gathers around a kitchen table with Greenwood at the head. They clasp hands, invoking Norman Rockwell's *Freedom from Want*, just in time for the chorus. Greenwood then tells listeners that he will "gladly stand up" and defend his country just as those fighting men had in past conflicts. Viewers eventually learn that Greenwood's biggest battle in the video's narrative is financial. His character seems to have lost his farm, and that is why the family has gathered and packed the truck. But nothing can shake his faith in freedom, even the freedom to fall into financial destitution. "Because," he lands his soaring chorus, "there ain't no doubt I love this land / God bless the U.S.A."[95]

Heard within the United States' rightward political trajectory during the 1980s, Greenwood delivered a slick, singable anthem to an American public primed for his unquestioning devotion to the nation. It received a boost when the Republican Party featured the video at its 1984 national convention in Dallas, and President Reagan soon adopted it as an exemplary expression of national pride.[96] Although Greenwood did not write "God Bless the U.S.A." with a partisan agenda in mind, the song complemented the president's image as a Cold Warrior who played to white America's nostalgia for an undefined simpler time and who equated "freedom" with the free market. The lyrics echoed the unshakeable optimism articulated in Reagan's 1984 campaign promise that it was "morning in America." With the "God Bless the U.S.A." music video's sunrise on the farm, tractors, family meal, prayer, and deference to the military, it could have doubled as one of Reagan's campaign ads. Both Greenwood and Reagan tied their patriotism to the mightiness and assumed righteousness of the US military. For Greenwood, that meant giving a lyrical nod to "the men who died" for the freedom he loves. For Reagan, that meant upholding soldiers as the nation's ideal citizens, embarking on a defense-industry spending spree that enriched private contractors, and expanding the size of the US Army, all of which promised to bring about what he called "peace through strength."[97]

The song won Greenwood accolades and opportunities from the country music industry, the military, and politicians. The CMA awarded him Song of the Year for "God Bless the U.S.A." while also nominating him for Entertainer of the Year and Male Vocalist of the Year, all in 1985.[98] He also began working as an Army National Guard television spokesman that year and appeared at installations around the country for concerts.[99] One visit to the USS *Kitty Hawk* on patrol in the Pacific ended with its crew standing in a formation like a marching band at halftime to spell out "PROUD TO BE AN AMERICAN!" on the deck.[100] Reagan invited Greenwood to the White House for a visit and taped a personal message at the beginning of the "God Bless the U.S.A." video to be played for the Paralyzed Veterans of America convention in 1984. The National Conference of Christians and Jews used Greenwood's video as well in conjunction with its conference theme of patriotism the same year.[101] Reagan quoted from the song again in his Thanksgiving address to the armed forces in 1985, saying, "All of us have much to be grateful for. As Lee Greenwood says in his song about being proud to be an American, we do live in a land where the flag still stands for freedom."[102] The president assumed that his military audience would

FIGURE 7.1 Sailors on the USS *Kitty Hawk* spell out the "Proud to Be an American" refrain from Lee Greenwood's "God Bless the U.S.A." as they return from the western Pacific and Indian Oceans in 1985. (PH3 Fred Brewer; National Archives at College Park—Still Pictures)

understand and appreciate the Greenwood reference. They may have, but PX record-sales data that year also suggested country music's diminishing presence in the armed forces—losing out to soul and pop.[103] Not only had "God Bless the U.S.A." become Greenwood's signature song; it helped solidify country music's reputation as the signature genre of US patriotism with the stamp of approval from the president himself.

As Reagan and Greenwood celebrated their shared vision of national pride, the US Air Force Recruiting Service ended its longtime connection with the country music industry. In 1985, the air force had issued a special series of its recruitment public service announcement show, *Country Music Time*, celebrating its twenty-fifth anniversary. The show still reached 2,300 civilian radio stations, as well as the AFRTS, and it still snagged the top country stars as musical guests. The air force recorded these shows in batches. Once every three months, the recruiting service would book two days of studio time in Nashville and cycle through fourteen artists recording their spots.[104] In the mid-1980s, the show's diverse lineup of artists included the Judds, Alabama, Rosanne Cash, Reba McEntire, Lyle Lovett, and, of course, Lee Greenwood.[105]

Despite the continued participation from contemporary country stars, the Air Force Recruiting Service canceled *Country Music Time* in 1987. US Air Force Lieutenant Colonel David C. Kraus sent a form letter to all the civilian station managers explaining that the service's "needs today are more focused": "We've redirected our resources to meet those needs." More specifically, he blamed economics: "Like many government agencies, we're faced with smaller budgets in the coming years. These factors changed our national advertising strategy and drove the decision to discontinue 'Country Music Time.'"[106] As the longest running country music recruitment program, the cancellation of *Country Music Time* signaled a sea change in military priorities as the air force recognized the new ineffectiveness of this campaign.

The country music industry, however, still found ways to promote its artists with the help of the armed forces through the relatively new models of home video sales and cable television. Hank Williams Jr. released his USS *Constellation* concert on VHS in 1986 under the title *A Star-Spangled Country Party*, showing him performing to an adoring crowd of sailors and civilian guests underneath the giant eagle on the ship's deck.[107] The Nashville Network (TNN), a country-music-themed network, had gone on air in 1983 and steadily grown its viewership through talk shows like Ralph Emery's *Nashville Now* and *Crook and Chase*. In 1985, TNN partnered with the USO to broadcast a television special documenting Loretta Lynn's tour of installations in South Korea and the Philippines. Chuck Hagel, the USO president, claimed that his organization was "impressed with the quality of management of TNN" and "by their engineering and producing qualities." Following Lynn's tour, Hagel made TNN the official network of the USO. If country performers toured for the USO, then they could bet that TNN audiences would see coverage of their performances and the specials produced around their interactions with the troops. In the late 1980s, TNN televised USO concert events for Loretta Lynn's tour of Asia, Lee Greenwood's concerts in the Mediterranean, and Charlie Daniels and the Judds from Guantanamo Bay.[108] Connie B. Gay could have only dreamed of having a full camera crew to document his base tours or an entire television network devoted to promoting country music when he started in the 1940s.

Country artists had always given their time for the USO, but the popularity of "God Bless the U.S.A." among politicians and military leaders made Greenwood a near-constant presence at military and political events. In the late 1980s and early 1990s, he averaged at least one USO tour per year, including multiple appearances with Bob Hope. He performed his signature song for crews aboard US aircraft carriers, before professional sporting events, at a memorial for the *Challenger* crew, for veterans' benefits, and in support of Republican politicians. It also earned him coveted recognition from the military when, at an Air National Guard convention in Jacksonville, Florida, US Air Force General John Conaway made him an honorary officer.[109] Greenwood knew he had tapped into something powerful with "God Bless the U.S.A.," something that overshadowed all other achievements of his career. As he told a reporter about the song, "It stands so high above everything else I've done. It is a powerful piece of material and it's almost impossible for me to do a show without it."[110]

The power of Greenwood's patriotism never strayed far from his pursuit of profit. In 1989, a charity organization called Veterans of the Vietnam War, Inc., sued the singer over a breach of contract for agreeing to and then refusing to perform at its event in Albany, Georgia. The veterans group issued Greenwood an advance check for $11,250 with the understanding that he would receive an undisclosed balance when he performed at the concert. The group also arranged for other musical acts to use Greenwood's sound and lighting equipment. However, on the day of the concert, Greenwood demanded the veterans pay him in cash rather than a check, as the contract stipulated. When the group could not produce the cash, Greenwood refused to play, and no other acts could use his equipment. Veterans of the Vietnam War alleged that Greenwood's actions cost it $228,000 in lost revenue and filed suit against him in the US district court in Pennsylvania.[111]

Greenwood's reputation would survive these allegations, and he continued to cultivate a relationship with the nation's most powerful Republican politicians. At the 1988 Republican National Convention, Greenwood performed "God Bless the U.S.A." onstage with President and First Lady Reagan standing by his side, signaling that the convention and George H. W. Bush, the presidential nominee, carried the blessing of the outgoing administration and country music's most patriotic ambassador. The three of them embraced in what looked like sincere affection when the song ended.[112] After Bush secured the nomination and hit the campaign trail that year, he used Greenwood and "God Bless the U.S.A." extensively in his campaign appearances and his inauguration, where the country singer led a forty-piece US Army Band in his signature song.[113] Bush, the Connecticut Yankee turned Texan, borrowed the populist appeal of country musicians like Greenwood to sell himself as a man of the people, despite his Yale education and careers in politics, the oil industry, and the Central Intelligence Agency.[114]

The Bush administration began with what looked like an era of peace and an end to the Cold War. On November 9, 1989, German citizens began tearing down the Berlin Wall, destroying a symbol of ideological divisions and checked aggression between the Soviet Union and the Western capitalist nations.[115] Yet, just as the Cold War subsided, Bush rushed to the defense of the oil-rich Kuwait to end Saddam Hussein's aggression against that country, pulling together an alliance of European and Middle Eastern nations to support the US-led attack that became the Persian Gulf War. An allied land assault began on February 24, 1991, only to end 100 hours later after driving Iraqi troops from Kuwait.[116] The AFRTS set up mobile radio stations in the desert to make sure that servicemembers remained entertained and informed. According to reports from these stations, the three most requested songs from US soldiers were Queen's "Another One Bites the Dust," Bruce Springsteen's "Born in the U.S.A.," and Greenwood's "God Bless the U.S.A."[117]

Greenwood finally had a war for his wartime song, and he jumped at the opportunity to support the military in the Persian Gulf. In February 1991, he recorded a special concert from Walt Disney World for the AFRTS with a "God Bless the U.S.A." finale.[118] US Army General Norman Schwarzkopf, commander in chief of Central Command, even used the song to motivate his staff. Just prior to the launch of the air attack on Iraqi forces, he read the orders, asked a chaplain to say a prayer, and then played Greenwood's song. Schwarzkopf would later laughingly call "God Bless the U.S.A." a "blatantly chauvinistic piece of music," but he added, "I think it characterized the pride that all of us have in our profession, and in what we were and there's a line in there that says 'I would proudly stand next to you, And defend her still today' and that's what it was all about." After the war, the general claimed that the song still made him feel "very emotional": "Particularly that business about, you know, men who have died. Because of course that brings back memories of Vietnam to me, as well as Desert Storm." Schwarzkopf noted, "There's a whole sort of emotional side of this military career that's expressed in that song, and it touches my heart every time I hear it."[119]

Apart from eliciting heartfelt reactions like Schwarzkopf's, Greenwood also saw a chance to make money on the nation's wartime fervor. He had recorded a series of disappointing albums with declining sales in the late 1980s and believed he saw an opening to renew listeners' love for his kind of country. In 1992, Greenwood released the album *American Patriot*, a collection of US-themed songs that included "God Bless the U.S.A." The press release for the album described the singer's many honors from the government, including his honorary rank in the air force and his role as a "mascot" for the USS *Theodore Roosevelt*. The album opens with children reciting the Pledge of Allegiance, setting a tone of innocence and reverence. The rest of the track list includes covers of Woody Guthrie's "This Land Is Your Land," "Dixie," "America the Beautiful," "God Bless America," and a new Greenwood original called "The Great Defenders," which salutes every branch of the service by name.[120]

Many reviewers panned the album, seeing it as a crass cash grab. One acerbic review from Canada called Greenwood "country's own king of cardigans" and described his late-1980s output as "flaccid and largely unlistenable songs." This same writer called *American Patriot* a "collection of toe-tappers for the Geritol crowd" and said that Greenwood appeared to be "jumping on the America-first bandwagon."[121] Following the celebrations for July 4, 1992, one critic complained that Greenwood received more television coverage than Wimbledon, "popping up everywhere to sing 'God Bless the U.S.A.'" He lamented that of all the beautiful, patriotic songs about the United States, Greenwood's "is just a shred of jingoistic fluff that captures neither the flavor nor the pulse of America, and it is upsetting that it has become THE patriotic song of choice during recent years."[122] Patriotic songs were fine for these critics, but they rolled their eyes at what they heard as the venal nationalism in "God Bless the U.S.A."

Greenwood paid little attention to these dissenters, as he enjoyed a level of popularity and cultural power that he had not seen in ten years. "War Launched Greenwood Revival," one headline from Gary, Indiana, proclaimed in September 1992. In the accompanying article, the Associated Press reporter Joe Edwards wrote that Greenwood's life was returning to its normal routine after singing "God Bless the U.S.A." almost every day for the previous year. At nearly fifty years old, Greenwood still maintained the performance pace of a younger man and did not take the renewed interest in his career for granted. He told Edwards, "Everywhere we went and I sang 'God Bless the U.S.A.,' people wanted me to be the spokesman to say 'support the troops.'" He claimed that whenever he traveled through the Los Angeles airport, "people from all walks of life, all colors" walk up to him and say, "You're Lee Greenwood. I like that song you sing." Edwards noted that the recent recognition for Greenwood had lit a spark under a lagging career "that surged in the early and mid-1980s, then faded." Now, Greenwood could bank on traveling the world as a patriotic star, often on behalf of the USO.[123] He also met his fourth wife, Kimberly Payne, a former Miss Tennessee twenty-five years his junior, on a USO tour.[124] Edwards searched for a way to describe Greenwood's career trajectory, landing on the idea that

FIGURE 7.2 Lee Greenwood performs a USO gig aboard the USS *Nashville* in 1987. (PH2 Don Koralewski; National Archives at College Park—Still Pictures)

the country star was "following in the footsteps of Bob Hope as the unofficial ambassador from show business to the armed forces."[125]

While Bob Hope made for an easy analogy, a more fitting one might have been Roy Acuff—or Faron Young or Jimmy Dean or Connie B. Gay. The real story was not only in the USO affiliation shared by Hope and Greenwood but also in the shared legacy of the country music industry's ability to link itself with the Defense Department to serve their overlapping goals. Like those other country artists and promoters before him, Greenwood found a way to meld the public and private sectors—the Pentagon and Music Row— to build a career that sustained his economic needs while serving the interest of the US government. The personnel makeup of the US military and the country industry had changed over the forty years since these two institutions began their relationship. That meant that Greenwood and other country artists did not have to serve in the same types of recruitment efforts that their predecessors had. But the evolution in country music militarization opened new opportunities for Nashville's artists to make a political statement and make a living by waving the flag.

Conclusion

· ·

In May 2003, the USO faced accusations of racial discrimination for the scarcity of Black hip-hop artists that it booked for tours of Iraq. Black troops constituted approximately 27 percent of the fighting force, and servicemembers of all races were fans of the genre. Still, their demands for more hip-hop fell on deaf ears. The USO denied any intentional wrongdoing and instead blamed hip-hop artists for not volunteering to go to the latest war zone. The rapper Coolio believed otherwise. He had volunteered for several USO tours and told *Billboard* magazine that he thought the USO was afraid the rappers would "get them in trouble," suggesting that hip-hop's reputation for controversy might not align with building troop morale or Pentagon-approved, wholesome entertainment. He certainly did not blame his fellow artists. Instead, Coolio accused the USO of not catering to servicemembers' tastes. "I can only guess they're not asking the troops who they want," he told the magazine, "because most of the cats in the service are young, and I'd say 75% of the troops listen to hip-hop and R&B."[1]

What the soldiers received instead was a predominance of white entertainers and a disproportionate number of country music artists. One veteran USO official commented on why country musicians volunteered to perform for the troops overseas more than other artists. He claimed that the "country music community is traditionally patriotic, with deep ties to the military." "It's that 'good old boy' thing," he explained, "and many musicians in the urban black community have long been distrustful of the military."[2]

That quick dismissal of the connection between Black artists and the US Armed Forces obscured the more complicated relationship between African American music and the military. The armed forces had functioned as a site of creativity and a target of critique for Black artists throughout the Cold War era, just as it had for white country musicians. Even during the rise of hip-hop, Black musicians made music and pursued professional music careers while in the service. The rap musicians DJ Mr. Mixx (David Hobbs) and Fresh Kid Ice (Chris Wong Won) met while stationed on March Air Force Base outside Los Angeles in the early 1980s. Together, they formed the group 2

Live Crew, moved to Miami, partnered with Luke "Skyywalker" Campbell, and made music that formed a flashpoint of debate over lyrical obscenity in the early 1990s. 2 Live Crew's bass-heavy, booty-shaking music also influenced the rap duo known as Duice, which consisted of L.A. Sno and Creo-D, two soldiers stationed at Fort Gordon, Georgia. Duice helped put southern hip-hop on the national stage with its dance-floor hit "Dazzey Duks" in 1993.[3] Meanwhile, the USO booked African American musicians for tours throughout the 1980s and 1990s, although those acts tended to be vocal groups that performed contemporary R&B and classic soul, including the legend Lou Rawls, rather than rap music.[4]

Black musicians did not necessarily feel any more or less "distrustful of the military" than white musicians. But their music did not receive the same level of support from the Pentagon that country music did, despite African Americans' long-standing commitment to the armed forces. It was true that the country music industry held "deep ties" to the military, but they were not the kind of bonds suggested by this USO official. By characterizing country fans as "good old boys" who just naturally joined the military and wanted country music as their in-country entertainment, the USO elided the business dealings at the heart of the Music Row–Pentagon connection. From Connie B. Gay and Faron Young to Elvis Presley and Joe Allison to Lee Greenwood and Toby Keith, the country music industry had found ways to profit from US military policies. Music Row's connection to patriotic armed service cannot be divorced from the economics of defense spending. Country music militarization had transformed the genre into the soundtrack of white devotion to the armed forces over the course of the late twentieth century to such an extent that what was actually a long-standing business model looked to be something "traditionally patriotic."

That conflation of race, genre, and US patriotism continues to shape country music's political affiliations into the recent past. On January 18, 2017, Thomas Barrack Jr., the chairman of Donald Trump's Presidential Inauguration Committee, commented that he had not asked Kanye West to perform at the inauguration ceremonies despite the hip-hop star's previous support for the new president. Barrack described what he saw as a conflict between the tone of the Trump festivities and West's music. "It's not the venue," Barrack reasoned. "The venue we have for entertainment is filled out. It's perfect. It's going to be typically and traditionally American." Instead of West, a Black artist from Chicago, Barrack booked several white country and rock music performers, including Lee Greenwood and Toby Keith. Greenwood, of course, performed "God Bless the U.S.A.," which candidate Trump used as his theme song at presidential campaign events.[5] Greenwood and Trump had known each other long before the inauguration. Greenwood had met with Trump's second wife, Marla Maples, several times in 1990 to discuss her music career, generating tabloid speculation about the possibility of a love affair between the singer and his protégé.[6] Additionally, Greenwood's fourth wife, Kimberly, the former Miss Tennessee, worked in the early 2010s as coordinator for the Tennessee and Georgia competitions for the Miss USA pageant that Trump owned.[7]

Keith played "Courtesy of the Red, White and Blue (The Angry American)," his rant of revenge against the nation's enemies released in the wake of 9/11, as well as "American Soldier," a more introspective musing on what it means to make self-sacrifice the driving motivation of one's work ethic.[8] With bigger names in popular music declining to participate, the Trump administration knew where to turn, and it turned south to Nashville.

And yet, like much of country music militarization, the truth behind Trump's use of the genre holds a more complicated history than its superficial appearance. Beginning in 2002 with the release of the hit "Courtesy of the Red, White and Blue (The Angry American)," Keith built an image as the most vocal patriot in a genre already known for its proud and pervasive support of the nation's military. "Courtesy of the Red, White and Blue" declared common Americans' devotion to the national defense and vowed to support the US military offensive against the terrorists who had attacked the United States. Keith gave Uncle Sam a cameo as a vengeful warrior. The Statue of Liberty stepped in as a fist-shaking Athena cheering soldiers into battle. Finally, in the culmination of the last verse, Keith promised the nation's enemies, "We'll put a boot in your ass / It's the American way."[9]

Although Keith was initially reluctant to record the song, he released it in May 2002, after being convinced to get it to the public by Marine Corps Commandant General James Jones, who had heard Keith perform the song at a Pentagon concert. In the early days of the war in Afghanistan, Keith considered "Courtesy" an anthem for a specific fight against a clear aggressor, not as blanket support for any and every US military action. There was no partisan message to the lyrics either, and Keith felt he was boosting troop morale more than anything else. The song also served as a memorial. Keith had lost his father, a US Army veteran, only six months before the 9/11 attacks. He remembered thinking, "What would the old angry American himself, the old one-eyed veteran, think about how soft our country got, to allow somebody to attack us on our own soil and kill this many innocent Americans?" The song hit number one on the *Billboard* country chart by

July 4 that summer and was placed in heavy rotation by country radio and music video channels.[10]

By 2005, Keith quietly but openly grappled with what his song had done to his career. "Now I know I get painted with a real broad brush [as] this Captain America, right-wing lunatic," he told *Billboard* magazine, "but the truth is, I knew there were a bunch of poor bastards that were gonna have to go into Afghanistan and give their all up for people who killed 3,000 Americans on 9-11." Keith chafed at being pigeonholed as country music's warmonger. At the time, the US invasion of Iraq had dragged into its second year, and Keith wanted no part in claiming support for that mission, although he still stood by the troops. In reference to "Courtesy," Keith reiterated its original context, claiming, "You don't have to listen but once to the words to understand that the song was strictly for Afghanistan." As for the expansion of the War on Terror to other fronts, the singer clarified, "I have no stance on the Iraq war, . . . but the second [that I say], 'I have no stance there, I'm not smart enough to tell whether we should be or not,' it becomes, 'Oh, he's trying to save his career now.'" Not exactly a right-winger, Keith was a registered Democrat until 2008, when he cut loose from any partisan affiliation, preferring to separate himself from the political fray. Members of the media still assumed that he supported the Republican Party because of his militaristic lyrical themes and his regular tour schedule with the USO. "I just start laughing," he said, when reporters make assumptions about his politics. "I can't support the troops and not be a Republican. That's impossible, right?"[11]

It did seem impossible in 2005. But Keith actually represented a fifty-year history of country music militarization that aligned genre, race, and armed service, regardless of partisan affiliation. Keith tried to honor the sacrifice of the "poor bastards," servicemembers like his father, who have to fight the war, citizens who may have joined the ranks in search of a better future only to be placed in the line of fire as part of the bargain.

Keith's support for the troops may have sounded predictably country and mistakenly partisan, but the militarization of American culture extended well beyond the bounds of country music and right-wing politics by the early twenty-first century. In the wake of 9/11 and the subsequent War on Terror, the Pentagon exerted a heavier influence than ever in creating positive pop-culture depictions of the US Armed Forces. Media scholars have noted the way procedural shows like *NCIS*, Marvel movies, *Top Gun: Maverick*, and even *The Price Is Right* work hand in hand with the Defense Department to edit scripts and curate portrayals of servicemembers. While conducted under the guise of assuring accuracy, the Pentagon's interference with film and television often sanitizes the brutal realities and ethical complexities of the military and wartime service.[12] Professional sports, particularly the NFL, emerged as a popular venue for militarization in the twenty-first century and led to lucrative deals between the Pentagon and teams that were willing to welcome the military at their games. The payment of taxpayer money to professional sports franchises led to an investigation into "paid patriotism" by Senators John McCain and Jeff Flake of Arizona in 2015. Their subsequent report revealed that the Defense Department paid around $10 million over four years to teams in exchange for promotional and recruitment opportunities.[13]

Country musicians are still playing a part in recruiting US soldiers and the militarization of pop culture in the present day. In the spring of 2020, as the COVID-19 pandemic shut down most in-person social interaction, the country singer Chuck Wicks began hosting informal, virtual performances on his Facebook page, which he called "Sunday Serenades." Many artists resorted to these internet concerts during the early days of the pandemic as a way to stay connected to fans, raise money for charities, and provide a bit of comfort during the public health crisis. Wicks, a midlevel artist with as much success competing on reality television and podcast hosting as on the country charts, jumped on this trend and used social media to reach his fans. Yet not everyone's streaming concerts carried the endorsement of the US Army as his did. Several episodes of Wicks's "Sunday Serenades" included a message about joining the military, sponsored by the US Army Recruiting for the Kentucky and Tennessee regions.[14]

While Wicks followed a long line of country artists by hosting these recruitment events, he has also participated in a business venture with his extended family to make money by cashing in on country music militarization. On November 5, 2021, Brittany Aldean, wife of the country star Jason Aldean, and Kasi Wicks, Chuck's wife and Jason's stepsister, announced the launch of "a clothing line based around patriotic values and being proud Americans!" on Instagram. Three days later, the four Aldeans and Wickses posed together on the social media site to model clothing with four different designs. Chuck Wicks sported a hooded sweatshirt bearing the slogan "Unsilent Majority Speaking Up to Protect Our Freedom." Jason Aldean wore a T-shirt with the words "We the people," taken from the Constitution, on the front and "This Is Our F***king Country" on the back, with a US flag censoring the three offending letters. Brittany Aldean modeled a sweatshirt that reads, "Unapologetically Conservative," while Kasi Wicks wore a long-sleeved T-shirt in dark olive green with the words "Military Lives Matter" across the chest.[15] Given that phrase's origin in the Black Lives Matter movement, which emerged to protest police brutality and the murder of African Americans by law enforcement, the co-optation of "Military Lives Matter" suggests that the real victims of violence in the world are members of the armed forces, while negating Black Lives Matter as a rallying cry for civil rights.

The Aldeans and Wickses initially planned the sale of this merchandise as a limited-time, three-day event, with a portion of the proceeds going to the Special Forces Charitable Trust, a veteran nonprofit, although it remains unclear just how much of the profits were allocated for the charity. However, the two wives of this foursome have started a website boutique called "Brittany and Kasi" that sells a variety of clothing and housewares emblazoned with these slogans. They have also added items that voice direct critiques of President Joe Biden. On the website for the store, Jason Aldean models a shirt that says, "I voted red, You voted blue, Don't blame me, This sh*ts on you," and the namesake proprietors pose in shirts that read, "Alexa, change the president."[16] The Aldeans have also clothed their young children, Memphis and Navy, in shirts from a different internet seller that read, "Hidin' from Biden."[17]

These country music couples have merged their professed support for the military with partisanship to gain notoriety and access to political power. Brittany and Kasi appeared for a meet and greet at the "AmericaFest" conference hosted by the right-wing propaganda organization Turning Point, USA in December 2021. Their promotion for the event featured the women wearing matching "Military Lives Matter" shirts.[18] Lee Greenwood performed for the conference attendees with several other country artists.[19] The Aldeans and the Wicks also spent New Year's Eve in 2021 at Mar-a-Lago with Donald Trump.[20]

By collapsing partisanship, genre, and support for the troops, members of this new generation of artists have found yet another way to profit from country music militarization. They have founded what amounts to a lifestyle brand that meshes well with Trump's "Make America Great Again" merchandise. In fact, Trump supporters have adopted "We the people" as a rallying cry of rebellion against what they see as an illegitimate executive in President Biden, including during the invasion of the US Capitol on January 6, 2021. It is part of a larger co-optation of symbols like the "Don't

Tread on Me" Gadsden flag, the Betsy Ross flag, and the year "1776" as a slogan for right-wing and white nationalist causes like the Oath Keepers, the Proud Boys, and the Three Percenters.[21]

In the hands of the Aldeans and the Wickses, country music militarization follows the transitive property that true conservatives support the military and that true conservatives also claim fealty to Trump. Therefore, fealty to Trump is akin to support for the military, so long as that military supports the political vision of conservative Americans. Subscribing to that lifestyle does not require one to serve in the military, play for the USO, or perform for recruitment events. You can just buy a shirt for $30. Through these circles, country music militarization has evolved into a fashion statement that announces more about people's political ideology than about their connections to the armed forces—though it did not start that way.

In the 1950s, the country music industry hitched the genre to the Cold War military as a means of boosting its visibility, record sales, and respectability. The music ended the century largely, although never fully, aligned with political conservatism as a result. There was nothing inevitable about the music's affiliation with the military or the Republican Party. Country music militarization reflected an economic opportunity for a white southern industry at midcentury. As the Vietnam War politicized the nation's cultural divisions, the country music industry broke right, and its products became the sound of the conservatives who claimed unyielding support for the military as a plank in the Republican Party platform. When we hear "God Bless the U.S.A." or country artists performing on a sandbag stage for a USO concert, we hear that history. It is the history of race-making, the commercial power of country music, and the expansion of the Cold War defense state. It is the history of how a devotion to US militarization developed a southern accent.

Acknowledgments

It is hard for me to express the amount of gratitude I have for the people who have helped me research, write, and publish this book. A true accounting of everyone who has assisted me along the way would be as long as the book itself. I will begin by thanking Mark Simpson-Vos and all at the University of North Carolina Press. It is a thrill to publish with the press, and I appreciate the patience, counsel, and understanding I have received there. I also appreciate the expert advice I received from the anonymous peer reviewers. It is a much stronger book for their suggestions, and all errors or lapses in judgment are mine alone.

Like many academic books, this one has been a long time in the making. I arrived at the University of Virginia with a desire to connect the history of popular music with political history. Luckily, I found myself surrounded by a dream team of brilliant, kind people who helped me work through what that might look like in practice. I had the great advantage of working closely with Grace Elizabeth Hale. Thanks to countless discussions with her, I began to focus on southern music in the late twentieth century and leaned into my love for and critical interest in country music. She made me a better writer, teacher, and person, and I am forever indebted to her. Brian Balogh pushed me to think about political history through the avenues of government spending and institutions. I hope that his immense influence is evident throughout the book. I could not believe my good fortune when Karl Hagstrom Miller moved to Charlottesville shortly after me. I was in his office every time the door was open, asking questions, kicking around ideas, and generally reveling the chance to talk about music with him. I also had the fantastic fortune of working with Claudrena Harold, and her class "From Motown to Hip Hop" remains the standard by which I measure all other lecture courses. Thanks to her for the inspiration and the dozens of lunches at Rev Soup.

I am also thankful for the incredible colleagues and friends at UVA who tolerated my ramblings about country music. My utmost thanks go to Sophie Abramowitz, Jim Ambuske, Monica Blair, Clayton Butler, Alicia Caticha, Kyle Chattleton, Swati Chawla, Amy Coddington, Benji Cohen, Jon Cohen, Alyssa Collins, Aldona Dye, Alexandra Evans, Erik Erlandson, Leif Frederickson, Jack Furniss, Justin Greenlee, Melissa Gismondi, Steven Lewis, Shira Lurie, Cecilia Márquez, Justin McBrien, Gillet Rosenblith, Abeer Saha, Emily Senefeld, and Lydia Warren. I appreciate the willingness of Sophie, Monica, Jon, Cecilia, and Gillet to read rough drafts and conference papers. I am especially thankful for Sophie and her insight into music history. My friendship with her and Nick Murray provided a much-needed community of country music obsessives in Charlottesville.

Other people around UVA offered their generous assistance during my time there, particularly Ed Barnaby, Jeremy Boggs, Lisa Goff, Jack Hamilton, Matt Hedstrom, Carmenita Higginbotham, Andrew Kahrl, Thomas Klubock, Phyllis Leffler, Kathleen Miller, Sarah Milov, Jennifer Via, Bill Wylie, and the members of the Prince Rogers Nelson Memorial Music Appreciation Society. I am also indebted to our friends and neighbors who made my family feel welcome in Charlottesville. Many thanks go to Kendra and David Aylor, Ed and Hannah Barnaby, Darian and Amy Cochran, Kathy Doby, Drew and Laura Duke, Dana Griffin, Sam and Megan Haas, Rosemarie Hanley, Kristen and Nate Ivanick, Jason and Margaux Jacks, Kyle and Kerri Kirkeide, Jeremy and Kristin Lynn, Kari Miller, Nathan Moore, and Germaine Porter.

The community of writers at Pop Con showed me kindness and encouragement when I began presenting the material that became this book. Thanks to David Cantwell, Daphne Carr, Steacy Easton, Nick Forster, Emily Gale, Jack Hamilton, Jewly Hight, Charles Hughes, Amanda Marie Martinez, Michaelangelo Matos, Charlie McGovern, Diane Pecknold, Ann Powers, Jody Rosen, Barry Shank, Alfred Soto, Gus Stadler, Tyina Steptoe, David Suisman, Oliver Wang, and Eric Weisbard. An extra thanks goes to Amanda, who read an entire draft of the book at a late stage when I needed another set of eyes on it.

Several institutions provided funding while I conducted research for this project. This project enjoyed financial support from the Rose Library at Emory University, the UVA Scholars' Lab, the UVA Graduate School of Arts and Sciences, the Briscoe Center for American History at the University of Texas, the Southern Labor Archives at Georgia State University, the Wilson Library at UNC–Chapel Hill, and UVA's Corcoran Department of History. A fellowship from the Smithsonian Institution's National Museum of American History and the National Museum of African American History and Culture allowed me to spend much-needed time at archives in Washington, DC. Finally, a fellowship from the Andrew W. Mellon Foundation and the American Council of Learned Societies generously supported my last year at the University of Virginia.

Conducting historical research means relying on the expertise of archivists, curators, and librarians. This book would not have been possible without Kathleen Campbell, Patrick Huber, and John Rumble at the Frist Library and Archive at the Country Music Hall of Fame and Museum. I am also indebted to Jeff Kollath at the Stax Museum of American Soul Music for granting me access to the O. B. McClinton collection. And I had the great benefit of working with Stacy Kluck, Dwandalyn Reese, and John Troutman at the Smithsonian Institution, all of whom pointed me in the right direction when I needed guidance.

Thanks to all the folks who allowed me to crash on their couches and in their spare bedrooms while I researched this material: Lee Bains and Dawn Riley, Jerstin and Orvokki Crosby, Peter Stafford and Jessica Attie, and Shaye Cohen and Miriam May. A special thanks goes to Brigid McCarthy and Dan Charles (along with Molly and Nora) for inviting me into their home while I conducted research in Washington, DC.

My journey toward writing about music began long ago as an undergraduate at the University of Alabama. I will always value the people in the Departments of

Anthropology, American Studies, and History and at the Alabama Museum of Natural History who encouraged me to be a scholar, particularly Lynne Adrian, Ian Brown, Bill Dressler, Rose Gladney, John C. Hall, Rosa Hall, Rich Megraw, Stacy Morgan, Kathy Oths, Joshua Rothman, (the late, great) Jim Salem, and Edward Tang. My next stop in academia placed me in the Southern Studies Program at the University of Mississippi. The wonderful folks at the Center for the Study of Southern Culture helped me see myself as a historian. My special thanks go to Kathryn McKee, Ted Ownby, Zandria Robinson, Jodi Skipper, Jimmy Thomas, and Charles Reagan Wilson, as well as Oxford friends Scott Barretta, Rebecca Camarigg, Meghan Holmes Chien, Mel Lassiter, Kathryn Radishofski, and Joe York. I also thank Ruth Deason, Mona Hill, and Ida Terry, three early teachers who told me I could be a writer long before I knew what that meant.

I have been able to finish this book and begin life as a professor because of the support I have received from the kind people in the Department of History at Mississippi State University. I am especially appreciative of the following new friends and colleagues: Kathryn Barbier, Stephen Brain, Christian Flow, Jim Giesen, Brenda Harris, Mark Hersey, Alix Hui, Andy Lang, Matt Lavine, Alan Marcus, Anne Marshall, Peter Messer, Julia Osman, Judy Ridner, Morgan Robinson, Leigh Soares, Courtney Thompson, and Pam Wasson. Jim and Anne have been especially helpful as my family resettles in Mississippi. I am also grateful for folks around campus and in the broader Starkville community for their friendship. Thanks to Megan Bean, Taze and Polly Fulford, Brien Henry, Tom Holder, Michelle Jones, Walton Jones, David May, David Nolen, George Rambow, Becky Smith, JohnEric Smith, Bob and Meredith Swanson, and Eric Vivier. I have had the pleasure of working with fantastic graduate students at Mississippi State. A special thanks goes to Madeline Berry, Colin Campbell, Patricia McCourt, Ryan Reynolds, Xavier Sivels, Nate Smith, and the History AV Club for making teaching so rewarding.

My closest friends and family have provided emotional and financial support throughout this process. I am thankful for the love and encouragement from Claire and Kevin Cremeens, Lakin Garth, Andrew Beck Grace, Tony and my late sister Tabitha Johnson, Chris Paysinger, Judy Richardson, Wyn Smith, and Bill Withrow and Kristen Godwin. My parents, Joe and Vickie Thompson, instilled a love for history in me as a child, encouraged all my intellectual and creative efforts, and never faltered from showing me their care. My mom exemplifies a life of positivity and joy that inspires me every day. My dad was my first and best history teacher. He taught me how to treasure what the past can tell us about our present and, most importantly, how to have fun while learning that history.

My deepest and most heartfelt gratitude goes to Jennifer Thompson. She has sustained me in every way imaginable since we met on an archaeological excavation in Louisiana more than twenty years ago. She has been my first reader, my greatest friend, and the only person who could tolerate this rambling journey through life with me. Thanks to her unwavering love and support, we have been able to build a beautiful family together while I wrote this book. To our children, Evie, Virginia, and Joseph, I dedicate this work to y'all. Here's to the history that we have made together and all that lies ahead of us.

Notes

Abbreviations

ARA	Alabama Room Archives, Anniston-Calhoun County Public Library, Anniston, Alabama
CGC	Connie B. Gay Collection, Frist Library and Archive of the Country Music Hall of Fame and Museum, Nashville, Tennessee
CMFOHP	Country Music Foundation Oral History Project, Frist Library and Archive of the Country Music Hall of Fame and Museum, Nashville, Tennessee
CMMC	Country Music Magazine Collection, National Museum of American History, Smithsonian Institution, Washington, DC
DCC	Dick Curless Collection, Frist Library and Archive of the Country Music Hall of Fame and Museum, Nashville, Tennessee
FLA	Frist Library and Archive of the Country Music Hall of Fame and Museum, Nashville, Tennessee
HJA	Hogan Jazz Archive, Tulane University Special Collections, New Orleans, Louisiana
LGC	Lee Greenwood Collection, Frist Library and Archive of the Country Music Hall of Fame and Museum, Nashville, Tennessee
JFKPL	John F. Kennedy Presidential Library
MSCR	Memphis and Shelby County Room Special Collections, Memphis Public Library, Memphis, Tennessee
NARA-CP	National Archives and Records Administration II, College Park, Maryland
R&SVC	Rock 'n' Soul Videohistory Collection, 1990–1999, Archives Center, National Museum of American History, Smithsonian Institution, Washington, DC
RMAL	Stuart A. Rose Manuscript, Archives, and Rare Book Library, Emory University, Atlanta, Georgia
RSD-LOC	Recorded Sound Division, Library of Congress, Washington, DC
SDEC	The Sam DeVincent Collection of Illustrated American Sheet Music, Ephemera, Archives Center, National Museum of American History, Smithsonian Institution, Washington, DC
SFC	Southern Folklife Collection, University of North Carolina–Chapel Hill
SMASM	Stax Museum of American Soul Music Archives, Memphis, Tennessee

Introduction

1. "Ted Cruz: 'My Music Tastes Changed on 9/11.'"

2. Gilbert, "CMT News Special Explores Maines-Keith Controversy"; Laura Snapes, "The Chicks: 'We Were Used and Abused by Everybody Who Wanted to Make Money off Us,'" *The Guardian*, July 18, 2020, www.theguardian.com/music /2020/jul/18/dixie-chicks-used-and-abused-by-everybody-who-wanted-to-make -money-off-us; Rudder, "In Whose Name?"

3. Phyllis Stark and Deborah Evans Price, "Country Acts Feed Fans' Hunger for Patriotic Tunes," *Billboard*, May 3, 2003, 74.

4. Schulman, *Seventies*, 115–116; Cowie, *Stayin' Alive*, 167–176; Malone and Neal, *Country Music, USA*, 373, 431, 477.

5. I use the term "militarization" instead of "militarism" to distinguish between the influence of the Defense Department on civilian culture and the wholesale capture or domination of the culture by the military. In this regard, I follow the distinction made by the scholars Amy J. Rutenberg, Lisa M. Mundey, Aaron L. Friedberg, and others who have studied how military policies impacted private enterprise and US culture in the mid-twentieth century. Although the Defense Department wielded a powerful influence, the United States never adopted the complete regimentation of a garrison state that defines militarism. Using the term "militarization" better describes the way the economic and political priorities of national defense seeped into and shaped civilian life. For more on this distinction, see Rutenberg, *Rough Draft*, 10; Mundey, *American Militarism and Anti-Militarism*; Friedberg, *In the Shadow of the Garrison State*.

6. The AFRTS formed in 1942. Originally called the Armed Forces Radio Service, the network added television in 1953 and changed its name to the Armed Forces Radio and Television Service the following year. In 1969, the network changed its name to the American Forces Radio and Television Service. It changed back to "Armed Forces" in 1982, only to revert back to "American Forces" in 2000. In 2017, the network dropped the "Radio and Television Service" moniker to the shorter American Forces Network. See Lange, "AFN."

7. Omer Anderson, "Country Wins Europe GI's to Tune of $4.2 Mil. Yearly," *Billboard*, January 13, 1968, 1.

8. This ideological break did not always follow partisan lines. Liberal politicians often supported military spending when it benefited the defense industries that supplied the economic backbone of their states. See Brenes, *For Might and Right*; Lassiter, "Political History beyond the Red-Blue Divide."

9. Malone, *Don't Get above Your Raisin'*, 30; Fox, *Real Country*, 31, 43–44; Peterson, "Class Unconsciousness in Country Music."

10. Malone, *Don't Get above Your Raisin'*. For essays on constructions of gender in country music, see McCusker and Pecknold, *Boy Named Sue*.

11. Huebner, *Warrior Image*; Engelhardt, *End of Victory Culture*; Daddis, *Pulp Vietnam*; Self, *All in the Family*; Mundey, *American Militarism and Anti-Militarism*; Sturken, *Tangled Memories*; Gibson, *Warrior Dreams*; Samet, *Looking for the Good War*; Du Mez, *Jesus and John Wayne*.

12. Books by James N. Gregory and Peter La Chapelle deal with the intersection of the migration of Oklahomans to Southern California during the Great Depression and the development of their transplanted musical culture in that region. However, these works do not examine the intersection of the Nashville music industry and defense spending. For those studies, see Gregory, *American Exodus*; La Chapelle, *Proud to Be an Okie*. Additionally, James C. Cobb mentions that Earl Bolick of the Blue Sky Boys took a job at the Marietta, Georgia, Lockheed plant after retiring from music. See Cobb, "From Rocky Top to Detroit City," 72–73.

13. Recent scholarship has documented the interracial and transnational roots of the genre with productive challenges to the assertion that only white, rural Americans have performed the music. See Pecknold, *Hidden in the Mix*; Troutman, *Kīkā Kila*; Dubois, *Banjo*.

14. Miller, *Segregating Sound*. Other recent works have put the lie to the idea that country music has been a genre exclusively for white artists and fans. See Pecknold, *Hidden in the Mix*; Hughes, *Country Soul*. For more on how record labels and promoters have sold country music as the authentic sound of rural, white America for nearly a century since the birth of the recording industry, see Peterson, *Creating Country Music*.

15. Dalfiume, *Desegregation of the US Armed Forces*; MacGregor, *Integration of the Armed Forces*; Myers, *Black, White, and Olive Drab*; Kimberley Phillips, *War! What Is It Good For?*

16. Schulman, *From Cotton Belt to Sunbelt*, viii; Markusen et al., *Rise of the Gunbelt*, 3, 6, 244; Jewell, *Dollars for Dixie*. Scholars have debated whether the impact of defense spending actually delivered a disproportionate benefit to the South. The economic historian David Carlton has disputed Bruce Schulman's argument about regional disparity, specifically regarding the number of installations and arms contractors ("American South and the US Defense Economy"). For the purposes of my work, I believe it is sufficient to say that the Pentagon invested an unprecedented amount of money in the South, which transformed the region's economy, transportation infrastructure, institutions of higher learning, and residential landscapes.

17. Schulman, *From Cotton Belt to Sunbelt*, 109, 140; Daggett, "Cost of Major U.S. Wars"; Brad Plumer, "America's Staggering Defense Budget, in Charts," *Washington Post*, January 7, 2013, www.washingtonpost.com/news/wonk/wp/2013/01/07 /everything-chuck-hagel-needs-to-know-about-the-defense-budget-in-charts/?utm _term=.6bb142d6eb58.

18. Cobb, *Selling of the South*; Wright, *Old South, New South*.

19. Katznelson, *When Affirmative Action Was White*; Skocpol, "G.I. Bill and U.S. Social Policy"; Cohen, *Consumer's Republic*; Frydl, *GI Bill*.

20. Schulman, *From Cotton Belt to Sunbelt*; Sparrow, *Warfare State*; Lassiter and Kruse, "Bulldozer Revolution"; Frederickson, *Cold War Dixie*.

21. Mazor, *Ralph Peer*, 116.

22. McNeil, "Elton Britt," 49–50.

23. "Acuff Fans Beat Frankie," *Stars and Stripes* (European ed.), August 22, 1945, 3; Sgt. Barrett McGurn, "Song of the Islands," *Yank*, July 7, 1944, www.unz.com /print/Yank-1944jul07-00011/; "Acuff vs. Sinatra," *Grinder's Switch Gazette*,

May 1945, 6, Printed Materials, FLA, http://digi.countrymusichalloffame.org/cdm/ref/collection/Printed/id/3029.

24. *Soldier's Joy: A Fiddle Fit for Roy*, exhibit text, Country Music Hall of Fame and Museum, Nashville, TN, December 13, 2022.

25. For case studies of country music and the military, see Wolfe and Akenson, *Country Music Goes to War*; Lund, "Country Music Goes to War." For an overview of songs about military service, see Horstman, "Songs of War and Patriotism." On the full range of songs about the threat of nuclear war, see *Atomic Platters: Cold War Music from the Golden Age of Homeland Security*, Bear Family Records BCD 16065, 2005, CD/DVD.

26. Malone and Neal, *Country Music, U.S.A.*; Pecknold, *Selling Sound*; Havighurst, *Air Castle of the South*; Stimeling, *Nashville Cats*.

27. Hitchcock, *Age of Eisenhower*; Hooks, *Forging the Military-Industrial Complex*; Olin, "Globalization and the Politics of Locality," 146–149; Leslie, *Cold War and American Science*; McGirr, *Suburban Warriors*. C. Wright Mills identified the influence of military spending on US politics and culture well before Eisenhower coined the phrase "military-industrial complex." In *The Power Elite*, published originally in 1956, Mills recognized how the Pentagon had captured the budgetary priorities of politicians and corporations.

28. Balogh, *Associational State*, 3–6; Sparrow, *Warfare State*, 7. A forthcoming book on the social and sensory histories of military musicians promises to shed even more light on music as a tool of the state. See Suisman, *Instrument of War*.

29. In keeping these forces of cultural creation in tension, it is my hope that this book shows how and why the genre evolved the way that it did and how inextricable the military is from that story. To paraphrase Stuart Hall, popular culture is never simply imposed on people without resistance, and it is not merely a reflection of "the people's" desires and tastes. Popular culture is made in the push and pull between those forces. See Hall, "Notes on Deconstructing the 'Popular,'" 564–574.

30. Mittelstadt, *Rise of the Military Welfare State*; Bailey, *America's Army*.

31. Leffler, *For the Soul of Mankind*, 234–259.

32. Winkie, "Thin Red Lines."

33. Von Eschen, *Satchmo Blows Up the World*; Monson, *Freedom Sounds*; Davenport, *Jazz Diplomacy*; Fosler-Lussier, *Music in America's Cold War Diplomacy*.

34. This project does not attempt to cover all of the topical music about the military created by Black artists. Other authors have noted the numerous songs about military service and Cold War foreign policy written by Black artists in R&B and soul, the two genres that are closest to African American equivalents to country music with regard to class affiliation and popularity in the mid-twentieth century. See van Rijn, *Truman and Eisenhower Blues*.

Chapter 1

1. Connie B. Gay, interview by Douglas B. Green, October 18, 1974, Nashville, TN, OH62, CMFOHP.

2. Hank Burchard, "The Country Boy from Lizard Lick Was Always Tuned In," *Washington Post*, February 18, 1971, 1.

3. Gay interview, CMFOHP.

4. Pecknold, *Selling Sound*, 137, 141, 187; M. Jones, "Connie B. Gay," 196; Lornell, *Capital Bluegrass*, 45–50.

5. Mackenzie, *Directory of the Armed Forces Radio Service Series*.

6. Van Rijn, *Truman and Eisenhower Blues*; Kimberley Phillips, *War! What Is It Good For?*

7. Gay interview, CMFOHP.

8. Gay.

9. John Sherwood, "Connie B. Gay Reminisces," *Evening Star*, January 29, 1968, B-2, Box 5, Clippings, CGC.

10. Gay interview, CMFOHP; Ayers, *Promise of the New South*, 45–46, 412–420.

11. Loss, *Between Citizens and the State*, 60–61; Rasmussen, *Taking the University to the People*; Carpenter, *Forging of Bureaucratic Autonomy*.

12. Gay interview, CMFOHP.

13. Gay.

14. Carlin, *String Bands in the North Carolina Piedmont*; Gay interview, CMFOHP; R. Cantwell, *Bluegrass Breakdown*.

15. Gay interview, CMFOHP.

16. Gay.

17. Connie B. Gay, "Just Call Me Lu!," Box 14, Folder 14-4, CGC.

18. Gay interview, CMFOHP.

19. Gay.

20. Sparrow, "Nation in Motion," 177, 178–180.

21. Gay interview, CMFOHP.

22. Lornell, *Exploring American Folk Music*, 54, 93, 101.

23. Wolfe, *Good-Natured Riot*.

24. Gay interview, CMFOHP.

25. Robert W. Ruth, "Hillbillies Take Over Saturdays at D.A.R.'s Hall in Washington," *Baltimore Sun* (morning ed.), April 8, 1948, 4, Box 5, Clippings, CGC.

26. Ruth, 1.

27. Milton Berliner, "A Revolution at Constitution Hall," *Washington Daily News*, April 7, 1948, 13, Box 5, Clippings, CGC.

28. "Saturday Night Hill-Billy Shows Start Soon in Constitution Hall," *Evening Star*, April 7, 1948, B-10, Box 5, Clippings, CGC.

29. Anderson, *My Lord, What a Morning*; Arsenault, *Sound of Freedom*; Darden, *Nothing but Love*, 94.

30. Berliner, "Revolution at Constitution Hall," 13.

31. Sonia Stein, "HillBilly Music Shows Way on Television," *Washington Post*, August 1, 1948, 1L, Box 5, Clippings, CGC. NBC had picked up the show in an attempt to compete with ABC's *Hayloft Hoedown*.

32. Gay interview, CMFOHP.

33. Stein, "HillBilly Music Shows Way on Television," 4L.

34. "Grandpa Jones and His Grandchildren" press release, Box 17, Scrapbook, CGC; Louis Jones, *Everybody's Grandpa*, 90.

35. Louis Jones, *Everybody's Grandpa*, 90–91.

36. Arlie Kinkade, "This, That, 'n' the Other," *National Hillbilly News: The Entertainer's News*, May–June 1950, 12, SDEC.

37. "Musical Mountaineer," *Country Song Roundup*, February 1951, 8, Box 3, CMMC.

38. Louis Jones, *Everybody's Grandpa*, 124–125.

39. Lou Frankel, "AFRS Global Americanization," *Billboard*, February 5, 1944, 12.

40. History of Armed Forces Radio and Television Service, press release, Historical: "On the Air" Articles, Histories, Reports, and Program Records, 1942–1992, Historical Materials, Box 5, Records of the Office of the Secretary of Defense, RG 330, NARA-CP; Frankel, "AFRS Global Americanization," 12, 19.

41. Mackenzie, *Directory of Armed Forces Radio Service Series*, 14.

42. Frankel, "AFRS Global Americanization," 3.

43. Frankel, 12.

44. Wm. T. Allen, "The Editor's Tally Book," *Jamboree*, December 1948, 2, Printed Materials, Digital Archives, FLA, http://digi.countrymusichalloffame.org/cdm/ref /collection/Printed/id/3187; George Sanders, "Hollywood Hoedown Lowdown," *Country Song Roundup*, April 1950, 16, Box 3, CMMC.

45. *Redd Harper's Hollywood Roundup*, NCPC 03530, sound disc 1, 33 1/3 rpm, Armed Forces Radio and Television Service, X AFRTS (16-inch) EN-81 238, RSD-LOC.

46. *Redd Harper's Hollywood Roundup*.

47. "First Christian Western," *Time*, October 8, 1951.

48. Billy Robinson, interview by John W. Rumble, November 23, 1998, OHC242, Nashville, TN, CMFOHP.

49. The media scholar Susan J. Douglas has written about the communal experience of radio listening as opposed to other forms of media consumption. She argues that through the radio, listeners were "tied by the most gossamer connections to an imagined community of people we sensed loved the same music we did, and to a DJ who often spoke to us in the most intimate, confidential, and inclusive tones." She also suggests that "what radio really did (and still does today) was allow listeners to experience at the same time multiple identities—national, regional, local." Douglas, *Listening In*, 22, 24.

50. Minnie Pearl, "Up in the Air with Minnie," *Country Song Roundup*, August 1950, 12, 29, Box 3, CMMC.

51. "WSM Grand Ole Opry Takes Off for Alaska," *National Hillbilly News*, March–April 1950, 42, Box 57, Folder: "Feuding, Hillbilly, Honky Tonk," SDEC.

52. Luke the Drifter, "No, No, Joe" b/w "Help Me Understand," MGM 10806-A, 1950, 78 rpm. For a sampling of Korean War–themed songs, see *Battleground Korea: Songs and Sounds of America's Forgotten War*, Bear Family Records BCD17518, 2018, CD boxed set.

53. "'Barn Dance' Stars Leave for Far East," *Richmond News Leader*, Monday, March 5, 1951, Box 17, Scrapbook, CGC.

54. "Grandpa Jones Celebrity Unit" memo, General Headquarters, Far East Command, Special Services Section, Recreation Division, March 10, 1951, Box 17, Scrapbook, CGC.

55. "Hillbillies Play FEAF Theater," *Stars and Stripes* (Pacific), March 12, 1951, Box 17, Scrapbook, CGC.

56. "Grandpa Jones and His Grandchildren in Tokyo—Part 1," 1951-03-10, Digital Archives, FLA, http://digi.countrymusichalloffame.org/cdm/singleitem/collection /musicaudio/id/2270/rec/7.

57. "Grandpa Jones and His Grandchildren in Tokyo—Part 1."

58. "Grandpa Jones and His Grandchildren in Tokyo—Part 2," 1951-03-10, Digital Archives, FLA, http://digi.countrymusichalloffame.org/cdm/singleitem/collection /musicaudio/id/2271/rec/8.

59. Daily report, Special Services Section, Staff Section Report, March 1951, Eighth US Army Special Services Section, Staff Section Reports, 1950–58, Declassified (EUAK Special Services Reports, Declassified), January 1950 to October 1951, Records of US Army Operational, Tactical, and Support Organizations (World War II and Thereafter), RG 338, NARA-CP; First Lt. Stewart N. Powell, "Grandpa Jones Tour of Korea 15–29 March 1951" memo, Headquarters, Eighth United States Army Korea, Office of the Special Services Officer, June 23, 1951, Box 17, Scrapbook, CGC.

60. Powell, "Grandpa Jones Tour of Korea 15–29 March 1951."

61. "Connie B. Gay Interviews Eighth United States Army Korean War Soldiers," Digital Archives, FLA, http://digi.countrymusichalloffame.org/cdm/singleitem /collection/musicaudio/id/2273/rec/4.

62. Mrs. Sawyers letter, January 23, 1951, 330.11 1951, Jan.–Feb., Box 216, General Correspondence, Jan. 1951–Jan. 1953, Office of the Secretary of the Army, RG 335, NARA-CP.

63. "Connie B. Gay Interviews Eighth United States Army Korean War Soldiers."

64. Powell, "Grandpa Jones Tour of Korea 15–29 March 1951."

65. "Connie B. Gay Korean tour report," Digital Archives, FLA, http://digi .countrymusichalloffame.org/cdm/singleitem/collection/musicaudio/id/2272/rec/5.

66. "Connie B. Gay Korean tour report."

67. "Plea for More Country Music Brings Op'ry Stars Half-Way 'Round World to Korea; 75,000 United Nations Men Entertained by Tubb, Childre, Snow," *Pickin' and Singin' News: The Nation-Wide Country Music Newspaper* (Audition ed.), 1, 8, Box: Oversized (J8b19), SFC; "Breakfast at the Opry," Part 1, Digital Archives, FLA, http:// digi.countrymusichalloffame.org/cdm/singleitem/collection/musicaudio/id/529 /rec/1.

68. Daily Activity Reports, March 1953, EUAK Special Services Reports, Declassified, RG 338, NARA-CP.

69. Sonia Stein, "He's Gay in Foxhole or Foyer," *Washington Post*, July 22, 1951, Section IV, 1, Box 5, Clippings, CGC.

70. Stein, 1.

71. "Grandpa Jones Group Given 'Can Do' Awards," press release, General Headquarters, Far East Command, Public Information Office, March 28, 1951, Box 17, Scrapbook, CGC.

72. Major General Edward F. Witsell to Connie B. Gay, April 26, 1951, Box 14, Folder 9, CGC.

73. Pecknold, *Hidden in the Mix*; Miller, *Segregating Sound*.

74. "Elton Britt Brings Folk Music to the Troops in Korea," *Country Song Roundup*, December 1951, 5, Box 3, CMMC; Hatchett and McNeil, "There's a Star Spangled Banner Waving Somewhere."

75. Louvin, *Satan Is Real*, 138–140. The Korean War proved to be particularly tough on brother duos. Bobby Osborne of the Osborne Brothers fought in Korea with the US Marine Corps, earning several medals including a Purple Heart. See Mullins, "Veterans' Day Tribute at SOIMF."

76. "Spots for Rice Paddy Ranger," DCC.

77. Dick Curless, "The Baron of Country Music," press release, DCC; Linda S. Corey, "Dick Curless: Still Beckoned by Maine," *Bangor Daily News*, October 17, 1972, Clippings Folder, DCC.

78. "Europe Goes Hillbilly," *Country Song Roundup*, June 1952, 16, Box 60, Folder F, SDEC.

79. "Show Biz," *Army Times*, October 25, 1952, 10. Cotton also toured US installations in Korea as part of an AFRS road show in December 1952. See *Army Times*, December 20, 1952, 1.

80. Tribe, "Carolina Cotton," 79.

81. Daily Activities Report of "Carolina Cotton Show," February 1, 1953, January 1953, EUAK Special Services Reports, Declassified, RG 338, NARA-CP.

82. Daily Activity Reports, October 1951, EUAK Special Services Reports, Declassified, RG 338, NARA-CP.

83. *Carolina Cotton Calls*, 83 (AFRTS16-10900), RSD-LOC.

84. Sklaroff, *Black Culture and the New Deal*, 191.

85. Dalfiume, *Desegregation of the US Armed Forces*; MacGregor, *Integration of the Armed Forces*; McMillen, *Remaking Dixie*; Myers, *Black, White, and Olive Drab*; Kimberley Phillips, *War! What Is It Good For?*; Schulman, *From Cotton Belt to Sunbelt*, 137.

86. Mackenzie, *Directory of the Armed Forces Radio Service Series*, 182.

87. For a compilation of these war-themed blues songs, see various artists, *Back to Korea Blues*, JASMCD 3150 (Jasmine Records, 2020), CD. For more on Hopkins's critiques of the US military, see Specht, "War News Blues."

88. James G. Thompson, "Should I Sacrifice to Live 'Half-American'?: Suggest Double VV for Double Victory against Axis Forces and Ugly Prejudices on the Home Front," *Pittsburgh Courier*, January 31, 1942.

89. "Author of Juke Hit Finds Legal Trouble," *Billboard*, September 2, 1944, 62; "Private Cecil 'I Wonder' Gant," *Billboard*, November 10, 1945, 36; "Apollo's Feature," *New York Amsterdam News*, December 1, 1945, 25.

90. Russell, "Cecil Gant," 213; *Billboard*, February 3, 1945, 16.

91. Pvt. Cecil Gant, "I Wonder," Gilt-Edge Records 500 CG1, 1944, 78 rpm.

92. Russell, "Cecil Gant," 213.

93. Jim Bulleit, interview by John W. Rumble, OHC47, May 9, 1983, Nashville, TN, CMFOHP; Hawkins, *Shot in the Dark*.

94. Ernie Newton, interview by Douglas Green, OH136-LC, September 24, 1974, Nashville, TN, CMFOHP.

95. Bill Holder, "Bullet Hits the Bull's Eye," *The Tennessean*, March 28, 1948, 70, 71.

96. "Cecil 'I Wonder' Gant Dies of a Heart Attack," *Chicago Defender*, February 17, 1951.

97. "Cecil 'I Wonder' Gant Dies of a Heart Attack."

98. "Top Hillbilly Impresario and Troupe Scheduled Here for Show Oct. 14," *Caribbean Breeze*, October 6, 1951, Box 5, Clippings, CGC.

99. "Connie B. Gay & Troupe Caribbean Tour," press release, September 19, 1951, Information Branch, Special Services Division, Department of the Army, Box 17, Scrapbook, CGC.

100. Gay interview, CMFOHP.

101. "Hillbillies Sweep Isthmus," *The Nation*, October 19, 1951, Box 17, Scrapbook, CGC.

102. George Forsythe, "Service Gave Jimmy Start," *Boston Traveler*, May 2, 1957, Section B, 50, Box 5, Clippings, CGC.

103. Gay interview, CMFOHP.

104. June Bundy, "C&W. Music Holds Line in Video Battle," *Billboard*, March 3, 1956, 63.

105. Lawrence Laurent, "Then Came the Dawn: CBS Finds Corn Field," *Washington Post and Times Herald*, April 9, 1957, B15, Box 5, Clippings, Gay collection, FLA; Gay interview, CMFOHP.

106. "Festival of the Fleets," *New York Times Magazine*, June 16, 1957, 4, Box 5, Clippings, CGC.

107. "TV and the Naval Review: Jimmy Dean and Arlene Francis Shows Come to Area for Network Telecasts," *Norfolk Ledger-Portsmouth Star*, Television Guide, June 8, 1957, Box 5, Clippings, CGC.

108. "The Joy of Corn," *Newsweek*, 1957, 46, Box 5, Clippings, CGC.

109. George Forsythe, "Service Gave Jimmy Start," *Boston Traveler*, May 2, 1957, Section B, 50, Box 5, Clippings, CGC.

110. Gay interview, CMFOHP.

111. McCandlish Phillips, "Country Stylist, Connie B. Gay Discusses Lucrative Formula," *New York Times*, September 8, 1957, X17.

112. Form S-1, Connie B. Gay Broadcasting Corporation, Securities and Exchange Commission, Washington, DC, Box 2, Folder 6, CGC.

113. M. Phillips, "Country Stylist," X17.

114. "Gay Jamboree for Military Jaunt Abroad," *Billboard*, October 15, 1955, 17.

115. Bob Freund, "Four Saints Really Five," *Fort Lauderdale News*, November 20, 1964, 61.

116. "Gay Jamboree for Military Jaunt Abroad," 17.

117. "Bouillet Joins Gay to Take CW Tunes to World," *Country Music Reporter*, October 20, 1956, 1, 20, FLA.

Chapter 2

1. *Amendment to Communications Act of 1934 (Prohibiting Radio and Television Stations from Engaging in Music Publishing or Recording Business): Hearings before the Senate Subcommittee on Communications of the Committee on Interstate and Foreign Commerce*, 85th Cong., 2nd sess. on S. 2834 (1958), 478; John Ryan, *Production of Culture in the Music Industry*; Pecknold, *Selling Sound*, 106–111.

2. *Amendment to Communications Act of 1934*, 490.

3. Linn, *Elvis's Army*, 16, 27, 22; Flynn, *Draft*, 98–103.

4. Faron Young, interview, Cradle of the Stars, Louisiana Hayride Interview, 1984, FV.2012.2018, FLA.

5. Young; Diekman, *Live Fast, Love Hard*, 18, 19.

6. Diekman, *Live Fast, Love Hard*, 23.

7. Quoted in Diekman, 26.

8. Whitburn, *Hot Country Songs*, 484.

9. Johnny Havlicek, "Faron Young Finds Army 'Variation on Old Theme,'" *The Tennessean*, April 15, 1953, 25.

10. "Singin' Soldier, Faron Young," *Country Song Roundup*, March–April 1954, 13, FLA; MacDonald, *Television and the Red Menace*, 114.

11. "More than 1400 Radio Stations to Share RS Spots," *Recruiting Journal*, June 1950, 1, April to August 1950, Monthly Publication "Recruiting Journal" with Related Source Material, 1950–1954, Recruiting Journal Files, Military Personnel Procurement Division Publicity Branch, Records of the Adjutant General's Office (TAGO), RG 407, NARA-CP.

12. "Publicity 'Props,'" *Recruiting Journal*, June 1950, 16, April to August 1950, Recruiting Journal Files, TAGO, RG 407, NARA-CP.

13. Kelly, "Study of the Role of Broadcasting," 2–3.

14. Kelly, 26, 33.

15. Kelly, 34–36.

16. MacDonald, *Television and the Red Scare*, 111–113.

17. MacDonald, 119.

18. "Publicity 'Props,'" 16.

19. "Chanted Jingles Added to Radio Spots," *Recruiting Journal*, June 1950, 16, April to August 1950, Recruiting Journal Files, TAGO, RG 407, NARA-CP.

20. "Fort Mason Band Aid to Recruiters," *Recruiting Journal*, August 1950, 10, April to August 1950, Recruiting Journal Files, TAGO, RG 407, NARA-CP.

21. "New Radio Officer Joins Publicity Branch," *Recruiting Journal*, September 1950, 1, September to December 1950, Recruiting Journal Files, TAGO, RG 407, NARA-CP.

22. "Army Band Dance Group in Network Radio Show," *Recruiting Journal*, February 1951, 17, January to April 1951, Recruiting Journal Files, TAGO, RG 407, NARA-CP.

23. "New RS TV Show Set for Early June," *Recruiting Journal*, May 1951, 16, May to August 1951, Recruiting Journal Files, TAGO, RG 407, NARA-CP.

24. "'Songs by Fisher' Aired on ABC," *Recruiting Journal*, July 1952, 17, June to December 1951, Recruiting Journal Files, TAGO, RG 407, NARA-CP.

25. Fisher, *Been There, Done That*, 41.

26. Fisher, 42–43.

27. AP, "Eddie Fisher Denies Army Coddled Him," *Detroit Free Press*, May 7, 1954, 6.

28. "At Ease with Pvt. Eddie Fisher," *Billboard*, September 22, 1951, 11.

29. Fisher, *Been There, Done That*, 43.

30. "Pfc. Eddie Fisher on Far East Tour; Sings for UN Troops in Korea," *Recruiting Journal*, September 1952, 17, June to December 1951, Recruiting Journal Files, TAGO, RG 407, NARA-CP.

31. Fisher, *Been There, Done That*, 46.

32. Bob Thomas, "Eddie Fisher Credits Army with Helping His Career," *Indiana Gazette*, June 29, 1954, 11.

33. "New Television Show Planned for Recruiting Service," *Recruiting Journal*, January 1953, 3, January to July 1953, Recruiting Journal Files, TAGO, RG 407, NARA-CP.

34. "'Talent Patrol' New Army and Air Force TV Show," *Recruiting Journal*, February 1953, January to July 1953, Recruiting Journal Files, TAGO, RG 407, NARA-CP.

35. "'Talent Patrol' to Continue through the Fall," *Recruiting Journal*, August 1953, 14, August to December 1953, Recruiting Journal Files, TAGO, RG 407, NARA-CP.

36. "New Recruit Wins Contest," *Billboard*, April 11, 1953, 43.

37. "Folk Talent and Tunes," *Billboard*, May 2, 1953, 48.

38. "Pvt. Young's Art Pleases Army Brass; On TV," *Pickin' and Singin' News: The Nation-Wide Country Music Newspaper* (Audition ed.), 1, 4, Box: Oversized (J8b19), SFC.

39. "Pfc. Faron Young, Hogtied," *Hoedown: The Magazine of Hillbilly and Western Stars*, October 1953, 26, Box 65, Folder V, Series 16, SDEC.

40. "Pvt. Young's Art Pleases Army Brass."

41. "Singin' Soldier, Faron Young," *Country Song Roundup*, March–April 1954, 15, 13, FLA.

42. Roberts, *Tell Tchaikovsky the News*.

43. John Ryan, *Production of Culture*, 16–30.

44. John Ryan, 1. For more on the importance of the ASCAP-BMI rivalry and its relationship to country music, see Pecknold, *Selling Sound*, 106–111.

45. John Ryan, *Production of Culture*, 109–125.

46. Diekman, *Live Fast, Love Hard*, 30. The Circle A Wranglers would continue at Fort McPherson even after Young's discharge. They went on to enlist then Pfc. Roger Miller as a fiddle player, giving him his first gig as a professional country musician.

47. "3d Army Shows to Entertain on Maneuvers," *Army Times*, April 17, 1954, 29.

48. "Third Army Show, Aug. 27, to Recall the Old South," *Army Times*, August 21, 1954, 22.

49. Diekman, *Live Fast, Love Hard*, 30, 35.

50. "Third Army Area Producing Six Radio Shows for Army Recruiting," *Recruiting Journal*, September 1954, 16, July to December 1954, Recruiting Journal Files, TAGO, RG 407, NARA-CP.

51. "Commendation for Third Army Recruiters," *Recruiting Journal*, September 1954, 17, July to December 1954, Recruiting Journal Files; TAGO, RG 407, NARA-CP.

52. "Featuring Town and Country Time Folk Music Style," *Recruiting Journal*, August 1953, 15, July to December 1954, Recruiting Journal Files, TAGO, RG 407, NARA-CP.

53. "Folk Music Production Town and Country Time Radio Series Begins This Month," *Recruiting Journal*, June 1953, 15, January to July 1953, Recruiting Journal Files, TAGO, RG 407, NARA-CP.

54. "Featuring Town and Country Time Folk Music Style," *Recruiting Journal*, August 1953, 15, August to December 1953, Recruiting Journal Files, TAGO, RG 407, NARA-CP.

55. "The Army Goes Country & Western," *Country & Western Jamboree*, July 1955, 17. *Town and Country Time* featured a young multi-instrumentalist named Roy Clark, who landed in the DC area thanks to his father's job at the Washington Naval Yard and would go on to host *Hee Haw* with Buck Owens. See Lornell, *Exploring American Folk Music*.

56. "Elliot to Welcome Faron Back from Army," *Atlanta Journal-Constitution*, November 17, 1954, 16; Dave Dexter Jr., "Glenn E. Wallichs—A Fond Farewell," *Billboard*, January 8, 1972, 3, 46.

57. *Country & Western Jamboree*, March 1955, 10, Box 62, Folder N, SDEC; Diekman, *Live Fast, Love Hard*, 36.

58. Diekman, *Live Fast, Love Hard*, 42–43.

59. Denning, *Cultural Front*; Lipsitz, *Time Passages*.

60. Dinerstein, *Swing the Machine*.

61. Miller, *Segregating Sound*; Pecknold, *Hidden in the Mix*.

62. Sugrue, *Origins of the Urban Crisis*; Kruse and Sugrue, *New Suburban History*; Nickerson and Dochuk, *Sunbelt Rising*.

63. Pecknold, *Selling Sound*, 66, 71.

64. Pecknold, 71.

65. Diekman, *Live Fast, Love Hard*, 27.

66. Pecknold, *Selling Sound*, 71.

67. "C&W Goes Big in Germany," *Country & Western Jamboree*, June 1955, 11, Box 56, Country and Western Jamboree, 1955–1959, SFC.

68. "GI Hillbillies Prove Germans Dig Hoedowns," *Army Times*, September 4, 1954, 17.

69. Ed (Tiny) Tims, letter to *Country & Western Jamboree*, August 1955, 4, Box 56, Country and Western Jamboree, 1955–1959, SFC.

70. Ed (Tiny) Tims, letter to *Country & Western Jamboree*, December 1955, 31, Box 56, Country and Western Jamboree, 1955–1959, SFC.

71. Cpl. Anthony Warrenfelt, letter to *Country & Western Jamboree*, August 1955, 4, Box 56, Country and Western Jamboree, 1955–1959, SFC.

72. M. V. Hinorn, letter to *Country & Western Jamboree*, October 1955, 4, Box 56, Country and Western Jamboree, 1955–1959, SFC.

73. Kelly, "Study of the Role of Broadcasting," 42–44.

74. Kelly, 44–47.

75. "New Army TV Show to Aid Recruiting," *Army Times*, June 15, 1957, 34; *Country Style, U.S.A.*, season 1 liner notes.

76. "Your United States Army Presents Transcribed 'Front and Center,'" emceed by Charlie Applewhite, featuring Bob Dini on vocals, 2478554-3-1, RSD-LOC.

77. "New Army TV Show to Aid Recruiting," *Army Times*, June 15, 1957, 34.

78. "Bradley Film Studios Get Army Contract," *The Tennessean*, January 29, 1957, 19.

79. Oermann, "Owen Bradley," 50–51.

80. *Country Style, U.S.A.*, episode 8, featuring Marty Robbins and Joyce Paul.

81. Buchanan Brothers, "Atomic Power," b/w "Singing an Old Hymn," RCA Victor 20-1850, 1946, 78 rpm; Louvin Brothers, "The Great Atomic Power" b/w "Insured beyond the Grave," MGM Records 11277, 1952, 78 rpm. The Louvin Brothers continued to perform and record military-themed songs throughout their career, including a compilation of patriotic songs. See the Louvin Brothers, *Weapon of Prayer*, Capitol Records ST 1721, 1962, 33 1/3 rpm. On the trend of atomic-themed songs in country music, see Wolfe, "Jesus Hits Like an Atom Bomb." For a compilation of these country tunes, pop songs, and public service announcements about the atomic bomb, see *Atomic Platters: Cold War Music from the Golden Age of Homeland Security*, Bear Family Records BCD 16065, 2005, CD/DVD boxed set.

82. *Country Style, U.S.A.*, episode 34, featuring Marty Robbins and the Anita Kerr Singers.

83. Canaday, *Straight State*; Morden, *Women's Army Corps*. For more on the military as an employment option for women, see Roth, *Her Cold War*.

84. "Pace, Hallaren on Mutual Network Broadcast for WAC Recruiting," *Recruiting Journal*, May 1951, 17, May to August 1951, Recruiting Journal Files, TAGO, RG 407, NARA-CP.

85. "WAC Honored in Special 'SOP' Radio Show; New Program: 'March Time Down South,'" *Recruiting Journal*, August 1951, 18, May to August 1951, Recruiting Journal Files, TAGO, RG 407, NARA-CP.

86. "Patti Page Compliments WACs," *Recruiting Journal*, December 1952, June to December 1952, Recruiting Journal Files, TAGO, RG 407, NARA-CP.

87. *Country Style, U.S.A.*, episode 19, featuring Faron Young and Skeeter Davis.

88. *Country Style, U.S.A.*, episode 19.

89. *Country Style, U.S.A.*, episode 19.

90. "Army's Country Style Television Series Assists in Bringing Music to the People," *Country & Western Jamboree*, August 1957, 18–19, Box 56, Country and Western Jamboree, 1955–1959, SFC.

91. *Country Hoedown*, 11 (2478554-3-2), RSD-LOC.

92. *Country Hoedown*, 11.

93. *Country Hoedown*, 11.

94. The historian Bill C. Malone situates these themes in the southern culture of bad-man braggadocio that runs from folk songs like "Wild Bill Jones" to the Outlaw movement of the 1970s to the alternative country rebellion of the 1990s. See Malone, "When the Lord Made Me, He Made a Rambling Man," chap. 5 in *Don't Get above Your Raisin'*, 117–148.

95. Quoted in Pecknold, "I Wanna Play House," 86.

96. *Country Hoedown*, 11.

97. Greene, *Lead Me On*; Adamson, "Few Black Voices Heard."

98. Pecknold, *Selling Sound*, 72, 80.

99. "Country Hoedown on Madison Avenue," *Country & Western Jamboree*, August 1956, 28–29, Box 56, Country and Western Jamboree, 1955–1959, SFC.

100. "Country Music Is a Way of Life," *Country & Western Jamboree*, June 1957, 21, Box 56, Country and Western Jamboree, 1955–1959, SFC.

101. Jack Setters, "Country Music Crusade," *Country & Western Jamboree*, July 1957, 25, Box 56, Country and Western Jamboree, 1955–1959, SFC.

102. *Amendment to Communications Act of 1934*.

103. John Ryan, *Production of Culture*, 114.

104. *Country & Western Jamboree*, Yearbook 1959, 15, 17, Box 56, Country and Western Jamboree, 1955–1959, SFC.

105. *Country & Western Jamboree*, Yearbook 1959, 22.

106. *Country & Western Jamboree*, Yearbook 1959, 27.

107. *Country & Western Jamboree*, Yearbook 1959, 23.

108. *Country & Western Jamboree*, Yearbook 1959, 20.

109. Young interview, FLA.

Chapter 3

1. "Conway Twitty Magnolia Stater," *Billboard*, October 20, 1958, 7; Ren Grevatt, "On the Beat," *Billboard*, January 26, 1959, 10.

2. "Conway Twitty Magnolia Stater," 7; Grevatt, "On the Beat," 10.

3. Grevatt, "On the Beat," 10.

4. Country Music Hall of Fame and Museum, "Conway Twitty."

5. Guralnick, *Last Train to Memphis*; Pecknold, *Selling Sound*, 89–94; Morrison, *Go Cat Go!*

6. Daniel, *Lost Revolutions*; Morrison, *Go Cat Go!*

7. Frank, "Memphis Naval Air Station, Millington"; "Pontoon Parts Repaired Here," *Memphis Press-Scimitar*, January 5, 1951, 1, MSCR; Williamson, *Elvis*, 119.

8. Bernard Lansky, interview, August 14, 1992, Box 5, R&SVC.

9. Lansky.

10. Williamson, *Elvis*, 119; Lansky interview, R&SVC.

11. Guralnick, *Last Train to Memphis*, 52.

12. Michael Finger, "Big Empties: Memphis Landmarks That Have Stood Vacant for Years, Waiting for Someone to Bring Them Back to Life," *Memphis Flyer*, December 4, 1997, www.memphisflyer.com/backissues/issue459/cvr459.htm; Wayne Risher, "Union Selling Old UAW Union Hall in Frayser, 30-Plus Years after Harvester

Plant Closing," *Memphis Commercial Appeal*, May 30, 2017, www.commercialappeal
.com/story/money/real-estate/2017/05/30/union-selling-old-uaw-union-hall
-frayser-30-plus-years-after-harvester-plant-closing/319965001/.

13. Firestone Files, Memphis Public Library, MSCR.

14. Daniel, *Lost Revolutions*, 39–60.

15. US Census Bureau, "Table 46: Population Rank of Incorporated Places."

16. Finger, "Big Empties."

17. Frank, "Memphis Naval Air Station, Millington."

18. "GIs Now Getting 'Quick Release' Sleeping Bags," *Memphis Press-Scimitar*, January 4, 1951, 9, MSCR.

19. "Pontoon Parts Repaired Here," *Memphis Press-Scimitar*, January 5, 1951, 1, MSCR.

20. Williamson, *Elvis*, 119.

21. Lansky interview, R&SVC.

22. Moore, *Scotty and Elvis*, 15–16.

23. Scotty Moore, interview, Box 6, R&SVC.

24. President Harry S. Truman, Executive Order 9981, "Establishing the President's Committee on Equality of Treatment and Opportunity in the Armed Services," July 26, 1948, www.trumanlibrary.org/9981.htm.

25. Moore, *Scotty and Elvis*, 17–22.

26. Moore, 21.

27. Moore, 26.

28. Moore interview, R&SVC.

29. Moore, *Scotty and Elvis*, 29.

30. Moore, 43.

31. Billy Lee Riley, interview, Box 8, R&SVC.

32. Riley, "Flyin' Saucer Rock 'n' Roll," 131.

33. Riley interview, R&SVC.

34. Riley.

35. Sun Records, "Billy Lee Riley."

36. Cash, *Cash*, 80.

37. Cash, 81.

38. Cash, 81, 82.

39. H. C. Holland to Hon. James C. Davis, January 8, 1952, Box 80, Folder "1952–Universal Military Training," James C. Davis Papers, RMAL.

40. Hon. R. F. Sams to Hon. James C. Davis, June 14, 1952, Box 80, Folder "1952–Universal Military Training," Davis Papers, RMAL.

41. Hon. James C. Davis to Mrs. Jack B. Cowan, March 8, 1952, Box 80, Folder "1952–Universal Military Training," Davis Papers, RMAL.

42. Kimberley Phillips, *War! What Is It Good For?*; Bristol and Stur, *Integrating the Military*; MacGregor, *Integration of the Armed Forces*; Myers, *Black, White, and Olive Drab*.

43. Bussey, *Firefight at Yechon*.

44. A. M. Rivera Jr., "REBEL FLAGS IN KOREA! Confederate Banners Fly Anywhere!!!," *Pittsburgh Courier*, September 29, 1951, 1.

45. Walter White, "Confederate Flags! A Fad or Revival of Fanaticism," *Chicago Defender*, October 6, 1951, 7.

46. "Johnny Cash: Too Much Talent to Head in Any One Direction," *Country Song Roundup*, February 1968, FLA.

47. "Johnny Cash," *Country Song Roundup*, April 1956, 20, CMMC.

48. "Johnny Cash," *Country & Western Jamboree*, Spring 1958, 84, Box 56, Country and Western Jamboree, 1955–1959, SFC.

49. Cash, *Cash*, 79.

50. Stan Kesler, interview, Box 5, R&SVC.

51. Bowman, "Stan Kesler," 280; Matt Sexton, "Bartlett Man Recalls Writing Rock's Past," *Bartlett (TN) Express*, May 23, 2013, http://bartlett-express.com/2013/05/23/bartlett-man-recalls-writing-rocks-past/.

52. Sonny Burgess, interview, Box 1, R&SVC; Schwartz, *We Wanna Boogie*.

53. "Report on Conditions of Military Service for the President's Commission on Veterans' Pension, Section 7," Professional Entertainment Services, World War II, 1, Historical Summaries of Major Events, 1955–1960, Special Services Division, Special Services Branch, TAGO, RG 407, NARA-CP.

54. Camfield, "Will to Win."

55. "Report on Conditions of Military Service."

56. "Report on Conditions of Military Service."

57. "Report on Conditions of Military Service."

58. "Army Entertainment Is a Hit," 1956 All-Army Entertainment Contest Finals program, Special Services Division, Historical Major Events and Problems, 1955–1960, 1 July 1955 to 30 June 1956, Box 1, TAGO, RG 407, NARA-CP.

59. "Report on Conditions of Military Service."

60. 1955 All-Army Contest program, Box 1, Special Services Division, Special Services Branch, Historical Summaries of Major Events and Problems, 1955–1960, TAGO, RG 407, NARA-CP.

61. "Discrimination in the Employment of Negroes in Special Services," Summary, July 1955–June 1956, Historical Summaries of Major Events and Problems, 1955–1960, Special Services Division, Special Services Branch, TAGO, RG 407, NARA-CP.

62. "Powell Airs Army Bias!," *Pittsburgh Courier*, April 28, 1956, 20.

63. "Discrimination in the Employment of Negroes in Special Services."

64. "Summary of Major Events," July 1956–June 1957, Historical Summaries of Major Events and Problems, 1955–1960, Special Services Division, Special Services Branch, TAGO, RG 407, NARA-CP.

65. Charlie Rich, interview, Box 8, R&SVC.

66. Rich.

67. Jim Stewart, interview, Box 8, R&SVC.

68. Stewart.

69. Hughes, *Country Soul*; Bowman, *Soulsville, U.S.A.*; Gordon, *Respect Yourself*.

70. Winford Turner, "Country Amusement Park Plan Is Revealed by Gordon Terry," *Decatur Daily*, March 11, 1964, A-12.

71. Diekman, *Live Fast, Love Hard*, 24.

72. Diekman, 29.

73. Turner, "Country Amusement Park Plan Is Revealed," A-12; Samuelson, "Gordon Terry," 534–535.

74. Bayne Hughes, "Gordon Terry Dies at 74," *Decatur Daily*, April 10, 2006, http://legacy.decaturdaily.com/decaturdaily/news/060410/terry.shtml.

75. "Pfc. Wynton Kelly Joins Army Group for TV Shot," *Chicago Defender*, February 13, 1954, 18.

76. Mark Gardner, "Wynton Kelly," *Coda*, June 1971, 37.

77. "Pfc. Wynton Kelly Joins Army Group for TV Shot," 18.

78. "Jazz Pianist Wynton Kelly Discharged by the Army," *New York Amsterdam News*, September 11, 1954, 20.

79. "Third Army Show, Aug. 27, to Recall the Old South," *Army Times*, August 21, 1954, 22.

80. Gardner, "Wynton Kelly."

81. See Von Eschen, *Satchmo Blows Up the World*; Monson, *Freedom Sounds*.

82. "Singer Sheds GI Uniform," *Baltimore Afro-American*, April 29, 1956, 7.

83. Rock and Roll Hall of Fame, "Elvis Presley."

84. Escott, *All Roads Lead to Rock*.

85. "'Galveston Blues' Catches On; Sells 100,000 Platers [sic]," *Baltimore Afro-American*, April 19, 1952, 6; Texas State University, "Clarence 'Candy' Green," https://gato-docs.its.txst.edu/jcr:b416dde1-c0d8-457f-af70-2ef1be028fe2/Clarence%20Candy%20Green.pdf.

86. Bowman, *Soulsville, U.S.A.*, 3–4.

87. Guralnick, *Last Train to Memphis*, 117–119.

88. Stewart interview, R&SVC.

89. Guralnick, *Last Train to Memphis*, 119–120.

90. Cowboy Jack Clement, interview, Box 2, R&SVC.

91. Doug Poindexter and Starlite Wranglers, "Now She Cares No More" b/w "My Kind of Carrying On," Sun Records 202, 1954, 78 rpm.

92. "Review of New C&W Records," *Billboard*, May 29, 1954, 60.

93. Guralnick, *Last Train to Memphis*, 89–90.

94. Guralnick, 89–90.

95. Guralnick, 89–97.

96. Hale, *Nation of Outsiders*, 62–72.

97. Moore interview, R&SVC.

98. Guralnick, *Last Train to Memphis*, 109–111.

99. Stewart interview, R&SVC.

100. Clement interview, R&SVC.

101. Guralnick, *Last Train to Memphis*, 127–130.

102. *Billboard*, October 6, 1954.

103. Guralnick, *Last Train to Memphis*, 135–140.

104. Tom Perryman, interview by John Rumble, OHC221, June 19, 1990, Nashville, TN, CMFOHP.

105. Leo Zabelin, "Upsets Mark First Readers' Poll," *Country & Western Jamboree*, December 1955, 8, Box 56, Country and Western Jamboree, 1955–1959, SFC.

106. Clement interview, R&SVC.

107. Guralnick, *Last Train to Memphis*, 129–130.

108. Hugh Cherry, oral history interview by John Rumble, OHC57, February 28, 1996, Nashville, TN, CMFOHP.

109. Charlie Louvin, oral history interview by Douglas B. Green, OH338, January 11, 1972, Nashville, TN, CMFOHP.

110. "Folk Music Fireball," *Country Song Roundup*, September 1955, 14, CMMC.

111. "New Policy Combines Pops-C&W," *Country & Western Jamboree*, December 1955, 13, Box 56, Country and Western Jamboree, 1955–1959, SFC.

112. Jack Stapp, oral history interview by Bill Ivey, OH373, August 8, 1972, Nashville, TN, CMFOHP.

113. Jon Pareles, "The Media Business: CBS Records to Buy Tree, Ending an Era in Nashville," *New York Times*, January 4, 1998.

114. Guralnick, *Last Train to Memphis*, 258.

115. Gay interview, CMFOHP.

116. Peter Golkin, "Elvis on the Potomac," *Washington City Paper*, February 19, 2007.

117. Moore, *Scotty and Elvis*, 109.

118. Hale, *Nation of Outsiders*, 62–72.

Chapter 4

1. Kelly, Bane, and Matson to Eisenhower, undated, White House Central Files (Eisenhower Administration, 1953–1961), Series: Alphabetical Files, 1953–1961, Dwight D. Eisenhower Library, https://catalog.archives.gov/id/594359; Levy, *Operation Elvis*.

2. Linn, *Elvis's Army*, 1–6.

3. Tosches, *Country*, 39–57; Pecknold, *Selling Sound*, 90–91.

4. George, *Death of Rhythm and Blues*; LeRoi Jones, *Blues People*, 222–223.

5. Hale, *Nation of Outsiders*, 62–72.

6. The military historian Brian Linn has noted that military service led to Presley's ascendance in respectability as well. However, Linn focuses on the conflict between the modernization of the Cold War nuclear army and the need for young men capable of operating such machinery. Presley functions as a brief example of this broader trend. See Linn, *Elvis's Army*.

7. "Army to Give Elvis Presley a G.I. Haircut," *Billboard*, October 27, 1956, 1; Levy, *Operation Elvis*, 3–10.

8. "It Ain't True. Elvis Is Not in the Army," *Army Times*, October 13, 1956, 21.

9. "Elvis Must Have a Good Press Agent," *Army Times*, October 20, 1956, 17.

10. Guralnick, *Last Train to Memphis*, 349–363.

11. "Minister Likens Elvis Presley to the Golden Calf," *Kingsport (TN) Times*, April 9, 1957, 8.

12. Quoted in Levy, *Operation Elvis*, 32.

13. "Elvis Hair Styles Take a Cropping," *The Tennessean*, December 24, 1956, 16.

14. UP, "Newest Hairdo Is 'Oooh, Elvis,'" *Montgomery Advertiser*, August 19, 1956, 49.

15. "The Presley Cut," *The Tennessean*, February 28, 1957, 9; Jack Bloom, "Girls Ape Elvis Hairdo, Barber Predicts Wide Popularity," *Lansing State Journal*, February 28, 1957, 12.

16. Hale, *Nation of Outsiders*, 67–72.

17. George, *Death of Rhythm and Blues*.

18. "Beat? For Elvis It's Army 1-2-3-4," *The Tennessean*, January 5, 1957, 1, 2.

19. Paul Vanderwood, "Elvis Scores Hit with Army—He's 1-A," *Memphis Press-Scimitar*, January 8, 1957, Memphis-Biography files, MSCR.

20. "Beat? For Elvis It's Army 1-2-3-4," 1, 2.

21. "Relax Girls; Presley May Keep Long Hair Even If Drafted," *Jackson (TN) Sun*, January 6, 1957, 23.

22. *Army Times*, January 12, 1957, 1.

23. Jim G. Lucas, "Elvis' 'Male Appeal' Rated 'Not Much,'" *Pittsburgh Press*, February 13, 1957, 22.

24. Goluboff, *Lost Promise of Civil Rights*, 5. On the construction of Jim Crow society, see Woodward, *Strange Career of Jim Crow*; Hale, *Making Whiteness*.

25. Bill Simon, "Boundaries between Music Types Fall; Deejays Spin Them All," *Billboard*, November 12, 1955, 34, 36.

26. Pee Wee King, "Pee Wee King's Corn Fab," *Country Song Roundup*, October 1956, 12, CMMC.

27. Quoted in Bertrand, *Race, Rock, and Elvis*, 164.

28. Louvin, *Satan Is Real*, 178.

29. Eskew, *But for Birmingham*, 114; Roche, "Asa/Forrest Carter and Regional/Political Identity," 238–239.

30. "Citizens' Unit Slates First Rally Saturday," *Anniston (AL) Star*, February 23, 1956; "Citizens' Council First Rally Set at VFW Hall Saturday Night," *Anniston (AL) Star*, February 24, 1956.

31. Spears, *Baptized in PCBs*, 85.

32. On remembrances of the military's experiments in integration at Fort McClellan, see the recollections of Mississippi governor William Winter, who spent time at the fort during World War II. Bolton, *William F. Winter and the New Mississippi*, 49, 55.

33. "Fort McClellan," *The Southerner: News of the Citizens' Council*, February 1956, 3, ARA.

34. Schulman, *From Cotton Belt to Sunbelt*, 136–137.

35. "Army Nears Full Integration," *Army Times*, September 19, 1953, 16. The army counted eighty-eight all-Black units, and only thirty-nine of those were stationed in the United States. James P. Mitchell, assistant secretary of the army, claimed, "Army policy is one of complete integration and it is to be accomplished as soon as possible."

36. Nichols, *Breakthrough on the Color Front*; Bob Horowitz, "Services Lead US in Racial Mixing," *Army Times*, February 20, 1954, 11.

37. Quoted in MacGregor, *Integration of the Armed Forces*, 492.

38. MacGregor, 496.

39. "3rd Army Chief, General Truman, Lauds WAC Facility," *Anniston (AL) Star*, May 23, 1954; "WAC Ready to Dedicate Giant Center Tomorrow," "WAC Has Vital Role in Uncle Sam's Army," and "Rules Given on Joining WAC," *Anniston (AL) Star*, September 26, 1954. On the history of the WAC and the gender assumptions that accompanied serving, see Canaday, *Straight State*; Morden, *Women's Army Corps*.

40. "Charge Jim Crow at Army Station," *Chicago Defender*, February 26, 1955, 4.

41. "Fort McClellan," *The Southerner: News of the Citizens' Council*, February 1956, 3, ARA.

42. Cody Hall, "Opposition to 'Rock 'n Roll Meets Cool Reception Here," *Anniston (AL) Star*, March 29, 1956. A similar article followed the next day, picked up from the UP. It also mentions Carter's campaign. See "Disc Jockey Defends 'Rock 'n Roll Hits," *Anniston (AL) Star*, March 30, 1956; "'Rock and Roll' Fighter Finds No Help in Ranks," *Birmingham World*, April 3, 1956.

43. Ward, "Civil Rights and Rock and Roll"; Ward, *Just My Soul Responding*, 95–105; Epstein, *Nat King Cole*, 251–256; Gourse, *Unforgettable*, 176–180; Haskins, *Nat King Cole*, 138–140; Sprayberry, "Town among the Trees"; Sprayberry, "Interrupted Melody"; Tosches, *Unsung Heroes of Rock 'n' Roll*, 36–37.

44. Whitburn, *Hot Country Songs*, 242.

45. Hank Locklin, "Geisha Girl," RCA Victor Records 447-0795, 1957, 45 rpm. This was not the first geisha-themed song. The country and western artist Danny Dill had released "Geisha Sweetheart" in 1956, but his version failed to make much of an impact.

46. "C&W Best Sellers in Stores," *Billboard*, November 25, 1957, 78; Trott, "Hank Locklin," 300–301.

47. Bobby Helms, "Fraulein," Decca Records 9-30194, 1957, 45 rpm; Escott, "Bobby Helms," 236.

48. Hank Locklin, *Foreign Love*, RCA Victor LP 1673, 1958, 33 1/3 rpm.

49. Skeeter Davis, "Lost to a Geisha Girl," RCA Victor 7084, 1957, 45 rpm; "Review Spotlight on C&W Records," *Billboard*, November 11, 1957, 124.

50. Kitty Wells, "(I'll Always Be Your) Fraulein," Decca 30415, 1957, 45 rpm.

51. Jimmie Skinner, "I Found My Girl in the USA," Mercury-Starday 71192, 1957, 45 rpm.

52. The McCoys, "Daddy's Geisha Girl," RCA Victor 47-7204, 1958, 45 rpm.

53. Jan Howard and Wynn Stewart, "Yankee Go Home," *Foreign Love Affairs*, Bear Family Records CD 16336, 2004. The original single was released in 1959.

54. "Harlan Howard, a Country Music Lover," *Country Song Roundup*, March 1968, 12, FLA; "Harlan Howard (in His Own Words)," *Country Song Roundup*, May 1970, 30, FLA.

55. Hank Locklin, "Foreign Car," RCA Victor 47-7472, 1959, 45 rpm.

56. Tsuchiya, "Interracial Marriages," 62.

57. Tsuchiya, 69–70. Whites made up 73 percent of the marrying males, followed by 15 percent nisei, while African Americans made up 12 percent.

58. "13 Japanese Attend School for Brides," *Army Times*, December 1, 1956, 33.

59. "Do Japanese Women Make Better Wives?," *Jet*, November 12, 1953, 18–21.

60. "Japanese Brides Take Lessons in American Way of Life," *Army Times*, June 15, 1957, 35.

61. "Japanese Brides Take Lessons in American Way of Life," 77. On the scale of Japanese abortion in the early 1950s, see James A. Michener, "The Facts about GI Babies," *Reader's Digest*, March 1954.

62. Library of Congress, "Shenandoah"; Frederic Knight Logan, *Fallen Leaf: An Indian Love Song*, voice and piano, lyrics by Virginia K. Logan (Chicago: Forster, 1922), Vocal Popular Sheet Music Collection, Score 418, University of Maine, https://digitalcommons.library.umaine.edu/mmb-vp/418/; Richmond F. Hoyt, *Princess Pocahontas*, march and two-step, arranged by Hugo O. Marks, for piano solo (New York/Chicago: Windsor Music, 1903), Frances G. Spencer Collection of American Popular Sheet Music, Baylor University, http://digitalcollections.baylor.edu/cdm/ref/collection/fa-spnc/id/6271.

63. Bob Wills and the Texas Playboys, "Cherokee Maiden," OKeh Records 6568, 1941, 78 rpm; Hank Thompson and His Brazos Valley Boys, "Squaws along the Yukon," Capitol Records F4017, 1958, 45 rpm; George Jones, "Eskimo Pie," Mercury Records 71257X45, 1958, 45 rpm.

64. Marty Robbins, *Gunfighter Ballads and Trail Songs*, Columbia Records CL 1349, 1959, 33 1/3 rpm; Benny Martin and the Whippoorwills, "Border Baby," Decca Records 9-30712, 1958, 45 rpm.

65. Charles K. Harris, "Ma Filipino Baby" (New York: Charles K. Harris, 1898), Charles Templeton Sheet Music Collection, Mississippi State University Digital Collections, http://digital.library.msstate.edu/cdm/ref/collection/SheetMusic/id/25439; J. A. Shipp and Tom Lemonier, "My Dear Luzon" (New York: F. A. Mills, 1904), Frances G. Spencer Collection of American Popular Sheet Music, Baylor University, http://digitalcollections.baylor.edu/cdm/ref/collection/fa-spnc/id/72566; Paul A. Rubens, "The Queen of the Philippine Islands" (London: Francis, Day, and Hunter, 1900), Frances G. Spencer Collection of American Popular Sheet Music, Baylor University, http://digitalcollections.baylor.edu/cdm/compoundobject/collection/fa-spnc/id/53363/rec/1; Don Ignacio, "On to Cuba, or, The Cuban Girl's Song to Her Lover" (Philadelphia: J. L. Carncross, 1869), Lester S. Levy Collection of Sheet Music, Johns Hopkins University, https://levysheetmusic.mse.jhu.edu/collection/129/121.

66. Dick Curless, "China Nights" b/w "Blues in My Mind," Event Records E-4266, 1957, 45 rpm; Marty Robbins, "I-Eish-Tay, Mah-Su," Columbia Records 4-43196, 1964, 45 rpm; Buck Owens and the Buckaroos, "Made in Japan," Capitol Records 3314, 1972, 45 rpm; John Anderson, *Tokyo, Oklahoma*, Warner Brothers Records 9-25211, 1985, 33 1/3 rpm.

67. Ricky Nelson, "Hello Mary Lou" b/w "Travelin' Man," Imperial Records 5741, 1961, 45 rpm.

68. Merle Haggard, "Irma Jackson," *Let Me Tell You about a Song*, Capitol Records ST-882, 1972, 33 1/3 rpm; Billy Joe Shaver, "Black Rose," Monument Records ZS7 8593, 1973, 45 rpm.

69. Marty Robbins, *Island Woman*, Columbia Records CS 8976, 1964, 33 1/3 rpm.

70. *Country Style, U.S.A.*, episode 18, featuring Johnny Cash and Carolee Cooper.

71. Whitburn, *Hot Country Songs*, 84.

72. M. Hamilton, *In Search of the Blues*; Johnny Cash, *Johnny Cash with His Hot and Blue Guitar*, Sun Records, 1957, 33 1/3 rpm.

73. Johnny Cash and the Tennessee Two, "Hey, Porter!," Sun Records 221, 1955, 45 rpm.

74. Randolph, *For Jobs and Freedom*.

75. Miller, *Segregating Sound*, 216.

76. *Johnny Cash: The First 25 Years*, directed by Walter C. Miller, aired on May 8, 1980, on CBS.

77. *Country Style, USA*, episode 18.

78. Guralnick, *Last Train to Memphis*, 445–446.

79. "Drafting Elvis Cause of Woe for His Draftboard," *Memphis Commercial Appeal*, January 5, 1958, Memphis-Biography files, MSCR.

80. *Country Song Roundup*, November 1958, FLA.

81. Louis Silver, "Inductees Haven't Any Gripe at Sharing Army with Elvis," *Memphis Commercial Appeal*, March 20, 1958, 47; Bill Burke, "Officially, Pvt. Presley! Sworn into the Army," *Memphis Press-Scimitar*, March 24, 1958; "Elvis Passes First Test: 'I'll Learn—I've Got To,'" *Memphis Press-Scimitar*, March 25, 1958, MSCR; "Private Presley's Debut," *Life*, April 7, 1958, 118.

82. Guralnick, *Last Train to Memphis*, 462.

83. Louis Silver, "Pvt. Elvis Begins Army Life in Sentry-Guarded Barracks," *Memphis Commercial Appeal*, March 25, 1958, 8, Memphis-Biography files, MSCR.

84. "Private Presley's Debut," 118.

85. Silver, "Pvt. Elvis Begins Army Life in Sentry-Guarded Barracks," 1.

86. The Threeteens, "Dear 53310761" b/w "Doowaddie," Rev Records 3516, 1958, 45 rpm.

87. June Bundy, "Deejay Competition Booms Stunts, Contests, Gimmicks," *Billboard*, June 2, 1958, 15.

88. "Vox Jox," *Billboard*, June 16, 1958, 39.

89. "Teeners Dog Elvis Tags," *Billboard*, June 23, 1958.

90. Bill Parsons, "All American Boy" b/w "Rubber Dolly," Fraternity Records JO8W-2324, 1958, 45 rpm.

91. *Responsibilities of Broadcasting Licensees and Station Personnel: Hearings Before a Subcommittee of the Committee on Interstate and Foreign Commerce, House of Representatives, Eighty-Sixth Congress, Second Session, on Payola and Other Deceptive Practices in the Broadcasting Field* (1960).

92. Grandpa Jones, "All American Boy" b/w "Pickin' Time," Decca 9-030823, 1959, 45 rpm.

93. "Weary Presley Reaches Post; Fans By-Passed," *Memphis Commercial Appeal*, March 29, 1958, 11, Memphis-Biography files, MSCR.

94. Bill Burke, "Elvis Gets His Order: Sails Sept. 22 to Post in Germany," *Memphis Press-Scimitar*, September 11, 1958, Memphis-Biography files, MSCR.

95. Bill Burke, "Elvis Will Let Army Call Tune about His Singing," *Memphis Press-Scimitar*, June 3, 1958; "Rock 'N' Roll King Saddened: Elvis Presley's Mother Succumbs to Illness," *Memphis Press-Scimitar*, August 14, 1958, Memphis-Biography files, MSCR.

96. Williamson, *Elvis Presley*, 177–188; Guralnick, *Careless Love*, 36–47.

97. Bill Burke, "Army Losing a National Institution," *Memphis Press-Scimitar*, February 16, 1960.

98. Steve Sholes, "The New Stars Determine Evolution of C&W Music," *Country & Western Jamboree*, Spring 1958, 42, Box 56, Country and Western Jamboree, 1955–1959, SFC.

99. "Elvis Presley: A Teenage Tradition," *Country Song Roundup*, November 1959, 6–7, CMMC.

100. "Country Music's King for 1959 Is Johnny Cash," *Country Song Roundup*, November 1959, 26–27, CMMC.

101. Bobby Bare, "I'm Hanging Up My Rifle," Fraternity Records F-861, 1959, 45 rpm. Bare would maintain a long, hit-making career in country music, often singing songs written by Shel Silverstein. Silverstein, who made a name for himself as a children's author and illustrator, received his professional start as a cartoonist for *Stars and Stripes* while stationed in the Pacific with the US Army. Silverstein would also write songs for Johnny Cash, Waylon Jennings, Loretta Lynn, Kris Kristofferson, and Dr. Hook and the Medicine Show. Bart Barnes, "Author Shel Silverstein Dies," *Washington Post*, May 11, 1999; "Shel Silverstein's Unlikely Rise to Kid Lit Stardom."

102. "*Billboard* Spotlight Pick," *Billboard*, March 9, 1959, 46.

103. Oscar Godbout, "Presley Flies In to Drop the 'Sgt.,'" *New York Times*, March 4, 1960, 27.

104. Guralnick, *Careless Love*, 6.

105. John P. Shanley, "Presley Performs on the Sinatra Show," *New York Times*, May 13, 1960, 63.

106. "Zest Triumphs over Skimpy Book," *Billboard*, April 25, 1960, 21.

107. Sidney, *Bye Bye Birdie*.

108. Sidney.

109. Sidney.

110. Taurog, *GI Blues*.

111. Taurog.

112. Taurog.

113. "AFRTS: A Radio and Television Programming Chronicle," AFRTS Story, Histories, Reports, and Program Records, 1942–1992, Historical Materials, Box 4, Records of the Office of the Secretary of Defense, RG 330, NARA-CP.

114. Whitburn, *Hot Country Songs*, 329.

115. Whitburn, 329.

Chapter 5

1. Omer Anderson, "Army B'dcasts Boom Overseas C&W Sales," *Billboard*, August 1, 1960, 4.

2. Pecknold, *Selling Sound*, 135–143; Malone and Neal, *Country Music, U.S.A.*, 265–267.

3. Anderson, "Army B'dcasts Boom Overseas C&W Sales," 4.

4. Omer Anderson, "Country Wins Europe GI's to Tune of $4.2 Mil. Yearly," *Billboard*, January 13, 1968, 1.

5. Omer Anderson, "US Launches European Drive to Aid Country Music Image," *Billboard*, December 25, 1965, 24, 33.

6. Quoted in Pecknold, *Selling Sound*, 137.

7. Pecknold, 75.

8. Connie B. Gay, interview by Douglas B. Green, October 18, 1974, Nashville, TN, OH62, CMFOHP.

9. Pecknold, *Selling Sound*, 137.

10. Quoted in Pecknold, 138.

11. I draw from Michael Denning's definition of "cultural politics" here to understand how something as ephemeral as a logo could convey the alignment of the country music industry with the foreign policies of Cold War militarization. According to Denning, "cultural politics is at one level simply the politics of letterheads and petitions, the stances taken by artists and intellectuals, the pledges of allegiance and declarations of dissent. But it is also the politics of the cultural field itself, the history of the institutions and apparatuses in which artists and intellectuals work." Denning, *Cultural Front*, xix.

12. Gay interview, CMFOHP.

13. "CMA Annual Meeting Marks Beginning of Fourth Year," *Close-Up*, October 1961, 1, FLA.

14. Pecknold, *Selling Sound*, 139–141.

15. Gay interview, CMFOHP.

16. Pecknold, *Selling Sound*, 136.

17. *Close-Up*, April 29, 1960, 1, FLA.

18. Bill Sachs, "C.&W. DJ's Map Serious Event as 7th Annual WSM Festival," *Billboard*, November 17, 1958, 18, 24; Bill Sachs, "Fun and Frolic Dominates 7th C.&W. Deejay Festival," *Billboard*, November 24, 1958, 3, 14.

19. Sachs, "Fun and Frolic Dominates," 3.

20. Sachs, 3, 14.

21. "New Vast PX Wax Market," *Billboard*, September 20, 1947, 29.

22. "New Vast PX Wax Market," 29.

23. Tyler, *Music of the Postwar Era*; Millard, *America on Record*.

24. Delo, *Peddlers and Post Traders*; Wiley, *Life of Johnny Reb*, 163, 191; Lair, *Armed with Abundance*, 148–149.

25. Lair, *Armed with Abundance*, 148–149.

26. Ren Grevatt, "Overseas G.I. Puts Out Millions to Hear Music from Home," *Billboard*, February 9, 1957, 1, 20. Grevatt later worked as a publicist for the Grateful Dead, the Nitty Gritty Dirt Band, Linda Ronstadt, Alice Cooper, and others. See Grevatt, *Confessions of a Rock 'n' Roll PR Guy*.

27. Grevatt, "Overseas G.I.," 1.

28. Ted Sharpe, "Music on Record," *Army Times*, November 1, 1952, 10.

29. Keightley, "'Turn It Down!' She Shrieked," 149–177.

30. Grevatt, "Overseas G.I.," 1.

31. Grevatt, 1.

32. "New Army TV Show to Aid Recruiting," *Army Times*, June 15, 1957, 34.

33. June Bundy, "US Armed Forces Huge Wax Market," *Billboard*, December 15, 1958, 3.

34. "John J. Ryan, 55, Publisher; Wrote on Military Sales," *New York Times*, May 19, 1977, B12.

35. John J. Ryan, "Special Report: The Exchange Story, Background, Outlook," *Army Times*, March 16, 1957.

36. Bundy, "US Armed Forces Huge Wax Market," 3.

37. Bundy, 3, 85.

38. "US Army and Air Force," *Close-Up*, July 11, 1960, 2, FLA.

39. "International Flavor," *Close-Up*, July 11, 1960, 2, FLA.

40. "International," *Close-Up*, December 31, 1960, 2, FLA. *Close-Up* featured requests for more records and publicity materials from foreign markets. For examples, see the semiregular "International" column, as well as specific articles like "Austrian & Australian Country Music Men Drop a Line . . . ," *Close-Up*, March 1961, 1, FLA.

41. "Country Music Round Up—Word from CMA'ers," *Close-Up*, October 1961, 2, FLA.

42. "Swing to C&W Bugs Commies," *Close-Up*, November 1961, 4, FLA.

43. "Berlin Lad Number 1 C&W Fan, He Wants CMA Membership," *Close-Up*, November 1961, 4, FLA.

44. "Top Talent Carries C&W to European, Pacific Outposts," *Close-Up*, November 1961, 4, FLA.

45. "AFN Boosts C&W Output," *Close-Up*, November 1961, 4, FLA.

46. "More Country Music Fills AFN Air," *Billboard*, September 25, 1961, 3.

47. Anderson, "Army B'dcasts Boom Overseas C&W Sales," 4.

48. "News from Stations," *Close-Up*, December 1962, 1, FLA.

49. "Country Music Roundup—Word from and about CMA'ers," *Close-Up*, June 1962, 3, FLA.

50. "Country Music Has Biggest Year among Forces Stationed in Europe," *Billboard*, December 25, 1961, 5. The PXs supplemented their record supplies with German country music platters. This led to a dispute between the European Exchange Service and US record companies, which insisted that the PXs sell US products. See "'Buy American' Push Ups Armed Forces PX Sales," *Billboard*, January 20, 1962, 5.

51. Vernon Scott, "Twang, Twang, Twang," UPI, *Stars and Stripes* (Europe), September 15, 1961, 14.

52. *Stars and Stripes* published four other letter writers who echoed Graupp's complaints with varying degrees of grievance.

53. "More Country Music Fills AFN Air," *Billboard*, September 25, 1961, 3.

54. "Bavarians Make Pitch as Europe's Nashville," *Billboard*, March 10, 1962, 20; "More Country Music Fills AFN Air," 3.

55. Branch, *Parting the Waters*, 268, 274–275, 278–280, 295.

56. Frederickson, *Dixiecrat Revolt*.

57. Kimberley Phillips, *War! What Is It Good For?*, 112–187.

58. Dudziak, *Cold War Civil Rights*, 152–158, 186; Branch, *Parting the Waters*, 827–828.

59. MacGregor, *Integration of the Armed Forces*, 530–535.

60. Bruce Lambert, "Judge Gerhard Gesell Dies at 82; Oversaw Big Cases," *New York Times*, February 21, 1993, Section 1, 39; MacGregor, *Integration of the Armed Forces*, 535–536.

61. President's Committee on Equal Opportunity in the Armed Forces (Gesell Committee), "Initial Report: Equality of Treatment and Opportunity for Negro Military Personnel Stationed within the United States," June 13, 1963, 5, Box 023, Papers of John F. Kennedy, Presidential Papers, White House Staff Files of Lee C. White, Civil Rights File, 1961–1963, President's Committee on Equal Opportunity in the Armed Forces: Proposals, 1963: 24 June–9 October (2 of 2 folders), JFKPL.

62. Gesell Committee, 8, Table I.

63. "Country Music Round Up—Word from CMA'ers," *Close-Up*, April 1961, 3, FLA.

64. "Old Year Was Big Year for Country Music Industry as C&W Steals the Show on Stage, Record & Radio-TV," *Close-Up*, January 1962, 3, FLA; "Country Music Round Up—Word from CMA'ers," *Close-Up*, April 1962, 3, FLA.

65. "Country Music Round Up—Word from CMA'ers," *Close-Up*, June 1962, 1, Transcription Records, FLA.

66. Gesell Committee, "Initial Report," 12–13, JFKPL.

67. Gesell Committee, 15.

68. Gesell Committee, 15.

69. Chief of Naval Personnel to Distribution List, "Appointment/enlistment of qualified members of the non-caucasian manpower pool in the US Navy" memo, February 19, 1963, Series 1: President's Committee on Equal Opportunity in the Armed Forces Files, 1944–1963, Box 001, Folder 2: Directives on Equal Opportunities in the Armed Forces—Hewe's copy, 1948–1963, Laurence I. Hewes Personal Papers, JFKPL.

70. "A suggested letter of transmittal to the President containing a summary of findings and recommendations," Box 002, Folder 3: Initial report, President's Committee on Equal Opportunity in the Armed Forces, 6/21/63, Hewes Papers, JFKPL.

71. Gesell Committee, "Initial Report," 68, JFKPL.

72. Gesell Committee, 37.

73. Gesell Committee, 74; United Service Organization, Implementation of Policy #22 "Services to all Members of the Armed Forces," Box 001, Folder 2: Directives on Equal Opportunities in the Armed Forces—Hewe's copy, 1948–1963, Hewes Papers, JFKPL.

74. MacGregor, *Integration of the Armed Forces*, 539–540.

75. Cross, "Brother Wild," in *Room Full of Mirrors*, 84–107; Official Military Personnel File for James M. Hendrix, NAID: 57288864, Folders: Service Documents (May 1961–June 1962), Disciplinary (March 31, 1962–May 23, 1962), Medical Records (May 1961–June 1962), NARA-CP; https://catalog.archives.gov/id/57288864.

76. Toussaint credited his mother, Naomi Neville, as the composer of "Whipped Cream" in order to avoid contract disputes. Allen Toussaint, interview by Robert Palmer, 1987, Box 38 (ID: 1589), HJA; Allen Toussaint, interview by Tad Jones,

March 13, 1979, Box 33 (ID:1253–1255), HJA; Broven, *Rhythm and Blues in New Orleans*, 263.

77. Ruth Brecher and Edward Brecher, "The Military's Limited War against Segregation," *Harper's*, September 1963, 79, 80.

78. Brecher and Brecher, 81.

79. Brecher and Brecher, 92.

80. Rumble, "Joe Allison," 11.

81. Diekman, *Live Fast, Love Hard*, 40. Allison described finding inspiration for the song while watching a gangster movie featuring John Derek, whose character wanted "to die young and leave a good-looking corpse." Ken Nelson, a producer for Capitol Records, gave the song to Young, pairing the song's hell-raising message with the newly discharged and famously rebellious singer.

82. *Billboard*, May 21, 1955, 32, 34; Diekman, *Live Fast, Love Hard*, 70.

83. Joe Allison, "Music City USA," *Country Song Roundup*, December 1951, 11, CMMC.

84. Rumble, "Joe Allison," 11.

85. La Chapelle, *Proud to Be an Okie*; Gregory, *American Exodus*; Dochuck, *From Bible Belt to Sunbelt*; McGirr, *Suburban Warriors*.

86. Simpson, *Early '70s Radio*, 11–13, 157.

87. Simpson, 157.

88. Weisbard, *Top 40 Democracy*, 2–5.

89. "Folk Talent and Tunes," *Billboard*, May 31, 1952, 82; "Folk Talent and Tunes," *Billboard*, November 15, 1952, 59.

90. "KRKD Format Shift: 100% C.&W. Music," *Billboard*, October 13, 1956, 53.

91. Joe Allison, interview by John W. Rumble, OHC6, May 27, 1994, Nashville, TN, CMFOHP.

92. Allison.

93. *Country Corner* (#1108 RU-29-7-15 A [Jan. 1967]), Part 1, and *Country Corner* (#1109 RU-29-7-15 B [Jan. 1967]), Part 1, LPA 50031, RSD-LOC.

94. "Country Music Goes International," *Billboard: The World of Country Music*, November 2, 1963, 166.

95. Omer Anderson, "US Launches European Drive to Aid Country Music Image," *Billboard*, December 25, 1965, 24, 33.

96. Heil, *Voice of America*; Krugler, *Voice of America*; Puddington, *Broadcasting Freedom*; Von Eschen, *Satchmo Blows Up the World*.

97. "CMA Members Invited to Support Radio Free Europe," *Close-Up*, June 1962, 1.

98. Omer Anderson, "Country Wins Europe GI's to Tune of $4.2 Mil. Yearly," *Billboard*, January 13, 1968, 1.

Chapter 6

1. "Country Music Album Salutes Armed Forces," *Close-Up*, February 1968, 1, FLA.

2. Newport and Carroll, "Iraq versus Vietnam."

3. Young, *Vietnam Wars*, 225–231.

4. Pecknold, *Selling Sound*, 218; La Chapelle, *I'd Fight the World*.

5. McClinton and Wood, *Hard Way to Go.*

6. Other scholars have argued that country music did not become more politically conservative in the 1960s but that the conservative movement adopted country music. While true, that analysis misses how the institutional connection between Music Row and the Pentagon primed the genre for that adoption. See Pecknold, *Selling Sound*, 219; Hughes, *Country Soul*, 131.

7. Schulman, *Seventies*, 115–116; Cowie, *Stayin' Alive*, 167–176.

8. Caro, *Passage of Power.*

9. Hemmer, *Messengers of the Right*; Richardson, *How the South Won the Civil War*; Phillips-Fein, *Invisible Hands.*

10. *Life*, November 1963.

11. "Country Music Roundup," *Close-Up*, October 1963, 1, FLA.

12. "C&W Goes to Holland," *Music City News*, November 1963, 4, FLA; "Country Music Roundup," *Close-Up*, November 1963, 2, FLA; "Country Music Roundup," *Close-Up*, December 1963, 1, FLA.

13. "LBJ Taps Gay for Goodwill Mission," *Music City News*, July 1964, 7, FLA.

14. *Music City News*, October 1964, 16, FLA.

15. "Barry Goldwater America's #1 Radio Fan," *Music City News*, October 1964, 3, FLA.

16. Hemmer, *Messengers of the Right.*

17. "President Proclaims November National Country Music Month," *Music City News*, November 1964, 27, FLA.

18. Leffler, *For the Soul of Mankind*, 151–157; Young, *Vietnam Wars*, 103.

19. Rutenberg, *Rough Draft.*

20. USO itineraries, Roy Acuff Scrapbooks, 1961–1965, FLA; "Acuff Joins Country Song Hall of Fame," *Stars and Stripes*, November 13, 1962, Roy Acuff Scrapbooks, 1961–1965, FLA.

21. "Country Music Stays Aboard Navy's Fleet of Stations," *Music City News*, March 1964, 11.

22. Young, *Vietnam Wars*, 158–163; National Archives, "Vietnam War US Military Fatal Casualty Statistics."

23. "Roy Acuff's Grand Ole Opry Opens in Santo Domingo," *United States Forces News*, June 17, 1965, 4, Acuff Scrapbooks, FLA. *Music City News* republished this article for civilian country music audiences. See "Country Ballads and Rebel Bullets Ring Out in Santo Domingo," *Music City News*, July 1965, 1, 14. For President Johnson's public message regarding this military action, see Johnson, "May 2, 1965."

24. Red O'Donnell, "Whatever Happened to Melancholy Baby?," *Nashville Banner*, December 4, 1965, Acuff Scrapbooks, FLA.

25. Maj. H. E. Swinney, USAF, "Roy's for the Troops—All the Way," *Stars and Stripes* (Pacific), December 26, 1965, Acuff Scrapbooks, FLA.

26. Swinney.

27. "Hometowners, USA Scores," *Music City News*, April 1965, 9.

28. Tom T. Hall, interview by Cecil Whaley, July 22, 1969, Nashville, TN, OH322, CMFOHP.

29. Hall; "A Conversation with Tom T. Hall," *Country Song Roundup*, May 1969, 33, FLA.

30. Hall interview, CMFOHP; Geoffrey Himes, "Who Needs Country Radio? Not Tom T. Hall," *New York Times*, January 13, 2008.

31. Whitburn, *Hot Country Songs*, 477.

32. "Decca—Johnny Wright Answer Viet Nam Plea," *Music City News*, December 1965, 30, FLA.

33. Rossinow, *Politics of Authenticity*; Gitlin, *Sixties*.

34. Whitburn, *Hot Country Songs*, 131.

35. Dave Dudley, *There's a Star-Spangled Banner Waving Somewhere*, Mercury Records SR 61057, 1965, 33 1/3 rpm.

36. Larry Arnett, "Stranger than Fiction—The Real Life Adventures of Songwriter Kris Kristofferson," *Country Song Roundup*, April 1969, 17–18, FLA; Geoff Lane, "Kris Waited until the Music Tides Turned," *Music City News*, June 1973, 25–26, 29, FLA.

37. Kubrick, *Full Metal Jacket*.

38. Elton Whisenhunt, "Nashville Scene," *Billboard*, January 1, 1966, 29.

39. Hall interview, CMFOHP.

40. Fry, *American South and the Vietnam War*, 148, 149.

41. Harris Martin, "Music City News Goes to Viet Nam," *Music City News*, January 1966, 1, 11, 16, FLA.

42. Omer Anderson, "US Launches European Drive to Aid Country Music Image," *Billboard*, December 25, 1965, 24, 33; "Military Brass Gives C&W 'Class,'" *Music City News*, January 1966, 1, 4, FLA.

43. "Opry Stars Send TV Special to Vietnam," *Close-Up*, February 1966, 5, FLA.

44. Bill Williams, "Country Music Goes to Viet Nam," *Country Song Roundup*, December 1966, 6, FLA.

45. "WSM Names New Promotion–Public Relations Manager," *Music City News*, November 1964, 4, FLA.

46. Williams, "Country Music Goes to Viet Nam," 6.

47. Williams, 6.

48. "CMA to Salute Military," *Close-Up*, August 1967, 7, FLA.

49. "Twenty-Five Years of Country Music Rewarded," *Close-Up*, October 1967, 5, FLA.

50. "Professional and Command Military Touring Shows," Folder: Chronological Lists of Professional and Command Military Touring Shows in Vietnam, 1 April 1966–31 March 1969, USARV, SSA (Prov)/Athletic, Rec., and Ent. Div., Entertainment Branch, Container 64, General Administrative Records, 04/1966–06/1972, RG 472, NARA-CP; Kramer, *Republic of Rock*, 170.

51. "Professional and Command Military Touring Shows." On the Cascades and their ties to the US Navy, see "The Cascades," *San Diego Reader*, accessed October 25, 2022, https://www.sandiegoreader.com/bands/cascades/.

52. Kramer, *Republic of Rock*, 170.

53. Kramer, *Republic of Rock*; J. Hamilton, *Just around Midnight*; Bradley and Werner, *We Gotta Get Outta This Place*.

54. Kramer, *Republic of Rock*, 167–187. Kramer has described the military's attempts to absorb and adopt elements of the counterculture, from loosening hair-length restrictions to booking psychedelic bands, as "hip militarism." Although there is plenty of evidence to suggest that servicemembers enjoyed these counterculture-adjacent acts, Kramer's tight focus on rock and soul misses the prominence of country musicians within the CMTS.

55. For the itineraries, after-action reports, evaluations, and other paperwork connected to the CMTS in these years, see USARV, SSA (Prov)/Athletic, Rec., and Ent. Div., Entertainment Branch, Containers 39 and 40: Records Regarding Command Military Touring Show (CMTS) Tours in Vietnam, 09/25/1966–12/22/1971, RG 472, NARA-CP.

56. Folder: CMTS Tours—Jamboree (3)—Feb. 18, 1967, USARV, SSA (Prov)/Athletic, Rec., and Ent. Div., Entertainment Branch, Containers 39: Records Regarding Command Military Touring Show (CMTS) Tours in Vietnam, 09/25/1966–12/22/1971, RG 472, NARA-CP.

57. "CMA Military Awards Get Top Priority," *Close-Up*, November 1967, 2, FLA.

58. "CMA Military Awards Get Top Priority," 2.

59. "Country Music Album Salutes Armed Forces," *Close-Up*, February 1968, 1, FLA.

60. "CMA Coordinates AFRTS TV," *Close-Up*, November 1967, 6, FLA.

61. Tom Grein, "Artifact Donations Reflect Country's Hall of Fame Growth," *Music City News*, April 1968, 14, FLA.

62. Whitburn, *Hot Country Songs*, 367.

63. Stonewall Jackson, "The Minute Men (Are Turning in Their Graves)," Columbia 4-43552, 1966, 45 rpm.

64. Stonewall Jackson, "The Stonewall Jackson Story," *Country Song Roundup*, May 1969, 9, FLA.

65. Newport and Carroll, "Iraq versus Vietnam."

66. Merle Haggard and the Strangers, "Okie from Muskogee," Capitol Records 2626, 1969, 45 rpm.

67. Rubin, *33 1/3*.

68. D. Cantwell, *Running Kind*.

69. Merle Haggard and the Strangers, "The Fightin' Side of Me," Capitol Records 2719, 1970, 45 rpm.

70. Ernest Tubb, "It's America (Love It or Leave It)," *A Good Year for the Wine*, Decca Records DL-75222, 1970, 45 rpm.

71. Whitburn, *Hot Country Songs*, 429.

72. Seymour M. Hersh, "Coverup," *New Yorker*, January 22, 1972.

73. Hughes, *Country Soul*, 142.

74. "Terry Nelson: The All-American Boy," *Country Song Roundup*, November 1971, 16–17, FLA.

75. Loretta Lynn, "Dear Uncle Sam" b/w "Hurtin' for Certain," Decca 31893, 1966, 45 rpm.

76. Tillis, *Stutterin' Boy*, 72–84; Whitburn, *Hot Country Songs*, 420; Mel Tillis, "Stateside," Kapp Records 722, 1967, 45 rpm.

77. Tillis, *Stutterin' Boy*, 170–171; Whitburn, *Hot Country Songs*, 360.

78. Tom T. Hall, "Mama Bake a Pie (Daddy Kill a Chicken)," *100 Children*, Mercury SR 61307, 1970, 33 1/3 rpm.

79. "Hank Snow Eager for More Viet Nam," *Close-Up*, February 1967, 6, FLA; "An Interview with Bill Anderson," *Country Song Roundup*, February 1968, 15–17, FLA; Bill Anderson, "My German Tour," *Country Song Roundup*, March 1968, 17–18, FLA; Saburo Kawahara, "Special Report on Country Music in Japan," *Country Song Roundup*, February 1968, 43–44, FLA; "To Tokyo, Taiwan and Thailand with Jeannie Seely," *Country Song Roundup*, November 1969, 8–11, FLA; "A Picture Story: 'Red Sovine in Vietnam,'" *Country Song Roundup*, April 1970, 10–13, FLA; "We Talk to Justin Tubb," *Country Song Roundup*, June 1968, 42–43, FLA.

80. "Roy Acuff . . . Country Music's Bob Hope," *Country Song Roundup*, June 1970, 18, 47, FLA.

81. Flood, *My Walk among the Stars*, 1–19, 35.

82. Everett J. Corbin, "The Flood That Brought Country-Western Music," *Music City News*, October 1966, 56, FLA.

83. Vuic, *Girls Next Door*, 184–215; Stur, *Beyond Combat*, 90–97; "Professional and Command Military Touring Shows," Folder: Chronological Lists of Professional and Command Military Touring Shows in Vietnam, 1 April 1966–31 March 1969, USARV, SSA (Prov)/Athletic, Rec., and Ent. Div., Entertainment Branch, Container 64, General Administrative Records, 04/1966–06/1972, RG 472, NARA-CP.

84. "Pat Campbell . . . TNT," *Country Song Roundup*, December 1968, 16, FLA.

85. "Pat Campbell . . . TNT," 16.

86. Spector, *After Tet*, 247. In a study of southern veterans, James R. Wilson called white southerners' use of country music in Vietnam a "provincial hallmark," noting that "Armed Forces radio blanketed Vietnam with the lonesome, often propagandistic wail of country music." Wilson suggests that country music's patriotic songs created a "social and political milieu that generally made it easier for southern veterans to come home than their comrades from other parts of the world." Although this probably conflates "southern" and "white," his point about the pervasiveness of country music and its connection to political attitudes that supported US militarism remains correct. See Wilson, *Landing Zones*, xi. For an analysis of how army brass attempted to deal with the "racial tension" among troops during Vietnam and the Black political response to those measures, see Bailey, *Army Afire*.

87. Kramer, *Republic of Rock*, 167–187.

88. "After Action Report 'Soul Coordinators,'" CMTS Tours—Soul Coordinators (78)—Aug. 10, 1970, Records Regarding Command Military Touring Shows (CMTS) Tours in Vietnam, USARV, SSA (Prov)/Athletic, Rec. and Ent. Division, Entertainment Branch, Container 44, Records of the US Forces in Southeast Asia, 1950–1976, RG 472, NARA-CP.

89. James Brown to Lyndon Johnson, June 11, 1968, 723-01 Rec & Entertainment Case Files, James Brown File, Morale SUPP Mixed FLS 68, Acc. 73-0010, Container 1, TAGO, RG 407, NARA-CP.

90. Brown to Johnson.

91. Cloteal Fitzpatrick (McClinton's sister), interview by the author, March 4, 2016.

92. McClinton and Wood, *Hard Way to Go*, 25.

93. McClinton and Wood, 37–46.

94. McClinton and Wood, 61–69.

95. Bowman, "O. B. McClinton," 26.

96. McClinton and Wood, *Hard Way to Go*, 101–103; Bowman, "O. B. McClinton," 26.

97. "O. B. McClinton, the 'Black Country Irishman,'" Stax press release, SMASM.

98. O. B. McClinton, "Obie from Senatobie," *Obie from Senatobie*, Enterprise Records ENS-1029, 1973, 33 1/3 rpm.

99. McClinton promotional materials, SMASM; Hughes, "I'm the Other One."

100. Bowman, "O. B. McClinton."

101. *Music City News*, February 1968, 20, FLA; "CMA's Director—Honorary AF Recruiter," *Close-Up*, July 1968, 8, FLA.

102. "Air Force Produces Country Music Time," *Music City News*, October 1969, 26-B, FLA; "Hall of Fame Museum Obtains Air Force Records," *Close-Up*, December 1969, 3, FLA; "USAF Presents Music to CM Hall of Fame," *Music City News*, January 1970, 6, FLA.

103. "Charlie Walker/Bob Luman," *Country Music Time*, 110605, 342-CMT-1/2, Audio Recordings from the "Country Music Time" Program Series, 1961–1986, Records of US Air Force Commands, Activities, and Organizations, 1900–2003, RG 342, NARA-CP. Charlie Walker had worked as a DJ in Texas since the early 1940s, and while stationed in Japan during World War II, Walker had made a name for himself by broadcasting American hillbilly music from Tokyo on the Armed Forces Radio Network. After the war, he returned to his stateside radio job in San Antonio, where he reigned as one of the top ten most popular DJs in the country for ten consecutive years from 1952 to 1962. See Bill Sachs, "Folk Talent and Tunes," *Billboard*, February 10, 1962, 46; Pugh, "Charlie Walker," 567.

104. Bartlett, "Operation Bootstrap."

105. "Little Jimmy Dickens/O. B. McClinton," *Country Music Time*, 111074, 342-CMT-923/924, Audio Recordings from the "Country Music Time" Program Series, 1961–1986, RG 342, NARA-CP.

106. "Margaret Lewis/The Carter Family and Dave Dudley," *Country Music Time*, 110621, 342-CMT-19/20, Audio Recordings from the "Country Music Time" Program Series, 1961–1986, RG 342, NARA-CP; J. H. McNaughton, "The Faded Coat of Blue" (Caledonia, NY: J. H. McNaughton, 1865), notated music, LOC, www.loc.gov/item/ihas.200001608/.

107. "Jeannie C. Riley," *Country Music Time*, 110622, 342-CMT-21, Audio Recordings from the "Country Music Time" Program Series, 1961–1986, RG 342, NARA-CP.

108. *The United States Army Recruiting Command Presents It's Music*, US Army Recruiting Command Broadcast Center, Show #9-68 & 10-68, 1968, 33 1/3 rpm.

109. *The United States Army Recruiting Command Presents It's Music*, US Army Recruiting Command Broadcast Center, Show #17-71, 1971, 33 1/3 rpm.

110. *United States Army Recruiting Command Presents It's Music*, Show #17-71.

111. "Johnny Darrell/Stonewall Jackson," *Country Music Time*, 110649, 342-CMT-61/62, Audio Recordings from the "Country Music Time" Program Series, 1961–1986, RG 342, NARA-CP.

112. "Billie Jo Spears and Barry Sadler/Ray Stevens," *Country Music Time*, 110617, 342-CMT-13/14, Audio Recordings from the "Country Music Time" Program Series, 1961–1986, RG 342, NARA-CP.

113. "Johnny Darrell/Stonewall Jackson."

114. Omer Anderson, "Country Wins Europe GI's to Tune of $4.2 Mil. Yearly," *Billboard*, January 13, 1968, 1.

115. "CMA Pioneer Honored by Invite to Vietnam," *Close-Up*, May 1968, 2, FLA.

116. "LBJ Likes Country Music," *Close-Up*, August 1968, 2, FLA.

117. "Owens Performs for LBJ Party," *Music City News*, October 1968, 8, FLA.

118. "Presidential Appeal for CMA," *Close-Up*, April 1968, 1, FLA.

119. La Chapelle, *I'd Fight the World*, 208–212.

120. "Gov. Wallace Alabama's # One Citizen, Country & Gospel Fan," *Music City News*, July 1965, 8, FLA.

121. "Gov. Wallace Visits Backstage at Opry," *Music City News*, July 1966, 21, FLA.

122. Carter, *Politics of Rage*.

123. Kazin, *Populist Persuasion*.

124. "Hal Cass Has Great Patriotic Record in 'Stand Up for America,'" *Music City News*, August 1967, 26, FLA; "Col. Hal Sings the Blues," *Music City News*, May 1967, 22, FLA; "Col. Hal Sings," *Music City News*, June 1967, 19, FLA.

125. "Faron Breaks into Show Business," *Music City News*, October 1967, 6B, FLA.

126. La Chapelle, *I'd Fight the World*, 213; Carter, *Politics of Rage*, 424.

127. "Artists Campaign for Alabama Winner," *Close-Up*, July 1970, 7, FLA.

128. Quoted in Carter, *Politics of Rage*, 425.

129. McGinnis, *Selling of the President, 1968*; Brownell, *Showbiz Politics*.

130. Cowie, *Stayin' Alive*, 165; Schulman, *Seventies*; Self, *All in the Family*; Kevin Phillips, *Emerging Republican Majority*.

131. "White House Hears Cash's Country Music," *Close-Up*, May 1970, 5, FLA; "White House Newsmen Hear Best of Country," *Close-Up*, July 1971, 1, FLA.

132. Cash, *Man in Black*, 173–175; Cash, "Johnny Cash Performs at the White House."

133. "President Continues Use of Country Artists," *Close-Up*, July 1971, 12.

134. Richard Nixon to Charley Pride, October 26, 1971, National Museum of African American History and Culture, https://nmaahc.si.edu/object/nmaahc_2012 .125.82.

135. Young, *Vietnam Wars*, 235–238.

136. "AFRTS Receives Special Merit Award," *Music City News*, November 1969, 30, FLA; "The Early Days and Early Dollars Paved the Way for the Bustling ACM of Today," *Billboard*, April 28, 1990, A-3.

137. "USN Presents Award at CMA Banquet," *Close-Up*, November 1969, 7, FLA.

138. "Proof Positive of Country Music Appeal," *Close-Up*, June 1970, 8, FLA.

139. "Country Music in Vietnam," *Music City News*, October 1971, 12-A, FLA.

140. "Servicemen 'Dig' Country Music," *Close-Up*, February 1972, 2, FLA.

141. Young, *Vietnam Wars*, 261–262.

142. "Nixon Cites Patriotic Song," *Close-Up*, July 1972, 4, FLA.

143. "Lynn Anderson Opens GOP Convention," *Close-Up*, October 1972, 12, FLA.

144. "Country/Politics," *Music City News*, August 1972, 4, FLA.

145. Cowie, *Stayin' Alive*, 167–168.

146. Quoted in Young, *Vietnam Wars*, 262.

147. Gallup, "Presidential Approval Ratings"; Saad, "Gallup Vault."

148. Richard Nixon, "Remarks at the Grand Ole Opry House, Nashville, Tennessee," March 16, 1974, American Presidency Project, www.presidency.ucsb.edu /documents/remarks-the-grand-ole-opry-house-nashville-tennessee.

149. Pecknold, *Selling Sound*, 224.

150. Nixon, "Remarks at the Grand Ole Opry House." Haggard had appeared before, in 1973, to sing "Okie from Muskogee" and "The Fightin' Side of Me."

151. Nixon.

152. Les Bridges, "Tom T. Hall: When the Women Hiss, He Says . . . ," *Rolling Stone*, June 21, 1973, Box 53, Folder L, SDEC.

Chapter 7

1. *25th Anniversary of the Country Music Association*, directed by Dwight Hemion, written by Chet Hagan and Barry Adelman, aired 1983, FV.2009.0630, DVD00634, FLA; Richard Harrington, "Country Music Gala Set for Constitution Hall," *Washington Post*, February 10, 1983.

2. *25th Anniversary of the Country Music Association*.

3. *25th Anniversary of the Country Music Association*.

4. Ronald Reagan, "Remarks by President Reagan during country music reception. East Room," March 15, 1983, Ronald Reagan Presidential Library and Museum, https://www.reaganlibrary.gov/archives/audio/remarks-president-reagan-during -country-music-reception-east-room; Collis, "25th Anniversary of the Country Music Association."

5. Mittelstadt, *Rise of the Military Welfare State*, 8, 77–78.

6. Leffler, *For the Soul of Mankind*, 234–259.

7. Simpson, *Early '70s Radio*, 155; Weisbard, *Top 40 Democracy*, 91.

8. "Country Soars to Highest Sales Ever," *Close-Up*, October 1981, 1, 9; Gerry Wood, Sally Hinkle, and Kip Kirby, "Top Disk Executives Boost Country Gains," *Billboard*, November 4, 1978, 1; Martinez, "Redneck Chic."

9. Edward Morris, "Soul Leads Armed Forces Record Sales," *Billboard*, December 7, 1985, 57.

10. Young, *Vietnam Wars*.

11. Claude Hill, "Vietnam: A Major Market Fades," *Billboard*, May 17, 1975, 1.

12. Hill, 14.

13. "CMA Receives Navy Award," *Close-Up*, November 1974, 7.

14. "Country Music Aids Army Recruiting," *Close-Up*, June 1975, 3.

15. Mittelstadt, *Rise of the Military Welfare State*, 23–28; Bailey, *America's Army*.

16. Mittelstadt, *Rise of the Military Welfare State*, 7, 23–28.

17. *United States Air Force Presents . . . Roland Bynum Soul in Motion*, US Air Force Recruiting Service Directorate of Advertising, Series #4-1, April 1973, 33 1/3 rpm.

18. *Army ROTC Presents "Soul Line,"* Army ROTC, January 1976, 33 1/3 rpm.

19. "US Exports Country Music to Russia," *Close-Up*, September 1974, 6, FLA; "Country Wows Russians," *Close-Up*, October 1974, 7, FA.

20. Patrick Carr, "Opryland in Russia," *Country Music*, February 1975, 28, Box: 30015, SFC Radio and Television Files, Folder: WSM Radio AM 650, SFC.

21. Leffler, *For the Soul of Mankind*, 234–259.

22. Von Eschen, *Satchmo Blows Up the World*; "Country Wows Russians," *Close-Up*, October 1974, 7, FLA.

23. Carr, "Opryland in Russia," 28.

24. "Country Special Filmed in Soviet Union," *Close-Up*, January 1975, 2, FLA.

25. Connie B. Gay, "President's Press Secretary a Country Music Pioneer," *Close-Up*, November 1974, 10, FLA.

26. "Country Special Filmed in Soviet Union," 2.

27. Carr, "Opryland in Russia," 33.

28. "Voice of America Talks Country," *Close-Up*, May 1975, 1, FLA.

29. "New Atlanta PX Buying Hdqrs, Opens Apr. 27; To Add DC Area Record/Tape Buying by July 27," *Billboard*, February 2, 1974, 3; John Sippel, "Armed Forces Sales Spurt," *Billboard*, August 28, 1977, 1, 75.

30. Earl Paige, "Exchanges Build Civilian Sales," *Billboard*, January 25, 1975, 36, 40.

31. Sippel, "Armed Forces Sales Spurt," *Billboard*, August 28, 1977, 1, 75.

32. "A Management Study of American Forces Radio and Television," September 1974, Management Study of AFRTS—BC, 1974, Armed Forces Radio and Television Service, Histories, Reports, and Program Records, Box 3: Special Reports, RG 330, NARA-CP.

33. "Management Study."

34. "Management Study."

35. Dan Abramson, "Dual Personality Stars in Country Syndication Set," *Billboard*, February 22, 1975, 28, 33; "Jerry Naylor Jackson 1939–2019," *Yamhill County's News-Register*, December 17, 2019, https://newsregister.com/article?articleTitle =jerry-naylor-jackson-1939-2019-1575913365--35426.

36. 1985 AFRTS schedules, Armed Forces Radio and Television Service, Histories, Reports, and Program Records, Box 4: Historical Materials, RG 330, NARA-CP.

37. Jim Melanson, "'King Biscuit' Rates High in Youth Recognition," *Billboard*, February 2, 1975, 24.

38. "AFRTS: A Radio and Television Programming Chronicle," 1980, AFRTS Story, Armed Forces Radio and Television Service, Histories, Reports, and Program Records, Box 4: Historical Materials, RG 330, NARA-CP.

39. Lon Helton, "A Tale of Two Countdowns," *Radio and Records*, September 30, 1983, 66.

40. "Audio Cassette Broadcast System," AFRTS Special Report, Issue 6, July 15, 1977, AFRTS History, Special Reports, 1974–1977, Armed Forces Radio and Television

Service, Histories, Reports, and Program Records, Box 3: Special Reports, RG 330, NARA-CP.

41. "Management Study."

42. Simpson, *Early '70s Radio*, 155; Weisbard, *Top 40 Democracy*, 91.

43. Waylon Jennings, Willie Nelson, Jessi Colter, and Tompall Glaser, *Wanted! The Outlaws*, RCA Victor, AAL1-1321, 1976, 33 1/3 rpm.

44. Malone and Neal, *Country Music, U.S.A.*, 398–404; Mellard, *Progressive Country*; Stimeling, *Cosmic Cowboys and New Hicks*. Although *Wanted! The Outlaws* has received designation as the first country record to go platinum, Ray Charles's *Modern Sounds in Country and Western* actually achieved that distinction first in 1962. However, the industry did not classify Charles's influential album as country music at the time. See Pecknold, "Making Country Modern."

45. Malone and Neal, *Country Music, U.S.A.*, 378–382; Weisbard, *Top 40 Democracy*.

46. Oermann, "Barbara Mandrell," 309–310.

47. Schulman, *Seventies*, 115–116; Cowie, *Stayin' Alive*, 167–176; Malone and Neal, *Country Music, U.S.A.*, 373, 431, 477.

48. Schulman, *From Cotton Belt to Sunbelt*.

49. Martinez, "Redneck Chic."

50. Lechner, *South of the Mind*.

51. "Roy Clark on 18-Day Russian Concert Tour," *Close-Up*, February 1976, 4, FLA.

52. "President Sends Telegram to CMA," *Close-Up*, November 1975, 2, FLA.

53. "CMA Board Meets in Washington," *Close-Up*, May 1978, 7, FLA.

54. Leffler, *For the Soul of Mankind*, 263–267.

55. Jimmy Carter, "Address at Commencement Exercises at the University of Notre Dame," May 22, 1972, American Presidency Project, www.presidency.ucsb.edu /documents/address-commencement-exercises-the-university-notre-dame.

56. Perlstein, *Reaganland*, 107.

57. "Country at Carnegie," *Close-Up*, June 1977, 2, FLA; Gerry Wood, "Giant Net for N.Y. Concert," *Billboard*, May 14, 1977, 26, 62.

58. Pat Nelson, "Halsey's Event Generates Estimated $1.5 Mil. Action," *Billboard*, September 24, 1977, 30; Ellis Winder, "Halsey Sets Nov. 3–5 for Tulsa Intl. Fest," *Billboard*, May 6, 1978, 84; Gerry Wood, "TV to Tape Tulsa Fest," *Billboard*, October 21, 1978, 23; Gerry Wood, "Tulsa International Music Festival," *Billboard*, November 4, 1978, 85, 87.

59. "Montreux: 65 Fly Out," *Billboard*, July 14, 1979, 34.

60. "Country on the Tube," *Close-Up*, October 1977, 2, FLA.

61. "Armed Forces to Air CMA Awards Show," *Close-Up*, December 1977, 2, FLA.

62. "CMA Honors President Carter," *Close-Up*, June 1979, 1, 9, FLA.

63. "Chinese Ambassador Visits Nashville," *Close-Up*, December 1979, 1, 9, FLA.

64. Harold Kennedy, "America Sings Along with Country Music," *US News and World Report*, June 21, 1982.

65. Leffler, *For the Soul of Mankind*, 260; Cowie, *Stayin' Alive*.

66. Reagan, "Inaugural Address."

67. Jacobs and Zelizer, *Conservatives in Power*.

68. "Former CMA President Heads Civil Aeronautics Board," *Close-Up*, October 1981, 13, FLA; Jeanette Steele, "Dan McKinnon: Navy Pilot, Radio, Airline Executive," *San Diego Union-Tribune*, November 26, 2012, www.sandiegouniontribune.com/sdut-dan-mckinnon-navy-pilot-radio-airline-executive-2012nov26-story.html; S.2493—Airline Deregulation Act, 95th Cong. (1977–1978). McKinnon possessed all the credentials of a Southern California conservative. He had served as a pilot in the US Navy in the 1950s. He bought the San Diego station KSON in 1962 and converted it to a country format. He counted Billy Graham as a friend and served as chairman of Graham's 1976 "Crusade" revival at Jack Murphy Stadium in San Diego. In addition to his CMA presidency, McKinnon also served on the board of the National Association of Recording Manufacturers.

69. California State University, Northridge, "Mike Curb Biography."

70. "Country Soars to Highest Sales Ever," *Close-Up*, October 1981, 1, 9, FLA.

71. "CMA Survey Shows Half US Radio Stations Program Country Music," *Close-Up*, May 1982, 1, FLA.

72. AFRTS—Programming Center, AM Radio Program Index, Fall 1985, Folder: AFRTS Information, 1942–1986, Armed Forces Radio and Television Service, Histories, Reports, and Program Records, Box 5: Historical Materials, RG 330, NARA-CP.

73. Duplication and Packing List, Armed Forces Radio and Television Service, January 27, 1986, Folder: AFRTS Information, 1942–1986, Armed Forces Radio and Television Service, Histories, Reports, and Program Records, Box 5: Historical Materials, RG 330, NARA-CP.

74. John Sippel, "Military PX Sales Thriving," *Billboard*, September 20, 1980, 1, 61.

75. "Top 10 Disks Pushed to O'seas PX Shops," *Billboard*, March 28, 1981, 58.

76. Rose Clayton, "Georgia: State's Stock Rises as World Distrib, Sales Hub," *Billboard*, September 26, 1981, G-6.

77. Jim Sampson, "Country in German Spotlight," *Billboard*, January 30, 1982, 10, 70.

78. "Savoy Planning Cutbacks as Black Retail Sales Sag," *Billboard*, January 8, 1983, 64; Edward Morris, "Armed Forces Record Sales Up in 1982," *Billboard*, June 11, 1983, 37.

79. Enrique Fernandez, "Menudo Fever Grips New RCA Division VP," *Billboard*, January 7, 1984, 41; John Sippel, "Military Purchases Increase," *Billboard*, December 1, 1984.

80. Morris, "Soul Leads Armed Forces Record Sales," 57.

81. Rose Clayton, "6 Fresh Acts—And the Key to Their Success," *Billboard*, October 4, 1980, 44.

82. Quoted in Bego, *George Strait*, 9–12; Bob Allen, "George Strait and the Ace in the Hole Band Pick Up the Pieces Where Bob Wills Left Off," *Country Music*, September–October 1988, FLA.

83. "Newsline," *Close-Up*, January 1982, 20, FLA; Kip Kirby, "Nashville Scene," *Billboard*, February 20, 1982, 60; Kip Kirby, "Nashville Scene," *Billboard*, December 4, 1982, 42; "International," *Close-Up*, July 1982, 19, FLA.

84. Thomas K. Arnold, "Showtime for Hank Williams, Jr.," *Billboard*, March 31, 1984, 43; "*Constellation* III (CVA-64), 1961–2003," Naval History and Heritage

Command, https://www.history.navy.mil/research/histories/ship-histories/danfs/c/constellation-iii.html.

85. Lee Greenwood, "It Turns Me Inside It" b/w "Thank You for Changing My Life," MCA 51159, 1981, 45 rpm; Whitburn, *Billboard Country*; Greenwood and McLin, *God Bless the U.S.A.*

86. Bob Millard, "Lee Greenwood: Surviving a Hard and Lonely Road to the Top," *Country Song Roundup*, December 1983, LGC; Greenwood and McLin, *God Bless the U.S.A.*

87. Millard, "Lee Greenwood: Surviving." Del Reeves had started playing professionally while serving in the US Air Force and pursued a rockabilly career after his discharge before landing a string of trucker-themed country hits in the 1960s. See "Del Reeves: The Early Years," *Music City News*, December 1966, 4, FLA.

88. Greenwood and McLin, *God Bless the U.S.A.*, 53–55.

89. Bob Millard, "Lee Greenwood: Our Man from Las Vegas," *Country Music*, March–April 1984, LGC; Greenwood and McLin, *God Bless the U.S.A.*, 89–117.

90. Millard, "Lee Greenwood: Our Man"; John Kiely, "If Hollywood Made a Movie of Lee Greenwood's Life, No One Would Believe It," *Kitchener-Waterloo Record*, February 2, 1984, LGC; Lee Greenwood publicity fact sheet, n.d., LGC.

91. Greenwood and McLin, *God Bless the U.S.A.*, 138.

92. Greenwood and McLin, 138. On the religious content of the song, see Shearon, "Sacred in Country Music," 405; Lee Greenwood, "God Bless the U.S.A.," MCA 52386, 1983, 45 rpm.

93. "Lee Greenwood Chart History," *Billboard*, accessed July 11, 2022, www.billboard.com/artist/lee-greenwood/chart-history/tlp/.

94. Kip Kirby, "Music Row Construction Boom Brings New Blood to Nashville," *Billboard*, August 25, 1984, 54; "Factfile," *Close-Up*, June 1984, 17.

95. Greenwood, "Lee Greenwood—God Bless the U.S.A."

96. Kip Kirby, "Nashville Scene," *Billboard*, September 1, 1984, 44.

97. On Reagan's idealization of the citizens soldier, see Mittelstadt, *Rise of the Military Welfare State*, 9.

98. "Awards Show Finalist Announced," *Close-Up*, October 1985, 12, FLA; "CMA Presents: 'Country's Brightest Stars,'" *Close-Up*, November–December 1985, 15, FLA.

99. "Newsline," *Close-Up*, October 1985, 9, FLA.

100. Greenwood and McLin, *God Bless the U.S.A.*, 172.

101. Kip Kirby, "Nashville Scene," *Billboard*, August 4, 1984, 42; Kip Kirby, "Nashville Scene," *Billboard*, September 1, 1984, 44.

102. Kip Kirby, "Nashville Scene," *Billboard*, November 23, 1985, 44A.

103. Morris, "Soul Leads Armed Forces Record Sales," 57.

104. "Armed Forces Show Marking 25th Year," *Billboard*, October 26, 1985, 64.

105. Country Music Time Transcription Series, 12 Inch Radio Transcriptions, A—Country Music Binder, FLA.

106. David C. Kraus, Lt. Col., USAF, Deputy Director, Advertising and Publicity to Station Managers, July 16, 1987, 12 Inch Radio Transcriptions, A—Country Music Binder, FLA.

107. "Behind the Lens," *Close-Up*, February 1986, 15.

108. "TNN to Air Specials, Expand Quiz Show Focus," *Billboard*, November 22, 1986, 41; Edward Morris, "Independent TV Producers Offer TNN a Variety of Creative Programs," *Billboard*, April 23, 1988, TNN-6, TNN-22.

109. "Lee Greenwood Sings for Corker," *Chattanooga News-Free Press*, October 17, 1988, LGC; Tracy Wenzel, "Star-filled Night Shines with Hope," *Northwest Florida News*, October 6, 1989, LGC; Leslie Welch, "Country Star Croons for Politicos," *Little Rock Gazette*, November 19, 1989, LGC; Greenwood and McLin, *God Bless the U.S.A.*, 202.

110. Joe Edwards, "The Singer George Bush Just Can't Get Enough Of," AP, *Bridgeport Telegram*, September 14, 1989, LGC.

111. "Veterans Group Sues Singer," *Columbus Ledger-Enquirer*, December 16, 1989, LGC; "Wilkes-Barre Vets Sue Singer Who Didn't Sing," *Morning Call*, December 14, 1989, A2.

112. Reagan Library, "Celebration after President Reagan's Speech."

113. "Country Stars Shine during Inauguration," *Close-Up*, February 1989, 2, FLA.

114. Edwards, "Singer George Bush Just Can't Get Enough Of."

115. Leffler, *For the Soul of Mankind*, 422–448.

116. Engel, *When the World Seemed New*.

117. Phyllis Stark, "Desert Shield Net Dodges Obstacles in Saudi Arabia," *Billboard*, February 9, 1991, 18.

118. Greenwood and McLin, *God Bless the U.S.A.*, 251–254.

119. *Frontline*, "Oral History: Norman Schwarzkopf."

120. *American Patriot*, Liberty Records press release, LGC.

121. James O'Connor, "Lee Greenwood, *American Patriot*," *Winnipeg Sun*, June 5, 1992, LGC.

122. Jack Burditt, "Don't Bother Me When I'm Bothered," *Signal and Saugus Enterprise*, July 10, 1992, LGC.

123. Joe Edwards, "War Launched Greenwood Revival," *Post-Tribune*, September 4, 1992, LGC.

124. Gallagher, "Lee Greenwood on Why the Fourth Time's the Charm."

125. Edwards, "War Launched Greenwood Revival."

Conclusion

1. Bill Holland, "Rap, Hip-Hop AWOL in Iraq," *Billboard*, May 24, 2003, 66. In fact, hip-hop and heavy metal rose as two of the most popular genres among troops in the War on Terror. See Gilman, *My Music, My War*; Pieslak, *Sound Targets*.

2. Holland, "Rap, Hip-Hop AWOL in Iraq," 66.

3. Sarig, *Third Coast*, 17, 33; *Urban Daily* Staff, "Duice—'Dazzey Duks.'"

4. *Billboard* regularly mentioned R&B USO tours in the 1990s in the column "The Rhythm and the Blues." On Lou Rawls and the USO, see Moira McCormick, "After 30 Years of Recording, Renewal and Reward," *Billboard*, October 20, 1990.

5. Jon Caramanica, "Concert for Trump Misses an Opportunity," *New York Times*, January 19, 2017, www.nytimes.com/2017/01/19/arts/music/trump-make-america-great-again-concert-review.html.

6. David Zimmerman, "Greenwood Lends Maples a Hand," *USA Today*, May 21, 1990, 2D, LGC.

7. Gallagher, "Lee Greenwood on Why the Fourth Time's the Charm."

8. Caramanica, "Concert for Trump Misses an Opportunity."

9. Toby Keith, "Courtesy of the Red, White, and Blue (The Angry American)," DreamWorks Nashville, 2002, CD.

10. Ray Waddell, "Red, White, & True Blue," *Billboard*, June 18, 2005, 58. Keith followed that release with other military-themed songs like "American Soldier" and "The Taliban Song" from the album called *Shock'n Y'all*, itself a play on the Pentagon's "Shock and Awe" tactical campaign in Iraq. On the evolution of Keith's political views, see Spencer Kornhaber, "Toby Keith in Trump's America," *The Atlantic*, November 2017, www.theatlantic.com/magazine/archive/2017/11/toby-keith -the-bus-songs/540654/.

11. Waddell, "Red, White, & True Blue," 58.

12. Stahl, *Militainment, Inc.*; Stahl, *Theaters of War*.

13. Everett, "Report: Pentagon Spent Millions."

14. Joseph M. Thompson, "The Longtime Connection between Race, Country Music and Military Recruitment," *Washington Post*, June 9, 2020, www.washing tonpost.com/outlook/2020/06/09/long-connection-between-race-country-music -military-recruitment/.

15. Aldean, "Our site is LIVE!!"

16. Brittany and Kasi (website), accessed July 9, 2022, https://brittanyandkasi .com/.

17. M. Johnson, "Brittany Aldean and Her Kids Wear 'Anti-Biden' Clothing."

18. Aldean, "COME SEE US TOMORROW."

19. TPUSA Events, "Have Y'all Seen the Music Lineup for AMERICAFEST 2021?!"

20. Aldean, "Best New Years EVER"; Wicks, "Happy New Year from Mar a Lago!!"

21. *Washington Post* Staff, "Identifying Far-Right Symbols That Appeared at the US Capitol Riot," *Washington Post*, January 15, 2021, www.washingtonpost.com /nation/interactive/2021/far-right-symbols-capitol-riot/.

Bibliography

Archives and Collections

Alabama Room Archives, Anniston-Calhoun County Public Library, Anniston, Alabama

Archives Center, National Museum of American History, Smithsonian Institution, Washington, DC

Country Music Magazine Collection

Rock 'n' Soul Videohistory Collection, 1990–1999

The Sam DeVincent Collection of Illustrated American Sheet Music, Ephemera

Frist Library and Archive of the Country Music Hall of Fame and Museum, Nashville, Tennessee

Connie B. Gay Collection

Country Music Foundation Oral History Project

Dick Curless Collection

Lee Greenwood Collection

Hogan Jazz Archive, Tulane University Special Collections, New Orleans, Louisiana

John F. Kennedy Presidential Library, Boston, Massachusetts

Laurence I. Hewes Personal Papers

Lee C. White Staff Files

Library of Congress, Washington, DC

AFRTS Collection, Recorded Sound Division

Memphis and Shelby County Room Special Collections, Memphis Public Library, Memphis, Tennessee

Biographical Files

National Archives and Records Administration II, College Park, Maryland

Record Group 330: Records of the Office of the Secretary of Defense, 1921–2008

Record Group 335: Records of the Office of the Secretary of the Army, 1903–2007

Record Group 338: Records of US Army Operational, Tactical, and Support Organizations (World War II and Thereafter), 1917–1999

Record Group 342: Records of US Air Force Commands, Activities, and Organizations, 1900–2003

Record Group 407: Records of the Adjutant General's Office, 1905–1981

Record Group 472: Records of the US Forces in Southeast Asia, 1950–1976

Southern Folklife Collection, University of North Carolina—Chapel Hill
  Radio and Television Files
Stax Museum of American Soul Music Archives, Memphis, Tennessee
  O. B. McClinton Publicity Files
Stuart A. Rose Manuscript, Archives, and Rare Book Library, Emory University,
    Atlanta, Georgia
  James C. Davis Papers

Digital Archives

Alphabetical Files, 1953–1961, Dwight D. Eisenhower Library, Abilene, Kansas
The American Presidency Project, University of California–Santa Barbara
Charles Templeton Sheet Music Collection, Mississippi State University Digital
  Collections
Digital Archives, Country Music Hall of Fame and Archives
Frances G. Spencer Collection of American Popular Sheet Music, Baylor University
National Museum of African American History and Culture
Ronald Reagan Presidential Library and Museum
Song of America Project, Library of Congress
Vocal Popular Sheet Music Collection, University of Maine

Periodicals

Anniston (AL) Star
Army Times
Atlanta Journal-Constitution
The Atlantic
Baltimore Afro-American
Baltimore Sun
Bangor Daily News
Bartlett (TN) Express
Billboard
Birmingham World
Boston Traveler
Caribbean Breeze
Chicago Defender
Close-Up
Coda
Columbus Ledger-Enquirer
Country Music
Country Music Reporter
Country Song Roundup
Country & Western Jamboree
Decatur Daily
Detroit Free Press

Evening Star (Washington, DC)
Fort Lauderdale News
The Guardian
*Hoedown: The Magazine of Hillbilly
  and Western Stars*
Indiana Gazette
Jackson (TN) Sun
Jamboree
Jet
Kingsport (TN) Times
Kitchener-Waterloo Record
Lansing State Journal
Life
Memphis Commercial Appeal
Memphis Flyer
Memphis Press-Scimitar
Montgomery Advertiser
Morning Call
Music City News
Nashville Banner
The Nation
National Hillbilly News

Newsweek
New Yorker
New York Amsterdam News
New York Times
New York Times Magazine
Norfolk Ledger-Portsmouth Star
Pickin' and Singin' News: The Nation-Wide Country Music Newspaper
Pittsburgh Courier
Pittsburgh Press
Post-Tribune
Radio and Records
Reader's Digest
Recruiting Journal
Richmond News Leader
Rolling Stone
San Diego Reader

San Diego Union-Tribune
Signal and Saugus Enterprise
The Southerner: News of the Citizens' Council
Stars and Stripes
The Tennessean
Time
United States Forces News
USA Today
US News and World Report
Washington City Paper
Washington Daily News
Washington Post
Winnipeg Sun
Yamhill County's News-Register
Yank

Books, Articles, Films, Theses, and Dissertations

Adamson, June N. "Few Black Voices Heard: The Black Community and the Desegregation Crisis in Clinton, Tennessee, 1956." *Tennessee Historical Quarterly* 53 (1994): 30–41.

Aldean, Brittany (@brittanyaldean). "Best New Years EVER. Here's to 2022." Instagram, December 31, 2021. www.instagram.com/p/CYLRgFJtIco/.

——. "COME SEE US TOMORROW." Instagram, December 18, 2021. www .instagram.com/p/CXpdwYaL6kP/.

——. "Our site is LIVE!!" Instagram, November 8, 2021. www.instagram.com/p /CWBJ9hTFNiw/.

Altman, Robert, dir. *Nashville*. 1975. Paramount Pictures, 2021. DVD.

Anderson, Marian. *My Lord, What a Morning: An Autobiography*. New York: Viking, 1956.

Arsenault, Raymond. *The Sound of Freedom: Marian Anderson, the Lincoln Memorial, and the Concert That Awakened America*. New York: Bloomsbury, 2009.

Ayers, Edward L. *The Promise of the New South: Life After Reconstruction*. New York: Oxford University Press, 1992.

Bailey, Beth. *America's Army: Making the All-Volunteer Force*. Cambridge, MA: Harvard University Press, 2009.

——. *An Army Afire: How the US Army Confronted Its Racial Crisis in the Vietnam Era*. Chapel Hill: University of North Carolina Press, 2023.

Balogh, Brian. *The Associational State: American Governance in the Twentieth Century*. Philadelphia: University of Pennsylvania Press, 2015.

Bartlett, Richard Adams. "Operation Bootstrap: Teaching the Young Men of Today and Tomorrow." *American Association of University Professors Bulletin* 42, no. 3 (Autumn 1956): 482–487.

Bego, Mark. *George Strait: The Story of Country's Living Legend*. New York: Kensington Books, 1997.

Bertrand, Michael T. *Race, Rock, and Elvis*. Urbana: University of Illinois Press, 2000.

Bolton, Charles C. *William F. Winter and the New Mississippi*. Jackson: University Press of Mississippi, 2013.

Bowman, Rob. "O. B. McClinton: Country Music, That's My Thing." *Journal of Country Music* 14, no. 2 (January 1992): 23–29.

——. *Soulsville, U.S.A.: The Story of Stax Records*. New York: Schirmer Trade Books, 1997.

——. "Stan Kesler." In *The Encyclopedia of Country Music*, 2nd ed., edited by Paul Kingsbury, Michael McCall, and John W. Rumble, 263–264. New York: Oxford University Press, 2012.

Bradley, Doug, and Craig Werner. *We Gotta Get Outta This Place: The Soundtrack of the Vietnam War*. Amherst: University of Massachusetts Press, 2015.

Branch, Taylor. *Parting the Waters: America in the King Years, 1954–63*. New York: Simon and Schuster, 1988.

Brenes, Michael. *For Might and Right: Cold War Defense Spending and the Remaking of American Democracy*. Amherst: University of Massachusetts Press, 2020.

Bristol, Douglas Walter, Jr., and Heather Marie Stur, eds. *Integrating the Military: Race, Gender, and Sexual Orientation Since World War II*. Baltimore: Johns Hopkins University Press, 2017.

Broven, John. *Rhythm and Blues in New Orleans*. Rev. and updated 3rd ed. Gretna, LA: Pelican, 2016.

Brownell, Kathryn. *Showbiz Politics: Hollywood in American Political Life*. Chapel Hill: University of North Carolina Press, 2014.

Bussey, Lt. Col. Charles M. *Firefight at Yechon: Courage and Racism in the Korean War*. Washington, DC: Brassey's, 1991.

California State University, Northridge. "Mike Curb Biography." Accessed August 2, 2021. www.csun.edu/pubrels/MikeCurb/bio.html.

Camfield, Thomas M. "'Will to Win'—The US Army Troop Morale Program of World War I." *Military Affairs* 41, no. 3 (October 1977): 125–128.

Canaday, Margot. *The Straight State: Sexuality and Citizenship in Twentieth-Century America*. Princeton, NJ: Princeton University Press, 2009.

Cantwell, David. *The Running Kind: Listening to Merle Haggard*. Chicago: University of Chicago Press, 2022.

Cantwell, Robert. *Bluegrass Breakdown: The Making of the Old Southern Sound*. Urbana: University of Illinois Press, 1984.

Carlin, Bob. *String Bands in the North Carolina Piedmont*. Jefferson, NC: McFarland, 2004.

Carlton, David. "The American South and the US Defense Economy: A Historical View." In *The South, the Nation, and the World: Perspectives on Southern Economic Development*, edited by David L. Carlton and Peter A. Colcanis, 151–162. Charlottesville: University of Virginia Press, 2003.

Caro, Robert A. *The Passage of Power: The Years of Lyndon Johnson*. New York: Knopf, 2012.

Carpenter, Daniel P. *The Forging of Bureaucratic Autonomy: Reputations, Networks, and Policy Innovation in Executive Agencies, 1862–1928*. Princeton, NJ: Princeton University Press, 2001.

Carter, Dan T. *The Politics of Rage: George Wallace, the Origins of the New Conservatism, and the Transformation of American Politics*. New York: Simon and Schuster, 1995

Cash, Johnny. *Cash: The Autobiography*. With Patrick Carr. New York: HarperCollins, 1997.

———. "Johnny Cash Performs at the White House for President Nixon and Guests, April 17, 1970." Timeline. Accessed July 22, 2021. www.johnnycash .com/timeline/johnny-cash-performs-at-the-white-house-for-president-nixon -and-guests/.

———. *Man in Black*. Grand Rapids, MI: Zondervan, 1975.

Cobb, James C. "From Rocky Top to Detroit City: Country Music and the Economic Transformation of the South." In *You Wrote My Life: Lyrical Themes in Country Music*, edited by Melton A. McLaurin and Richard A. Peterson, 63–80. Yverdon, Switzerland: Gordon and Breach, 1992.

———. *The Selling of the South: The Southern Crusade for Industrial Development, 1936–1980*. Baton Rouge: Louisiana State University Press, 1982.

Cohen, Lizabeth. *A Consumer's Republic: The Politics of Mass Consumption in Postwar America*. New York: Vintage Books, 2003.

Collis, Rob. "25th Anniversary of the Country Music Association (1983)." YouTube, May 14, 2017. https://youtu.be/pqsdVGzvi7s.

Country Music Hall of Fame and Museum. "Conway Twitty." Accessed August 22, 2023. https://www.countrymusichalloffame.org/hall-of-fame/conway-twitty.

Country Style, U.S.A. 1957. Hambergen, Germany: Bear Family Records, 2007. DVD.

Cowie, Jefferson. *Stayin' Alive: The 1970s and the Last Days of the Working Class*. New York: New Press, 2010.

Cross, Charles R. "Brother Wild." In *Room Full of Mirrors: A Biography of Jimi Hendrix*, 84–107. New York: Hyperion, 2005.

Daddis, Gregory A. *Pulp Vietnam: War and Gender in Cold War Men's Adventure Magazines*. Cambridge: Cambridge University Press, 2020.

Daggett, Stephen. "Cost of Major U.S. Wars." *CRS Report for Congress*, Congressional Research Service, June 29, 2010. https://fas.org/sgp/crs/natsec/RS22926.pdf.

Dalfiume, Robert M. *Desegregation of the US Armed Forces: Fighting on Two Fronts, 1939–1953*. Columbia: University of Missouri Press, 1969.

Daniel, Pete. *Lost Revolutions: The South in the 1950s*. Chapel Hill: University of North Carolina Press, 2000.

Darden, Robert. *Nothing but Love in God's Water: Black Sacred Music from the Civil War to the Civil Rights Movement*. University Park: Pennsylvania State University Press, 2014.

Davenport, Lisa E. *Jazz Diplomacy: Promoting America in the Cold War Era*. Jackson: University Press of Mississippi, 2013.

Delo, David Michael. *Peddlers and Post Traders: The Army Sutler on the Frontier.* Salt Lake City: University of Utah Press, 1992.

Denning, Michael. *The Cultural Front: The Laboring of American Culture in the Twentieth Century.* London: Verso, 1997.

Diekman, Diane. *Live Fast, Love Hard: The Faron Young Story.* Urbana: University of Illinois Press, 2007.

Dinerstein, Joel. *Swing the Machine: Modernity, Technology, and African American Culture between the World Wars.* Amherst: University of Massachusetts Press, 2003.

Dochuck, Darren. *From Bible Belt to Sunbelt: Plain-Folk Religion, Grassroots Politics, and the Rise of Evangelical Conservatism.* New York: Norton, 2011.

Douglas, Susan J. *Listening In: Radio and the American Imagination, from Amos 'n' Andy and Edward R. Murrow to Wolfman Jack and Howard Stern.* New York: Times Books, 1999.

Dubois, Laurent. *The Banjo: America's African Instrument.* Cambridge, MA: Harvard University Press, 2016.

Dudziak, Mary L. *Cold War Civil Rights: Race and the Image of American Democracy.* Princeton, NJ: Princeton University Press, 2000.

Du Mez, Kristin Kobes. *Jesus and John Wayne: How White Evangelicals Corrupted a Faith and Fractured a Nation.* New York: Norton, 2020.

Engel, Jeffrey A. *When the World Seemed New: George H. W. Bush and the End of the Cold War.* Boston: Houghton Mifflin Harcourt, 2017.

Engelhardt, Tom. *The End of Victory Culture: Cold War America and the Disillusioning of a Generation.* Rev. and exp. ed. Amherst: University of Massachusetts Press, 2007.

Epstein, Daniel Mark, *Nat King Cole.* New York: Farrar, Straus and Giroux, 1999.

Escott, Colin. *All Roads Lead to Rock: Legends of Rock and Roll: A Bear Family Reader.* New York: Schirmer Books, 1999.

——. "Bobby Helms." In *The Encyclopedia of Country Music*, 2nd ed., edited by Paul Kingsbury, Michael McCall, and John W. Rumble, 219. New York: Oxford University Press, 2012.

Eskew, Glenn T. *But for Birmingham: The Local and National Movements in the Civil Rights Struggle.* Chapel Hill: University of North Carolina Press, 1997.

Everett, Burgess. "Report: Pentagon Spent Millions on 'Paid Patriotism' with Pro Sports Leagues." *Politico*, November 4, 2015. www.politico.com/story/2015/11/pentagon-contracts-sports-teams-215508.

Fisher, Eddie. *Been There, Done That.* With David Fisher. New York: St. Martin's, 1999.

Flood, Dick. *My Walk among the Stars: Rubbing Shoulders with Country Giants.* Morrisville, NC: Lulu, 2019.

Flynn, George Q. *The Draft, 1940–1973.* Lawrence: University of Kansas Press, 1993.

Fosler-Lussier, Danielle. *Music in America's Cold War Diplomacy.* Oakland: University of California Press, 2015.

Fox, Aaron A. *Real Country: Music and Language in Working-Class Culture.* Durham, NC: Duke University Press, 2004.

Frank, Ed. "Memphis Naval Air Station, Millington." In *The Tennessee Encyclopedia of History and Culture*. Accessed August 30, 2019. http://tennesseeencyclopedia.net/entry.php?rec=921.

Frederickson, Kari. *Cold War Dixie: Militarization and Modernization in the American South*. Athens: University of Georgia Press, 2013.

———. *The Dixiecrat Revolt and the End of the Solid South, 1932–1968*. Chapel Hill: University of North Carolina Press, 2001.

Friedberg, Aaron L. *In the Shadow of the Garrison State: America's Anti-Statism and Its Cold War Grand Strategy*. Princeton, NJ: Princeton University Press, 2000.

Frontline. "Oral History: Norman Schwarzkopf." *The Gulf War: An In-Depth Examination of the 1990–1991 Persian Gulf Crisis*. PBS. Accessed June 30, 2021. www.pbs.org/wgbh/pages/frontline/gulf/oral/schwarzkopf/1.html.

Fry, Joseph A. *The American South and the Vietnam War: Belligerence, Protest, and Agony in Dixie*. Lexington: University Press of Kentucky, 2015.

Frydl, Kathleen J. *The GI Bill*. New York: Cambridge University Press, 2009.

Gallagher, Pat. "Lee Greenwood on Why the Fourth Time's the Charm." *The Boot*, March 3, 2010. https://theboot.com/lee-greenwood-wife/.

Gallup. "Presidential Approval Ratings: Gallup Historical Statistics and Trends." Accessed October 22, 2017. http://news.gallup.com/poll/116677/presidential-approval-ratings-gallup-historical-statistics-trends.aspx.

George, Nelson. *The Death of Rhythm and Blues*. New York: Pantheon Books, 1988.

Gibson, James William. *Warrior Dreams: Violence and Manhood in Post-Vietnam America*. New York: Hill and Wang, 1994.

Gilbert, Calvin. "CMT News Special Explores Maines-Keith Controversy." *CMT*, June 20, 2003. www.cmt.com/news/1473071/cmt-news-special-explores-maines-keith-controversy/.

Gilman, Lisa. *My Music, My War: The Listening Habits of US Troops in Iraq and Afghanistan*. Middleton, CT: Wesleyan University Press, 2016.

Gitlin, Todd. *The Sixties: Years of Hope, Days of Rage*. New York: Bantam Books, 1987.

Goluboff, Risa L. *The Lost Promise of Civil Rights*. Cambridge, MA: Harvard University Press, 2007.

Gordon, Robert. *Respect Yourself: Stax Records and the Soul Explosion*. New York: Bloomsbury, 2013.

Gourse, Leslie. *Unforgettable: The Life and Mystique of Nat King Cole*. New York: St. Martin's, 1991.

Greene, Lee Seifert. *Lead Me On: Frank Goad Clement and Tennessee Politics*. Knoxville: University of Tennessee Press, 1982.

Greenwood, Lee. "Lee Greenwood—God Bless the U.S.A." Directed by Gary Burden. 1984. YouTube, July 1, 2021. https://youtu.be/-KoXt9pZLGM.

Greenwood, Lee, and Gwen McLin. *God Bless the U.S.A.: Biography of a Song*. Gretna, LA: Pelican, 2002.

Gregory, James N. *American Exodus: The Dust Bowl Migration and Okie Culture in California*. New York: Oxford University Press, 1989.

Grevatt, Ren. *Confessions of a Rock n' Roll PR Guy: Can I Get Back to You?* AuthorHouse, 2015.

Guralnick, Peter. *Careless Love: The Unmaking of Elvis Presley.* Boston: Back Bay Books, 1999.

———. *Last Train to Memphis.* Boston: Back Bay Books, 1994.

Hale, Grace Elizabeth. *Making Whiteness: The Culture of Segregation in the South, 1890–1940.* New York: Vintage Books, 1999.

———. *A Nation of Outsiders: How the White Middle Class Fell in Love with Rebellion in Postwar America.* New York: Oxford University Press, 2011.

Hall, Stuart. "Notes on Deconstructing the 'Popular.'" In *Cultural Theory and Popular Culture: A Reader,* 5th ed., edited by John Storey, 564–574. New York: Routledge, 2019.

Hamilton, Jack. *Just around Midnight: Rock and Roll and the Racial Imagination.* Cambridge, MA: Harvard University Press, 2016.

Hamilton, Marybeth. *In Search of the Blues.* New York: Basic Books, 2009.

Haskins, James. *Nat King Cole.* With Kathleen Benson. New York: Stein and Day, 1984.

Hatchett, Louis, and W. K. McNeil. "'There's a Star Spangled Banner Waving Somewhere': The Story behind Its Success." In *Country Music Goes to War,* edited by Charles K. Wolfe and James E. Akenson, 33–42. Lexington: University Press of Kentucky, 2005.

Havighurst, Craig. *Air Castle of the South: WSM and the Making of Music City.* Urbana: University of Illinois Press, 2007.

Hawkins, Martin. *A Shot in the Dark: Making Records in Nashville, 1945–1955.* Nashville: Vanderbilt University Press and the Country Music Foundation Press, 2006.

Heil, Alan L., Jr. *Voice of America: A History.* New York: Columbia University Press, 2003.

Hemmer, Nicole. *Messengers of the Right: Conservative Media and the Transformation of American Politics.* Philadelphia: University of Pennsylvania Press, 2016.

Hitchcock, William I. *The Age of Eisenhower: American and the World in the 1950s.* New York: Simon and Schuster, 2018.

Hooks, Gregory. *Forging the Military-Industrial Complex: World War II's Battle of the Potomac.* Urbana: University of Illinois Press, 1991.

Horstman, Dorothy. "Songs of War and Patriotism." In *Sing Your Heart Out, Country Boy,* rev. and exp. ed., 266–286. Nashville, TN: Country Music Foundation Press, 1996.

Huebner, Andrew J. *The Warrior Image: Soldiers in American Culture from the Second World War to the Vietnam Era.* Chapel Hill: University of North Carolina Press, 2008.

Hughes, Charles. *Country Soul: Making Music and Making Race in the American South.* Chapel Hill: University of North Carolina Press, 2015.

———. "'I'm the Other One': O. B. McClinton and the Racial Politics of Country Music in the 1970s." In *The Honky Tonk on the Left: Progressive Thought in*

Country Music, edited by Mark Allan Jackson, 121–146. Amherst: University of Massachusetts Press, 2018.

Jacobs, Meg, and Julian E. Zelizer. *Conservatives in Power: The Reagan Years, 1981–1989.* Boston: Bedford, 2010.

Jewell, Katherine Rye. *Dollars for Dixie: Business and the Transformation of Conservatism in the Twentieth Century.* Cambridge: Cambridge University Press.

Johnson, Lyndon B. "May 2, 1965: Report on the Situation in the Dominican Republic." Presidential Speeches, UVA Miller Center. Accessed June 23, 2021. https://millercenter.org/the-presidency/presidential-speeches/may-2-1965-report-situation-dominican-republic.

Johnson, Megan. "Brittany Aldean and Her Kids Wear 'Anti-Biden' Clothing on Instagram," *Yahoo!*, September 26, 2021. www.yahoo.com/lifestyle/brittany-aldean-anti-biden-clothing-201838794.html.

Jones, LeRoi. *Blues People: Negro Music in White America.* New York: Harper Perennial, 2002.

Jones, Louis M. *Everybody's Grandpa: Fifty Years behind the Mike.* With Charles K. Wolfe. Knoxville: University of Tennessee Press, 1984.

Jones, Margaret. "Connie B. Gay." In *The Encyclopedia of Country Music*, 2nd ed., edited by Paul Kingsbury, Michael McCall, and John W. Rumble, 184–185. New York: Oxford University Press, 2012.

Katznelson, Ira. *When Affirmative Action Was White: An Untold History of Racial Inequality in Twentieth-Century America.* New York: Norton, 2005.

Kazin, Michael. *The Populist Persuasion: An American History.* New York: Basic Books, 1995.

Keightley, Keir. "'Turn It Down!' She Shrieked: Gender, Domestic Space, and High Fidelity, 1948–1959." *Popular Music* 15, vol. 2 (May 1996): 149–177.

Kelly, William P. "A Study of the Role of Broadcasting in the US Army Recruiting Program." Master's thesis, American University, 1962.

Kramer, Michael J. *The Republic of Rock: Music and Citizenship in the Sixties Counterculture.* New York: Oxford University Press, 2013.

Krugler, David F. *The Voice of America and the Domestic Propaganda Battles, 1945–1953.* Columbia: University of Missouri Press, 2000.

Kruse, Kevin M., and Thomas J. Sugrue. *The New Suburban History.* Chicago: University of Chicago Press, 2006.

Kubrick, Stanley, dir. *Full Metal Jacket.* 1987. Burbank, CA: Warner Home Video, 2001. DVD.

La Chapelle, Peter. *I'd Fight the World: A Political History of Old-Time, Hillbilly, and Country Music.* Chicago: University of Chicago Press, 2019.

———. *Proud to Be an Okie: Cultural Politics, Country Music, and Migration to Southern California.* Berkeley: University of California Press, 2007.

Lair, Meredith H. *Armed with Abundance: Consumerism and Soldiering in the Vietnam War.* Chapel Hill: University of North Carolina Press, 2014.

Lange, Katie. "AFN: Keeping Military Troops, Families Informed since 1942." *Inside DOD* (US Department of Defense blog), April 26, 2021. www.defense.gov

/News/Inside-DOD/Blog/Article/2584742/afn-keeping-military-troops-families
-informed-since-1942/.

Lassiter, Matthew D. "Political History beyond the Red-Blue Divide." *Journal of American History* 98, no. 3 (December 2011): 760–764.

Lassiter, Matthew D., and Kevin Kruse. "The Bulldozer Revolution: Suburbs and Southern History since World War II." *Journal of Southern History* 75, no. 3 (August 2009): 691–706.

Lechner, Zachary J. *The South of the Mind: American Imaginings of White Southernness, 1960–1980.* Athens: University of Georgia Press, 2018.

Leffler, Melvyn P. *For the Soul of Mankind: The United States, the Soviet Union, and the Cold War.* New York: Hill and Wang, 2007.

Leslie, Stuart W. *The Cold War and American Science: The Military-Industrial-Academic Complex at MIT and Stanford.* New York: Columbia University Press, 1993.

Levy, Alan. *Operation Elvis.* New York: Holt, 1960.

Library of Congress. "Shenandoah." *Song of America Project.* Accessed March 5, 2018. www.loc.gov/creativity/hampson/about_shenandoah.html.

Linn, Brian. *Elvis's Army: Cold War GIs and the Atomic Battlefield.* Cambridge, MA: Harvard University Press, 2016.

Lipsitz, George. *Time Passages: Collective Memory and American Popular Culture.* Minneapolis: University of Minnesota Press, 1990.

Lornell, Kip. *Capital Bluegrass: Hillbilly Music Meets Washington, DC.* New York: Oxford University Press, 2019.

———. *Exploring American Folk Music: Ethnic, Grassroots, and Regional Traditions in the United States.* 3rd ed. Jackson: University of Mississippi Press, 2012.

Loss, Christopher P. *Between Citizens and the State: The Politics of American Higher Education in the 20th Century.* Princeton, NJ: Princeton University Press, 2011.

Louvin, Charlie. *Satan Is Real: The Ballad of the Louvin Brothers.* With Benjamin Whitmer. New York: HarperCollins, 2012.

Lund, Jens. "Country Music Goes to War: Songs for the Red-Blooded American." *Popular Music and Society* 1, no. 4 (Summer 1972): 210–230.

MacDonald, J. Fred. *Television and the Red Menace.* New York: Praeger, 1985.

MacGregor, Morris J., Jr. *Integration of the Armed Forces, 1940–1965.* Washington, DC: Center for Military History, 1981.

Mackenzie, Harry, comp. *The Directory of the Armed Forces Radio Service Series.* Westport, CT: Greenwood, 1999.

Malone, Bill C. *Don't Get above Your Raisin': Country Music and the Southern Working Class.* Urbana: University of Illinois Press, 2002.

Malone, Bill C., and Jocelyn R. Neal. *Country Music, U.S.A.* 3rd rev. ed. Austin: University of Texas Press, 2015.

Markusen, Ann, Peter Hall, Scott Campbell, and Sabina Deitrick. *The Rise of the Gunbelt: The Military Remapping of Industrial America.* New York: Oxford University Press, 1991.

Martinez, Amanda Marie. "Redneck Chic: Race and the Country Music Industry in the 1970s." *Journal of Popular Music Studies* 32, no. 2 (June 2020): 128–143.

Mazor, Barry. *Ralph Peer and the Making of Popular Roots Music*. Chicago: Chicago Review Press, 2015.

McClinton, O. B., and Gerry Wood. *Hard Way to Go: The O. B. McClinton Autobiography*. Self-published by Gerry Wood, 1991.

McCusker, Kristine M., and Diane Pecknold, eds. *A Boy Named Sue: Gender and Country Music*. Jackson: University Press of Mississippi.

McGinnis, Joe. *The Selling of the President, 1968*. New York: Trident, 1969.

McGirr, Lisa. *Suburban Warriors: The Origins of the New American Right*. Princeton, NJ: Princeton University Press, 2002.

McMillen, Neil R., ed. *Remaking Dixie: The Impact of World War II on the American South*. Jackson: University of Mississippi Press, 1997.

McNeil, W. K. "Elton Britt." In *The Encyclopedia of Country Music*, 2nd ed., edited by Paul Kingsbury, Michael McCall, and John W. Rumble, 49–50. New York: Oxford University Press, 2012.

Mellard, Jason. *Progressive Country: How the 1970s Transformed the Texan in Popular Culture*. Austin: University of Texas Press, 2013.

Millard, Andre. *America on Record: A History of Recorded Sound*. 2nd ed. New York: Cambridge University Press, 2005.

Miller, Karl Hagstrom. *Segregating Sound: Inventing Folk and Pop Music in the Age of Jim Crow*. Durham, NC: Duke University Press, 2010.

Mills, C. Wright. *The Power Elite*. New ed. Oxford: Oxford University Press, 2000.

Mittelstadt, Jennifer. *The Rise of the Military Welfare State*. Cambridge, MA: Harvard University Press, 2015.

Monson, Ingrid. *Freedom Sounds: Civil Rights Call Out to Jazz and Africa*. New York: Oxford University Press, 2010.

Moore, Scotty. *Scotty and Elvis: Aboard the Mystery Train*. With James L. Dickerson. Jackson: University Press of Mississippi, 2013.

Morden, Bettie J. *The Women's Army Corps, 1945–1978*. Washington, DC: Center of Military History, 1990.

Morrison, Craig. *Go Cat Go! Rockabilly Music and Its Makers*. Urbana: University of Illinois Press, 1999.

Mullins, Daniel. "Veterans' Day Tribute at SOIMF." *Bluegrass Today*, November 14, 2011. https://bluegrasstoday.com/veterans-day-tribute-at-soimf/.

Mundey, Lisa M. *American Militarism and Anti-Militarism in Popular Media, 1945–1970*. Jefferson, NC: McFarland, 2012.

Myers, Andrew H. *Black, White, and Olive Drab: Racial Integration at Fort Jackson, South Carolina, and the Civil Rights Movement*. Charlottesville: University of Virginia Press, 2006.

National Archives. "Vietnam War US Military Fatal Casualty Statistics." Accessed October 22, 2017. www.archives.gov/research/military/vietnam-war/casualty -statistics.

Naval History and Heritage Command. "*Constellation* III (CVA-64), 1961–2003." April 8, 2020. www.history.navy.mil/research/histories/ship-histories/danfs/c /constellation-iii.html.

Newport, Frank, and Joseph Carroll. "Iraq versus Vietnam: A Comparison of Public Opinion." Gallup, August 24, 2005. https://news.gallup.com/poll/18097 /iraq-versus-vietnam-comparison-public-opinion.aspx.

Nichols, Lee. *Breakthrough on the Color Front*. New York: Random House, 1954.

Nickerson, Michelle, and Darren Dochuk, eds. *Sunbelt Rising: The Politics of Space, Place, and Region*. Philadelphia: University of Pennsylvania Press, 2011.

Oermann, Robert K. "Barbara Mandrell." In *The Encyclopedia of Country Music*, 2nd ed., edited by Paul Kingsbury, Michael McCall, and John W. Rumble, 309–310. New York: Oxford University Press, 2012.

———. "Owen Bradley." In *The Encyclopedia of Country Music*, 2nd ed., edited by Paul Kingsbury, Michael McCall, and John W. Rumble, 47–48. New York: Oxford University Press, 2012.

Olin, Spencer C. "Globalization and the Politics of Locality: Orange County, California, in the Cold War Era." *Western Historical Quarterly* 22, no. 2 (May 1991): 143–161, https://doi.org/10.2307/969203.

Pecknold, Diane, ed. *Hidden in the Mix: The African American Presence in Country Music*. Durham, NC: Duke University Press, 2013.

———. "'I Wanna Play House': Configurations of Masculinity in the Nashville Sound Era." In *A Boy Named Sue: Gender and Country Music*, edited by Kristine M. McCusker and Diane Pecknold, 86–106. Jackson: University Press of Mississippi, 2004.

———. "Making Country Modern in Country and Western Music." In *Hidden in the Mix: The African American Presence in Country Music*, edited by Diane Pecknold, 82–99. Durham, NC: Duke University Press, 2013.

———. *The Selling Sound: The Rise of the Country Music Industry*. Durham, NC: Duke University Press, 2007.

Perlstein, Rick. *Reaganland: America's Right Turn, 1976–1980*. New York: Simon and Schuster, 2020.

Peterson, Richard A. "Class Unconsciousness in Country Music." In *You Wrote My Life: Lyrical Themes in Country Music*, edited by Melton A. McLaurin and Richard A. Peterson, 35–62. Yverdon, Switzerland: Gordon and Breach, 1992.

———. *Creating Country Music: Fabricating Authenticity*. Chicago: University of Chicago Press, 1997.

Phillips, Kevin P. *The Emerging Republican Majority*. New Rochelle, NY: Arlington House, 1969.

Phillips, Kimberley L. *War! What Is It Good For? Black Freedom Struggles and the U.S. Military*. Chapel Hill: University of North Carolina Press, 2012.

Phillips-Fein, Kim. *Invisible Hands: The Businessmen's Crusade against the New Deal*. New York: Norton, 2009.

Pieslak, Jonathan. *Sound Targets: American Soldiers and Music in the Iraq War*. Bloomington: Indiana University Press, 2009.

Puddington, Arch. *Broadcasting Freedom: The Cold War Triumph of Radio Free Europe and Radio Liberty*. Lexington: University Press of Kentucky, 2000.

Pugh, Ronnie. "Charlie Walker." In *The Encyclopedia of Country Music*, 2nd ed., edited by Paul Kingsbury, Michael McCall, and John W. Rumble, 545. New York: Oxford University Press, 2012.

Randolph, A. Phillip. *For Jobs and Freedom: Selected Speeches and Writings of A. Philip Randolph*. Amherst: University of Massachusetts Press, 2014.

Rasmussen, Wayne D. *Taking the University to the People: Seventy-Five Years of Cooperative Extension*. Ames: Iowa University Press, 1989.

Reagan, Ronald. "Inaugural Address." January 20, 1981. Reagan Foundation. www.reaganfoundation.org/media/128614/inaguration.pdf.

Reagan Library. "Celebration after President Reagan's Speech at Republican National Convention on August 15, 1988." YouTube, November 5, 2018. https://youtu.be/-_neeH8pp34.

Richardson, Heather Cox. *How the South Won the Civil War: Oligarchy, Democracy, and the Continuing Fight for the Soul of America*. New York: Oxford University Press, 2020.

Riley, Billy Lee. "Flyin' Saucer Rock 'n' Roll." Interview by Ken Burke. In *Flying Saucers Rock 'n' Roll: Conversations with Unjustly Obscure Rock 'n' Soul Eccentrics*, edited by Jake Austen, 128–189. Durham, NC: Duke University Press, 2011.

Roberts, Michael James. *Tell Tchaikovsky the News: Rock 'n' Roll, the Labor Question, and the Musicians Union, 1942–1968*. Durham, NC: Duke University Press, 2014.

Roche, Jeff. "Asa/Forrest Carter and Regional/Political Identity." In *The Southern Albatross: Race and Ethnicity in the American South*, edited by Phillip D. Dillard and Randal L. Hall, 235–274. Macon, GA: Mercer University Press, 1999.

Rock and Roll Hall of Fame. "Elvis Presley." Accessed December 16, 2018. www.rockhall.com/inductees/elvis-presley.

Rossinow, Doug. *The Politics of Authenticity: Liberalism, Christianity, and the New Left in America*. New York: Columbia University Press, 1998.

Roth, Tanya L. *Her Cold War: Women in the U.S. Military, 1945–1980*. Chapel Hill: University of North Carolina Press, 2021.

Rubin, Rachel Lee. *33 1/3: Okie from Muskogee*. New York: Bloomsbury Academic, 2018.

Rudder, Randy. "In Whose Name? Country Artists Speak Out on Gulf War II." In *Country Music Goes to War*, edited by Charles K. Wolfe and James E. Akenson, 208–226. Lexington: University Press of Kentucky, 2005.

Rumble, John. "Joe Allison." In *The Encyclopedia of Country Music*, 2nd ed., edited by Paul Kingsbury, Michael McCall, and John W. Rumble, 9. New York: Oxford University Press, 2012.

Russell, Tony. "Cecil Gant." In *The Penguin Guide to Blues Recordings*, edited by Tony Russell, Chris Smith, Neil Slaven, Ricky Russell, and Joe Faulkner, 213–214. New York: Penguin Books, 2006.

Rutenberg, Amy J. *Rough Draft: Cold War Military Manpower Policy and the Origins of Vietnam-Era Draft Resistance*. Ithaca, NY: Cornell University Press, 2019.

Ryan, John. *The Production of Culture in the Music Industry: The ASCAP-BMI Controversy.* Lanham, MD: University Press of America, 1985.

Ryan, John J. *Selling the Armed Forces Consumer Market: The Military Market Handbook.* Washington, DC: Army Times, 1957.

Saad, Lydia. "Gallup Vault: Hawks v. Doves on Vietnam." Gallup, May 24, 2016. http://news.gallup.com/vault/191828/gallup-vault-hawks-doves-vietnam.aspx.

Samet, Elizabeth D. *Looking for the Good War: American Amnesia and the Violent Pursuit of Happiness.* New York: Farrar, Straus and Giroux, 2021.

Samuelson, Dave. "Gordon Terry." In *The Encyclopedia of Country Music*, 2nd ed., edited by Paul Kingsbury, Michael McCall, and John W. Rumble, 509. New York: Oxford University Press, 2012.

Sarig, Roni. *Third Coast: OutKast, Timbaland, and How Hip-Hop Became a Southern Thing.* New York: Da Capo, 1997.

Schulman, Bruce J. *From Cotton Belt to Sunbelt: Federal Policy, Economic Development, and the Transformation of the South, 1938–1910.* New York: Oxford University Press, 1991.

———. *The Seventies: The Great Shift in American Culture, Society, and Politics.* New York: Da Capo, 2001.

Schwartz, Marvin. *We Wanna Boogie: The Rockabilly Roots of Sonny Burgess and the Pacers.* Little Rock: Butler Center for Arkansas Studies, 2014.

Self, Robert O. *All in the Family: The Realignment of American Democracy since the 1960s.* New York: Hill and Wang, 2012.

Shearon, Stephen. "The Sacred in Country Music." In *The Oxford Handbook of Country Music*, edited by Travis D. Stimeling, 395–414. New York: Oxford University Press, 2017.

"Shel Silverstein's Unlikely Rise to Kid Lit Stardom." *Mental Floss*, June 22, 2014. www.mentalfloss.com/article/22470/shel-silversteins-unlikely-rise-kid-lit -superstardom.

Sidney, George, dir. *Bye Bye Birdie.* 1963. Culver City, CA: Columbia Pictures, 2006. DVD.

Simpson, Kim. *Early '70s Radio: The American Format Revolution.* London: Continuum, 2011.

Sklaroff, Lauren Rebecca. *Black Culture and the New Deal: The Quest for Civil Rights in the Roosevelt Era.* Chapel Hill: University of North Carolina Press, 2009.

Skocpol, Theda. "The G.I. Bill and U.S. Social Policy, Past and Future." *Social Philosophy & Policy* 14, no. 7 (1997): 95–115.

Sparrow, James T. "A Nation in Motion: Norfolk, the Pentagon, and the Nationalization of the Metropolitan South, 1941–1953." In *The Myth of Southern Exceptionalism*, edited by Matthew D. Lassiter and Joseph Crespino, 167–189. New York: Oxford University Press, 2010.

———. *Warfare State: World War II Americans and the Age of Big Government.* New York: Oxford University Press, 2011.

Spears, Ellen Griffith. *Baptized in PCBs: Race, Pollution, and Justice in an All-American Town.* Chapel Hill: University of Chapel Hill Press, 2014.

Specht, Joe W. "War News Blues: Lightnin' Hopkins, World War II, Korea, and Vietnam." *Journal of Texas Music* 21 (2021). https://www.txst.edu/ctmh /publications/journal/issues/jtmh-vol-21/vol-21-war-news-blues.html.

Spector, Ronald H. *After Tet: The Bloodiest Year in Vietnam.* New York: Free Press, 1993.

Sprayberry, Gary S. "'Interrupted Melody': The 1956 Attack on Nat 'King' Cole." *Alabama Heritage* 71 (Winter 2004): 16–24.

———. "'Town among the Trees': Paternalism, Class, and Civil Rights in Anniston, Alabama, 1872 to Present." PhD diss., University of Alabama, 2003.

Stahl, Roger. *Militainment, Inc.: War, Media, and Popular Culture.* New York: Routledge, 2010.

———, dir. *Theaters of War.* Media Education Foundation, 2022. https://vimeo.com /ondemand/theatersofwar?autoplay=1.

Stimeling, Travis D. *Cosmic Cowboys and New Hicks: The Countercultural Sounds of Austin's Progressive Country Music Scene.* New York: Oxford University Press, 2011.

———. *Nashville Cats: Record Production in Music City.* New York: Oxford University Press, 2020.

Stur, Heather Marie. *Beyond Combat: Women and Gender in the Vietnam War Era.* New York: Cambridge University Press, 2011.

Sturken, Marita. *Tangled Memories: The Vietnam War, the AIDS Epidemic, and the Politics of Remembering.* Berkeley: University of California Press, 1997.

Sugrue, Thomas J. *Origins of the Urban Crisis: Race and Inequality in Postwar Detroit.* Princeton, NJ: Princeton University Press, 1996.

Suisman, David. *Instrument of War: Music and the Making of America's Soldiers.* Chicago: University of Chicago Press, forthcoming.

Sun Records. "Billy Lee Riley." Accessed December 20, 2018. www.sunrecords .com/artists/billy-lee-riley.

Taurog, Norman, dir. *GI Blues.* 1960. Burbank, CA: Warner Brothers, 2014. DVD.

"Ted Cruz: 'My Music Tastes Changed on 9/11.'" CBS Mornings, YouTube, March 24, 2015. https://youtu.be/nik-UstmCjw.

Texas State University. "Clarence 'Candy' Green." Accessed September 14, 2022. https://gato-docs.its.txstate.edu/jcr:b416dde1-c0d8-457f-af70-2ef1be028fe2 /Clarence%20Candy%20Green.pdf.

Tillis, Mel. *Stutterin' Boy.* With Walter Wager. New York: Rawson Associates, 1984.

Tosches, Nick. *Country: The Biggest Music in America.* New York: Stein and Day, 1977.

———. *Unsung Heroes of Rock 'n' Roll: The Birth of Rock in the Wild Years before Elvis.* New York: Martin Secker and Warburg, 1991.

TPUSA Events (@tpusaevents). "Have Y'all Seen the Music Lineup for AMERICAFEST 2021?!" Instagram, October 28, 2021. www.instagram.com/p /CVlsaYBvn8_/?hl=en.

Tribe, Ivan M. "Carolina Cotton." In *The Encyclopedia of Country Music,* 2nd ed., edited by Paul Kingsbury, Michael McCall, and John W. Rumble, 73. New York: Oxford University Press, 2012.

Trott, Walt. "Hank Locklin." In *The Encyclopedia of Country Music*, 2nd ed., edited by Paul Kingsbury, Michael McCall, and John W. Rumble, 284. New York: Oxford University Press, 2012.

Troutman, John. *Kīkā Kila: How the Hawaiian Steel Guitar Changed the Sound of Modern Music*. Chapel Hill: University of North Carolina Press, 2016.

Tsuchiya, Tomoko. "Interracial Marriages between American Soldiers and Japanese Women at the Beginning of the Cold War." *Journal of American and Canadian Studies* 29 (2011): 59–84.

Tyler, Don. *Music of the Postwar Era*. Westport, CT: Greenwood, 2008.

Urban Daily Staff. "Duice—'Dazzey Duks.'" *Urban Daily*. November 14, 2022. https://theurbandaily.com/979235/duice-dazzey-duks-daily-one-hit-wonder/.

US Census Bureau. "Table 46: Population Rank of Incorporated Places of 100,000 Population or More, 1990; Population, 1790 to 1990; Housing Units: 1940 to 1990." In *1990 Census of Population and Housing: Population and Housing Unit Counts: United States*, 593–601. Washington, DC: US Department of Commerce, Economics and Statistics Administration. www2.census.gov/library/publications /decennial/1990/cph-2/cph-2-1-1.pdf.

van Rijn, Guido. *The Truman and Eisenhower Blues: African-American Blues and Gospel Songs, 1945–1960*. London: Continuum, 2004.

Von Eschen, Penny M. *Satchmo Blows Up the World: Jazz Ambassadors Play the Cold War*. Cambridge, MA: Harvard University Press, 2006.

Vuic, Kara Dixon. *The Girls Next Door: Bringing the Home Front to the Front Lines*. Cambridge, MA: Harvard University Press, 2019.

Ward, Brian. "Civil Rights and Rock and Roll: Revisiting the Nat King Cole Attack of 1956." *OAH Magazine of History*, April 2010, 21–24.

———. *Just My Soul Responding: Rhythm and Blues, Black Consciousness, and Race Relations*. Berkeley: University of California Press, 1998.

Weisbard, Eric. *Top 40 Democracy: The Rival Mainstreams of American Music*. Chicago: University of Chicago Press, 2014.

Whitburn, Joel, comp. *Hot Country Songs: Billboard 1944 to 2008*. Menomonee Falls, WI: Record Research, 2008.

Wicks, Chuck (@chuckwicks). "Happy New Year from Mar a Lago!! Here we go . . . may we all accomplish what we want as we reset for this new year ahead of us!! Love you." Instagram, December 31, 2021. www.instagram.com/p /CYLQR1hNgYz/.

Wiley, Bell Irvin. *The Life of Johnny Reb: The Common Soldier of the Confederacy*. Updated ed. Baton Rouge: Louisiana State University Press, 2008.

Williamson, Joel. *Elvis: A Southern Life*. With Donald L. Shaw. New York: Oxford University Press, 2015.

Wilson, James R. *Landing Zones: Southern Veterans Remember Vietnam*. Durham, NC: Duke University Press, 1990.

Winkie, J. Davis. "Thin Red Lines: Early Cold War Military Censorship of Hollywood War Movies." Master's thesis, University of North Carolina–Chapel Hill, 2019. https://doi.org/10.17615/3jjy-b862.

Wolfe, Charles K. *A Good-Natured Riot: The Birth of the Grand Ole Opry.* Nashville, TN: Country Music Foundation and Vanderbilt University Press, 1999.

——. "Jesus Hits Like an Atom Bomb: Nuclear Warfare in Country Music, 1944–1956." In *Country Music Goes to War,* edited by Charles K. Wolfe and James E. Akenson, 102–125. Lexington: University Press of Kentucky, 2005.

Wolfe, Charles K., and James E. Akenson, eds. *Country Music Goes to War.* Lexington: University Press of Kentucky, 2005.

Woodward, C. Vann. *The Strange Career of Jim Crow.* New York: Oxford University Press, 1955.

Wright, Gavin. *Old South, New South: Revolutions in the Southern Economy since the Civil War.* Baton Rouge: Louisiana State University Press, 1986.

Young, Marilyn B. *The Vietnam Wars, 1945–1990.* New York: HarperCollins, 1991.

Index

Italicized page numbers indicate illustrations

2 Live Crew, 252–253

Aaron, Hank, 224
Academy of Country Music (ACM), 213, 241
Acuff, Roy, 161, 189, 192, 220, 236, 251; Acuff-Rose, 66; military recruitment and, 70; political views, 180–181, 185; Richard Nixon and, 213, 216–217; USO and other military tours, 8, 9, 28–29, 78, 79–80, 147, 159, 182–185, 191, 201; Vietnam and, 9, 176, 184, 201; World War II and
Alabama (band), 238, 239, 246
Aldean, Jason (Brittany), 256–258
"All American Boy" (Bill Parsons/Bobby Bare), 137, 139
Allen, Steve, 52, 58, 69
Allied Forces Network (AFN), 36, 67, 146, 175, 189, 223
Allison, Joe, 76, 170, 253; *Country Corner*, 147, 171–173, 229; format radio, 170–171, 172
Allman Brothers Band, The, 233
all-volunteer force (AVF): country music and, 12–13, 220–223; demographics of, 12, 220, 224, 227, 235, 240; soul music and, 224, 239. *See also* Friedman, Milton
American Country Countdown, 230, 238
American Patriot (Lee Greenwood), 249–250
American Society of Composers, Authors, and Publishers (ASCAP),

47, 60–61, 79–81. *See also* Smathers Bill
American Top 40, 230
Anderson, Bill, 201, 206, 214
Anderson, John, 131
Anderson, Liz, 195
Anderson, Lynn, 215
Ann-Margaret, 140–141
Applewhite, Charlie, 70–72, 74, 132, 134
Armed Forces Radio and Television Service (AFRS/AFRTS), 4–5, 12–13, 34, 55, 75, 83, 206, 241, 246, 249; African American genres and, 38–39; AFN and, 67, 97, 146–148, 158–162; automation of, 221, 231, 240; country music programming during Korean War, 17, 27–31, 35–36, 38, 46, 67; country music programming during Vietnam War, 147, 170–175, 189, 190, 194–195, 204, 214–215, 222; country music programming during World War II, 17, 25, 36; labor and cost management, 228–229; Los Angeles studios, 171, 229; morale and, 26, 39, 174, 228, 229, 231; origins, 26–27; promoting sales and policing image of country music, 148, 156, 159, 160, 162, 173–175, 189, 195, 213–215, 229–232; rock and pop programming, 144, 229; syndication and adoption of tape machines, 221, 228–231, 234–235, 238–239. *See also* Allied Forces Network (AFN); Far East Network
Armstrong, Louis, 39, 103

Army and Air Force Post Exchange Service (PX), 96; introduction of record sales, 153–154, 287n55; origins, 154; genre and format preferences, 154–158, 239–240, 246; country music record sales, 4, 12, 148, 156–157, 160–162, 173–175, 190, 195, 214–215, 239, 246; consolidation and distribution of music sales, 221, 227–228, 238–239; morale and, 154, 157; Vietnam War revenue, 222
Arnold, Eddy, 15, 23, 33, 69, 79, 110, 180
At Ease with Pvt. Eddie Fisher, 56–57, 73
Atkins, Chet, 46, 91, 111, 128, 173
"Atomic Power" (Buchanan Brothers/ Fred Kirby), 71

"Back to Korea Blues" (Sunnyland Slim), 39, 270n87
"The Ballad of the Green Berets" (Sergeant Barry Sadler), 195, 209
Bare, Bobby, 137, 139, 176
Basie, Count, 38
"The Battle Hymn of Lt. Calley" (Terry Nelson and C Company), 198–199
Beatles, The, 192, 207, 208
Beaulieu, Priscilla (Priscilla Presley), 137
Bell, Al, 204–205
Bell, Tom, 208
Billy Adams and the Rock-A-Teens, 139
Birmingham civil rights movement, 169, 211
Bishop, Joey, 191
Black, Bill, 92, 105–106
bluegrass, 132, 159, 236
"Blue Moon of Kentucky" (Elvis Presley), 107, 109
Bolling, A. R., 61, 65, 102
Bolling Air Force Base, 43
Bouillet, Walter A., 45–46, 75
Bowman, Don, 230
Bowman, Rob, 204
Bradley, Owen, 41, 71–72, 75, 76, 83, 134, 165
Brasfield, Rod, 29

Brecher, Ruth and Edward, 168–170
Britt, Elton, 8, 35, 176, 179, 187
Broadcast Music, Incorporated (BMI), 47, 60–61, 79–81, 99, 235. *See also* Smathers Bill
Brown, Charles S., 158, 165
Brown, Charlie, 206
Brown, James, 203
Brown, Jerry, 237
Brown, Jim Ed, 195
Bryant, Boudleaux, 102
Bullet Records, 40–42
Burgess, Sonny, 85, 97–98
Burning Spear, 193
Bush, George H. W., 12, 13, 248–249
Bush, George W., 2
Buzz, 193
Bynum, Roland, 224

C. and W. Golds, 193
Camel Rock & Roll Party, 38
Campbell, Glen, 213, 214
Campbell, Pat, 202
Cam Ranh Bay, 203
Carrigan, Bill, 36, *37*
Carter, Asa, 122–123, 125, 131, 211. *See also* North Alabama Citizens' Council
Carter, Clarence, 204
Carter, Jimmy, 233–235, 236, 237
Carter, June, 165
Carter, Mother Maybelle, 189
Carter Family, 132, 158, 159, 189, 207, 209
Cascades, The, 191
Cash, Johnny, 4, 15, 71, 84, 85, 97, 102, 139, 188, 209, 214; US Air Force career, 93, 95–96, 133; US Army recruitment and, 133–134; politics and, 213, 236; rockabilly and, 105, 132–133, 139
Cash, Rosanne, 247
Chai Zemin, 235–236
Charles, Ray, 220
Cheatham Street Warehouse, 240
Chicago (band), 208
Chicks (Dixie), The, 1–2

Civil Aeronautics Board, 237
Civil Rights Act of 1964, 179
Clark, Roy, 15, 212, 219, 220, 233, 234, 235, 274n55
Clark Air Force Base, 201
Clement, Cowboy Jack, 85, 105, 108
Clement, Frank G., 47, 49, 77–80
Cline, Patsy, 15, 71, 165
Clooney, Rosemary, 70, 73, 155
Cold War: China and, 25, 90, 91, 236; containment, 47, 49, 81, 85, 115, 129, 148, 150, 234; détente, 12, 220, 225; economics of militarization, 3, 6, 8, 10, 16, 17, 48, 88, 233; end of, 249; human rights, 234; nuclear war, 147; political consensus, 5, 175, 177, 200, 218; propaganda, 13, 28, 52, 159, 180, 188, 224–226. *See also* country music militarization; Soviet Union; United States Department of Defense; United States Department of State
Cole, Nat "King," 39, 100, 125, 128
Collins, Jo, 202
Colter, Jessi, 231
Command Military Touring Shows (CMTS), 192–194, 203, 292nn54–55
Como, Perry, 156, 236
Confederate flag, 36, *37*, 95, *126*
Connally, John, 210
conservatism, 5, 12, 178, 206, 209, 218, 258
Coolio, 252
Cooper, Carolee, 132
Cooper, Wilma Lee and Stoney, 132, 165
Copas, Cowboy, 165
Cotton, Carolina, 36, 38, 202; *Carolina Cotton Calls*, 17, 36, 38
Council on Youth Opportunity, 210–211
counterculture, 178, 190, 192–194, 198, 208–209, 232–233
Country Hoedown, 46, 75–77
Country Jamboree, *64*, 69
country music: advertising potential, 21, 150, 152, 247; antiwar views and, 178, 187, 195–199, 206, 210, 212;

atomic warfare, 8, 61, 71–72, 266n25, 275n81; Christianity and, 3, 27–28, 30, 36, 38, 76, 122, 211, 183, 243; civilian radio, 75, 151–152, 206, 230, 238, 246; class politics of, 2, 4, 6, 17, 19, 45, 52, 76, 80–81, 119, 135, 142, 160–162, 218, 236; communism and, 8, 16, 28, 54, 101, 133, 148, 183, 186, 159, 174–175, 235–236; crossover success and economic growth, 60, 110, 128, 147, 155–156, 221, 231–233, 238; interracial sex and, 127–132; race and, 4, 6–7, 23–24, 42, 50, 82, 106, 108, 112, 115, 122, 162–163, 203, 205, 265nn13–14; popularity with international civilian audiences, 67, 158–162; popularity with military audiences, 67–68, 157, 214–215; Soviet Union and, 224–226, 233
country music and military recruitment programs. See *Country Hoedown*; *Country Jamboree*; *Country Music Time*; *Country Style, U.S.A.* (radio); *Country Style, U.S.A.* (television); *George Hamilton IV Show*; *Leatherneck Jamboree*; *Your Navy Country Music Show*
Country Music Association (CMA): 25th Anniversary Celebration, 219–220; formation of, 10, 146, 15, 16, 149–152, 219; global ambitions, *150*, 158–160, 170, 174–175, 238; military awards and publicity, 190, 193–194, 222–223; marketing to military audiences, 12, 146–147, 148–150, 156, 176, 193–195, 214, *215*; public-private partnership with the Defense Department, 11–12, 13, 146–147, 162, 170, 178, 194; political affiliations, 174–175, 177, 181, 210–211, 213, 226, 233–236, 237
Country Music Disc Jockey Association, 16, 66, 149
Country Music Hall of Fame, 10, 16, 84, 176, 195, *196*, 206, 235

country music militarization: concept of, 3, 4, 12–13, 15, 219, 264n5; commercial value of, 50, 150, 152–153, 194, *215*, 220–222, 239–241, 251, 253, 254, 255–256; songwriting and, 188, 209, 241; politics of, 176, 216, 251, 254, 255, 257–258; race and, 225, 253, 255, 258

Country Music Salutes the Armed Forces (various artists), 176

Country Music Television, 242

Country Music Time, 146, 177, 206–210, 246–247

Country Style, U.S.A. (radio), 69, 146, 165

Country Style, U.S.A. (television), 70–76, 77, 132, 134, 152, 156, 165, 217

"Courtesy of the Red, White and Blue (The Angry American)" (Toby Keith), 1, 3, 254–255

Cox, Billy, 167–168

Cramer, Floyd, 51, 111

Crook and Chase, 247

Cruz, Ted, 1

Cuban Missile Crisis, 182

Curb, Mike, 237

Curb Records, 2, 237

Curless, Dick, 35, 131

Cymande, 224

Daniels, Charlie, 234, 247

Daniels, Tom, 146, 159, 160, 206, 229

Darin, Bobby, 70

Darrell, Johnny, 200, 209

Davis, Skeeter, 74, 130, 173, 195

Dean, Jimmy, 15, 43–46, 63, 66, 75, 99, 111, 152, 201, 219, 241, 251

"Dear Uncle Sam" (Loretta Lynn), 199

Deen, Dixie, 189, 212; as Dixie Hall, 236

Delmore Brothers, The, 19

Del-Vikings, The, 162

Denny, Jim, 109, 159

Denver, Bob, 191

Denver, John, 232

Diamond, Neil, 208

Dickens, Little Jimmy, 28, 70, 79, 80–81, 201

Diggs, Charles, Jr., 124–125

Dobie, Frank, 130

Doggett, Bill, 156

Domino, Fats, 156

Donut Dollies, 202

Doors, The, 207

draft, 56, 57, 102, 104, 168; country artists and, 10, 11, 48, 51, 83, 85, 97, 100, 102, 137, 204; country music and, 45, 197; Elvis Presley and, 113–114, 116, 118–119, 134–135, 140–141, 144; race and class demographics, 7, 38, 189, 218; personnel policy, 12, 48–49, 53, 94, 189, 220, 223–224; resistance to, 223. *See also* Universal Military Training (UMT)

Dudley, Dave, 187–189, 223

Duice, 253

Dylan, Bob, 132, 188

"The East is Red," 236

Eby, Robert, 190, 194

Eighth US Army Korea (EAUK), 30, 33, 36

Electric Grunts, 193

Ellington, Duke, 38, 65

Enid Air Force Base, 100

Eshleman, Billie Jean, 51

Everly Brothers, The, 165

FAME Studios, 199, 204, 205

Far East Network (FEN), 30, 147

Farm Security Administration, 19, *20*

Fender, Freddy, 235, 241

"The Fightin' Side of Me" (Jeannie C. Riley), 207, 209

"The Fightin' Side of Me" (Merle Haggard), 1, 3, 178, 198, 210, 216

Fisher, Eddie, 49, 56–58, 64, 65, 73, 84

Five Star Jubilee, 161

Fixed Water, 193

Flake, Jeff, 256

Flatt and Scruggs, 165, 186

Flood, Dick, 201

Foley, Red, 28, 29, 33, 42, 110

"Folsom Prison Blues" (Johnny Cash), 96, 204

Fonda, Henry, 191

Ford, Gerald, 225, 233

Ford, Tennessee Ernie, 75, 76, 225, 226

Foreign Love (Hank Locklin), 115, 127–130, *128*, 187

Fort Benning, 94, 130

Fort Bliss, 130

Fort Bragg, 61, 85, 101, 197

Fort Campbell, 167, 193, 195–196

Fort Carson, 100–101, 116

Fort Chaffee, 97, 135–137

Fort Dix, 116, 139

Fort Gillem, 221, 227, 238–239

Fort Gordon, 253

Fort Hood, 56, 137, 168

Fort Jackson, 51–52, 102

Fort Knox, 85

Fort Lawton, 93

Fort Lee, 124

Fort Mason, 55

Fort McClellan, 102, 114, 122–125, *126*

Fort McPherson, 61, 62, 94, 102

Fort Meade, 207

Fort Myer, 56, 57, 73

Fort Ord, 167

Four Tops, The, 208

Francis, Arlene, 52, 58

Francis, Connie, 70, 191

Franklin, Aretha, 192

Fraternity Records, 137, 139

"Fraulein" (Bobby Helms), 115, 128

"Fraulein" (Dave Dudley), 187

"Fraulein" (Hank Locklin), 129

Friedman, Milton, 223–224, 237

Full Metal Jacket, 188

Gant, Cecil, 39–42, *41*

Garner, James, 191

Gay, Connie B., 10, 15–17, *20*, 40, 48, 66, 190, 201, 247; CMA and, 147, 150–151; Constitution Hall and, 22–24, 219–220; Country Music Disc Jockey Association, 16, 149; country music on television, 24, 44; country music radio in Washington DC, 21–22; early life and employment, 18, 21; Elvis Presley and, 111; Faron Young and, Hillbilly Cruise, 15, 111; Jimmy Dean and, 43–44; Korean War tour with Grandpa Jones, 24–25, *32*, 29–34, 78; media ownership, 44, 152; New Deal employment, 18–21, *20*; military recruitment and, 45–46, 63–64, 66, 69, 75–76, 158, 162; political connections, 179–180, 210, 226; relationship with US Armed Forces, 16, 17, 29–34, 43, 44–46, 48, 67, 68, 99, 251, 253

"Geisha Girl" (Dave Dudley), 187

"Geisha Girl" (Hank Locklin), 115, 127, 129, 130, 131

Gene Price's Country World, 229, 238

George, Nelson, 118

George Hamilton IV Show, 69

George Wallace Jr and His Governor's Five, 212

Germany, 36, 55, 94; country music fans, 67, 158, 159, 160, 162, 223; country music tours, 28–29, 78, 80, 185, 201; US military occupation of, 93, 96, 97, 124, 132, 137, 139, 180, 185–186; World War II, 8, 25

GI Bill, 4, 47, 49, 50, 69, 104, 105, 223, 240; racial discrimination and, 7–8, 82

"GI Blues" (Elvis Presley), 142

Gigandet, Joseph, 55–56, 58, 73

Gillespie, Dizzy, 102, 103

Gilley, Mickey, 220

Glaser, Tompall, 180, 231

"God Bless the U.S.A." (Lee Greenwood), 1, 3, 13, 221, 241–250, 253, 256; military uses, 243–246; music video, 243

Godfrey, Arthur, 56, 58

Goetz, Joseph F., 45

Goldwater, Barry, 177, 179–181, 237; Stars for Barry, 180–*181*

Grammer, Billy, 212

Grand Ole Opry, 15, 22–23, 24, 25, 30, 42, 50–51, 78, 102, 108–109; AFRS/AFRTS, 36, 38, 160, 189, 229; inspiration for country artists, 96, 203; military recruitment, 61, 63, 66, 75; military tours, 8, 9, 17, 28, 33, 48, 58, 67, 81; politics and, 77, 211, 216, 235; WSM, 66, 149, 152, 182, 189–190, 213

Grant, Marshall, 132

Grateful Dead, The, 198, 208

"The Great Atomic Power" (Louvin Brothers), 71

Green, Clarence "Candy," 104

Greenwood, Lee, 1, 13, 221, 241–251, *246*, *251*, 253, 255

Guarnieri, Johnny, 55

Gulf of Tonkin Resolution, 183, 241

Guthrie, Woody, 188

Hagel, Chuck, 247

Haggard, Merle, 1, 3, 12, 102, 111, 131, 178, 205, 210, 229; "Okie from Muskogee" and, 197–198; Richard Nixon and, 213, 216–217

Hall, Tom T., 178, 185–189, 198, 200, 210, 216, 218, 234

Halsey, Jim, 234–235, 243

Hamilton, George IV, 15, 69

Hamilton, Mark, 64

Hannon, Dennis, 2

Harper, Redd, 27, 36, 38

"Have You Forgotten?" (Darryl Worley), 1

Hawkins, Harold "Hawkshaw," 97, 165

"Heartbreak, USA" (Kitty Wells), 130

"Heartbreak Hotel" (Elvis Presley), 110–111, 116

Hee Haw, 214, 233, 238, 243

"Hello Vietnam" (Johnny Wright), 186–187, 188

Helms, Bobby, 115, 128

Hendrix, Jimi, 167–168, 203

Herb Alpert's Tijuana Brass, 168

Herndon, Mark, 240

"Hey, Porter!" (Johnny Cash),132–133

Higginsen, Vy, 224

Hillbilly Gasthaus, 36, *37*, 67

Hillbilly Reveille, 146, 160

Hip-hop, 252–253

Hit Country, 229

Hometowners, The, 185

Hope, Bob, 34, 80, 184, 191, 192, 201, 217, 248, 251

Horne, Lena, 38

Horton, Johnny, 139

"Hound Dog" (Elvis Presley), 116, 118, 132

Howard, Harlan, 130, 195

Howard, Jan, 130, 195

Humphrey, Hubert, 210

Huskey, Ferlin, 80

"(I'll Always Be) Your Fraulein" (Kitty Wells), 130

"It's America (Love It or Leave It)" (Ernest Tubb), 198

"It's for God, and Country, and You Mom (That's Why I'm Fighting in Viet Nam)" (Ernest Tubb), 198

It's Music, 207–208

"It Turns Me Inside Out" (Lee Greenwood), 241, 242

"It Wasn't God Who Made Honky Tonk Angels" (Kitty Wells), 130

"I Walk the Line" (Johnny Cash), 96, 132

"I Wonder" (Private Cecil Gant), 39–40

Jackson, Michael, 238

Jackson, Stonewall, 195–197, 209

Jamboree (band), 193

Japan, 94, 203; country music tours, 16, 25, 29–30, 33–34, 45, 80, 159, 176, 182, 184, 201; country music and servicemembers stationed in, 68, 83, 154; US military occupation of, 124. *See also* Japanese War Brides; "Geisha Girl" (Hank Locklin); *Foreign Love* (Hank Locklin)

Japanese War Brides, 129–130
jazz, 86, 161; AFRS/AFRTS programming and, 17, 38, 235; influence on country musicians, 100; military record sales, 155; military recruitment and, 55; United States Army Special Services Division, 102; State Department diplomacy tours, 13, 103, 174, 225, 266n33
Jefferson Airplane, 192
Jennings, Waylon, 84, 200, 231–232, 241
Johnson, Lyndon B., 147, 177, 179–183, 203, 210; Vietnam and, 182–183, 185, 210
Jones, George, 130, 159, 216
Jones, Louis Marshall "Grandpa," 15, 16, 137, 212, 219; military career, 24–25, 39, 48; Korean War tour with Connie B. Gay, 29–34, 32, 43; *Old Dominion Barn Dance*, 25, 29, 30
Jubilee, 38
Judds, The, 247

Kadena Air Base, 204
Kasem, Casey, 230
Keith, Toby, 1, 3, 253–255
Kelly, Wynton, 102–104
Kennedy, John F.: Cold War politics, 147, 179–180, 182; racial integration and the military, 148, 163–165. *See also* President's Committee on Equal Opportunity in the Armed Forces (Gesell Committee)
Kent, George, 200
Kesler, Stan, 85, 96–97, 110
King, B. B., 235
King, Pee Wee, 40, 60, 79, 120
King Biscuit Flower Hour, 230
Klick, Mary, 29, 30, 33, 34, 180
Korean War, 28, 38, 39, 45, 57, 98, 154; country music and, 29, 36, 187, 197; country music tours, 16, 17, 25, 29–35, 43, 78, 80–81, 159, 184; economic impact, 85, 88, 89, 142, 144; racial

integration and, 7, 94, 95, 163; recruitment and, 48, 52, 74
Kristofferson, Kris, 188, 209

Lackland Air Force Base, 204
Laird, Melvin, 228, 230
Lansky, Bernard, 85–86, 89, 138
Lawson, James, 163
Leatherneck Jamboree, 165
Ledbetter, Huddie "Lead Belly," 132
LeMay, Curtis, 211
Lewis, John, 163
Live from Gilley's, 238
Locklin, Hank, 115, 127–130, 185, 197. See also *Foreign Love* (Hank Locklin)
Loew's Theater, 86, 88
Lomax, John, 130, 132
Long, Hubert, 51, 210
Los Angeles Lakers, 191
Louisiana Hayride, 50, 108, 109
Louvin, Charlie, 35, 109–110, 180, 189, 223
Louvin, Ira, 121–122
Louvin Brothers, The, 35, 71, 121
Lovett, Lyle, 247
Luman, Bob, 206
Lynde, Paul, 140
Lynn, Loretta, 195, 199, 234, 247

Mack, Warner, 206
Malone, Bill C., 236
"Mama Bake a Pie (Daddy Kill a Chicken)" (Tom T. Hall), 200
Mandrell, Barbara, 232, 235
Mansfield, Jayne, 191
March Air Force Base, 252
Martin, Benny, 130, 165
Martin, Jimmy, 68, 159
McCain, John, 256
McClellan Air Force Base, 242
McClinton, Brock, 222–223
McClinton, O. B., 177, 178, 203–206, 207
McCoys, The, 130
McCrae, Jody, 72
McEntire, Reba, 247

McFaden, Larry, 242
McGraw, Tim, 130
McKinnon, Dan, 237
McNamara, Robert, 164, 169–170
McPhatter, Clyde, 103–104
McReynolds, Jesse, 35; Jim and Jesse, 35, 236
Melody Roundup, 17, 26
Memphis, 90, 108, 109, 117–119, 137, 204–205; Beale Street, 86; defense economy, 84–86, 87–88, *89*; industrialization of, 84, 87; postwar music scene, 92, 93, 96, 97, 100, 104, 105–107, 204; rockabilly and, 11, 83–84, 93, 108, 112, 134, 137. *See also* Presley, Elvis; rockabilly; Stax Records; Sun Records
Memphis State College (University of Memphis), 104, 105
militarism, 264n5. *See also* country music militarization
Miller, Roger, 111, 188, 200, 273n46
Millington Naval Air Station, 85, 88–89
"The Minute Men (Are Turning in Their Graves)" (Stonewall Jackson), 195, 209
Mitchum, Robert, 191
Mondale, Walter, 237
Monroe, Bill, 97, 102, 107, 109
Monroe Brothers, The, 19
Moody, Clyde, 40
Moore, Joyce, 183
Moore, Scotty, 85, 90; Elvis Presley and, 106–109, 142; naval career, 90–92, 110–111; Starlite Wranglers, 92, 105–106
Morgan, George, 159, 211, 212
Motown Records, 203
Music Row: as location of the country music industry, 5, 71, 148, 162, 163, 176, 195, 231, 243; as metonym for country music industry, 4, 13, 233; politics and, 179–182, 233. *See also* country music militarization; United States Department of Defense: country music industry and

Muskie, Edmund, 177, 206
My Lai Massacre, 198
Myrtle Beach, South Carolina, 240

Nash, Diane, 163
Nashville (film), 232
Nashville Cats (band), 193
The Nashville Network (TNN), 242, 247
Nashville Now, 206, 247
National Association for the Advancement of Colored People (NAACP), 95, 120
National Country Music Month, 181–182, 210, 233, 235
National Guard, 69–70, 77, 95, 122, 189, 190, 243, 248
Naval Air Technical Training Center, 88, *89*
Naylor, Jerry, 229
Nelson, Ricky, 131
Nelson, Terry, 198–199
Nelson, Willie, 71, 82, 111, 170, 231–233, 235
Newman, Jimmy C., 186, 236
Newton-John, Olivia, 232
Nixon, Richard, 177, 216; country music and, 3, 178, 197, 212–213, 215–218, 233; Vietnam and, 215. *See also* all-volunteer force (AVF); silent majority
"No, No Joe" (Hank Williams as Luke the Drifter), 29
North Alabama Citizens' Council, 122–123, 125, *126*. *See also* Carter, Asa

Oak Ridge Boys, The, 235
"Obie from Senatobie" (O. B. McClinton), 205–206
O'Jays, The, 224
"Okie from Muskogee" (Merle Haggard), 197–198, 205
Okinawa, 159, 160, 177, 199, 204
Operation Bootstrap, 207
Operation Christmas Star, 189
Operation Reindeer, 154

Opryland, USA, 216, 225, 226, 235
Osborne Brothers, The, 68, 212, 270n75
Owens, Buck, 111, 131, 173, 201, 210

Pace, Kelly, 132
Page, Patti, 60, 73, 121
Parker, Colonel Tom, 110, 111, 116
Parton, Dolly, 221, 232
Paulick, Michael, 193, 195
Payne, Kimberly, 250, 254
Pearl, Minnie, 15, 23, 28, 29, 40, 70, 75, 78, 211
Pearson, Duke, 102
Pecknold, Diane, 66
Perkins, Carl, 84, 97, 220
Perkins, Luther, 132
Persian Gulf War, 13, 221, 249
Phillips, Dewey, 86–87, 106, 107–108
Phillips, Sam, 79, 83, 106–107, 109, 119
Pierce, Webb, 50–51, 110, 211
Pink Floyd, 238
Plantation Records, 198
Pop Goes Country, 238
pop music, 121, 141; AFRS/AFRTS programming, 26, 214; class politics and, 11, 47, 60, 79, 81, 147; military recruitment, 55, 69–70, 73. See also *It's Music*
Post Exchange (PX): *See* Army and Air Force Post Exchange Service (PX)
Precision Tools (Memphis), 85, 88, 142, 144
President's Committee on Equal Opportunity in the Armed Forces (Gesell Committee), 164–167, 169
Presley, Elvis: army career and image transformation, 115–116, 141–145; army induction, 118–119, 134–136; backlash to, 109–110, 114, 117, 120–122; *Bye Bye Birdie* and, 140–141; country music press and, 110, 114, *142–143*; country radio and, 108–109; defense industry employment, 88–89, 142, 144; fan reaction to

military service, 113–114, 141; first performances in Memphis, 108; gender subversion, 116–118; *GI Blues*, 141–142, 144; hair, 113, 117–118, 136; high school and ROTC, 86–87, 89, 144; impact on country music industry, 110–112, 138–139; *Love Me Tender*, 117; *King Creole*, 134; relationship to African American music, 115, 121–122. *See also* White Citizens' Councils; rockabilly
Price, Ray, 173, 210
Pride, Charley, 178, 204, 213, 225, 235
Prince Albert Show, 28, 58
Putman, Curly, 209

Queen (band), 249

R&B/blues, 17, 40, 41, 86, 106, 120, 168, 266n34; AFRTS/AFRS programming, 38, 39, 155; influence on country musicians, 84, 100, 101, 106, 107, 108, 110, 114–115, 118; United States Army Special Services Division and, 99, 102, 104, 252, 253
racial integration of US Armed Forces, 82, 85, 177–178, 265n15, 281n32; discrimination from civilian communities, 11, 93–95, 114, 123, 166–167; morale, 164, 167, 169; on-base discrimination, 99, 167, 169; on-base school desegregation, 99, 124; positive coverage of military integration, 169, 281n32; Project Clear, 123–124; recruitment of African American servicemembers, 165–167, 224; Truman and Executive Order 9981, 7, 17, 163; WACs and, 124–125. *See also* President's Committee on Equal Opportunity in the Armed Forces (Gesell Committee)
Radio Ranch, 15, 22, 68
Randolph, A. Philip, 133
Rascals, The, 242
RCA Studios, 111, 144

RCA Victor Records, 110, 116, 138, 152, 190, 239

Reagan, Ronald, 5, 12, 220, 234, 237–238, 241; Lee Greenwood and, 13, 221, 243, 243–246, 248

Redd Harper's Hollywood Roundup, 17, 27

Redding, Otis, 101, 192

Reed, Jerry, 241

Reeves, Jim, 46, 69, 70, 78, 111, 139, 173

Republican Party, 5, 181, 215, 226, 235, 243, 248, 253, 256

"The Return of the All American Boy" (Billy Adams and the Rock-A-Teens), 139

Rice, Vernon, 75, 152–153

Rich, Charlie, 84, 85, 100

Riley, Billy Lee, 85, 92–93, 96

Riley, Jeannie C., 186, 198, 207, 212, 213

Ritter, Tex, 75, 161, 170, 193, 195

Robbins, Marty, 130, 131; military recruitment and, 71, 72; political views, 180

Robinson, Billy, 28

rockabilly, 139, 140; country music and, 83, 110; race and, 11, 84–85, 100, 112, 118, 121; musicians in the US military, 11, 82, 84, 85, 102, 132, 300n87. *See also* Memphis: rockabilly and; Presley, Elvis: impact on country music industry

rock and roll, 11, 79, 86, 103, 106, 111, 121, 149, 151; AFRTS programming, 144, 156. *See also* counterculture; Presley, Elvis; Smathers Bill; Vietnam War: rock and roll; White Citizens' Councils: backlash to rock and roll

Rodgers, Jimmie, 8, 76, 158, 220; Jimmie Rodgers Memorial Festival, 66, 77

Rogers, Kenny, 200, 219–220, 232

Ronstandt, Linda, 208

"Ruby, Don't Take Your Love to Town" (Johnny Darrell/Waylon Jennings/ Roger Miller/Kenny Rogers and First Edition/Mel Tillis), 199–200

Ryan, John J., 156–157

Ryman Auditorium, 22, 23, 36, 48, 51, 108, 211, 216

Sadler, Barry, 195, 209

"Sad News from Korea" (Lightnin' Hopkins), 39, 270n87

Satisfiers, The, 55

Savoy Records, 239

Schwarzkopf, Norman, 249

Seeger, Pete, 188

Seely, Jeannie, 201

Shaver, Billy Joe, 131

Shaw, Tom, 207

Sholes, Steve, 111, 138

silent majority, 2, 3, 178, 212, 216, 218

Silverstein, Shel, 285n101

Sinatra, Frank, 8, 139–140, 156

Sinatra, Nancy, 139, 191, 202

Skinner, Jimmie, 130

Smathers Bill, 47–48, 61, 79–82, 147, 149

Smith, Connie, 173, 189, 206

Smith, Margo, 241

Smith-Hughes Farm Vocational Education Act of 1917, 18

Snow, Hank, 110, 160, 180; military tours, 33, 78, 147, 159, 191, 193, 201; recruitment, 69

Soldier Brides Act, 130

"The Soldier's Sweetheart" (Jimmie Rodgers), 8

Soul in Motion, 224

Soul Line, 224

soul music, 85, 100–101, 103, 174, 192, 205, 232, 253, 266n34; AFRS/AFRTS programming, 230; military recruitment, 13, 221, 224; PX sales, 221, 239, 248; Command Military Touring Shows (CMTS), 193, 203–205

Southwest Texas State University (Texas State University), 240

Soviet Union, 12, 13, 52, 91, 182, 220, 234, 235, 243, 249; country music tours, 225–226, 233

Sovine, Red, 46, 201
Spinners, The, 224
Springsteen, Bruce, 249
Stalin, Joseph, 29, 96
Stapp, Jack: Tree Publishing, 110–111; CMA and, 149, 152
Stax Records, 85, 101, 204–205
Stewart, Jim, 85, 100–101, 104, 108
Stewart, Wynn, 130
Stickbuddy Jamboree (*Stick-Buddy Jamboree*), 67, 146, 159, 160, 206, 229
Storz, Todd, 171
Strait, George, 4, 240–241
String-A-Longs, The, 193
Sunbelt South, 8, 65, 212, 221, 232–233, 236, 265n16
"Sunday Morning Coming Down" (Sergeant Barry Sadler), 209
Sun Records, 83, 85, 93, 97, 100, 106–107, 132, 144

Taft-Hartley Act, 65
Talent Patrol, 52, 58, 61, 64, 103
television and military recruitment, 53–55. See also *Country Style, U.S.A.* (television); *Talent Patrol*; United States Department of Defense; United States Army and Air Force Recruiting Service
Terry, Gordon, 102
"That's All Right" (Elvis Presley), 107, 109–110, 132
"That's All Right Mama" (Arthur "Big Boy" Crudup), 107
"There's a Star-Spangled Banner Waving Somewhere" (Elton Britt), 8, 35, 176, 187
Third US Army, 58, 61, 102–103
Thompson, Hank, 68, 130, 212, 235
Threeteens, The, 136, 144
Thurmond, Strom, 163
Tillis, Mel, 4, 176, 199–200, 242
Tippin, Aaron, 1, 3, 14
The Tommy Hunter Show, 238
Toussaint, Allen, 168

Town and Country Time, 15, 22, 43, 63–64, 69, 76
Town Hall Party, 22
"The Town That Never Sleeps" (Charlie Walker), 207
"Travelin' Soldier" (The Chicks), 1–2
Travis, Merle, 225
Trump, Donald, 253–254, 257
Tubb, Ernest, 33, 75, 109, 198, 213, 223
Twitty, Conway (Harold Jenkins), 83–84, 111, 140, 234

United Service Organization (USO): country musicians and, 8, 9, 36, 43, 45, 147, 182–183, 190, 241, 242, 243, 247, 250, *251*, 253, 256; handshake tours, 191; morale and, 191, 192, 252; racial discrimination, 99, 167, 252–253, 255; War on Terror, 252; World War II, 8, 36, 98; Vietnam War, 9, 184, 191–193. *See also* Command Military Touring Shows (CMTS); Acuff, Roy: USO and other military tours
United States Air Force, 28, 43, 68, 93, 96, 100, 133, 162, 164, 177, 199, 204, 252. See also *Country Music Time*; *Soul in Motion*; United States Army Special Services; Army and Air Force Post Exchange Service (PX); United States Army and Air Force Recruiting Service
United States Air Force Service Band, 49, 54, 55
United States Army and Air Force Recruiting Service, 49, 52–55, 57–58, 69, 73, 165; country music and, 63–64, 66, 69, 73, 75–76, 134, 163, 165, 177, 246–247; *Recruiting Journal*, 56, 58, 63
United States Army Entertainment Branch, 43, 45, 119, 192
United States Army Recruiting Command, 207

United States Army Service Band, 49, 54–56

United States Army Special Services Division, 97, 36, 43, 45, 57, 61; African American music and, 102–104, 203; creation of, 98; country musicians and, 4, 11, 29, 33, 67, 97, 99–100, 102, 193, *194*, 240; Elvis Presley, 116, 119–120, 144; jazz bands, 100; morale and, 4, 98; racial discrimination and, 99–100, 124–125; rock and roll and, 193; rockabilly and, 83, 85, 92–93, 97, 100; servicemember talent shows, 98–99; United States Air Force, 11, 96, 100. *See also* Command Military Touring Shows (CMTS); United Service Organization (USO)

United States Department of Agriculture Soil Erosion Service, 18

United States Department of Defense, 10, 48, 139, 142, 145, 154, 185, 227; Pentagon creation, 21–22; country music industry and, 5, 11, 13–14, 43, 64, 148, 164, 175, 195, 213–214, 222, 251; military–industrial complex, 10, 148, 182, 209, 218, 266n27; military spending and the US South, 5, 84; pop culture and, 13, 52–54, 69–70, 191, 228–231, 255–256; race and, 94, 95, 136, 169, 178, 224. *See also* country music and military recruitment programs; country music militarization; United States Army and Air Force Recruiting Service: country music and

United States Department of State, 13, 79, 103, 174, 220, 225–226

United States Second Armored Division, 97, 137, 141

Universal Military Training (UMT), 94

Urban Cowboy, 221, 233

Vanderbilt University, 163

Van Dyke, Dick, 140

Van Dyke, LeRoy, 206

"Viet Nam Blues" (Dave Dudley), 188

Vietnam War: antiwar movement, 177, 178, 192, 195, 197, 206, 211, 216; country music fandom and promotion, 189–190, 193–195, *196*, 214, *215*; country music songs about, 1, 12, 177–178, 186–189, 194–200; country music tours, *9*, 184–185, 191, 201–202; gender and entertainment, 201–202; politics of, 3, 5, 178, 181, 210–218, 258; popular opinion regarding, 175, 176, 216; race and entertainment, 203–204, 206–210; recruitment during, 35, 177, 206–208; rock and roll, 192–193, 203; servicemembers demographics, 188–189, 192; strategy and cost, 179, 182–183; US withdrawal, 222; veterans of, 242, 248. *See also* Acuff, Roy: Vietnam and; country music militarization; Army and Air Force Post Exchange Service (PX); Command Military Touring Shows (CMTS); United Service Organization (USO): Vietnam War

Village Barn, 22

Voice of America (VOA), 79, 174, 226–227, 235

Wagon Wheels, The, 193, *194*

Walker, Charlie, 206–207, 294n103

Walker, Cindy, 129

Walker, Jo, 195, 235; as Jo Walker-Meador, 238

Wallace, George, 122, 177, 218; country music campaigning, 211–212

Wanted! The Outlaws, 231–232, 298n44

Ward, Clara, 191

War on Poverty, 210–211

War on Terror, 1–3, 255

Washington, Dinah, 102

WDIA, 204

Welch, Raquel, 202

"Welfare Cadillac" (Guy Drake), 213

Welk, Lawrence, 218

Wells, Kitty, 130, 159, 173
West, Ben, 163
West, Dottie, 189
West, Kanye, 253
Western Jamboree (band), front
     cover, 29
Western Swing (radio show), 67
western swing (style), 36, 79, 101,
     105, 217
"What is Truth" (Johnny Cash), 213
"What We're Fighting For" (Dave
     Dudley), 187–188, 189
"Where the Stars and the Stripes and
     the Eagle Fly" (Aaron Tippin), 1
"Where Were You (When the World
     Stopped Turning)" (Alan Jackson), 1
White, Walter, 95
White Citizens' Councils: formation of,
     120; backlash to rock and roll, 114–115,
     120–121, 122, 123, 125; backlash to
     military integration, 114–115, 123, 125,
     126, 131. *See also* Carter, Asa; North
     Alabama Citizens' Council
Wolfman Jack (radio show), 230
Wicks, Chuck (Kasi), 256–258
Wilburn Brothers, The, 212
William Morris Agency, 210
Williams, Bill, 189–190, 195
Williams, Charlie, 214
Williams, Don, 234
Williams, Hank, 28–29, 51, 66, 92, 93,
     105–106, 121, 139, 240
Williams, Hank, Jr., 241, 247

Williams, Lawton, 115, 128–130
Willis Brothers, The, 23, 180, 189
Wills, Bob, 36, 71, 105, 130
Withers, Bill, 224
Women's Army Corps (WAC): country
     music recruitment and, 72–74;
     integration and, 124–125; pop music
     recruitment and, 73, 208
Wonder, Stevie, 224
Wooley, Sheb, 40
World War II, 54, 85, 88, 94, 98, 153,
     190, 242, 243; African American
     music and, 38, 40, 65; country music
     and, 17, 35–36, 38, 80, 138, 152, 200,
     206, 209, 242; military spending and,
     16, 87, 123. *See also* Acuff, Roy: World
     War II and; United Service
     Organization (USO): World War II
Worley, Darryl, 1, 2
Wright, Johnny, 186–187

"Yankee Go Home" (Jan Howard and
     Wynn Stewart), 130
Young, Faron: army entertainment and
     Circle A Wranglers, 61–62, 62, 82,
     101, 103, 116, 231, 251; army recruit-
     ment and, 4, 10, 48–49, 52, 58–59,
     63–65, 70, 74–76, 165, 253; back-
     ground and style, 50–52, 66, 102,
     106, 109, 111, 170; post-army career,
     65, 82, 180, 212; Smathers Bill
     testimony, 47–48, 79, 81–82
Your Navy Country Music Show, 182–183